THE
DEATH-DEFYING
DOCTOR
MIRAGE

JEN VAN METER | ROBERTO DE LA TORRE | DAVID BARON | DAVE LANPHEAR

CONTENTS

Collection Cover Art: Travel Foreman

David Baron
Roberto de la Torre
Khari Evans
Travel Foreman
Stephanie Hans
Dave Johnson
Dave Lanphear
Jen Van Meter
Brian Reber
Kevin Wada
Patrick Zircher

Editor: Alejandro Arbona
Editor-in-Chief: Warren Simons

VALIANT.

The Death-Defying Dr. Mirage®. Published by Valiant Entertainment,
LLC. Office of Publication: 350 Seventh Avenue, New York, NY 10001.
Compilation copyright ©2015 Valiant Entertainment LLC. All rights
reserved. Contains materials originally published in single magazine
form as The Death-Defying Dr. Mirage #1-5 and Shadowman®
#5. Copyright ©2013, 2014 and 2015 Valiant Entertainment LLC.
All rights reserved. All characters, their distinctive likeness and
related indicia featured in this publication are trademarks of Valiant
Entertainment LLC. The stories, characters, and incidents featured in
this publication are entirely fictional. Valiant Entertainment does not
read or accept unsolicited submissions of ideas, stories, or artwork.
Printed in the U.S.A. Second Printing.
ISBN: 9781939346490.

VALIANT
1
THE DEATH-DEFYING
DOCTOR MIRAGE
JEN VAN METER | ROBERTO DE LA TORRE | DAVID BARON

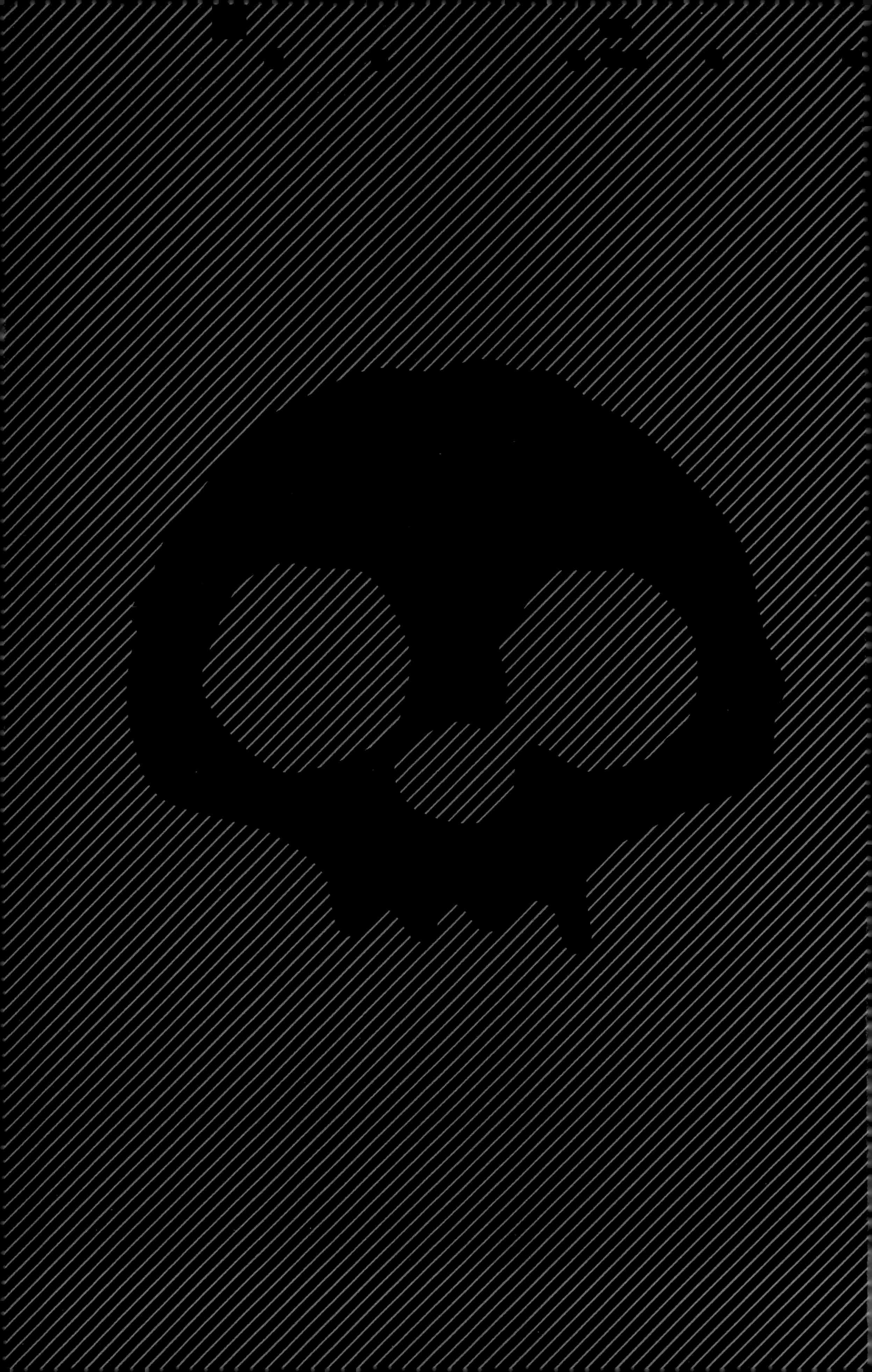

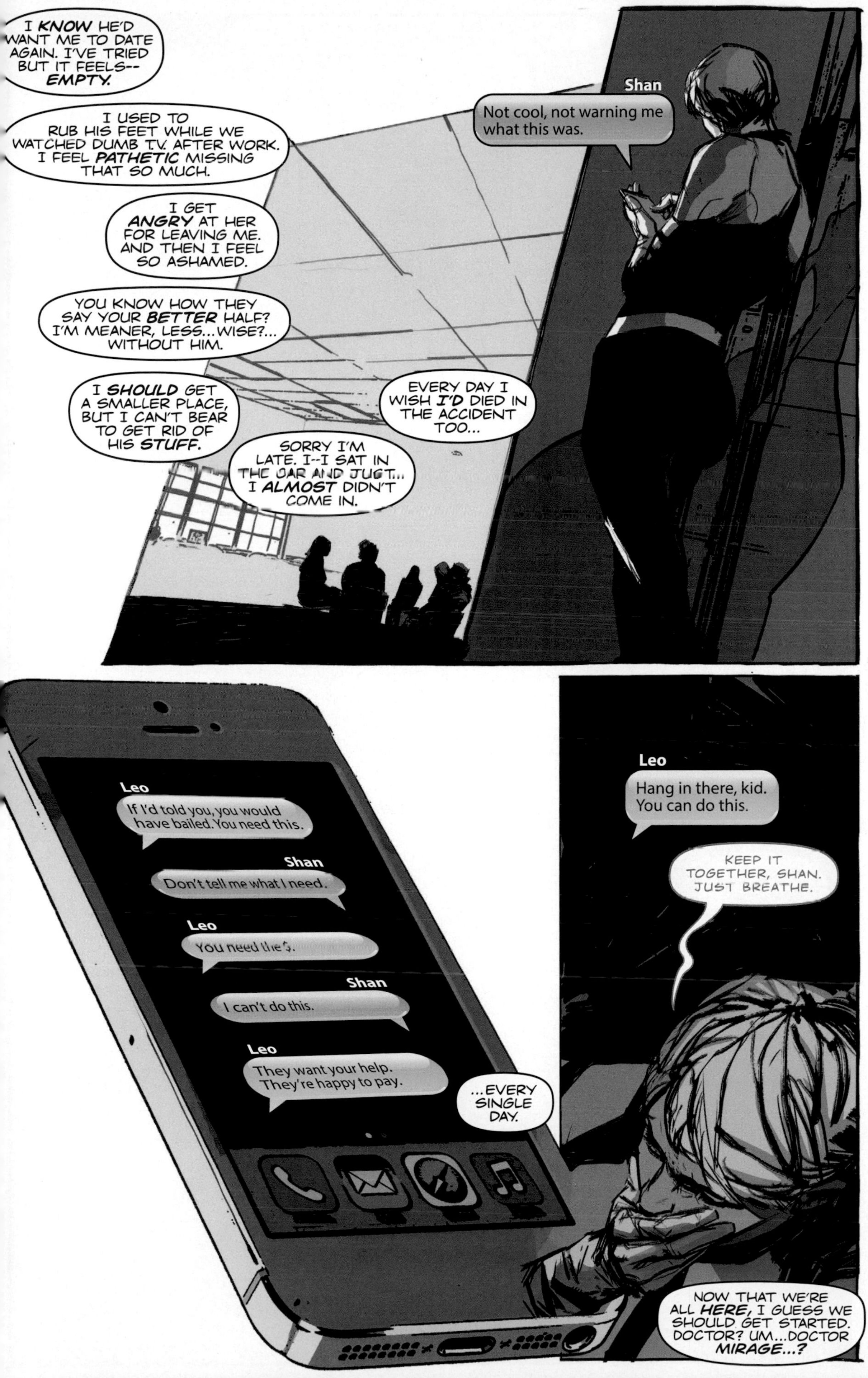
I KNOW HE'D WANT ME TO DATE AGAIN. I'VE TRIED BUT IT FEELS-- EMPTY.
I USED TO RUB HIS FEET WHILE WE WATCHED DUMB T.V. AFTER WORK. I FEEL PATHETIC MISSING THAT SO MUCH.
I GET ANGRY AT HER FOR LEAVING ME. AND THEN I FEEL SO ASHAMED.
YOU KNOW HOW THEY SAY YOUR BETTER HALF? I'M MEANER, LESS...WISE?... WITHOUT HIM.
I SHOULD GET A SMALLER PLACE, BUT I CAN'T BEAR TO GET RID OF HIS STUFF.
SORRY I'M LATE. I--I SAT IN THE CAR AND JUST... I ALMOST DIDN'T COME IN.
EVERY DAY I WISH I'D DIED IN THE ACCIDENT TOO...
Shan
Not cool, not warning me what this was.
Leo
If I'd told you, you would have bailed. You need this.
Shan
Don't tell me what I need.
Leo
You need this.
Shan
I can't do this.
Leo
They want your help. They're happy to pay.
...EVERY SINGLE DAY.
Leo
Hang in there, kid. You can do this.
KEEP IT TOGETHER, SHAN. JUST BREATHE.
NOW THAT WE'RE ALL HERE, I GUESS WE SHOULD GET STARTED. DOCTOR? UM...DOCTOR MIRAGE...?

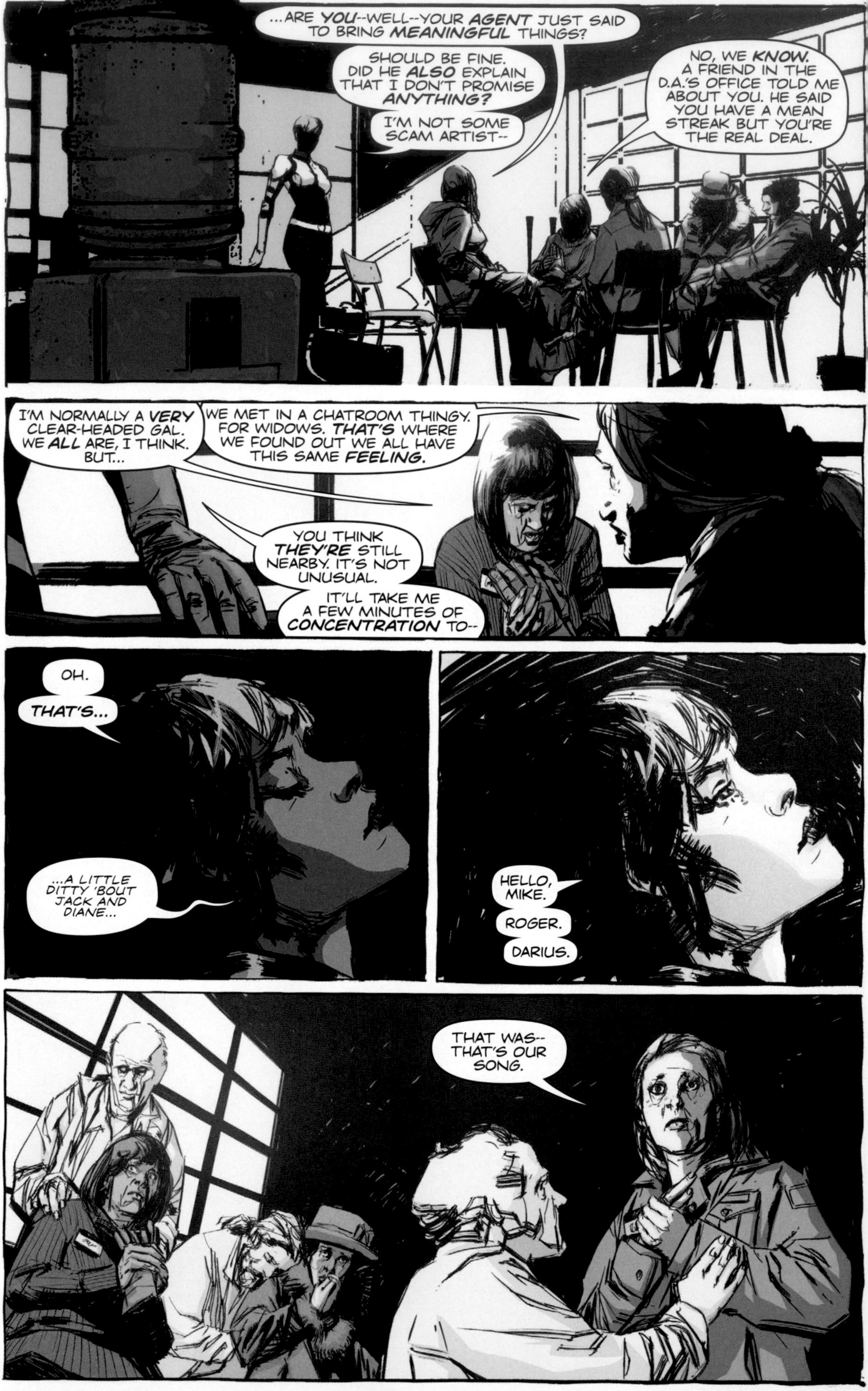
...ARE YOU--WELL--YOUR AGENT JUST SAID TO BRING MEANINGFUL THINGS?
SHOULD BE FINE. DID HE ALSO EXPLAIN THAT I DON'T PROMISE ANYTHING?
I'M NOT SOME SCAM ARTIST--
NO, WE KNOW. A FRIEND IN THE D.A.'S OFFICE TOLD ME ABOUT YOU. HE SAID YOU HAVE A MEAN STREAK BUT YOU'RE THE REAL DEAL.
I'M NORMALLY A VERY CLEAR-HEADED GAL. WE ALL ARE, I THINK. BUT...
WE MET IN A CHATROOM THINGY. FOR WIDOWS. THAT'S WHERE WE FOUND OUT WE ALL HAVE THIS SAME FEELING.
YOU THINK THEY'RE STILL NEARBY. IT'S NOT UNUSUAL.
IT'LL TAKE ME A FEW MINUTES OF CONCENTRATION TO--
OH.
THAT'S...
...A LITTLE DITTY 'BOUT JACK AND DIANE...
HELLO, MIKE.
ROGER.
DARIUS.
THAT WAS-- THAT'S OUR SONG.

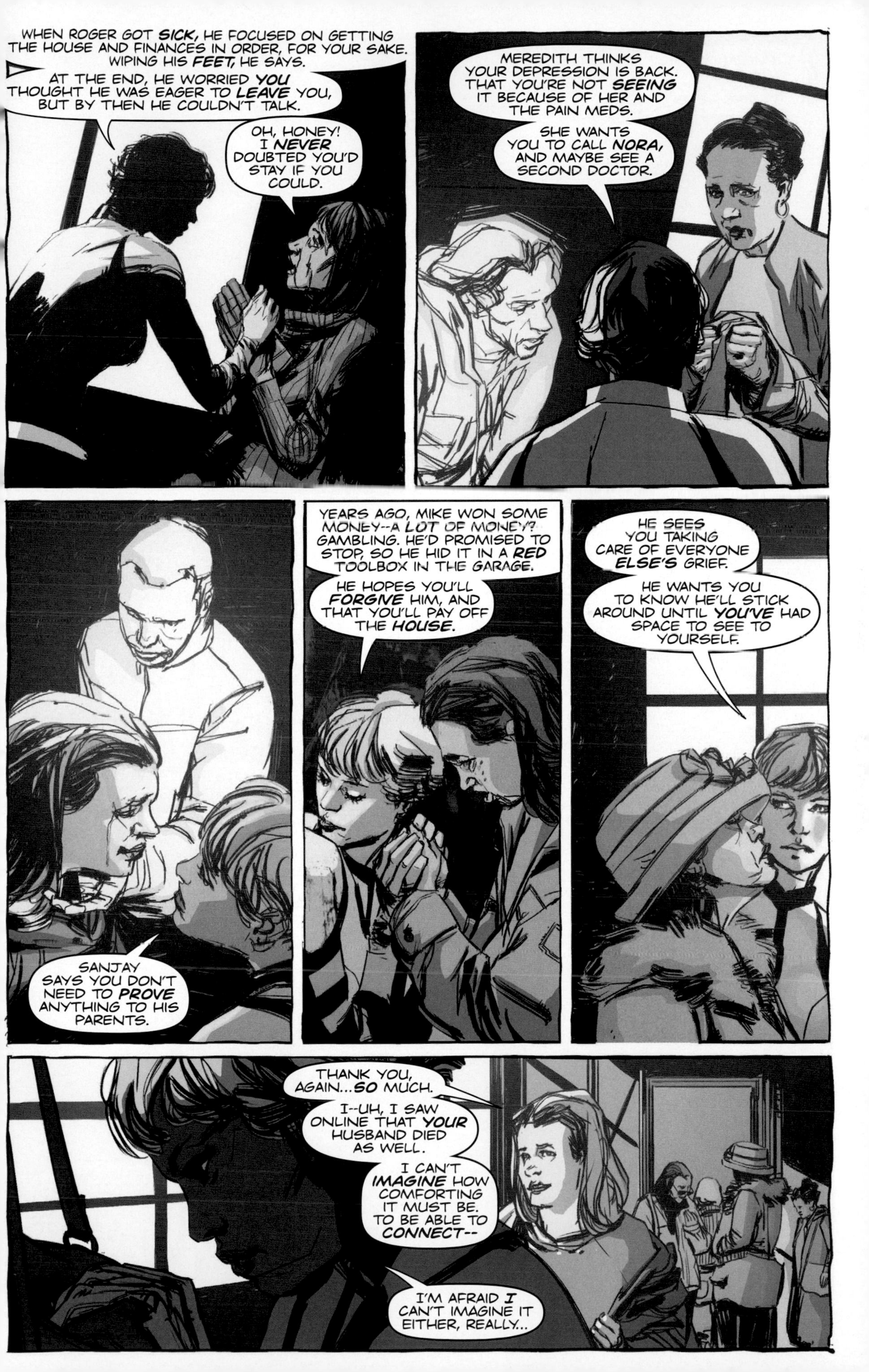

WHEN ROGER GOT SICK, HE FOCUSED ON GETTING THE HOUSE AND FINANCES IN ORDER, FOR YOUR SAKE. WIPING HIS FEET, HE SAYS.
AT THE END, HE WORRIED YOU THOUGHT HE WAS EAGER TO LEAVE YOU, BUT BY THEN HE COULDN'T TALK.
OH, HONEY! I NEVER DOUBTED YOU'D STAY IF YOU COULD.
MEREDITH THINKS YOUR DEPRESSION IS BACK. THAT YOU'RE NOT SEEING IT BECAUSE OF HER AND THE PAIN MEDS.
SHE WANTS YOU TO CALL NORA, AND MAYBE SEE A SECOND DOCTOR.
SANJAY SAYS YOU DON'T NEED TO PROVE ANYTHING TO HIS PARENTS.
YEARS AGO, MIKE WON SOME MONEY--A LOT OF MONEY--GAMBLING. HE'D PROMISED TO STOP, SO HE HID IT IN A RED TOOLBOX IN THE GARAGE.
HE HOPES YOU'LL FORGIVE HIM, AND THAT YOU'LL PAY OFF THE HOUSE.
HE SEES YOU TAKING CARE OF EVERYONE ELSE'S GRIEF.
HE WANTS YOU TO KNOW HE'LL STICK AROUND UNTIL YOU'VE HAD SPACE TO SEE TO YOURSELF.
THANK YOU, AGAIN...SO MUCH.
I--UH, I SAW ONLINE THAT YOUR HUSBAND DIED AS WELL.
I CAN'T IMAGINE HOW COMFORTING IT MUST BE. TO BE ABLE TO CONNECT--
I'M AFRAID I CAN'T IMAGINE IT EITHER, REALLY...

"...HWEN DOESN'T TALK TO ME. I DON'T KNOW WHERE HE IS."

SHAN? C'MON. YOU'VE *GOT* TO LET ME *IN.*

YOU SHOULDN'T HAVE COME, LEO. I'M IN A *MOOD* LIKE YOU WOULDN'T BELIEVE.

YOU WANT IN, COME ON IN. THE WARDS WON'T HURT. *MUCH.*

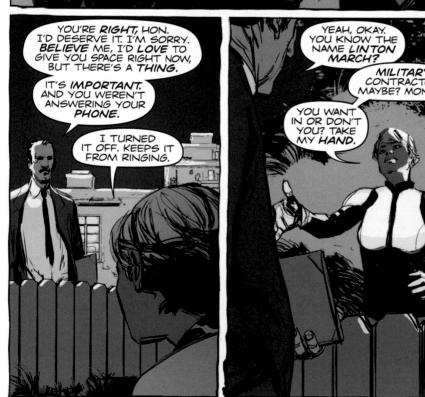

YOU'RE *RIGHT,* HON. I'D DESERVE IT. I'M SORRY. *BELIEVE* ME, I'D *LOVE* TO GIVE YOU SPACE RIGHT NOW, BUT THERE'S A *THING.*

IT'S *IMPORTANT.* AND YOU WEREN'T ANSWERING YOUR *PHONE.*

I TURNED IT OFF. KEEPS IT FROM RINGING.

YEAH, OKAY. YOU KNOW THE NAME *LINTON MARCH?*

MILITARY CONTRACTOR, MAYBE? MONEY?

YOU WANT IN OR DON'T YOU? TAKE MY *HAND.*

THAT, AND WIDOWED A YEAR BACK'S ABOUT ALL I GOT--VERY LOW PROFILE. BUT *LOTS* OF MONEY. *BILLIONS.*

SOME OF WHICH COULD BE *YOURS.* AS IN THIRTY THOU JUST FOR A *CONSULT.*

WHAT'S THE DOWNSIDE?

IT'S ME, HOUSE. ALL IS WELL.

RECLUSIVE BILLIONAIRE? WANTS TO HIRE A *PARANORMAL INVESTIGATOR...?*

HE *COULD* BE LOONY AS A DUCK FART, BUT *YOU* CAN HANDLE THAT.

I DON'T *WANT* TO TAKE ON A BIG JOB RIGHT NOW. THAT MONEY SOUNDS LIKE A *BIG JOB.*

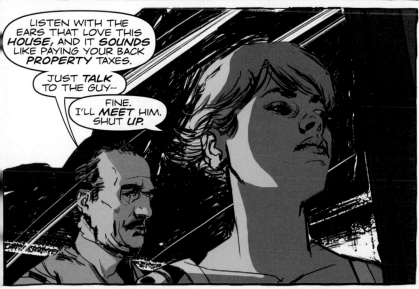

LISTEN WITH THE EARS THAT LOVE THIS *HOUSE,* AND IT *SOUNDS* LIKE PAYING YOUR BACK *PROPERTY* TAXES.

JUST *TALK* TO THE GUY--

FINE. I'LL *MEET* HIM. SHUT *UP.*

ATTA GIRL! I'LL GET IT SET UP. YOU *WON'T* REGRET IT, I SWEAR.

IF IT GOES LIKE THIS THING *TODAY,* THOUGH? I'M WALKING *AND* FIRING YOU.

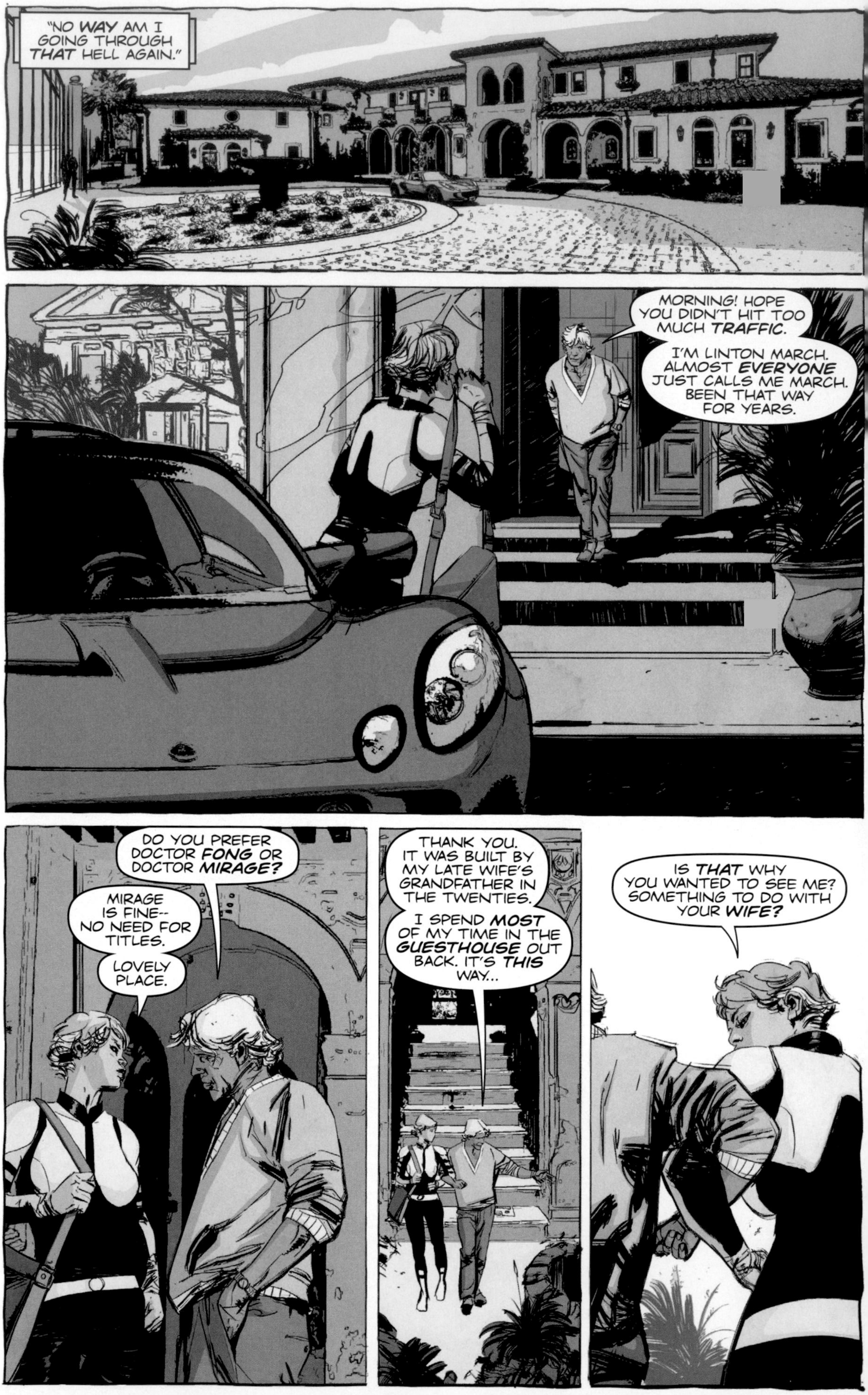
"NO WAY AM I GOING THROUGH THAT HELL AGAIN."
MORNING! HOPE YOU DIDN'T HIT TOO MUCH TRAFFIC.
I'M LINTON MARCH. ALMOST EVERYONE JUST CALLS ME MARCH. BEEN THAT WAY FOR YEARS.
DO YOU PREFER DOCTOR FONG OR DOCTOR MIRAGE?
MIRAGE IS FINE-- NO NEED FOR TITLES.
LOVELY PLACE.
THANK YOU. IT WAS BUILT BY MY LATE WIFE'S GRANDFATHER IN THE TWENTIES.
I SPEND MOST OF MY TIME IN THE GUESTHOUSE OUT BACK. IT'S THIS WAY...
IS THAT WHY YOU WANTED TO SEE ME? SOMETHING TO DO WITH YOUR WIFE?

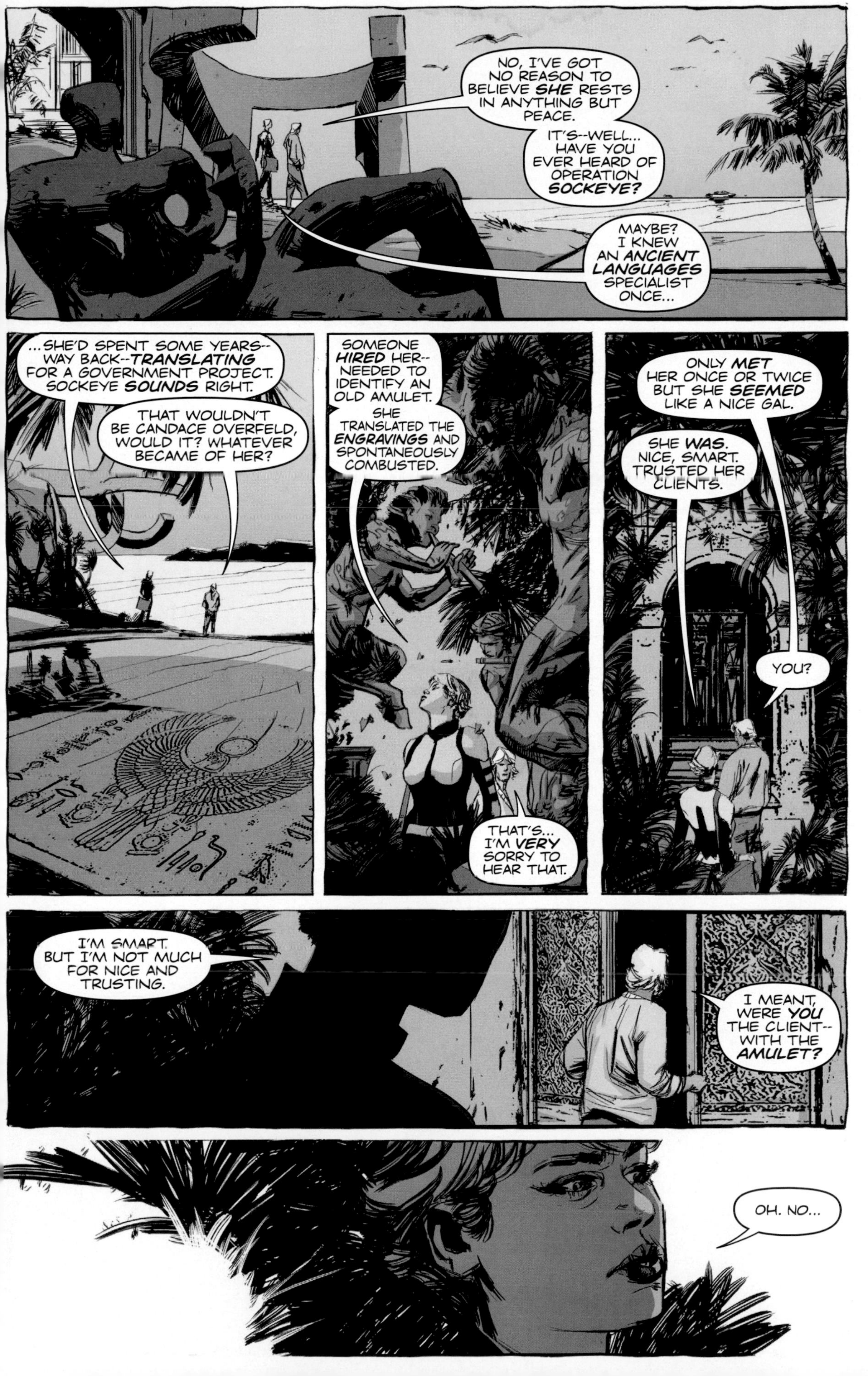
NO, I'VE GOT NO REASON TO BELIEVE SHE RESTS IN ANYTHING BUT PEACE.
IT'S--WELL... HAVE YOU EVER HEARD OF OPERATION SOCKEYE?
MAYBE? I KNEW AN ANCIENT LANGUAGES SPECIALIST ONCE...
...SHE'D SPENT SOME YEARS--WAY BACK--TRANSLATING FOR A GOVERNMENT PROJECT. SOCKEYE SOUNDS RIGHT.
THAT WOULDN'T BE CANDACE OVERFELD, WOULD IT? WHATEVER BECAME OF HER?
SOMEONE HIRED HER--NEEDED TO IDENTIFY AN OLD AMULET.
SHE TRANSLATED THE ENGRAVINGS AND SPONTANEOUSLY COMBUSTED.
THAT'S... I'M VERY SORRY TO HEAR THAT.
ONLY MET HER ONCE OR TWICE BUT SHE SEEMED LIKE A NICE GAL.
SHE WAS. NICE, SMART. TRUSTED HER CLIENTS.
YOU?
I'M SMART. BUT I'M NOT MUCH FOR NICE AND TRUSTING.
I MEANT, WERE YOU THE CLIENT--WITH THE AMULET?
OH. NO...

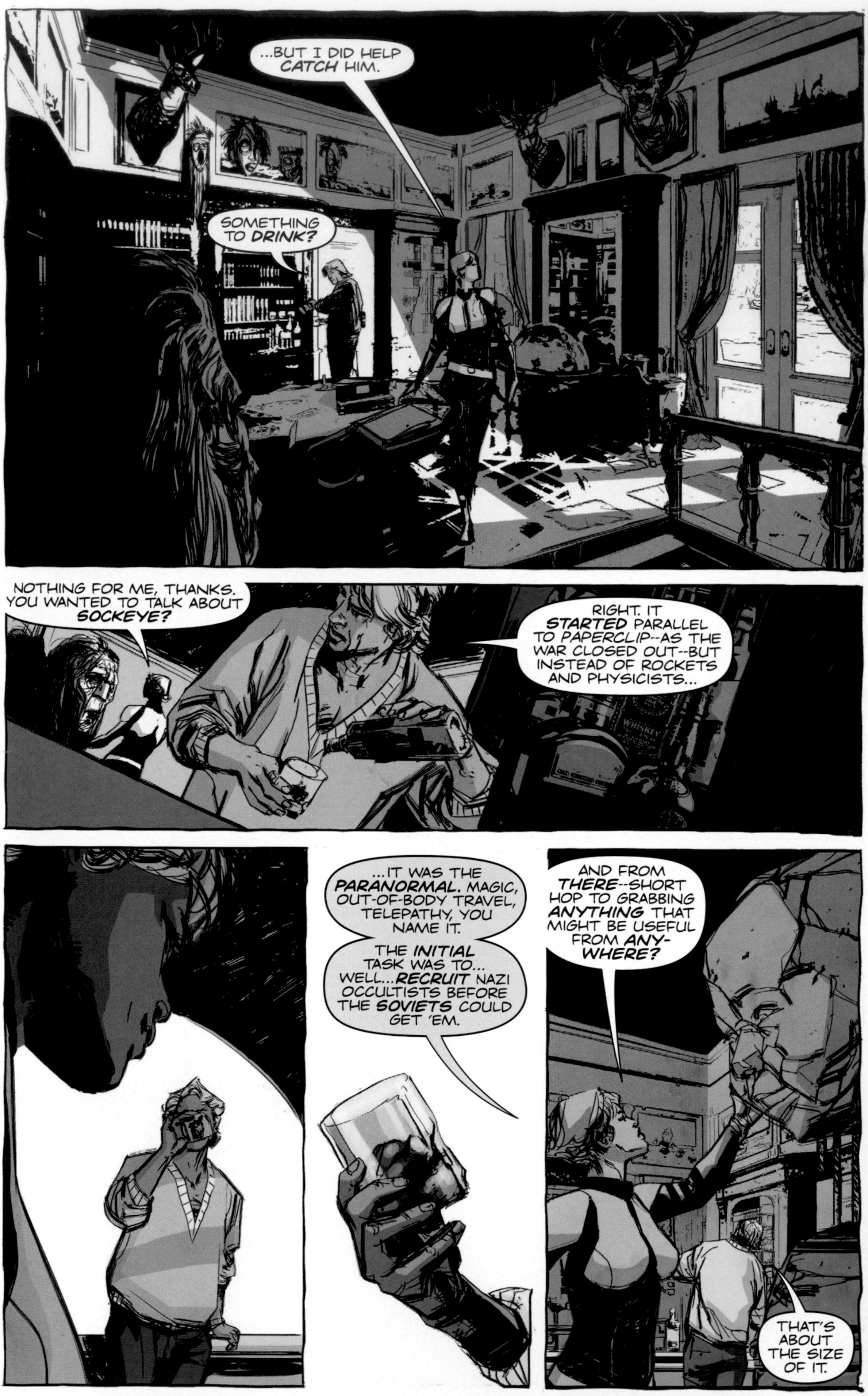
...BUT I DID HELP CATCH HIM.
SOMETHING TO DRINK?
NOTHING FOR ME, THANKS. YOU WANTED TO TALK ABOUT SOCKEYE?
RIGHT. IT STARTED PARALLEL TO PAPERCLIP--AS THE WAR CLOSED OUT--BUT INSTEAD OF ROCKETS AND PHYSICISTS...
WHISKEY
...IT WAS THE PARANORMAL. MAGIC, OUT-OF-BODY TRAVEL, TELEPATHY, YOU NAME IT.
THE INITIAL TASK WAS TO... WELL...RECRUIT NAZI OCCULTISTS BEFORE THE SOVIETS COULD GET 'EM.
AND FROM THERE--SHORT HOP TO GRABBING ANYTHING THAT MIGHT BE USEFUL FROM ANY-WHERE?
THAT'S ABOUT THE SIZE OF IT.

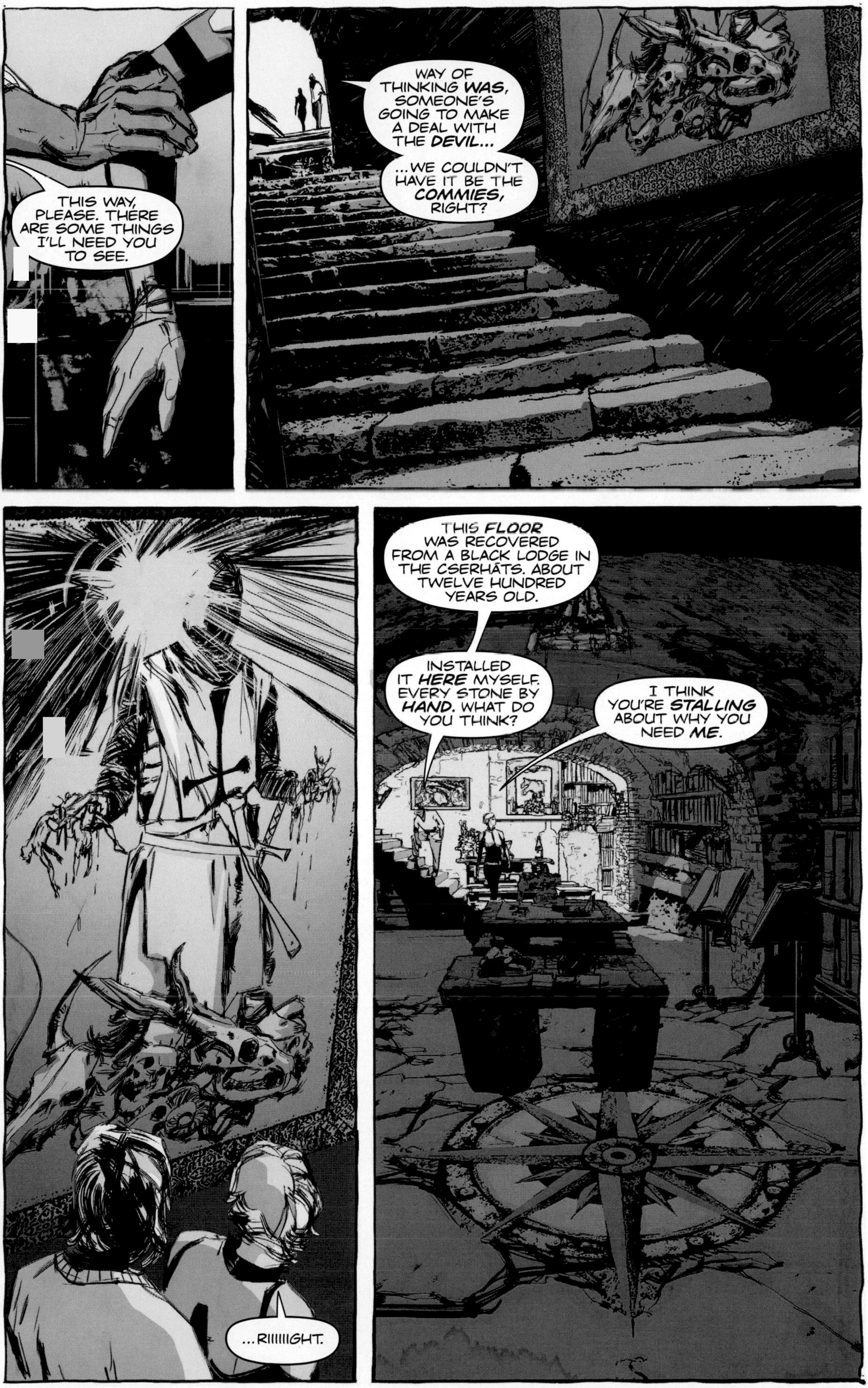
THIS WAY, PLEASE. THERE ARE SOME THINGS I'LL NEED YOU TO SEE.
WAY OF THINKING WAS, SOMEONE'S GOING TO MAKE A DEAL WITH THE DEVIL...
...WE COULDN'T HAVE IT BE THE COMMIES, RIGHT?
...RIIIIIIGHT.
THIS FLOOR WAS RECOVERED FROM A BLACK LODGE IN THE CSERHÁTS. ABOUT TWELVE HUNDRED YEARS OLD.
INSTALLED IT HERE MYSELF. EVERY STONE BY HAND. WHAT DO YOU THINK?
I THINK YOU'RE STALLING ABOUT WHY YOU NEED ME.

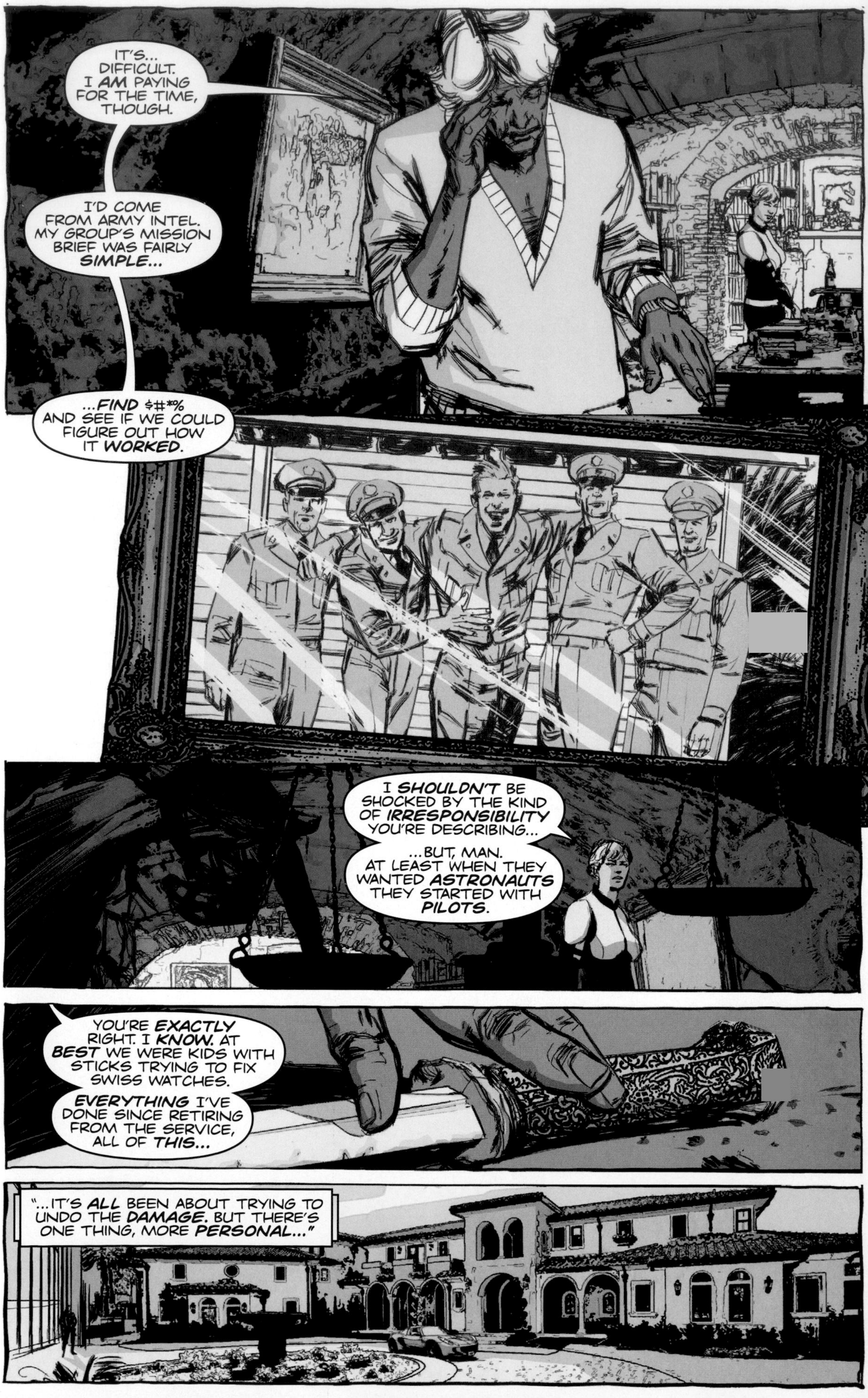
IT'S... DIFFICULT. I AM PAYING FOR THE TIME, THOUGH.
I'D COME FROM ARMY INTEL. MY GROUP'S MISSION BRIEF WAS FAIRLY SIMPLE...
...FIND $#*% AND SEE IF WE COULD FIGURE OUT HOW IT WORKED.
I SHOULDN'T BE SHOCKED BY THE KIND OF IRRESPONSIBILITY YOU'RE DESCRIBING...
...BUT, MAN. AT LEAST WHEN THEY WANTED ASTRONAUTS THEY STARTED WITH PILOTS.
YOU'RE EXACTLY RIGHT. I KNOW. AT BEST WE WERE KIDS WITH STICKS TRYING TO FIX SWISS WATCHES.
EVERYTHING I'VE DONE SINCE RETIRING FROM THE SERVICE, ALL OF THIS...
"...IT'S ALL BEEN ABOUT TRYING TO UNDO THE DAMAGE. BUT THERE'S ONE THING, MORE PERSONAL..."

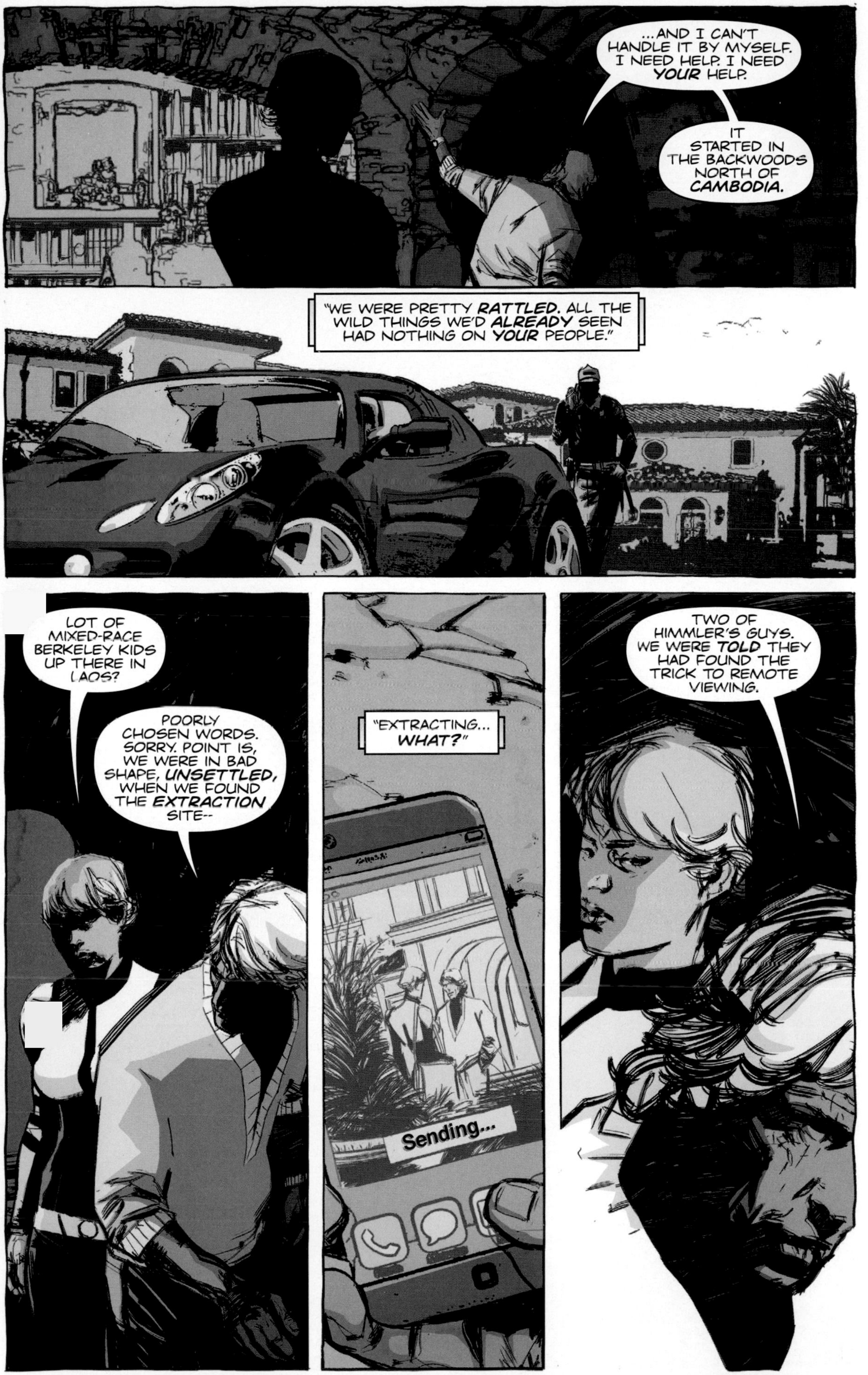
...AND I CAN'T HANDLE IT BY MYSELF. I NEED HELP. I NEED YOUR HELP.
IT STARTED IN THE BACKWOODS NORTH OF CAMBODIA.
"WE WERE PRETTY RATTLED. ALL THE WILD THINGS WE'D ALREADY SEEN HAD NOTHING ON YOUR PEOPLE."
LOT OF MIXED-RACE BERKELEY KIDS UP THERE IN LAOS?
POORLY CHOSEN WORDS. SORRY. POINT IS, WE WERE IN BAD SHAPE, UNSETTLED, WHEN WE FOUND THE EXTRACTION SITE--
"EXTRACTING... WHAT?"
Sending...
TWO OF HIMMLER'S GUYS. WE WERE TOLD THEY HAD FOUND THE TRICK TO REMOTE VIEWING.

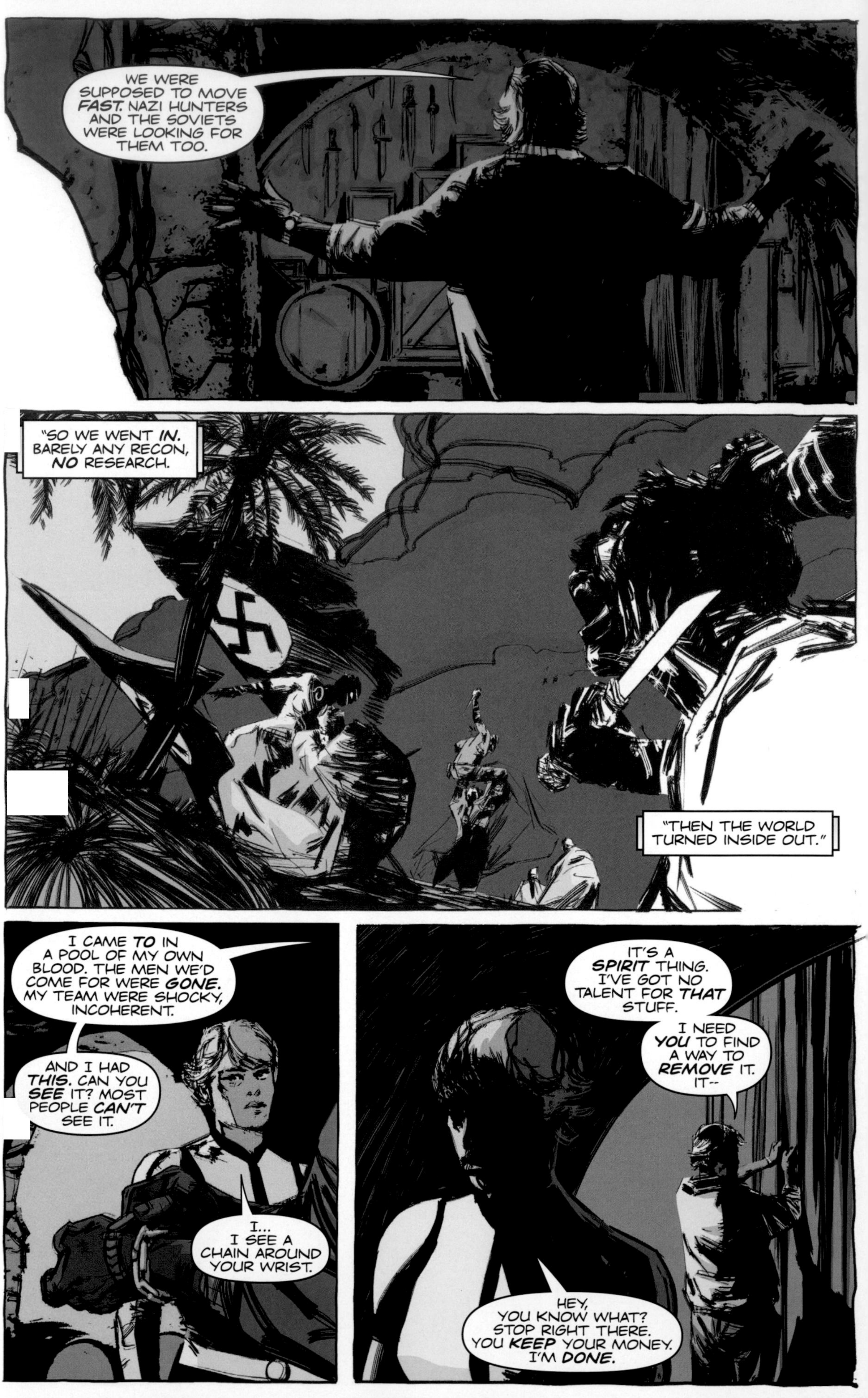
WE WERE SUPPOSED TO MOVE FAST. NAZI HUNTERS AND THE SOVIETS WERE LOOKING FOR THEM TOO.
"SO WE WENT IN. BARELY ANY RECON, NO RESEARCH.
"THEN THE WORLD TURNED INSIDE OUT."
I CAME TO IN A POOL OF MY OWN BLOOD. THE MEN WE'D COME FOR WERE GONE. MY TEAM WERE SHOCKY, INCOHERENT.
AND I HAD THIS. CAN YOU SEE IT? MOST PEOPLE CAN'T SEE IT.
I... I SEE A CHAIN AROUND YOUR WRIST.
IT'S A SPIRIT THING. I'VE GOT NO TALENT FOR THAT STUFF.
I NEED YOU TO FIND A WAY TO REMOVE IT. IT--
HEY, YOU KNOW WHAT? STOP RIGHT THERE. YOU KEEP YOUR MONEY. I'M DONE.

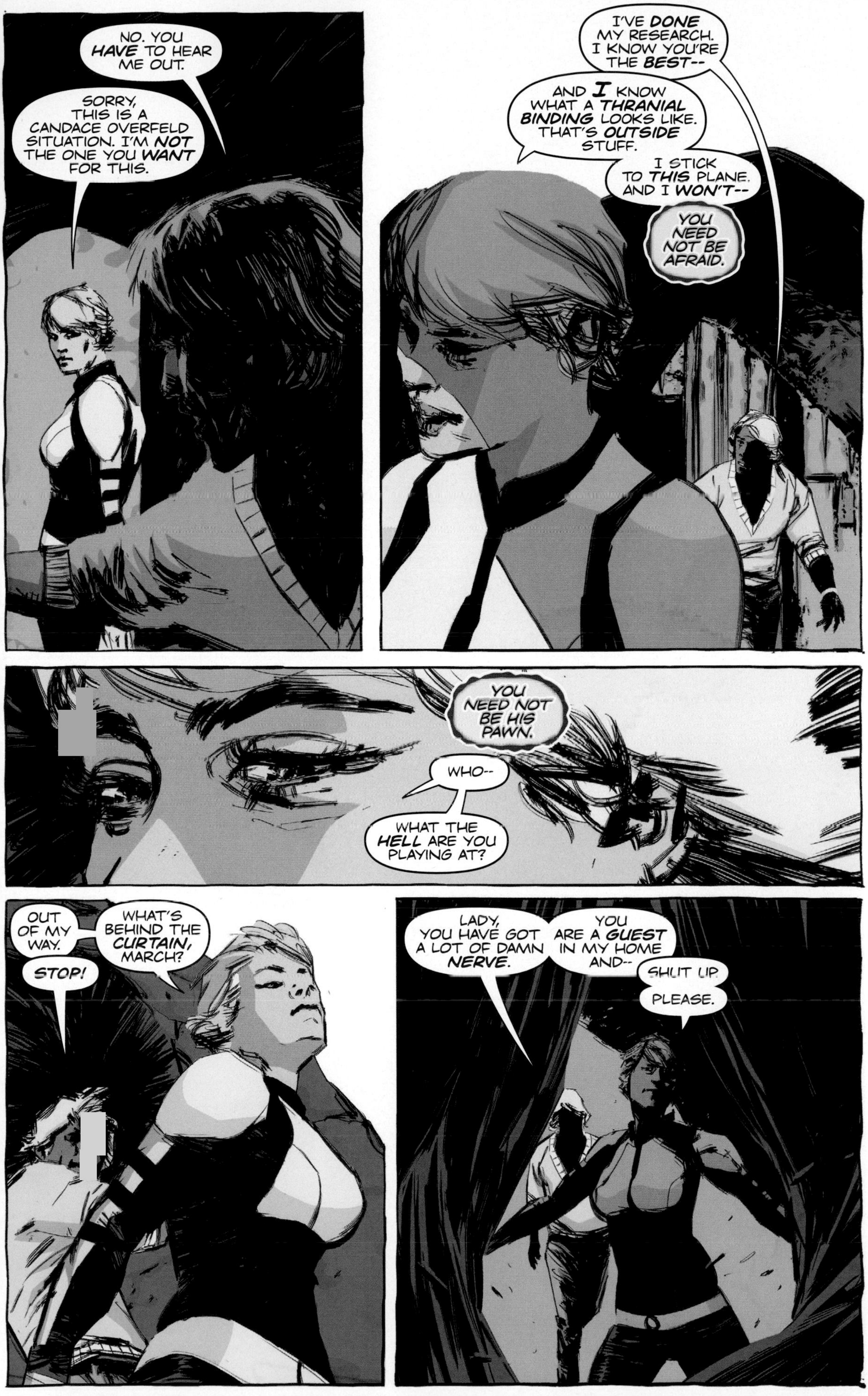
NO. YOU HAVE TO HEAR ME OUT.
SORRY, THIS IS A CANDACE OVERFELD SITUATION. I'M NOT THE ONE YOU WANT FOR THIS.
I'VE DONE MY RESEARCH. I KNOW YOU'RE THE BEST--
AND I KNOW WHAT A THRANIAL BINDING LOOKS LIKE. THAT'S OUTSIDE STUFF.
I STICK TO THIS PLANE. AND I WON'T--
YOU NEED NOT BE AFRAID.
YOU NEED NOT BE HIS PAWN.
WHO--
WHAT THE HELL ARE YOU PLAYING AT?
OUT OF MY WAY.
WHAT'S BEHIND THE CURTAIN, MARCH?
STOP!
LADY, YOU HAVE GOT A LOT OF DAMN NERVE.
YOU ARE A GUEST IN MY HOME AND--
SHUT UP.
PLEASE.

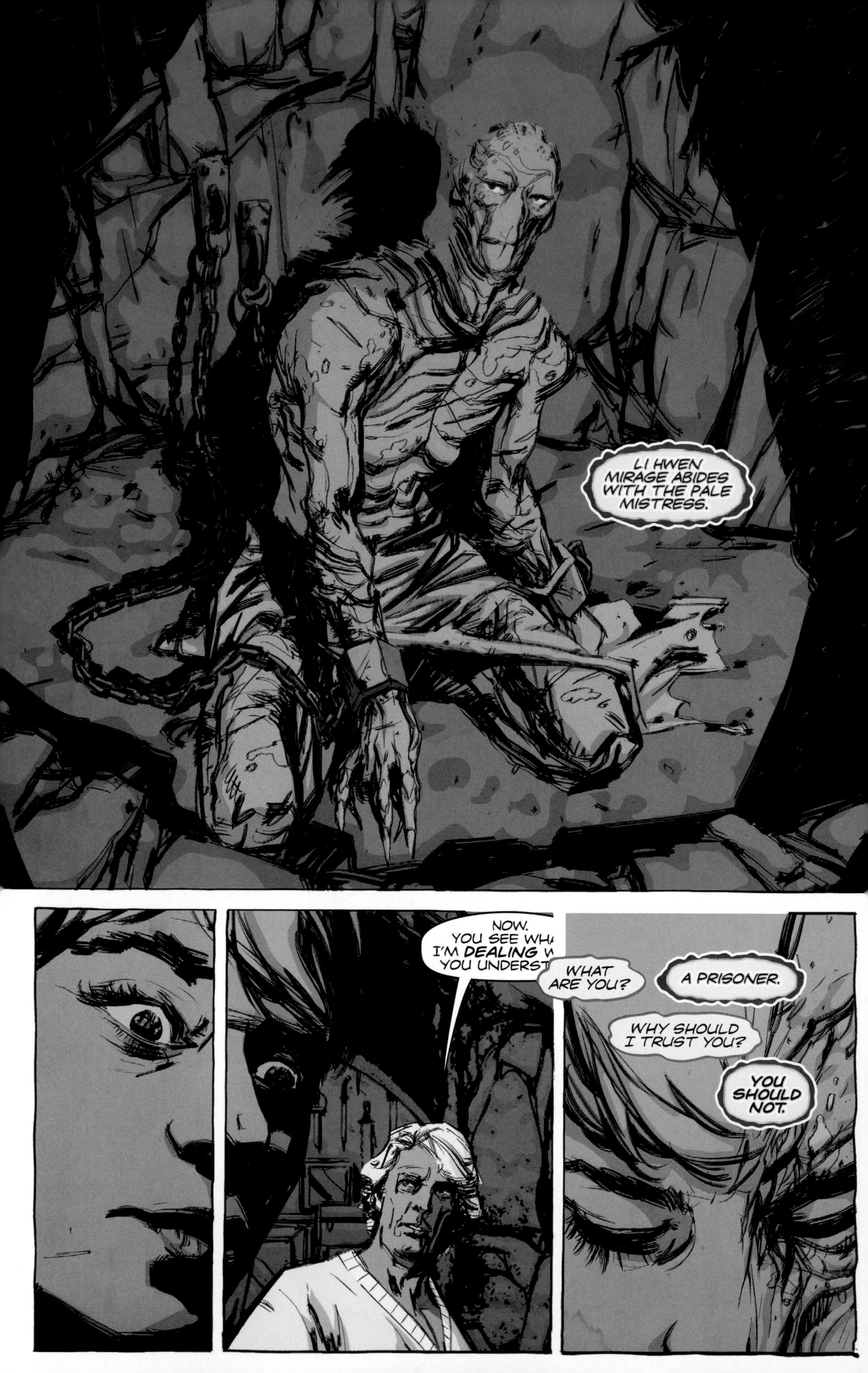
LI HWEN MIRAGE ABIDES WITH THE PALE MISTRESS.
NOW. YOU SEE WHA I'M DEALING W YOU UNDERST
WHAT ARE YOU?
A PRISONER.
WHY SHOULD I TRUST YOU?
YOU SHOULD NOT.

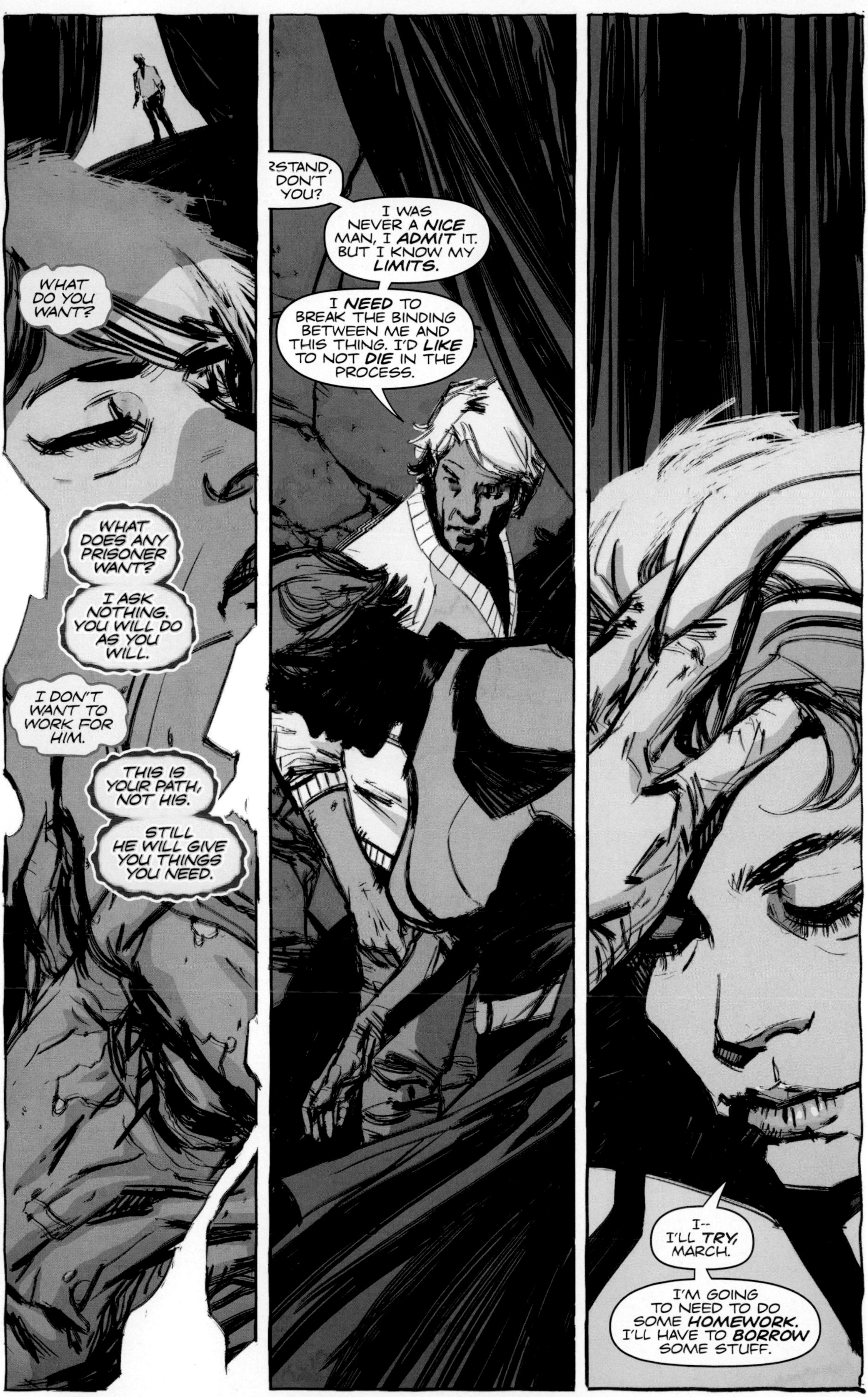
WHAT DO YOU WANT?
WHAT DOES ANY PRISONER WANT?
I ASK NOTHING. YOU WILL DO AS YOU WILL.
I DON'T WANT TO WORK FOR HIM.
THIS IS YOUR PATH, NOT HIS.
STILL HE WILL GIVE YOU THINGS YOU NEED.
RSTAND, DON'T YOU?
I WAS NEVER A NICE MAN, I ADMIT IT. BUT I KNOW MY LIMITS.
I NEED TO BREAK THE BINDING BETWEEN ME AND THIS THING. I'D LIKE TO NOT DIE IN THE PROCESS.
I-- I'LL TRY, MARCH.
I'M GOING TO NEED TO DO SOME HOMEWORK. I'LL HAVE TO BORROW SOME STUFF.

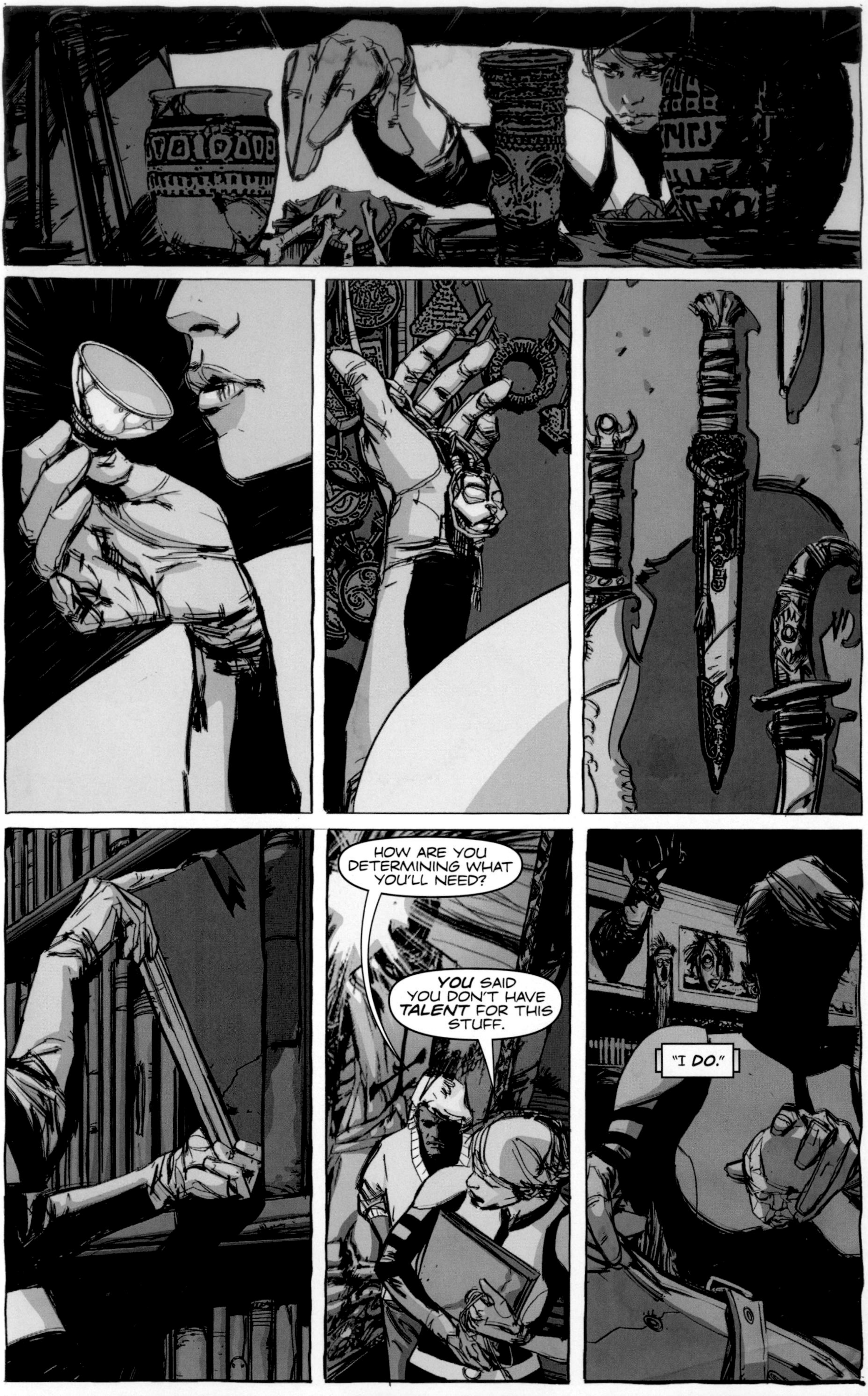
HOW ARE YOU DETERMINING WHAT YOU'LL NEED?
YOU SAID YOU DON'T HAVE **TALENT** FOR THIS STUFF.
"I ***DO.***"

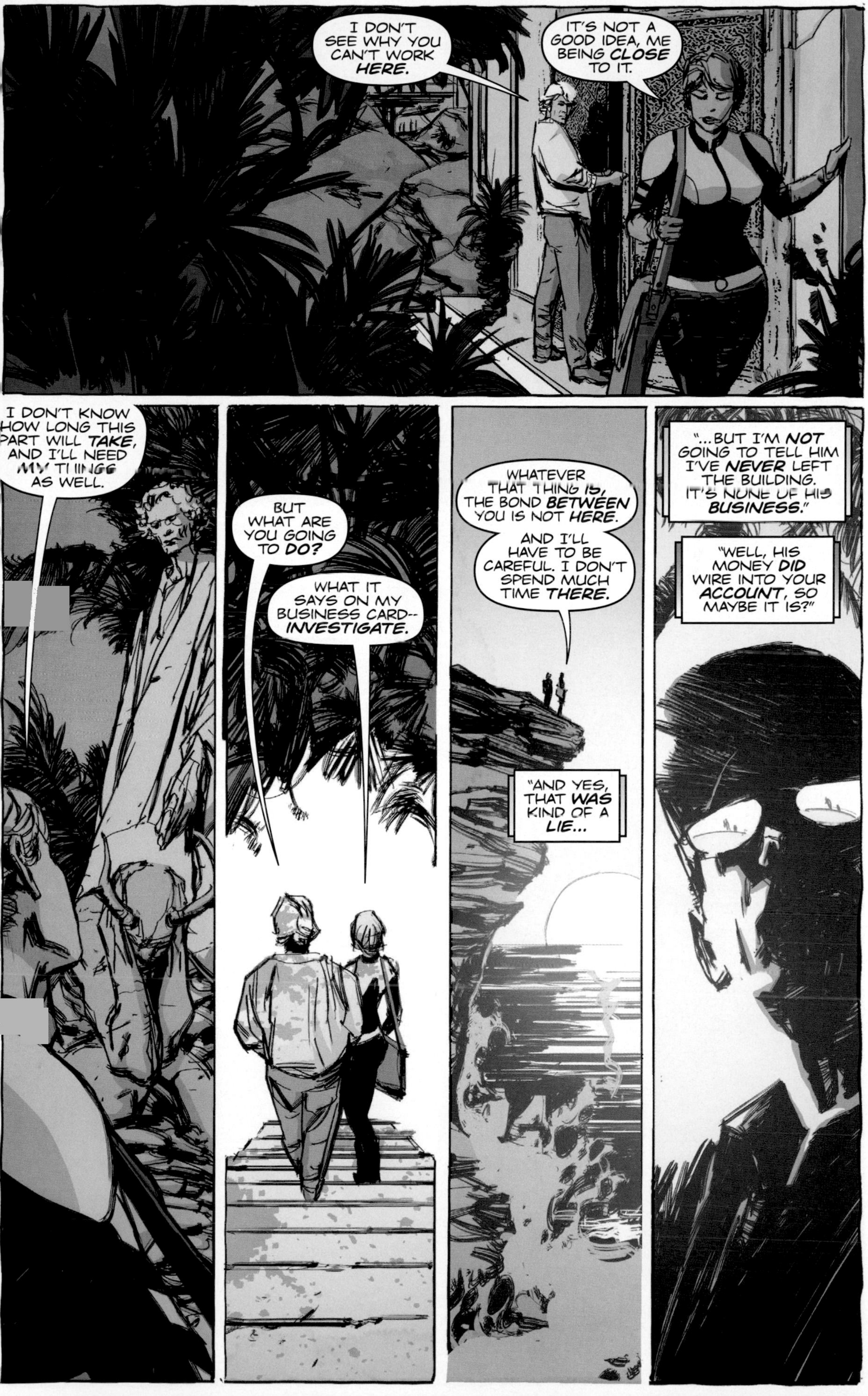
I DON'T SEE WHY YOU CAN'T WORK *HERE.*
IT'S NOT A GOOD IDEA, ME BEING *CLOSE* TO IT.
I DON'T KNOW HOW LONG THIS PART WILL *TAKE,* AND I'LL NEED MY THINGS AS WELL.
BUT WHAT ARE YOU GOING TO *DO?*
WHAT IT SAYS ON MY BUSINESS CARD-- *INVESTIGATE.*
WHATEVER THAT THING *IS,* THE BOND *BETWEEN* YOU IS NOT *HERE.*
AND I'LL HAVE TO BE CAREFUL. I DON'T SPEND MUCH TIME *THERE.*
"AND YES, THAT *WAS* KIND OF A *LIE...*
"...BUT I'M *NOT* GOING TO TELL HIM I'VE *NEVER* LEFT THE BUILDING. IT'S NONE OF HIS *BUSINESS.*"
"WELL, HIS MONEY *DID* WIRE INTO YOUR *ACCOUNT,* SO MAYBE IT IS?"

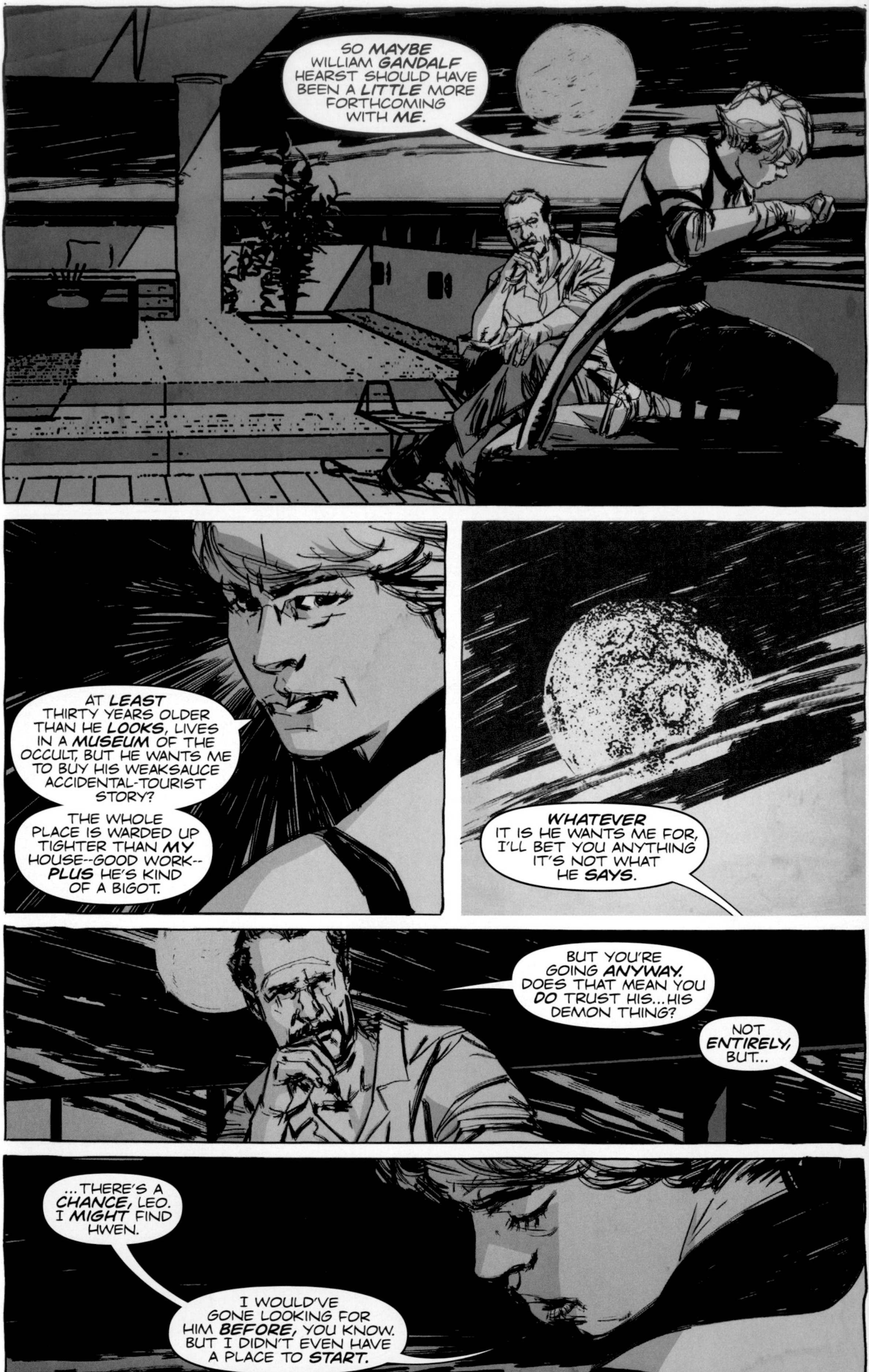
SO MAYBE WILLIAM GANDALF HEARST SHOULD HAVE BEEN A LITTLE MORE FORTHCOMING WITH ME.
AT LEAST THIRTY YEARS OLDER THAN HE LOOKS, LIVES IN A MUSEUM OF THE OCCULT, BUT HE WANTS ME TO BUY HIS WEAKSAUCE ACCIDENTAL-TOURIST STORY?
THE WHOLE PLACE IS WARDED UP TIGHTER THAN MY HOUSE--GOOD WORK-- PLUS HE'S KIND OF A BIGOT.
WHATEVER IT IS HE WANTS ME FOR, I'LL BET YOU ANYTHING IT'S NOT WHAT HE SAYS.
BUT YOU'RE GOING ANYWAY. DOES THAT MEAN YOU DO TRUST HIS...HIS DEMON THING?
NOT ENTIRELY, BUT...
...THERE'S A CHANCE, LEO. I MIGHT FIND HWEN.
I WOULD'VE GONE LOOKING FOR HIM BEFORE, YOU KNOW. BUT I DIDN'T EVEN HAVE A PLACE TO START.

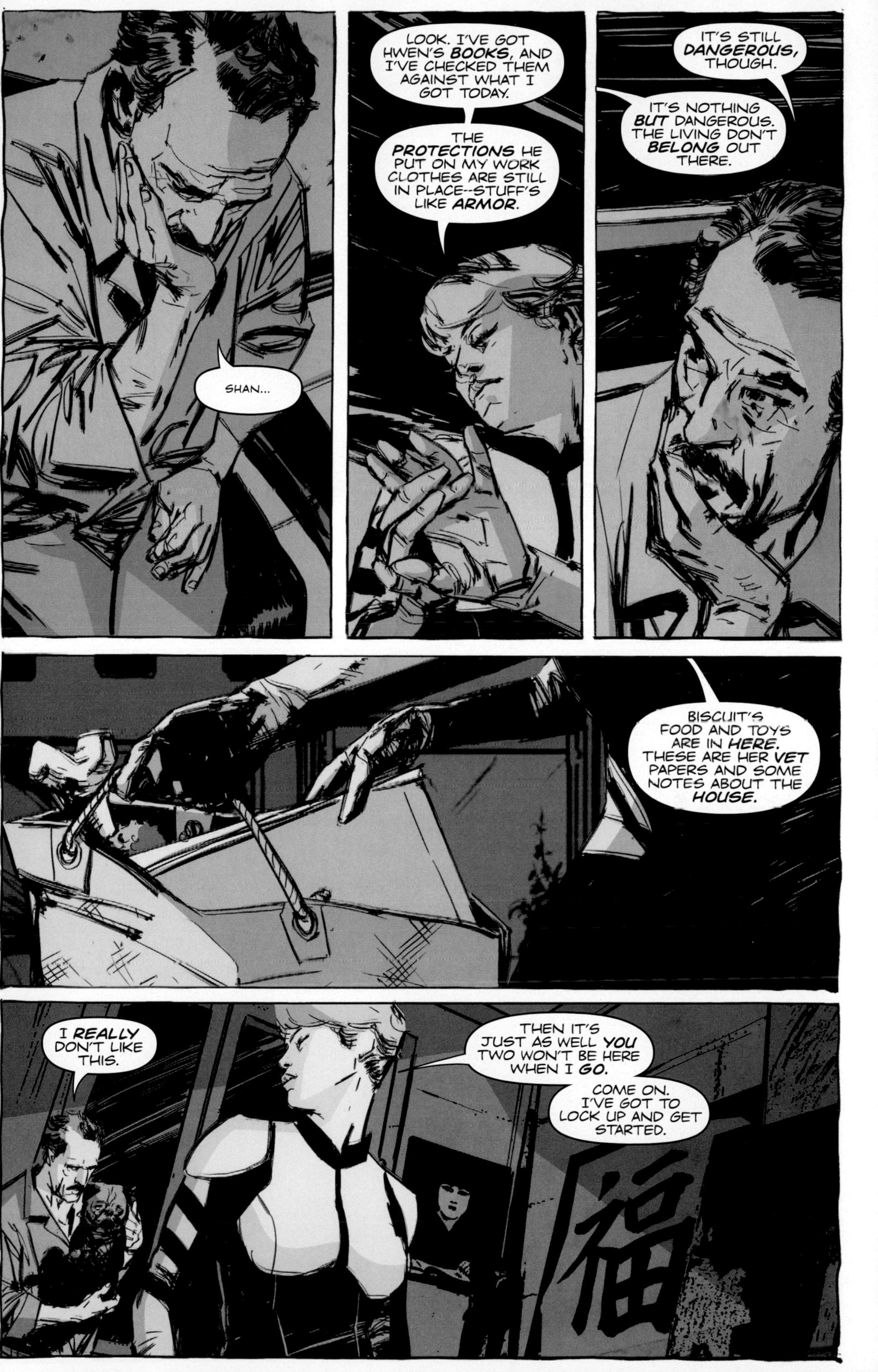
SHAN...
LOOK. I'VE GOT HWEN'S BOOKS, AND I'VE CHECKED THEM AGAINST WHAT I GOT TODAY.
THE PROTECTIONS HE PUT ON MY WORK CLOTHES ARE STILL IN PLACE--STUFF'S LIKE ARMOR.
IT'S STILL DANGEROUS, THOUGH.
IT'S NOTHING BUT DANGEROUS. THE LIVING DON'T BELONG OUT THERE.
BISCUIT'S FOOD AND TOYS ARE IN HERE. THESE ARE HER VET PAPERS AND SOME NOTES ABOUT THE HOUSE.
I REALLY DON'T LIKE THIS.
THEN IT'S JUST AS WELL YOU TWO WON'T BE HERE WHEN I GO.
COME ON. I'VE GOT TO LOCK UP AND GET STARTED.
福

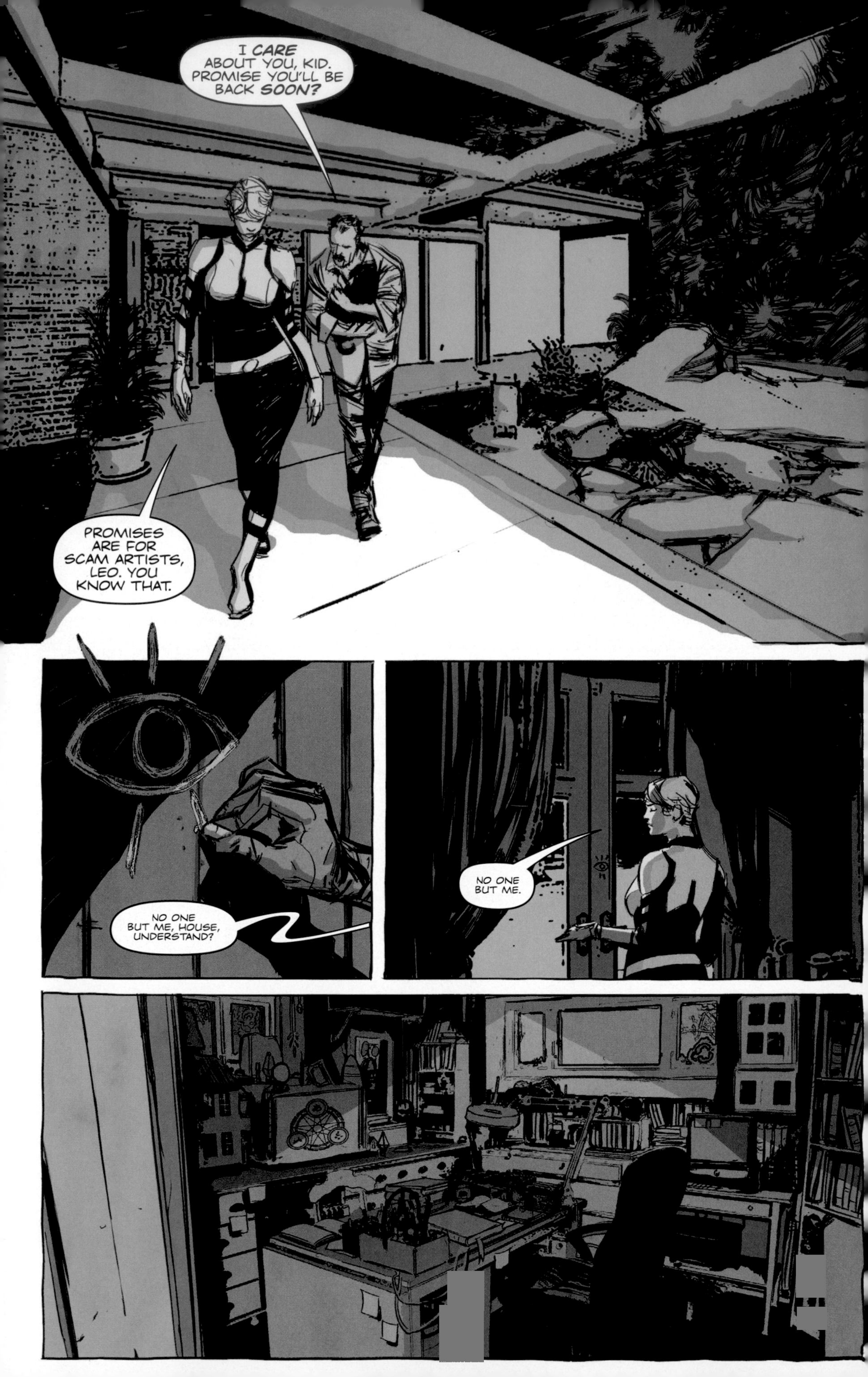
I CARE ABOUT YOU, KID. PROMISE YOU'LL BE BACK SOON?
PROMISES ARE FOR SCAM ARTISTS, LEO. YOU KNOW THAT.
NO ONE BUT ME, HOUSE, UNDERSTAND?
NO ONE BUT ME.

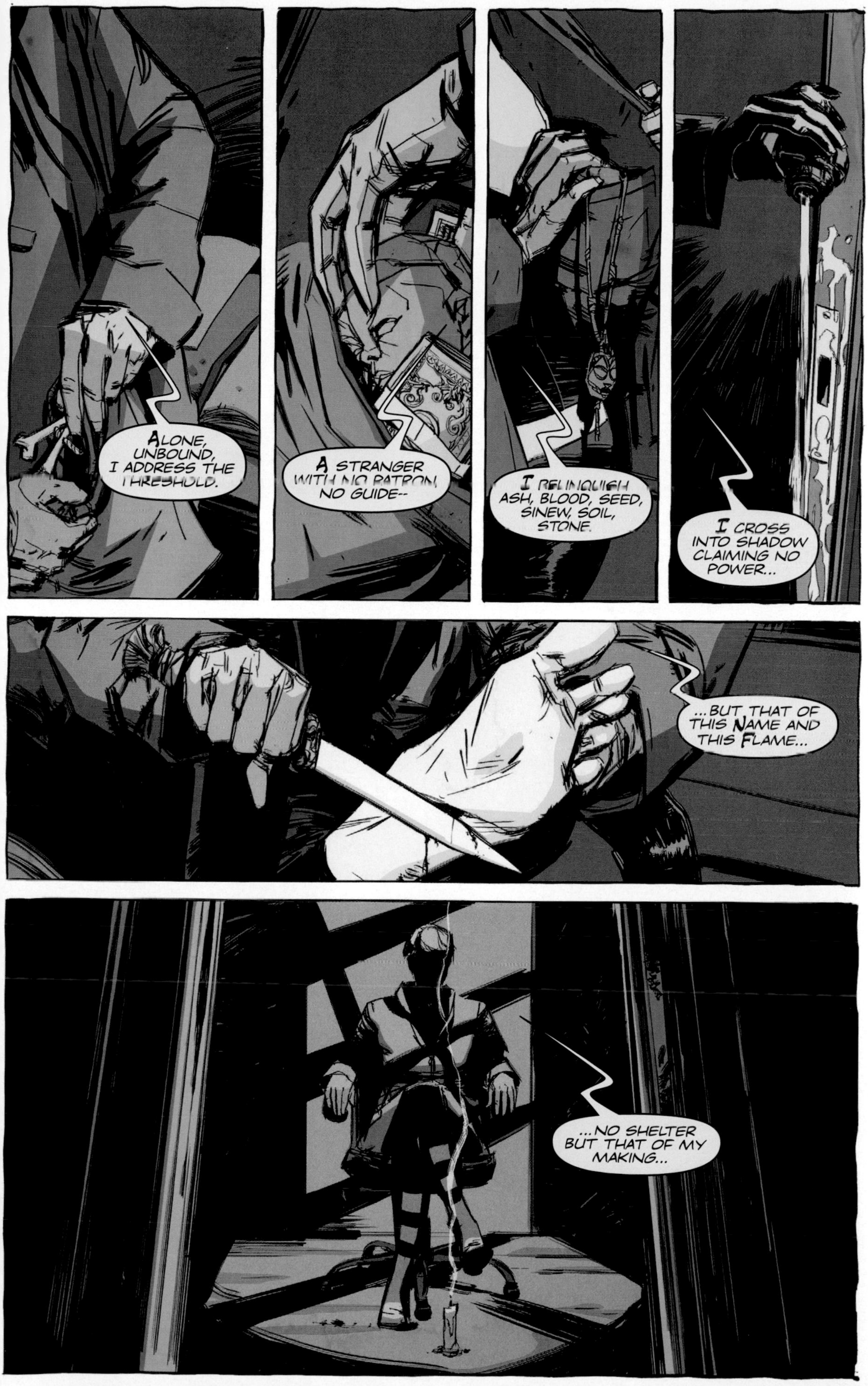
ALONE, UNBOUND, I ADDRESS THE THRESHOLD.
A STRANGER WITH NO PATRON, NO GUIDE--
I RELINQUISH ASH, BLOOD, SEED, SINEW, SOIL, STONE.
I CROSS INTO SHADOW CLAIMING NO POWER...
...BUT THAT OF THIS NAME AND THIS FLAME...
...NO SHELTER BUT THAT OF MY MAKING...

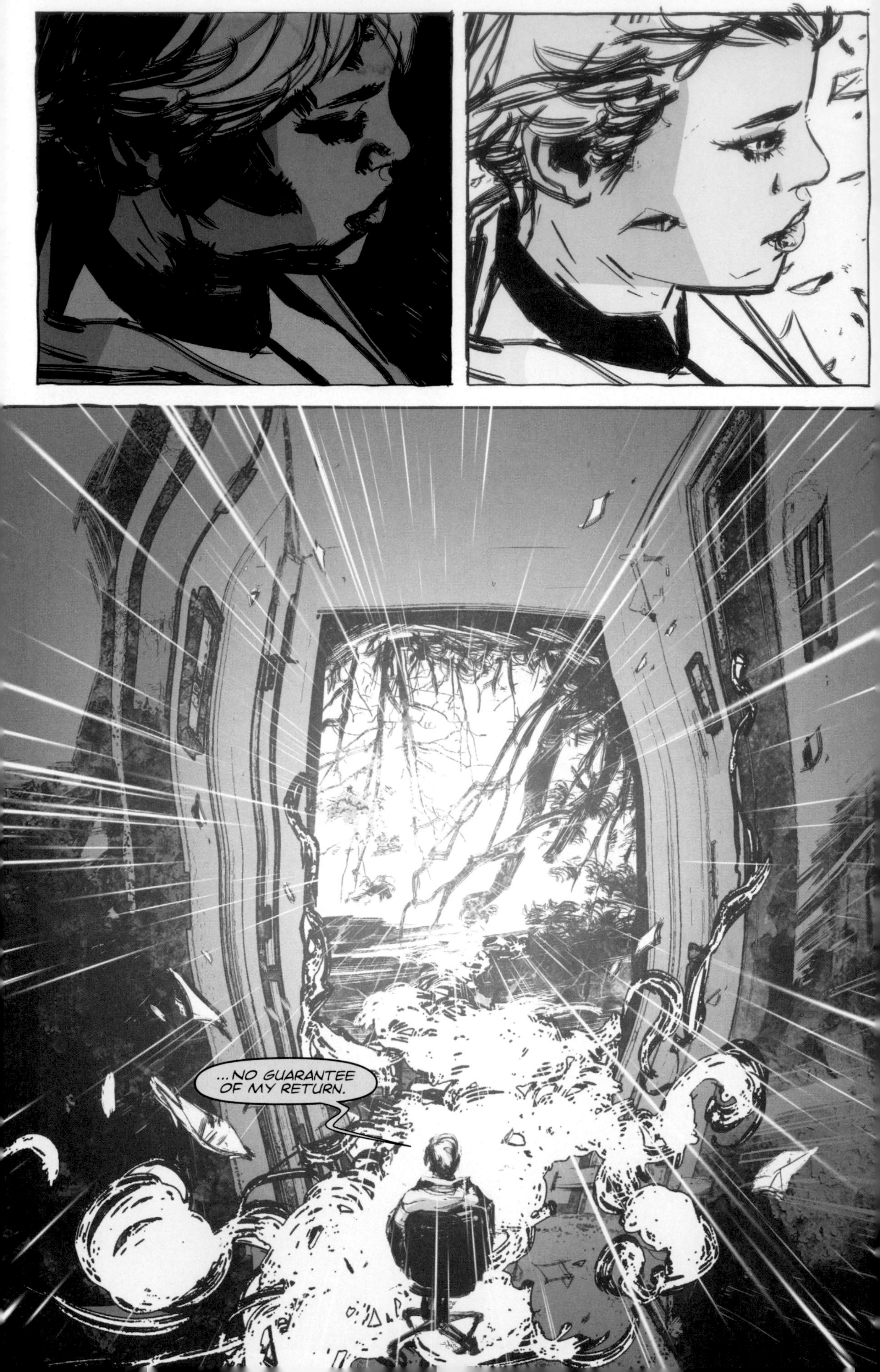
...NO GUARANTEE OF MY RETURN.

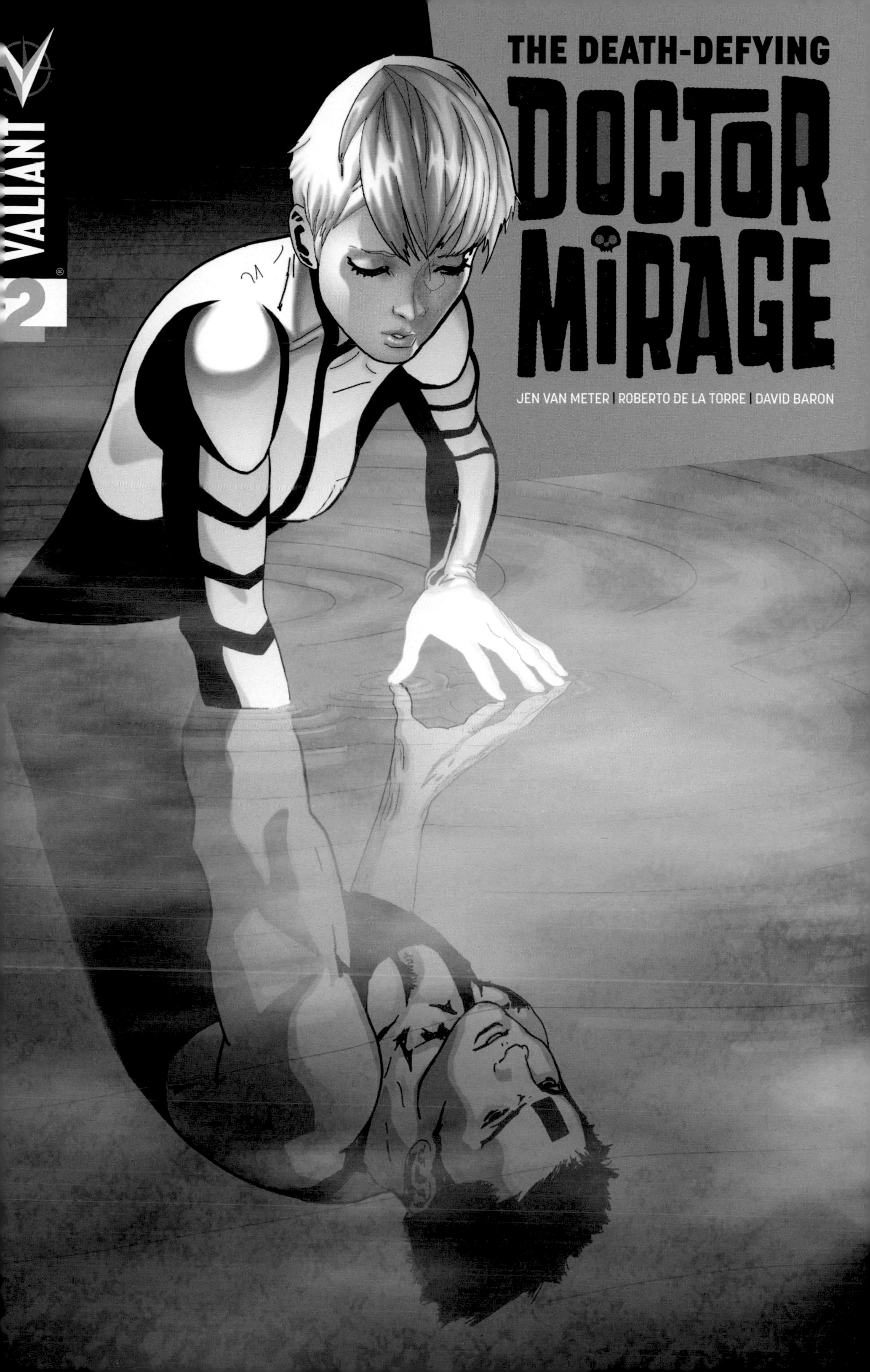
VALIANT
2
THE DEATH-DEFYING
DOCTOR MIRAGE
JEN VAN METER | ROBERTO DE LA TORRE | DAVID BARON

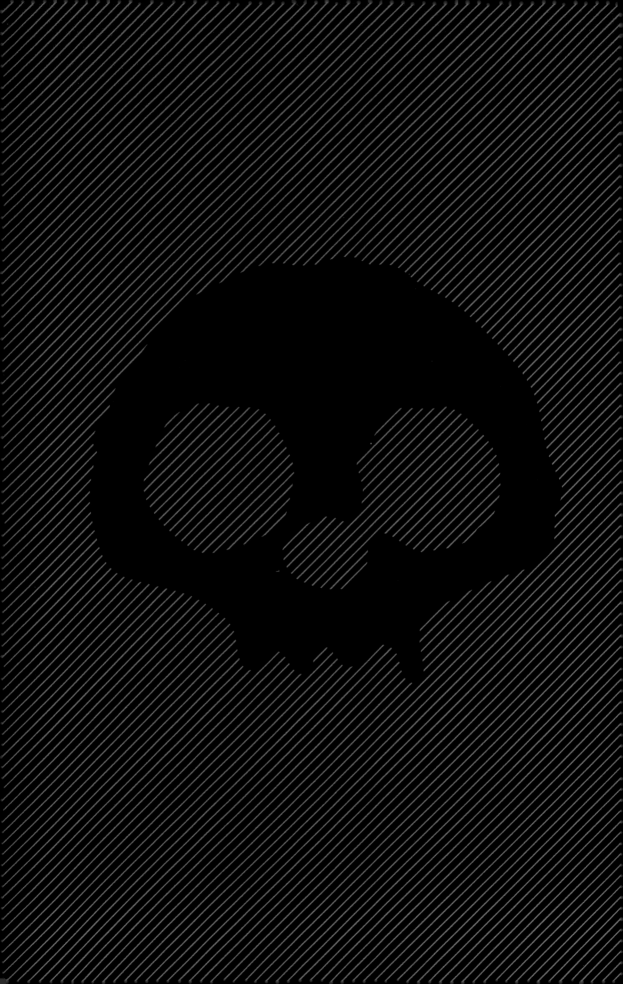

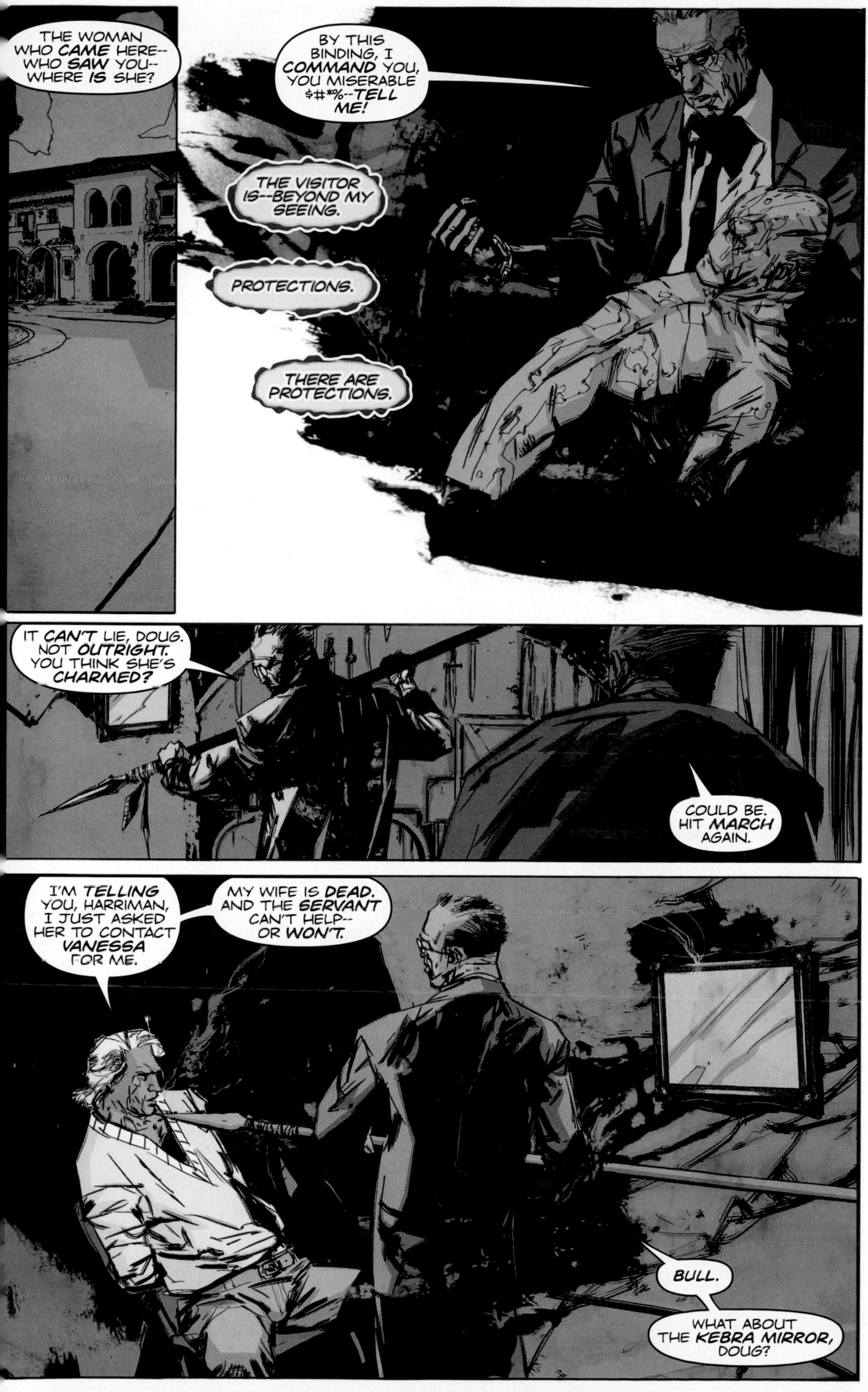
THE WOMAN WHO CAME HERE-- WHO SAW YOU-- WHERE IS SHE?
BY THIS BINDING, I COMMAND YOU, YOU MISERABLE $#*%--TELL ME!
THE VISITOR IS--BEYOND MY SEEING.
PROTECTIONS.
THERE ARE PROTECTIONS.
IT CAN'T LIE, DOUG. NOT OUTRIGHT. YOU THINK SHE'S CHARMED?
COULD BE. HIT MARCH AGAIN.
I'M TELLING YOU, HARRIMAN, I JUST ASKED HER TO CONTACT VANESSA FOR ME.
MY WIFE IS DEAD. AND THE SERVANT CAN'T HELP-- OR WON'T.
BULL.
WHAT ABOUT THE KEBRA MIRROR, DOUG?

WORTH A *TRY*.

DON'T *WET* YOURSELF, MARCH. YOU'RE HARDLY THE *FIRST* TO TRY AND GET *OUT* OF OUR LITTLE CLUB.

I WOULDN'T DO THAT TO THE *REST* OF YOU. I *SWEAR*.

YEAH, THAT'S WHAT *I* SAID. REMEMBER?

SERVANT, THIS IS A *SCRYING* TOOL. YOU ARE BOUND TO OBEY US...

...SO *SCRY*.

I WANT TO SEE SHAN FONG, WHO CALLS HERSELF *DOCTOR MIRAGE*.

ᕃᔕᑎᕋ ᐁᖁᔨᕋ ᑕᕃᔕ ᙉᔕᕐᕋᒣ ᘃᕋᔐᕋᒐᕋᖪ.

*%$#. SEE THE *CANDLE*? THE *BLOOD*?

WHAT? WHAT'S SHE *DOING*?

SHE'S #$&@ *PROJECTING* IS WHAT SHE'S DOING.

THAT'S JUST THE *MEAT*...

"...I WANT TO KNOW WHERE *THE REST OF HER* IS."

THE *NIGHT GARDEN* RECEIVES YOU STILL-TETHERED-TO-FLESH. BY *MISCHANCE...*?

OR BE YOU COURIER?

SUPPLICANT?

THIEF?

I'VE COME LOOKING FOR THE *PALE MISTRESS.*

I WAS TOLD SHE *HAS* SOMETHING OF MINE.

AH. SUPPLICANT. SO NOTED.

ARE YOU THREE-- WHAT *ARE* YOU? GUIDES?

WHILE YOU ARE *HERE*-- AND YOUR *FLESH* BREATHES *THERE...*

...YOUR GATE WEAKENS THE WALL BETWEEN *YOUR* HOME AND *OURS.*

WE DEFEND THE WALL.

YOU SEE TO YOURSELF.

OKAY, BUT DO I JUST GO ON MY *WAY?* ARE THERE *RULES* I SHOULD KNOW?

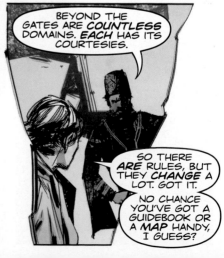

BEYOND THE GATES ARE *COUNTLESS* DOMAINS. *EACH* HAS ITS COURTESIES.

SO THERE *ARE* RULES, BUT THEY *CHANGE* A LOT. GOT IT.

NO CHANCE YOU'VE GOT A *GUIDEBOOK* OR A *MAP* HANDY, I GUESS?

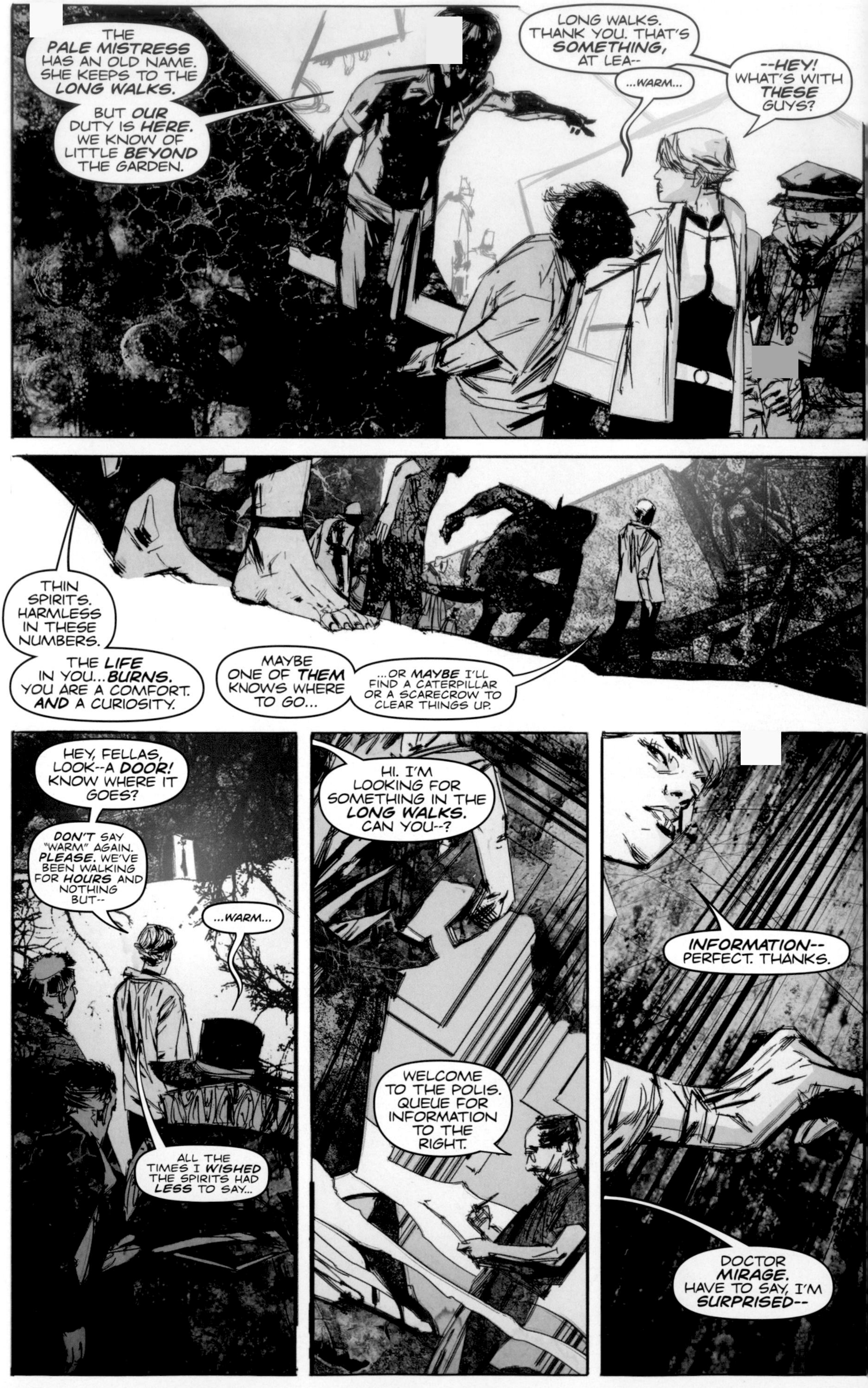

THE PALE MISTRESS HAS AN OLD NAME. SHE KEEPS TO THE LONG WALKS.
BUT OUR DUTY IS HERE. WE KNOW OF LITTLE BEYOND THE GARDEN.
LONG WALKS. THANK YOU. THAT'S SOMETHING, AT LEA--
...WARM...
--HEY! WHAT'S WITH THESE GUYS?
THIN SPIRITS. HARMLESS IN THESE NUMBERS.
THE LIFE IN YOU...BURNS. YOU ARE A COMFORT. AND A CURIOSITY.
MAYBE ONE OF THEM KNOWS WHERE TO GO...
...OR MAYBE I'LL FIND A CATERPILLAR OR A SCARECROW TO CLEAR THINGS UP.
HEY, FELLAS, LOOK--A DOOR! KNOW WHERE IT GOES?
DON'T SAY "WARM" AGAIN. PLEASE. WE'VE BEEN WALKING FOR HOURS AND NOTHING BUT--
...WARM...
ALL THE TIMES I WISHED THE SPIRITS HAD LESS TO SAY...
HI. I'M LOOKING FOR SOMETHING IN THE LONG WALKS. CAN YOU--?
WELCOME TO THE POLIS. QUEUE FOR INFORMATION TO THE RIGHT.
INFORMATION-- PERFECT. THANKS.
DOCTOR MIRAGE. HAVE TO SAY, I'M SURPRISED--

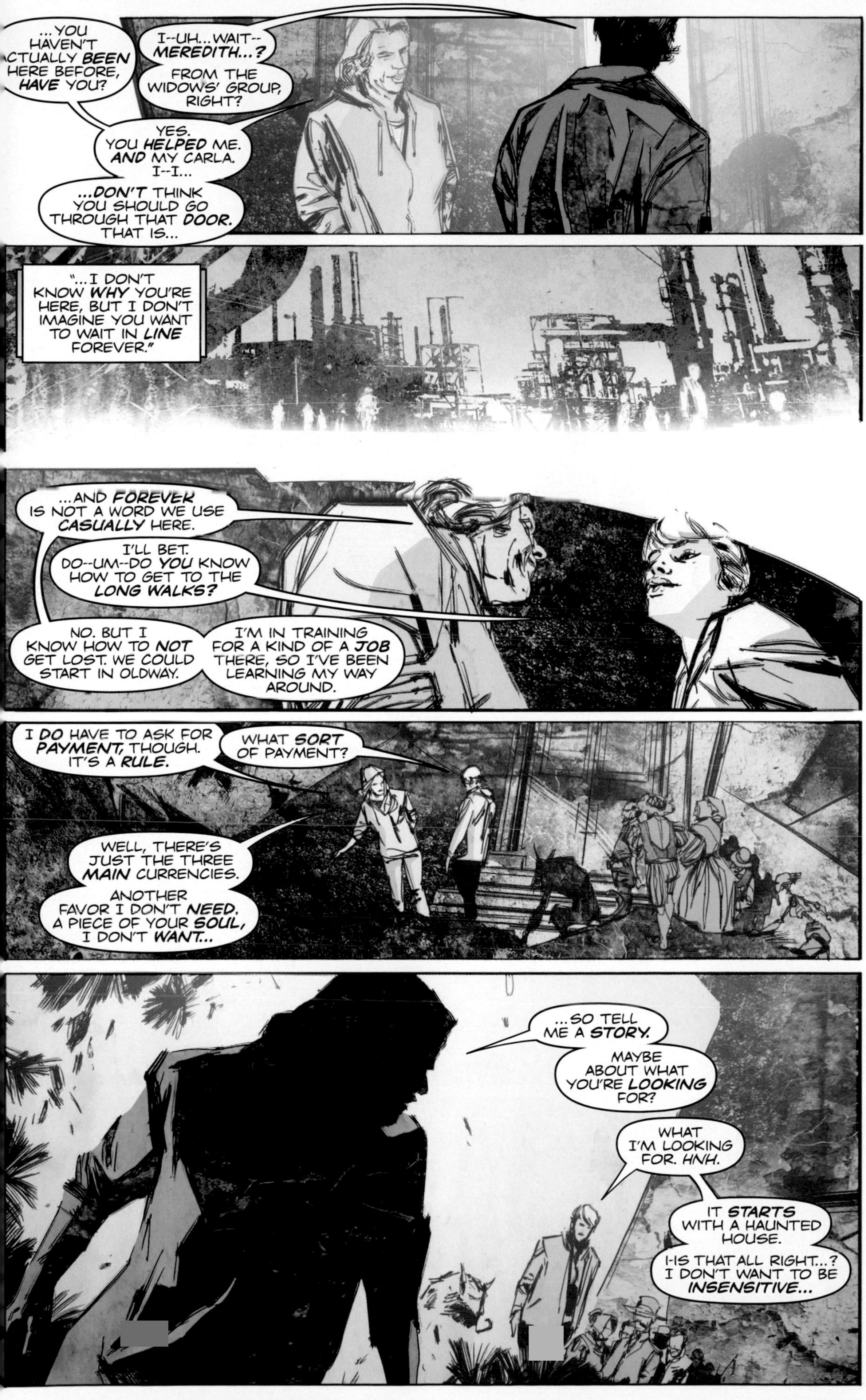
...YOU HAVEN'T ACTUALLY BEEN HERE BEFORE, HAVE YOU?
I--UH...WAIT-- MEREDITH...?
FROM THE WIDOWS' GROUP, RIGHT?
YES. YOU HELPED ME. AND MY CARLA. I--I...
...DON'T THINK YOU SHOULD GO THROUGH THAT DOOR. THAT IS...
"...I DON'T KNOW WHY YOU'RE HERE, BUT I DON'T IMAGINE YOU WANT TO WAIT IN LINE FOREVER."
...AND FOREVER IS NOT A WORD WE USE CASUALLY HERE.
I'LL BET. DO--UM--DO YOU KNOW HOW TO GET TO THE LONG WALKS?
NO. BUT I KNOW HOW TO NOT GET LOST. WE COULD START IN OLDWAY.
I'M IN TRAINING FOR A KIND OF A JOB THERE, SO I'VE BEEN LEARNING MY WAY AROUND.
I DO HAVE TO ASK FOR PAYMENT, THOUGH. IT'S A RULE.
WHAT SORT OF PAYMENT?
WELL, THERE'S JUST THE THREE MAIN CURRENCIES.
ANOTHER FAVOR I DON'T NEED. A PIECE OF YOUR SOUL, I DON'T WANT...
...SO TELL ME A STORY.
MAYBE ABOUT WHAT YOU'RE LOOKING FOR?
WHAT I'M LOOKING FOR. HNH.
IT STARTS WITH A HAUNTED HOUSE.
I-IS THAT ALL RIGHT...? I DON'T WANT TO BE INSENSITIVE...

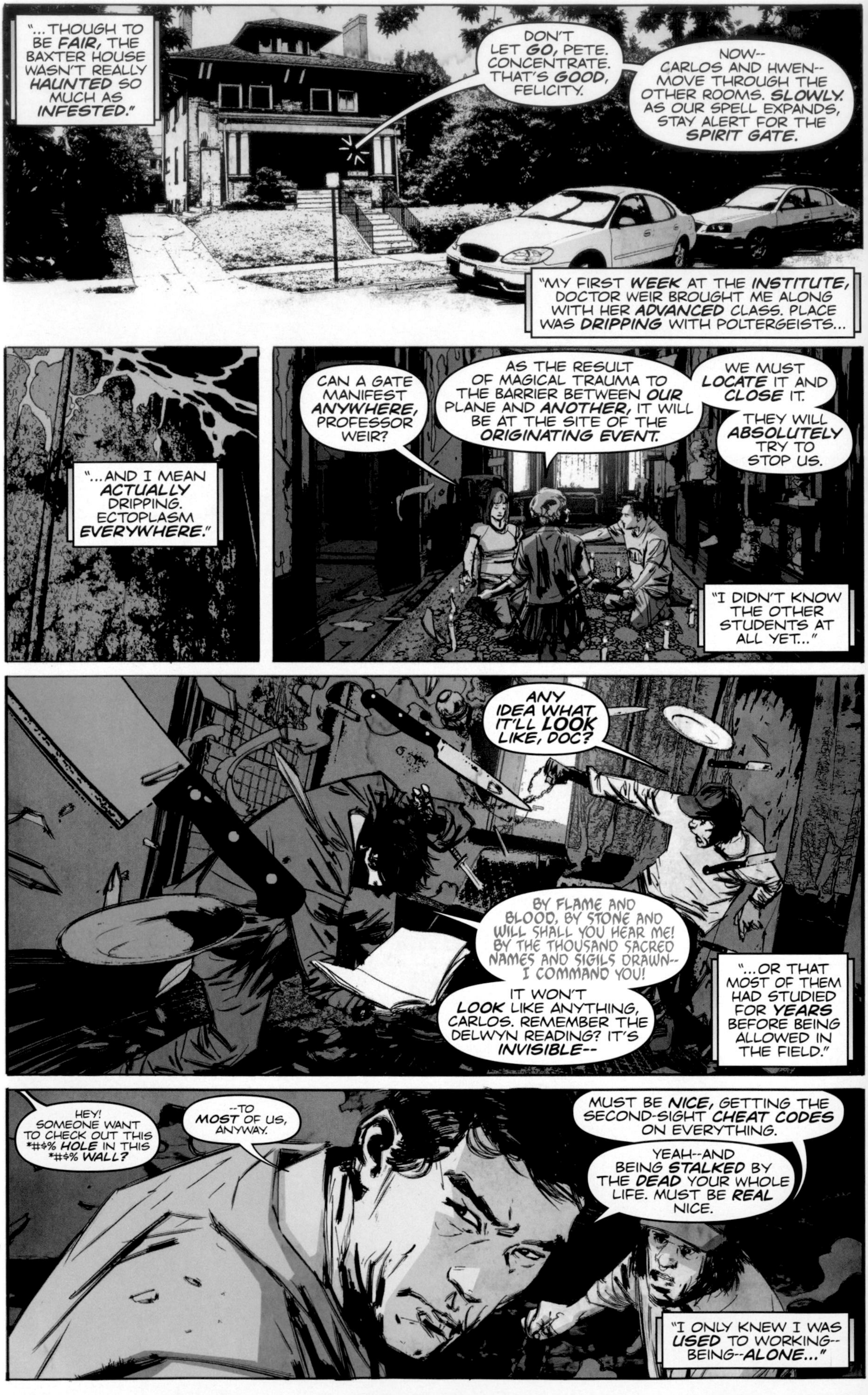
"...THOUGH TO BE FAIR, THE BAXTER HOUSE WASN'T REALLY HAUNTED SO MUCH AS INFESTED."
DON'T LET GO, PETE. CONCENTRATE. THAT'S GOOD, FELICITY.
NOW-- CARLOS AND HWEN-- MOVE THROUGH THE OTHER ROOMS. SLOWLY. AS OUR SPELL EXPANDS, STAY ALERT FOR THE SPIRIT GATE.
"MY FIRST WEEK AT THE INSTITUTE, DOCTOR WEIR BROUGHT ME ALONG WITH HER ADVANCED CLASS. PLACE WAS DRIPPING WITH POLTERGEISTS...
"...AND I MEAN ACTUALLY DRIPPING. ECTOPLASM EVERYWHERE."
CAN A GATE MANIFEST ANYWHERE, PROFESSOR WEIR?
AS THE RESULT OF MAGICAL TRAUMA TO THE BARRIER BETWEEN OUR PLANE AND ANOTHER, IT WILL BE AT THE SITE OF THE ORIGINATING EVENT.
WE MUST LOCATE IT AND CLOSE IT.
THEY WILL ABSOLUTELY TRY TO STOP US.
"I DIDN'T KNOW THE OTHER STUDENTS AT ALL YET..."
ANY IDEA WHAT IT'LL LOOK LIKE, DOC?
BY FLAME AND BLOOD, BY STONE AND WILL SHALL YOU HEAR ME! BY THE THOUSAND SACRED NAMES AND SIGILS DRAWN-- I COMMAND YOU!
IT WON'T LOOK LIKE ANYTHING, CARLOS. REMEMBER THE DELWYN READING? IT'S INVISIBLE--
"...OR THAT MOST OF THEM HAD STUDIED FOR YEARS BEFORE BEING ALLOWED IN THE FIELD."
HEY! SOMEONE WANT TO CHECK OUT THIS *#$% HOLE IN THIS *#$% WALL?
--TO MOST OF US, ANYWAY.
MUST BE NICE, GETTING THE SECOND-SIGHT CHEAT CODES ON EVERYTHING.
YEAH--AND BEING STALKED BY THE DEAD YOUR WHOLE LIFE. MUST BE REAL NICE.
"I ONLY KNEW I WAS USED TO WORKING-- BEING--ALONE..."

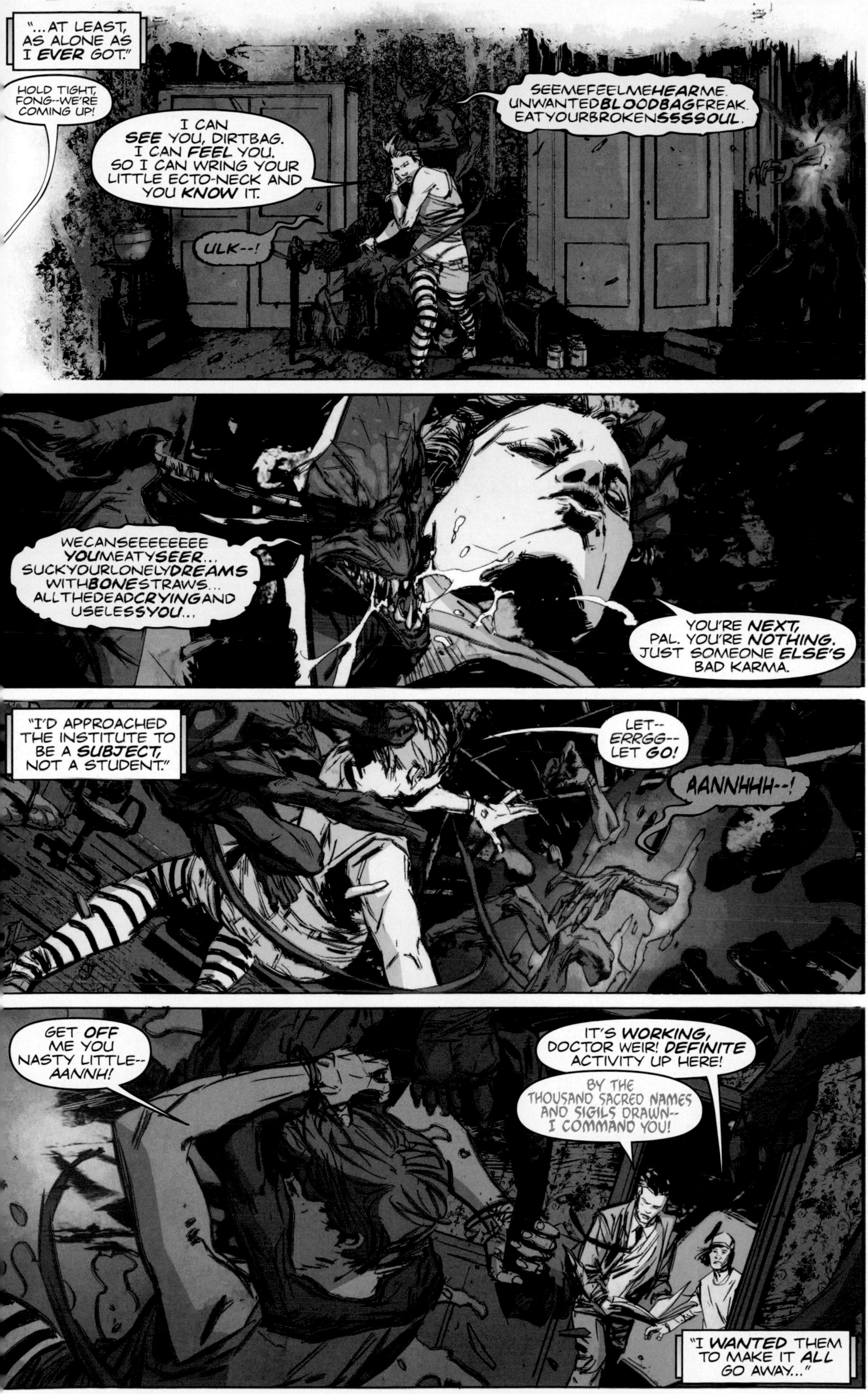
"...AT LEAST, AS ALONE AS I EVER GOT."
HOLD TIGHT, FONG--WE'RE COMING UP!
I CAN SEE YOU, DIRTBAG. I CAN FEEL YOU. SO I CAN WRING YOUR LITTLE ECTO-NECK AND YOU KNOW IT.
SEEMEFEELMEHEARME. UNWANTEDBLOODBAGFREAK. EATYOURBROKENSSSSOUL.
ULK--!
WECANSEEEEEEEE YOUMEATYSEER... SUCKYOURLONELYDREAMS WITHBONESTRAWS... ALLTHEDEADCRYINGAND USELESSYOU...
YOU'RE NEXT, PAL. YOU'RE NOTHING. JUST SOMEONE ELSE'S BAD KARMA.
"I'D APPROACHED THE INSTITUTE TO BE A SUBJECT, NOT A STUDENT."
LET-- ERRGG-- LET GO!
AANNHHH--!
GET OFF ME YOU NASTY LITTLE-- AANNH!
IT'S WORKING, DOCTOR WEIR! DEFINITE ACTIVITY UP HERE!
BY THE THOUSAND SACRED NAMES AND SIGILS DRAWN-- I COMMAND YOU!
"I WANTED THEM TO MAKE IT ALL GO AWAY..."

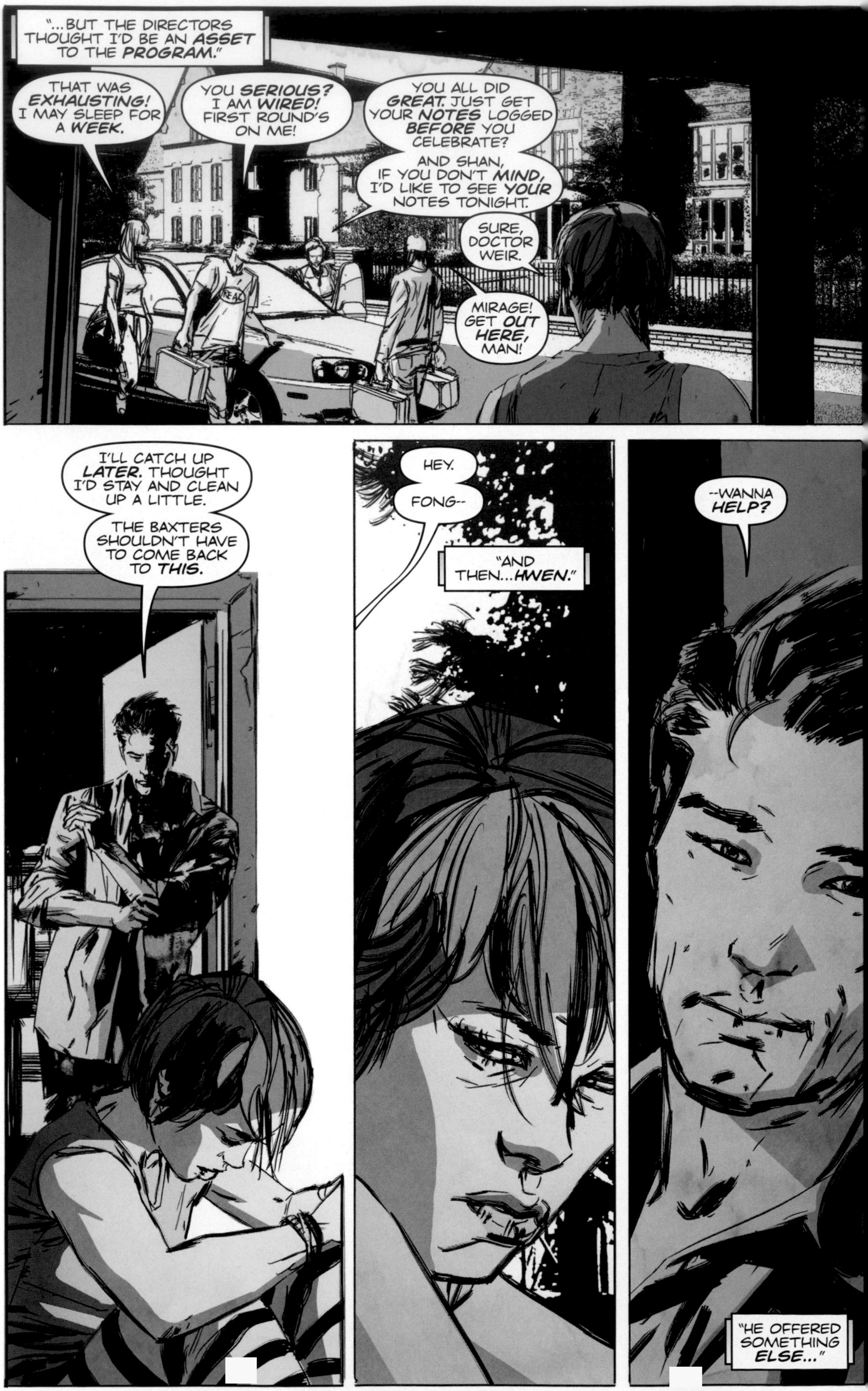
"...BUT THE DIRECTORS THOUGHT I'D BE AN ASSET TO THE PROGRAM."
THAT WAS EXHAUSTING! I MAY SLEEP FOR A WEEK.
YOU SERIOUS? I AM WIRED! FIRST ROUND'S ON ME!
YOU ALL DID GREAT. JUST GET YOUR NOTES LOGGED BEFORE YOU CELEBRATE?
AND SHAN, IF YOU DON'T MIND, I'D LIKE TO SEE YOUR NOTES TONIGHT.
SURE, DOCTOR WEIR.
MIRAGE! GET OUT HERE, MAN!
I'LL CATCH UP LATER. THOUGHT I'D STAY AND CLEAN UP A LITTLE.
THE BAXTERS SHOULDN'T HAVE TO COME BACK TO THIS.
HEY.
FONG--
"AND THEN...HWEN."
--WANNA HELP?
"HE OFFERED SOMETHING ELSE..."

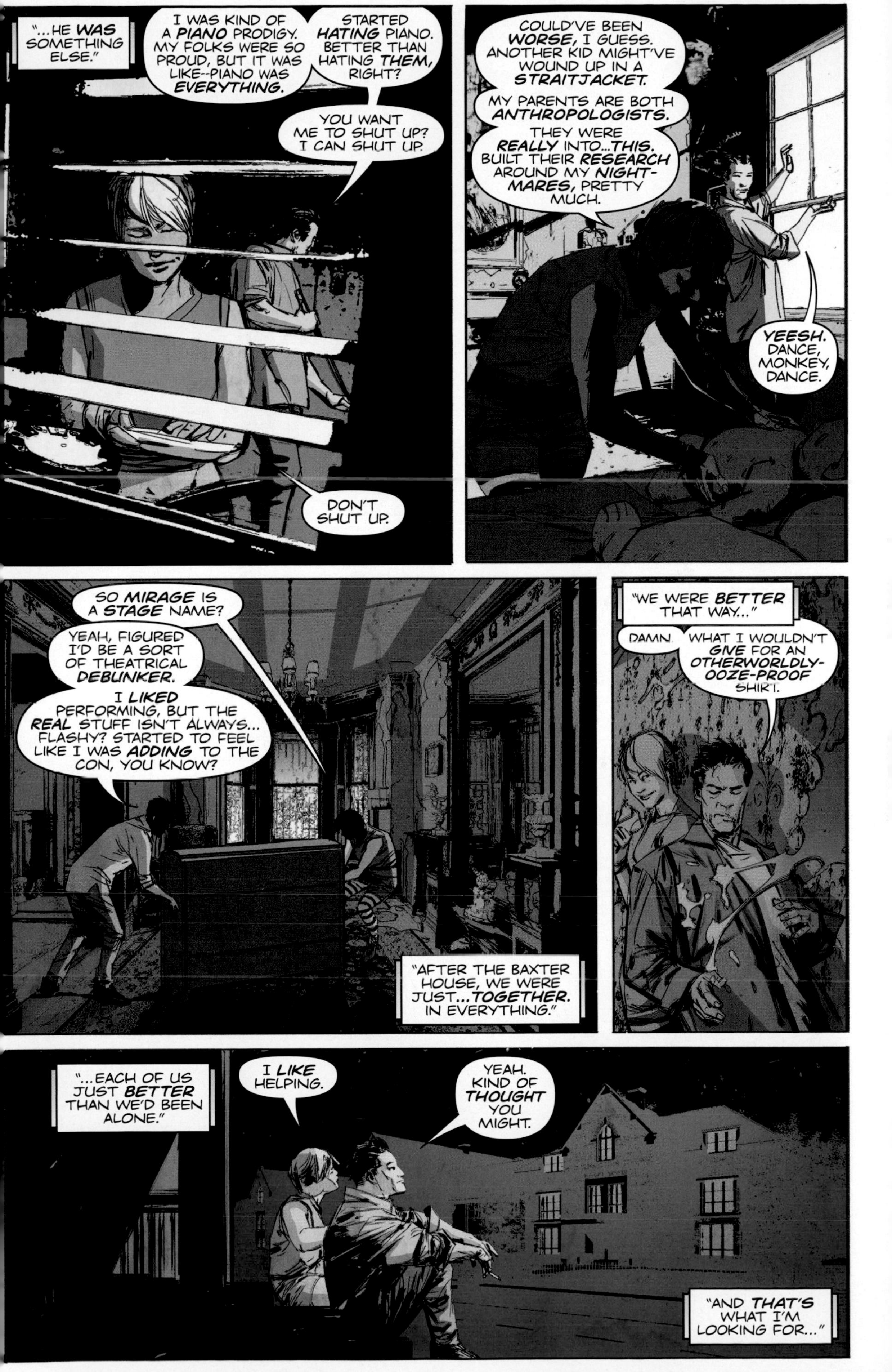
"...HE WAS SOMETHING ELSE."
I WAS KIND OF A PIANO PRODIGY. MY FOLKS WERE SO PROUD, BUT IT WAS LIKE--PIANO WAS EVERYTHING.
STARTED HATING PIANO. BETTER THAN HATING THEM, RIGHT?
YOU WANT ME TO SHUT UP? I CAN SHUT UP.
DON'T SHUT UP.
COULD'VE BEEN WORSE, I GUESS. ANOTHER KID MIGHT'VE WOUND UP IN A STRAITJACKET.
MY PARENTS ARE BOTH ANTHROPOLOGISTS.
THEY WERE REALLY INTO...THIS. BUILT THEIR RESEARCH AROUND MY NIGHT-MARES, PRETTY MUCH.
YEESH. DANCE, MONKEY, DANCE.
SO MIRAGE IS A STAGE NAME?
YEAH, FIGURED I'D BE A SORT OF THEATRICAL DEBUNKER.
I LIKED PERFORMING, BUT THE REAL STUFF ISN'T ALWAYS... FLASHY? STARTED TO FEEL LIKE I WAS ADDING TO THE CON, YOU KNOW?
"AFTER THE BAXTER HOUSE, WE WERE JUST...TOGETHER. IN EVERYTHING."
"WE WERE BETTER THAT WAY..."
DAMN.
WHAT I WOULDN'T GIVE FOR AN OTHERWORLDLY-OOZE-PROOF SHIRT.
"...EACH OF US JUST BETTER THAN WE'D BEEN ALONE."
I LIKE HELPING.
YEAH. KIND OF THOUGHT YOU MIGHT.
"AND THAT'S WHAT I'M LOOKING FOR..."

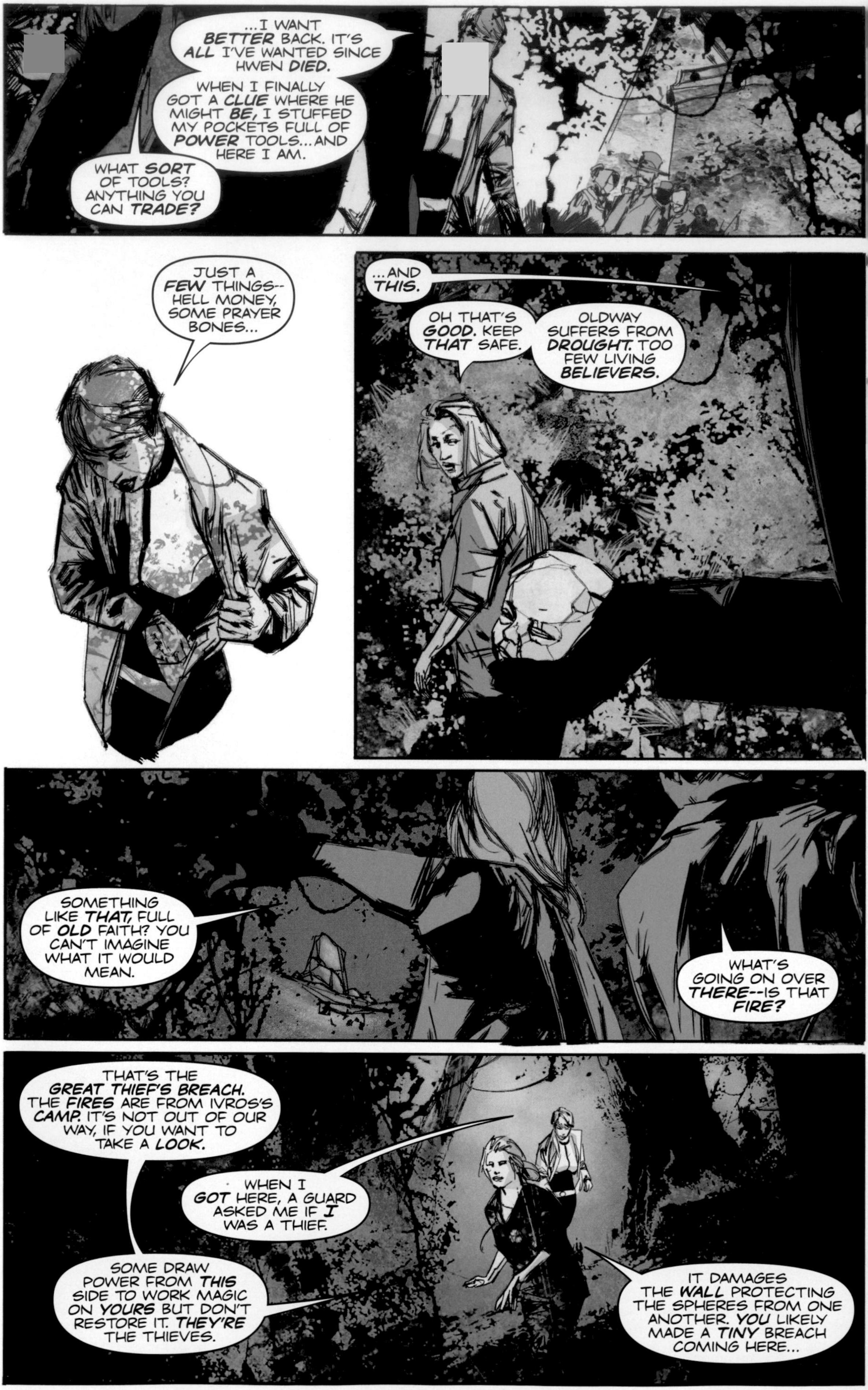
...I WANT BETTER BACK. IT'S ALL I'VE WANTED SINCE HWEN DIED.
WHEN I FINALLY GOT A CLUE WHERE HE MIGHT BE, I STUFFED MY POCKETS FULL OF POWER TOOLS...AND HERE I AM.
WHAT SORT OF TOOLS? ANYTHING YOU CAN TRADE?
JUST A FEW THINGS-- HELL MONEY, SOME PRAYER BONES...
...AND THIS.
OH THAT'S GOOD. KEEP THAT SAFE.
OLDWAY SUFFERS FROM DROUGHT. TOO FEW LIVING BELIEVERS.
SOMETHING LIKE THAT, FULL OF OLD FAITH? YOU CAN'T IMAGINE WHAT IT WOULD MEAN.
WHAT'S GOING ON OVER THERE--IS THAT FIRE?
THAT'S THE GREAT THIEF'S BREACH. THE FIRES ARE FROM IVROS'S CAMP. IT'S NOT OUT OF OUR WAY, IF YOU WANT TO TAKE A LOOK.
WHEN I GOT HERE, A GUARD ASKED ME IF I WAS A THIEF.
SOME DRAW POWER FROM THIS SIDE TO WORK MAGIC ON YOURS BUT DON'T RESTORE IT. THEY'RE THE THIEVES.
IT DAMAGES THE WALL PROTECTING THE SPHERES FROM ONE ANOTHER. YOU LIKELY MADE A TINY BREACH COMING HERE...

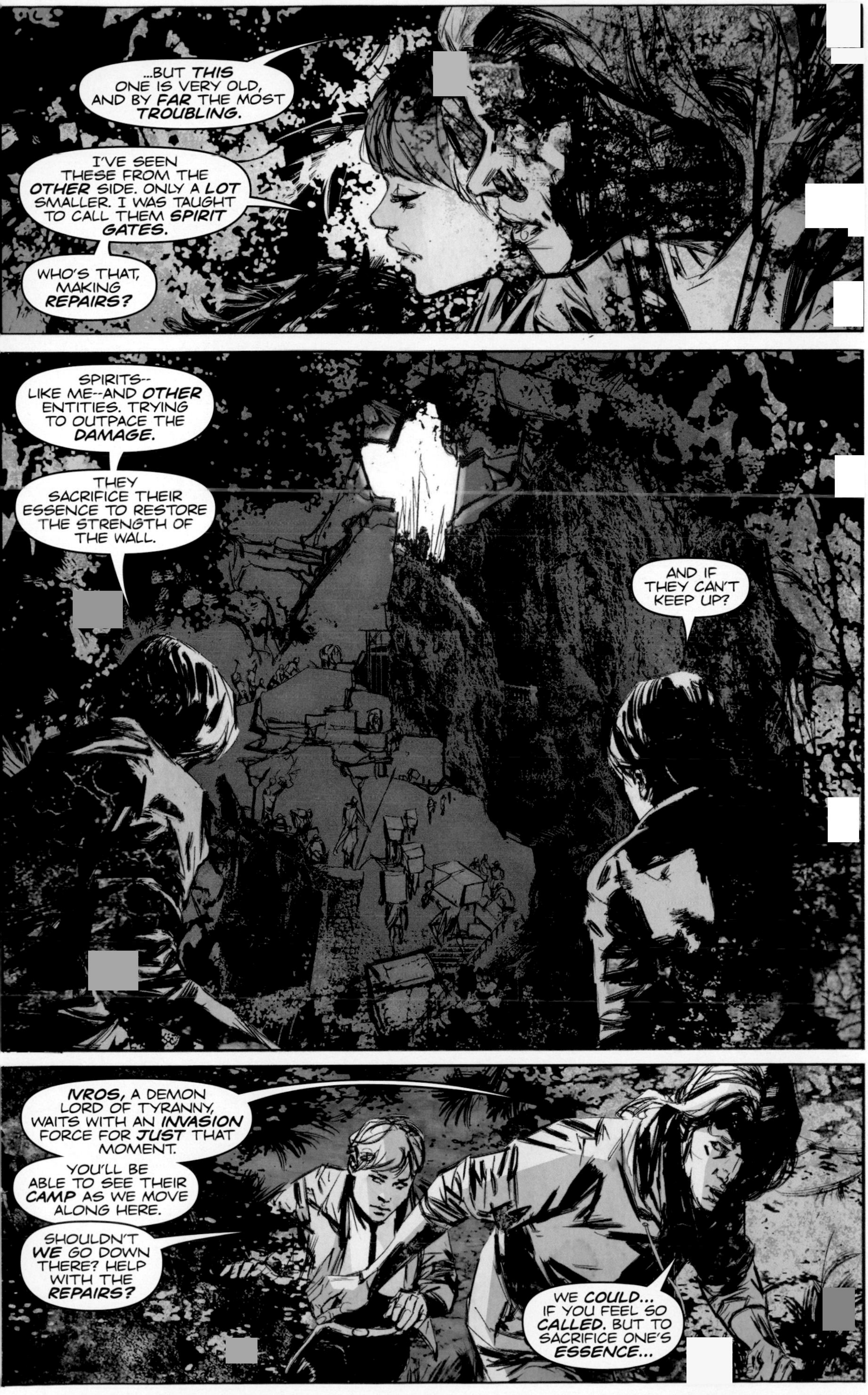
...BUT THIS ONE IS VERY OLD, AND BY FAR THE MOST TROUBLING.
I'VE SEEN THESE FROM THE OTHER SIDE. ONLY A LOT SMALLER. I WAS TAUGHT TO CALL THEM SPIRIT GATES.
WHO'S THAT, MAKING REPAIRS?
SPIRITS--LIKE ME--AND OTHER ENTITIES. TRYING TO OUTPACE THE DAMAGE.
THEY SACRIFICE THEIR ESSENCE TO RESTORE THE STRENGTH OF THE WALL.
AND IF THEY CAN'T KEEP UP?
IVROS, A DEMON LORD OF TYRANNY, WAITS WITH AN INVASION FORCE FOR JUST THAT MOMENT.
YOU'LL BE ABLE TO SEE THEIR CAMP AS WE MOVE ALONG HERE.
SHOULDN'T WE GO DOWN THERE? HELP WITH THE REPAIRS?
WE COULD... IF YOU FEEL SO CALLED. BUT TO SACRIFICE ONE'S ESSENCE...

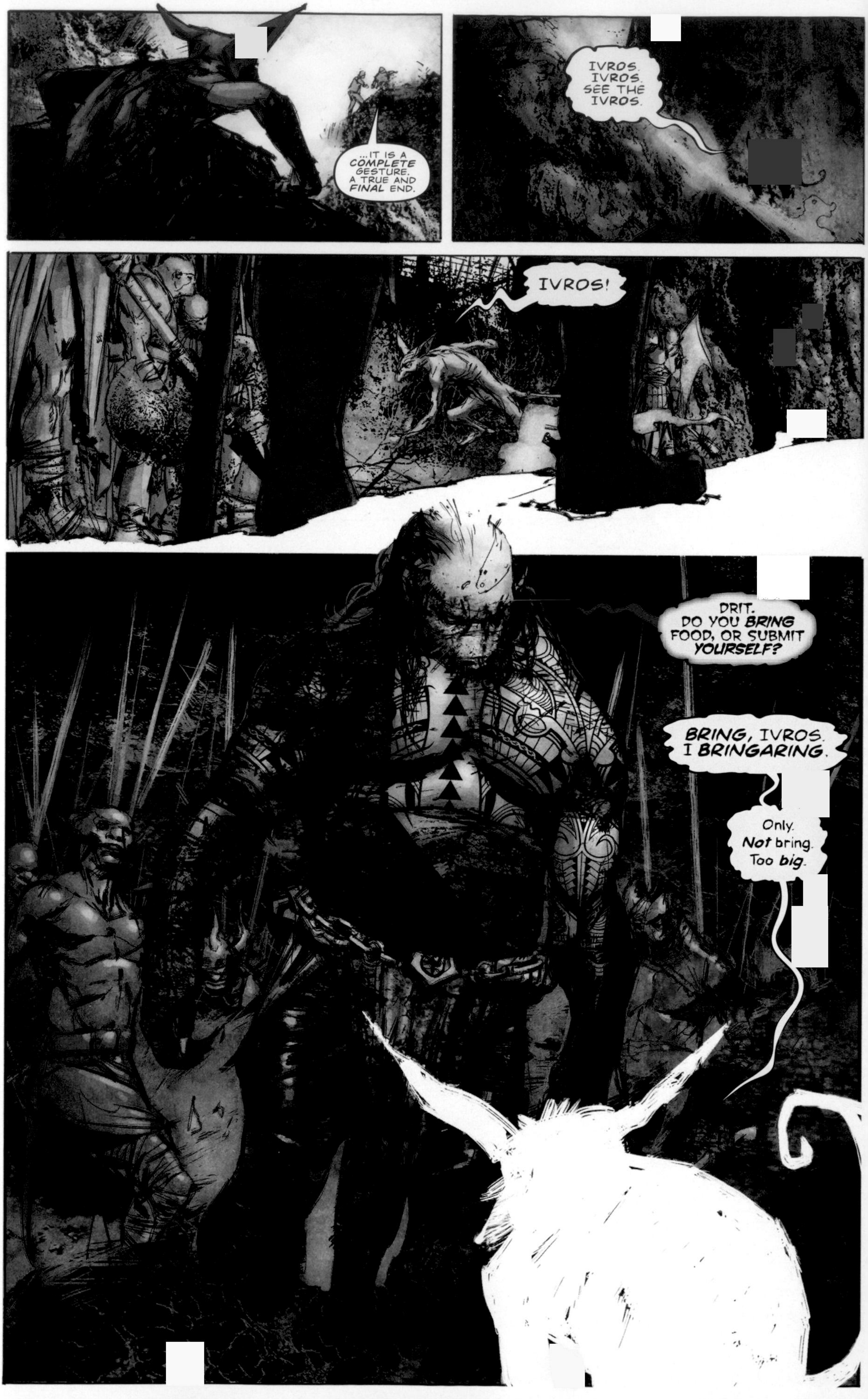

...IT IS A COMPLETE GESTURE. A TRUE AND FINAL END.
IVROS. IVROS. SEE THE IVROS.
IVROS!
DRIT. DO YOU BRING FOOD, OR SUBMIT YOURSELF?
BRING, IVROS. I BRINGARING.
Only. Not bring. Too big.

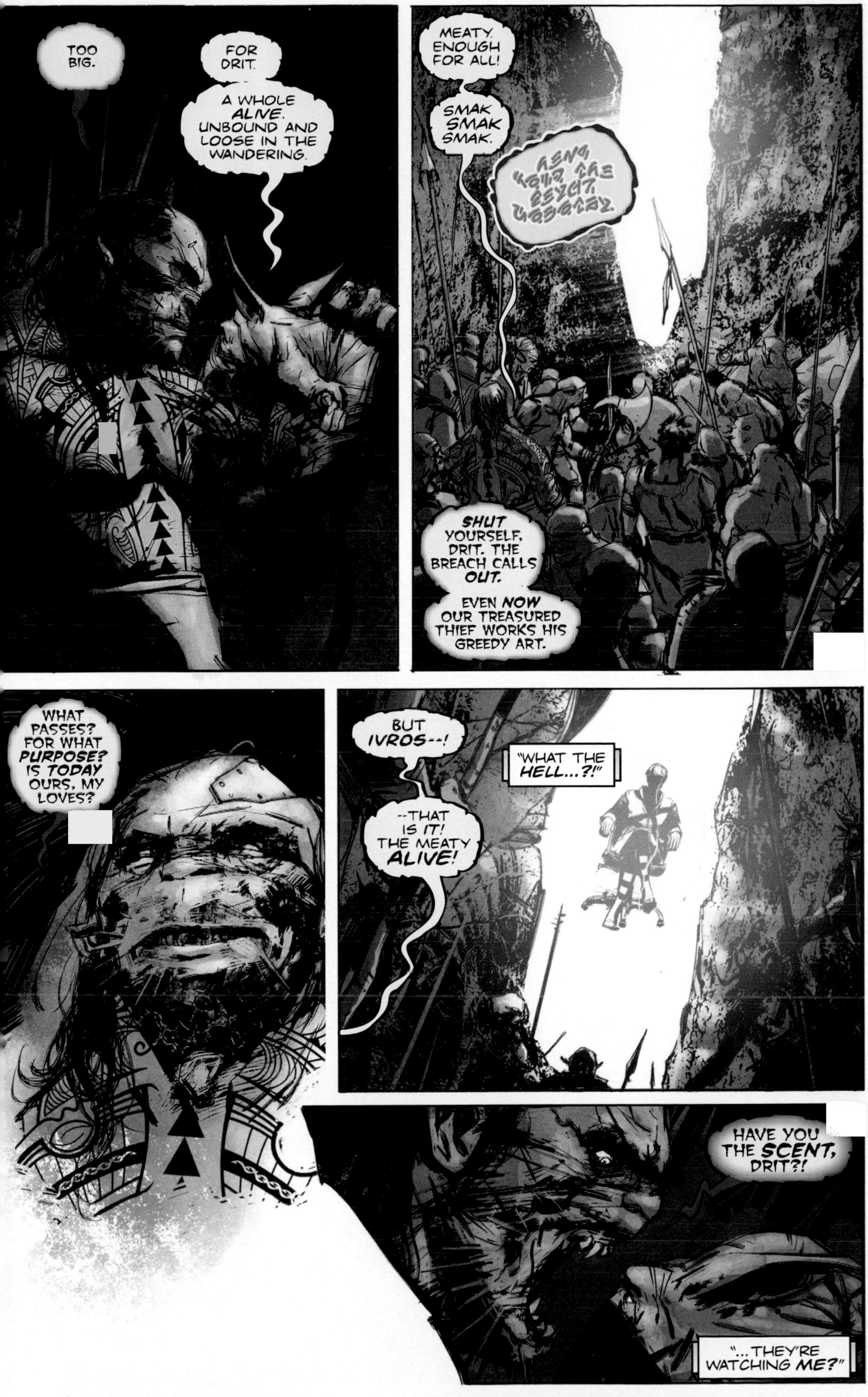
TOO BIG.
FOR DRIT.
A WHOLE ALIVE. UNBOUND AND LOOSE IN THE WANDERING.
MEATY. ENOUGH FOR ALL!
SMAK SMAK SMAK.
SHUT YOURSELF, DRIT. THE BREACH CALLS OUT.
EVEN NOW OUR TREASURED THIEF WORKS HIS GREEDY ART.
WHAT PASSES? FOR WHAT PURPOSE? IS TODAY OURS, MY LOVES?
BUT IVROS--!
"WHAT THE HELL...?!"
--THAT IS IT! THE MEATY ALIVE!
HAVE YOU THE SCENT, DRIT?!
"...THEY'RE WATCHING ME?"

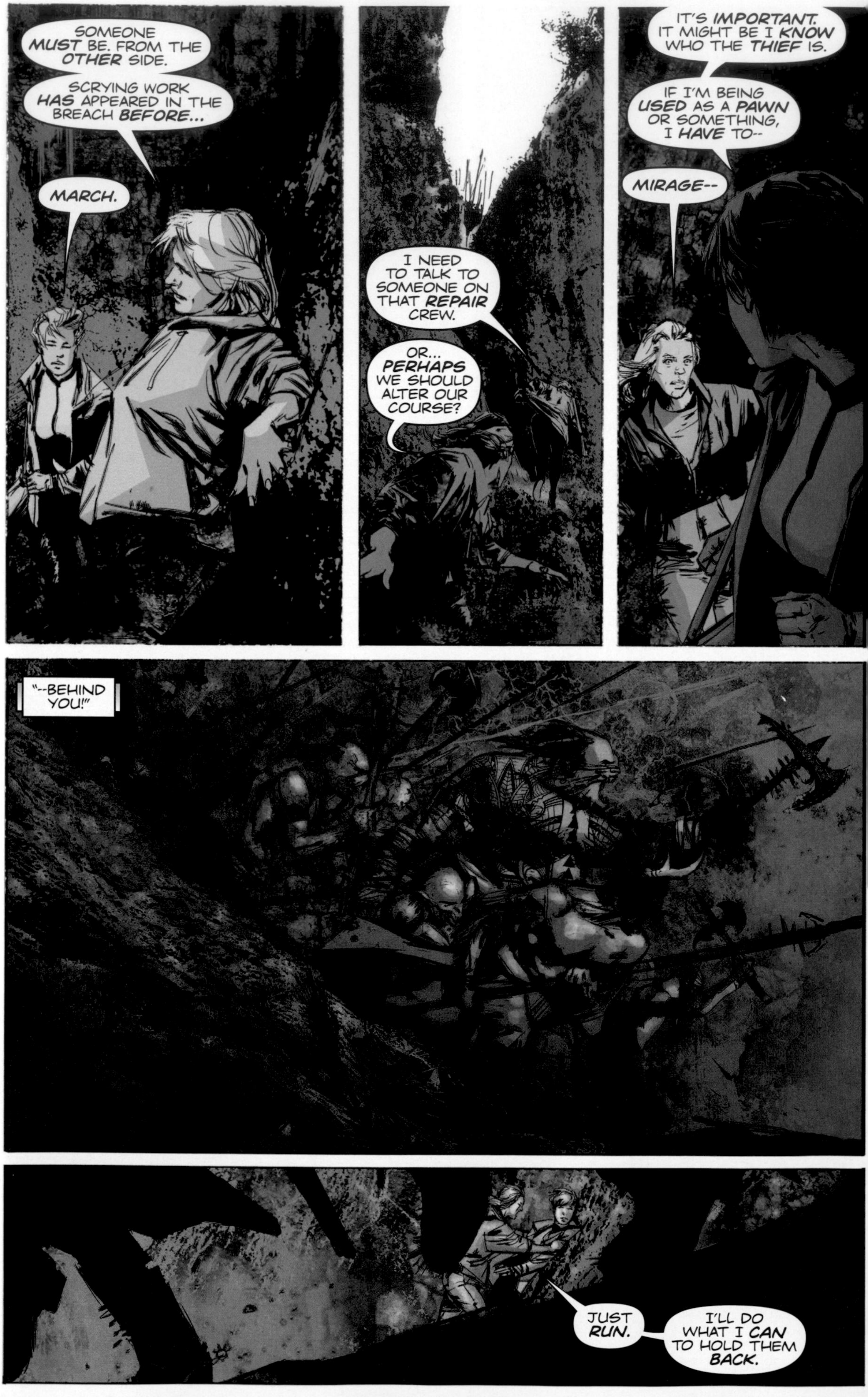
SOMEONE MUST BE. FROM THE OTHER SIDE.
SCRYING WORK HAS APPEARED IN THE BREACH BEFORE...
MARCH.
I NEED TO TALK TO SOMEONE ON THAT REPAIR CREW.
OR... PERHAPS WE SHOULD ALTER OUR COURSE?
IT'S IMPORTANT. IT MIGHT BE I KNOW WHO THE THIEF IS.
IF I'M BEING USED AS A PAWN OR SOMETHING, I HAVE TO--
MIRAGE--
"--BEHIND YOU!"
JUST RUN.
I'LL DO WHAT I CAN TO HOLD THEM BACK.

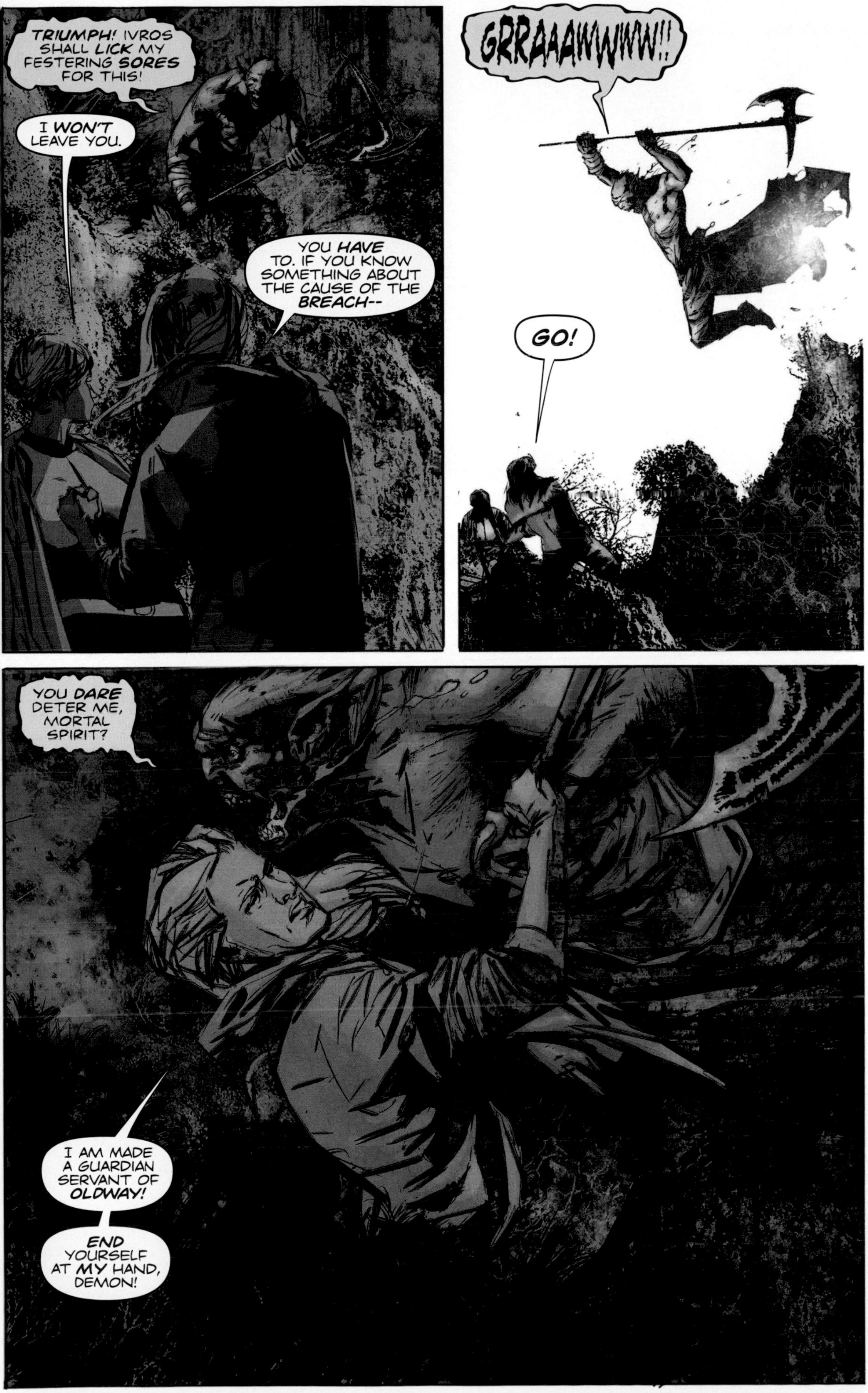
TRIUMPH! IVROS SHALL LICK MY FESTERING SORES FOR THIS!
I WON'T LEAVE YOU.
YOU HAVE TO. IF YOU KNOW SOMETHING ABOUT THE CAUSE OF THE BREACH--
GRRAAAWWWW!!
GO!
YOU DARE DETER ME, MORTAL SPIRIT?
I AM MADE A GUARDIAN SERVANT OF OLDWAY!
END YOURSELF AT MY HAND, DEMON!

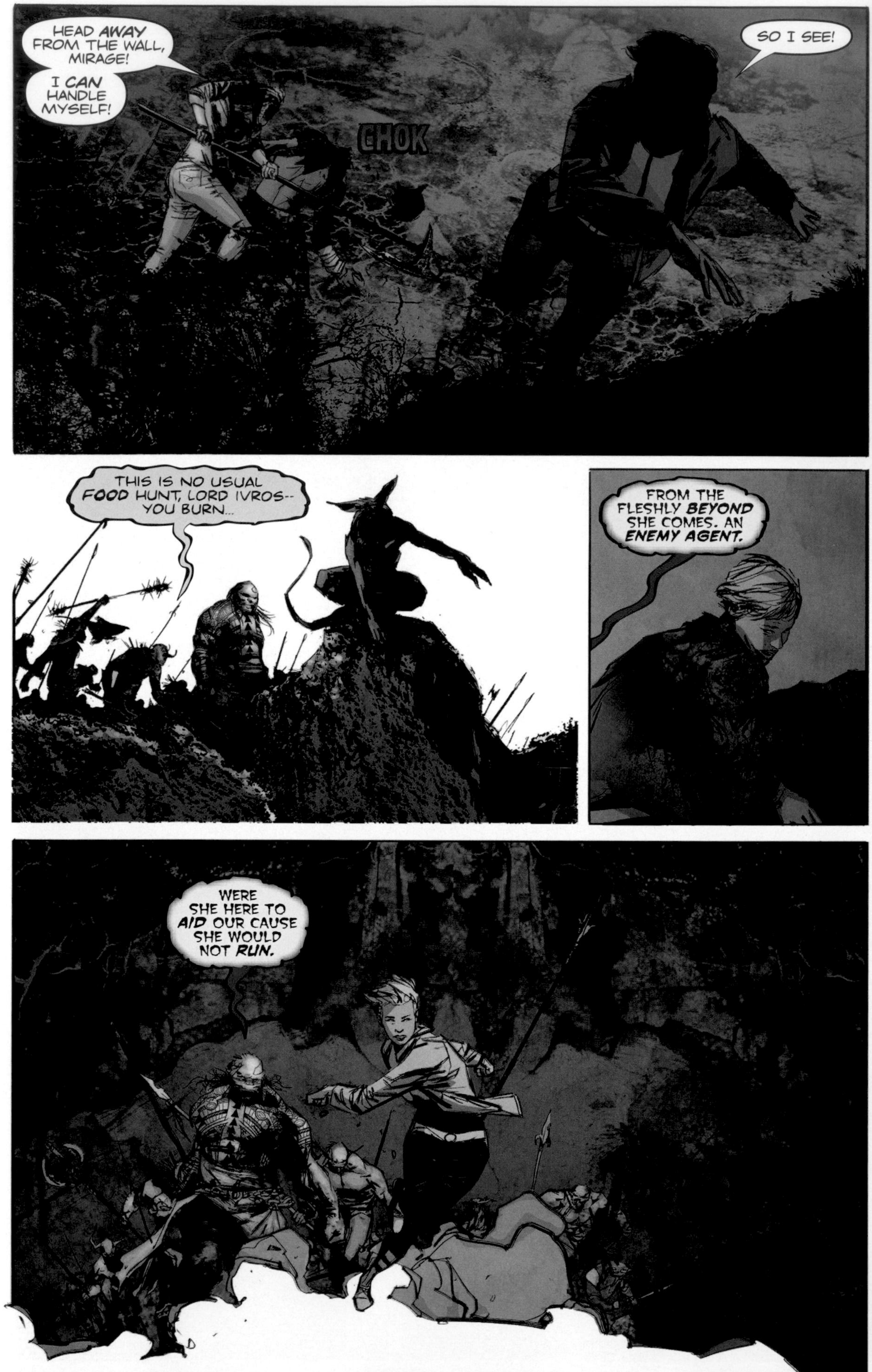
HEAD AWAY FROM THE WALL, MIRAGE!
I CAN HANDLE MYSELF!
SO I SEE!
CHOK
THIS IS NO USUAL FOOD HUNT, LORD IVROS-- YOU BURN...
FROM THE FLESHLY BEYOND SHE COMES. AN ENEMY AGENT.
WERE SHE HERE TO AID OUR CAUSE SHE WOULD NOT RUN.

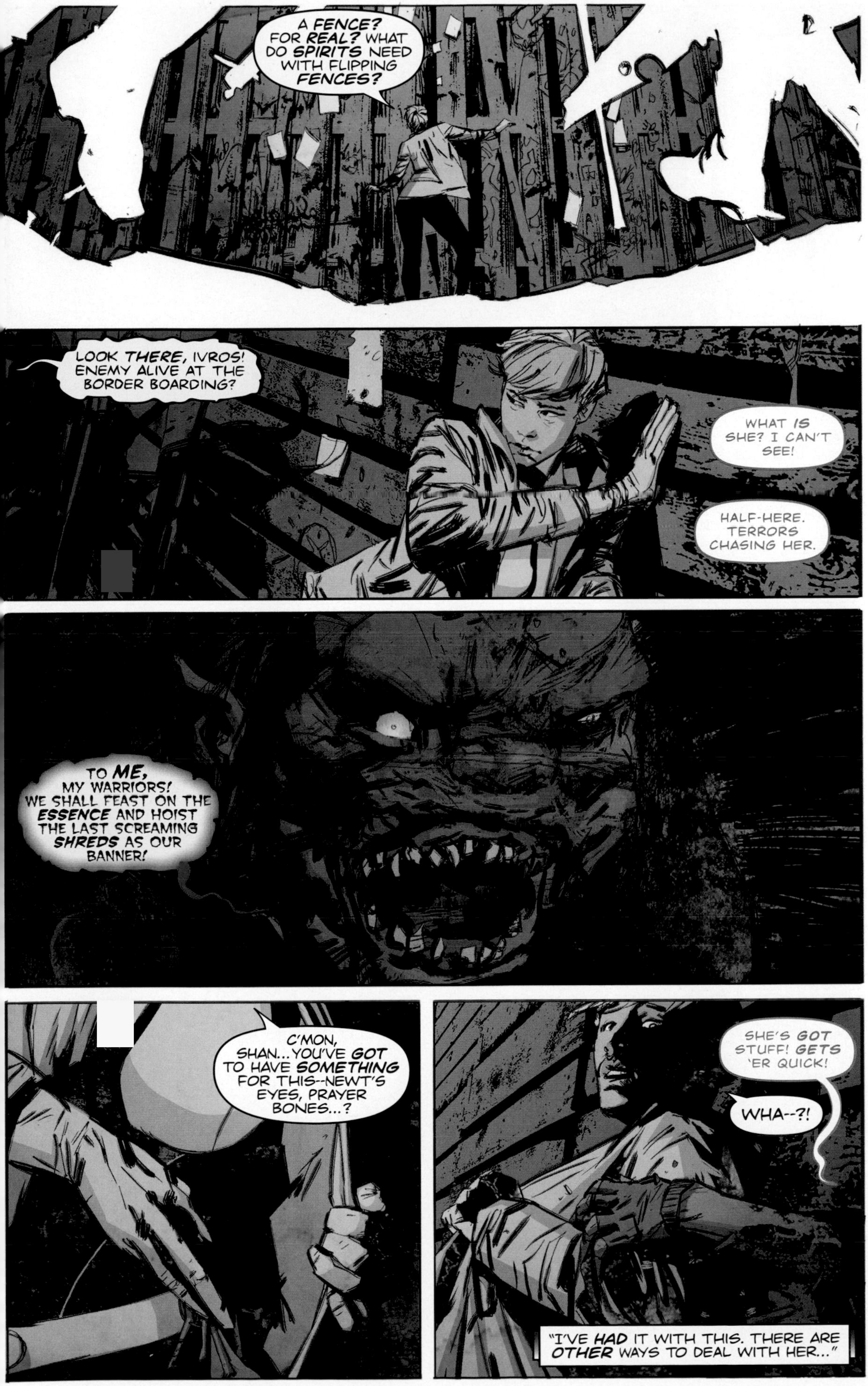
A FENCE? FOR REAL? WHAT DO SPIRITS NEED WITH FLIPPING FENCES?
LOOK THERE, IVROS! ENEMY ALIVE AT THE BORDER BOARDING?
WHAT IS SHE? I CAN'T SEE!
HALF-HERE. TERRORS CHASING HER.
TO ME, MY WARRIORS! WE SHALL FEAST ON THE ESSENCE AND HOIST THE LAST SCREAMING SHREDS AS OUR BANNER!
C'MON, SHAN...YOU'VE GOT TO HAVE SOMETHING FOR THIS--NEWT'S EYES, PRAYER BONES...?
SHE'S GOT STUFF! GETS 'ER QUICK!
WHA--?!
"I'VE HAD IT WITH THIS. THERE ARE OTHER WAYS TO DEAL WITH HER..."

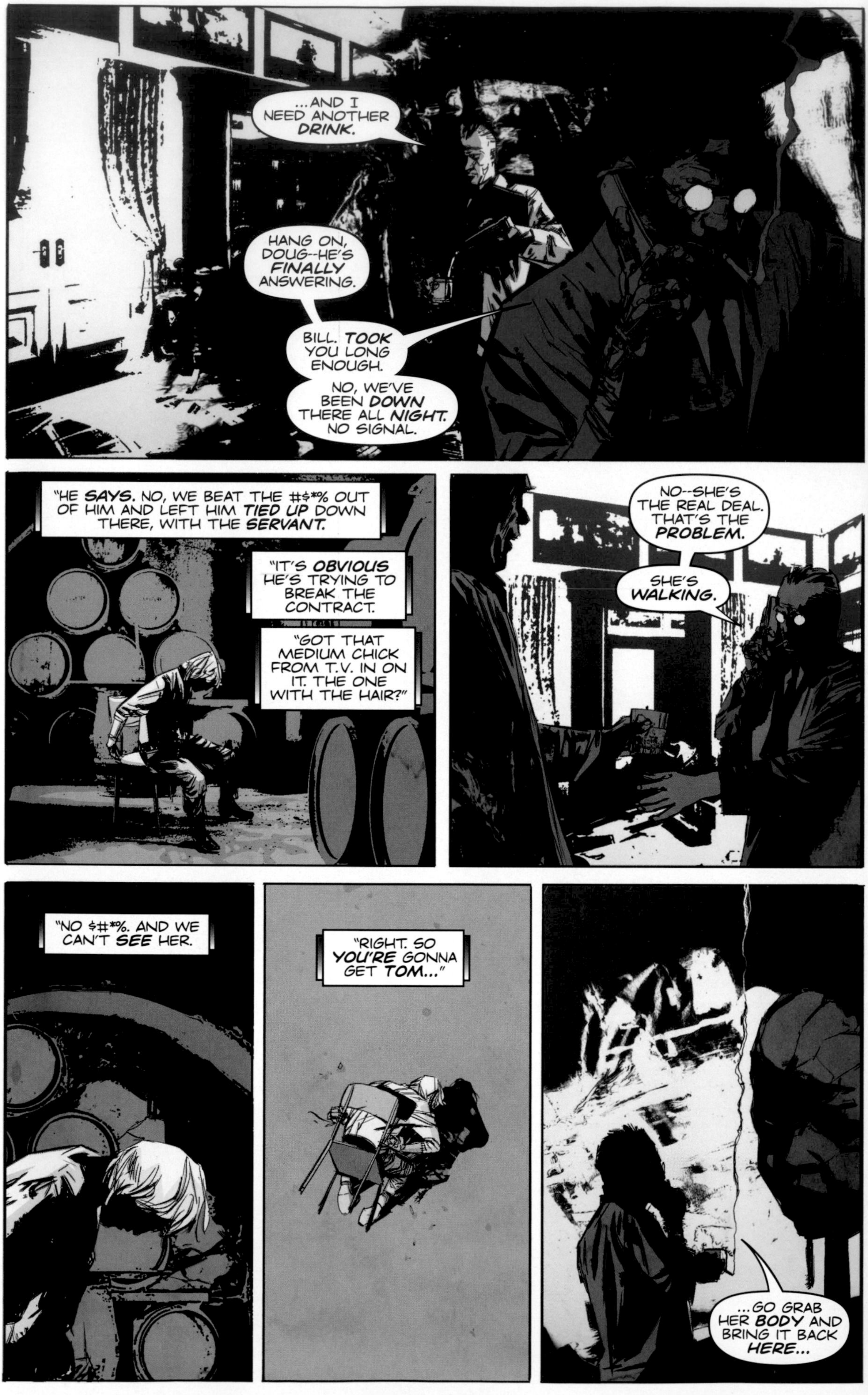
...AND I NEED ANOTHER DRINK.
HANG ON, DOUG--HE'S FINALLY ANSWERING.
BILL. TOOK YOU LONG ENOUGH.
NO, WE'VE BEEN DOWN THERE ALL NIGHT. NO SIGNAL.
"HE SAYS. NO, WE BEAT THE #$*% OUT OF HIM AND LEFT HIM TIED UP DOWN THERE, WITH THE SERVANT.
"IT'S OBVIOUS HE'S TRYING TO BREAK THE CONTRACT.
"GOT THAT MEDIUM CHICK FROM T.V. IN ON IT. THE ONE WITH THE HAIR?"
NO--SHE'S THE REAL DEAL. THAT'S THE PROBLEM.
SHE'S WALKING.
"NO $#*%. AND WE CAN'T SEE HER.
"RIGHT. SO YOU'RE GONNA GET TOM..."
...GO GRAB HER BODY AND BRING IT BACK HERE...

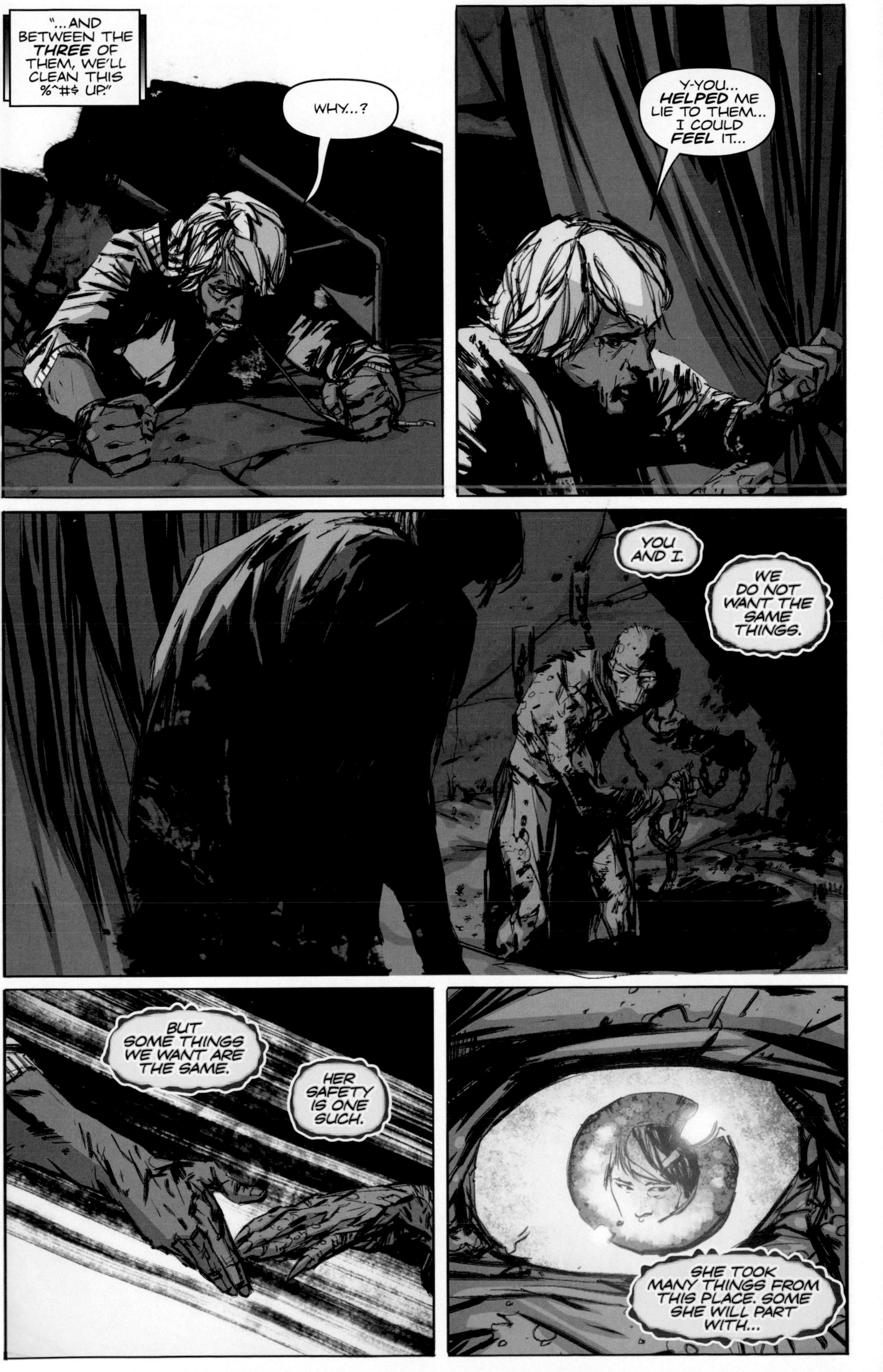
"...AND BETWEEN THE THREE OF THEM, WE'LL CLEAN THIS %^#$ UP."
WHY...?
Y-YOU... HELPED ME LIE TO THEM... I COULD FEEL IT...
YOU AND I.
WE DO NOT WANT THE SAME THINGS.
BUT SOME THINGS WE WANT ARE THE SAME.
HER SAFETY IS ONE SUCH.
SHE TOOK MANY THINGS FROM THIS PLACE. SOME SHE WILL PART WITH...

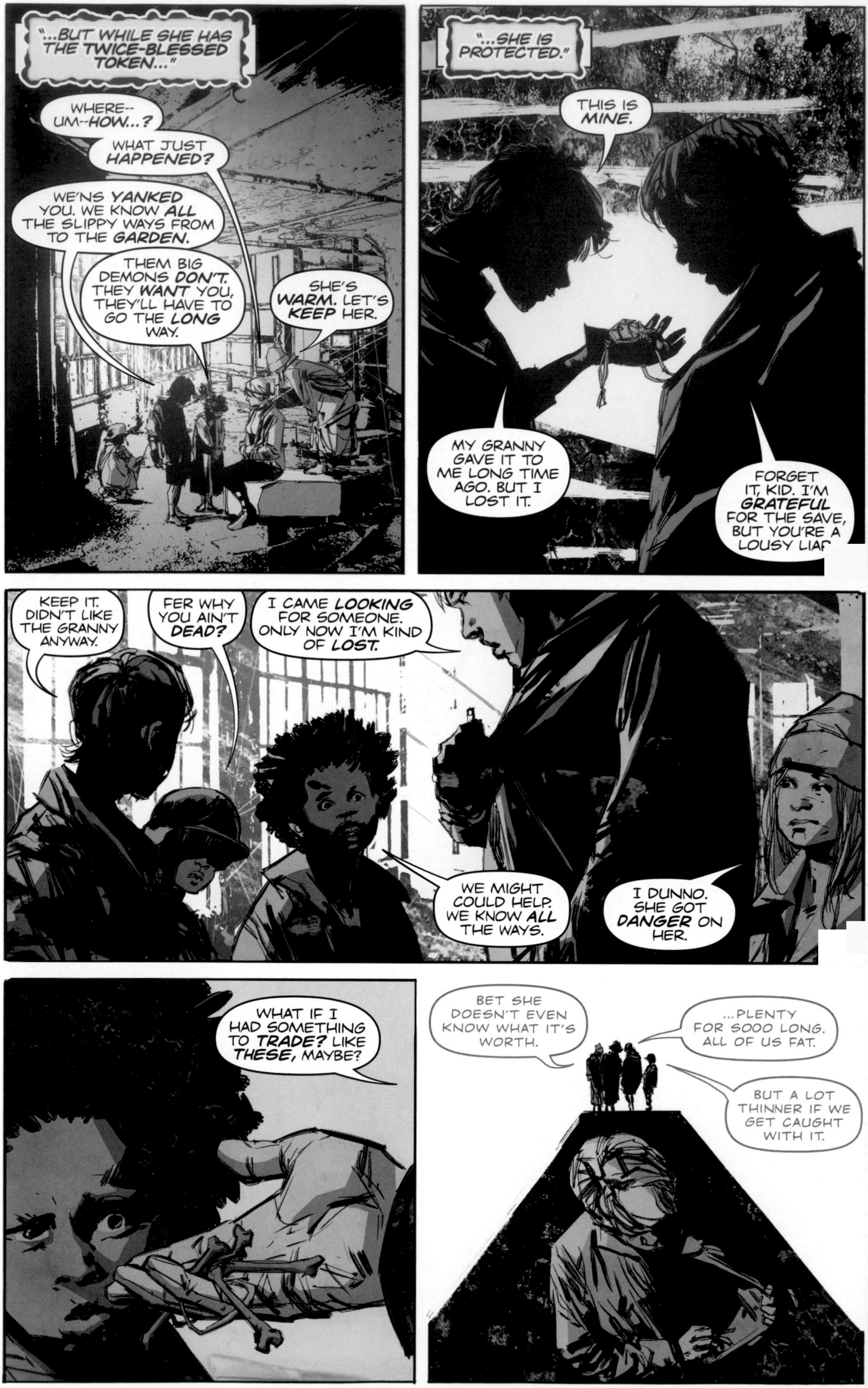
"...BUT WHILE SHE HAS THE TWICE-BLESSED TOKEN..."
WHERE-- UM--HOW...?
WHAT JUST HAPPENED?
WE'NS YANKED YOU. WE KNOW ALL THE SLIPPY WAYS FROM TO THE GARDEN.
THEM BIG DEMONS DON'T. THEY WANT YOU, THEY'LL HAVE TO GO THE LONG WAY.
SHE'S WARM. LET'S KEEP HER.
"...SHE IS PROTECTED."
THIS IS MINE.
MY GRANNY GAVE IT TO ME LONG TIME AGO. BUT I LOST IT.
FORGET IT, KID. I'M GRATEFUL FOR THE SAVE, BUT YOU'RE A LOUSY LIAR.
KEEP IT. DIDN'T LIKE THE GRANNY ANYWAY.
FER WHY YOU AIN'T DEAD?
I CAME LOOKING FOR SOMEONE. ONLY NOW I'M KIND OF LOST.
WE MIGHT COULD HELP. WE KNOW ALL THE WAYS.
I DUNNO. SHE GOT DANGER ON HER.
WHAT IF I HAD SOMETHING TO TRADE? LIKE THESE, MAYBE?
BET SHE DOESN'T EVEN KNOW WHAT IT'S WORTH.
...PLENTY FOR SOOO LONG. ALL OF US FAT.
BUT A LOT THINNER IF WE GET CAUGHT WITH IT.

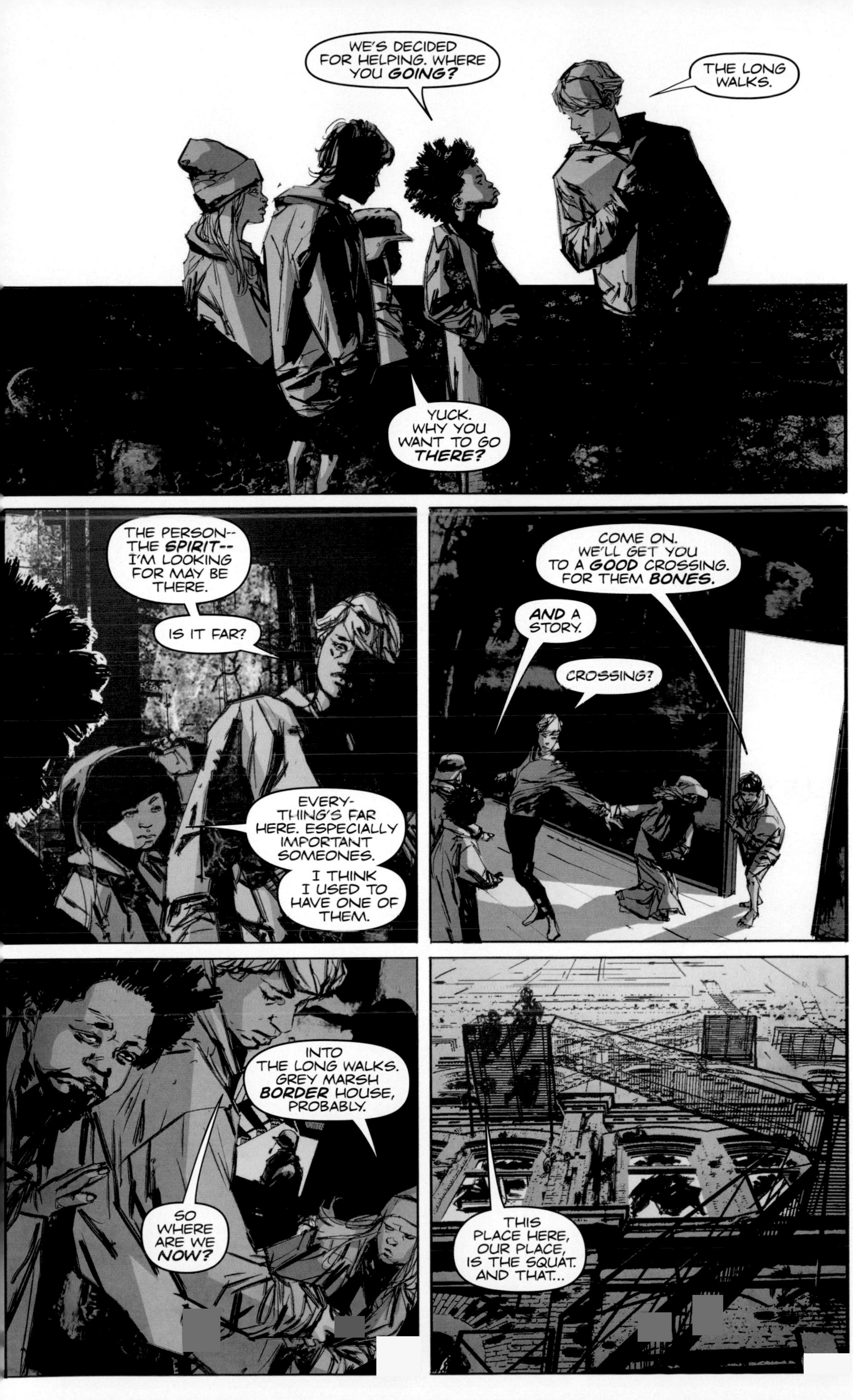
WE'S DECIDED FOR HELPING. WHERE YOU GOING?
THE LONG WALKS.
YUCK. WHY YOU WANT TO GO THERE?
THE PERSON-- THE SPIRIT-- I'M LOOKING FOR MAY BE THERE.
IS IT FAR?
EVERY-THING'S FAR HERE. ESPECIALLY IMPORTANT SOMEONES.
I THINK I USED TO HAVE ONE OF THEM.
COME ON. WE'LL GET YOU TO A GOOD CROSSING. FOR THEM BONES.
AND A STORY.
CROSSING?
INTO THE LONG WALKS. GREY MARSH BORDER HOUSE, PROBABLY.
SO WHERE ARE WE NOW?
THIS PLACE HERE, OUR PLACE, IS THE SQUAT. AND THAT...

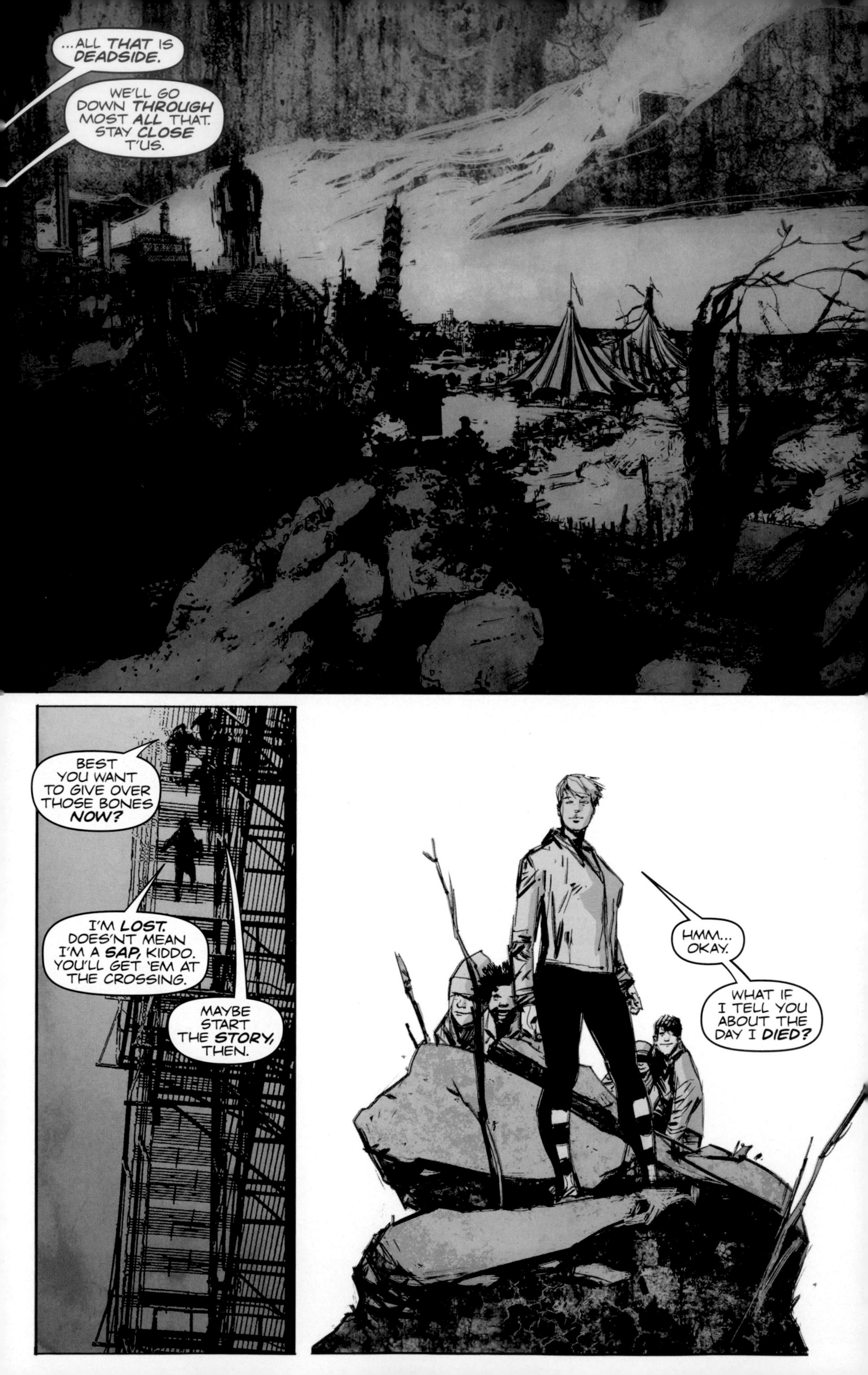
...ALL THAT IS DEADSIDE.
WE'LL GO DOWN THROUGH MOST ALL THAT. STAY CLOSE T'US.
BEST YOU WANT TO GIVE OVER THOSE BONES NOW?
I'M LOST. DOES'NT MEAN I'M A SAP, KIDDO. YOU'LL GET 'EM AT THE CROSSING.
MAYBE START THE STORY, THEN.
HMM... OKAY.
WHAT IF I TELL YOU ABOUT THE DAY I DIED?

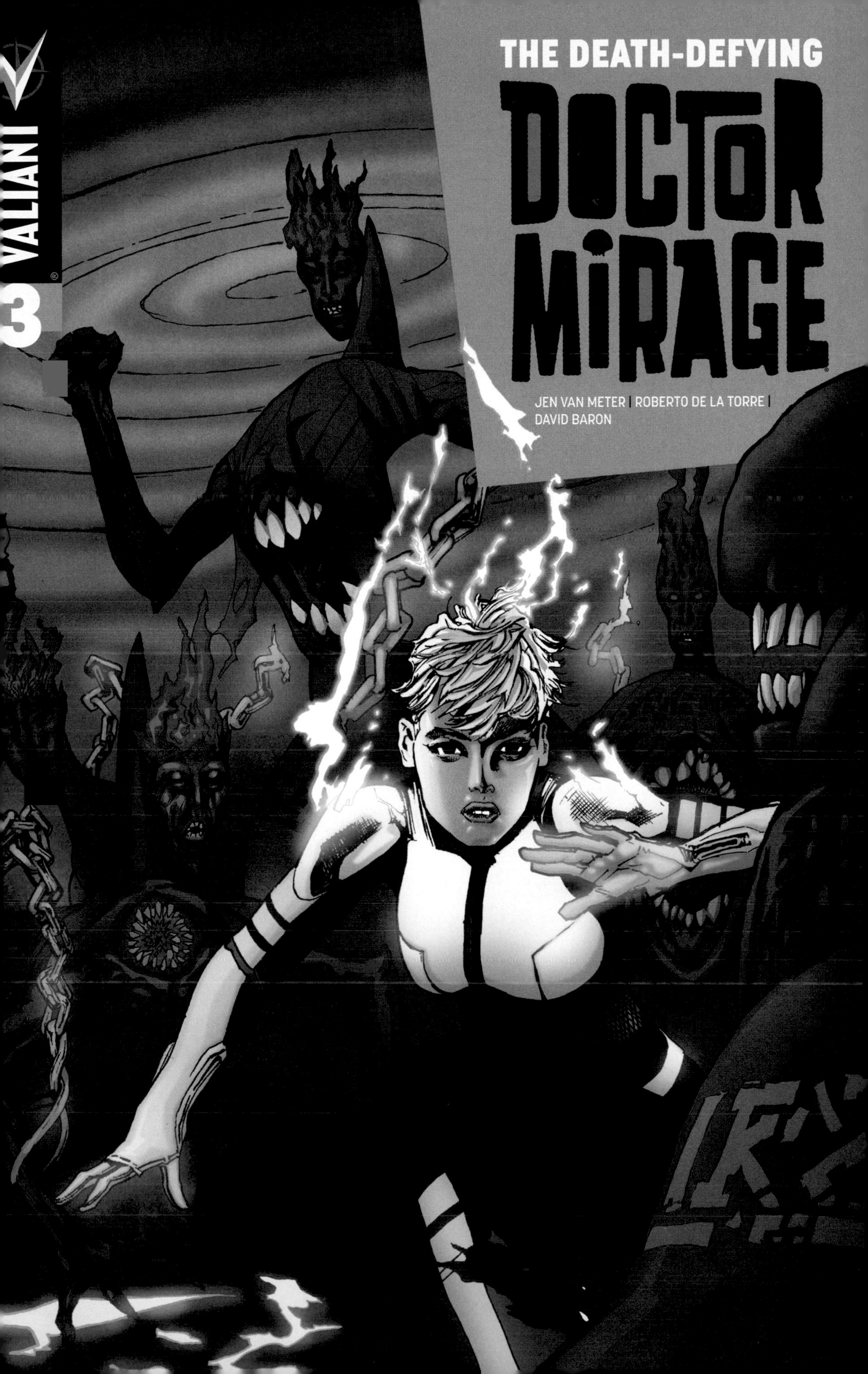
VALIANT
3
THE DEATH-DEFYING
DOCTOR MIRAGE
JEN VAN METER | ROBERTO DE LA TORRE | DAVID BARON

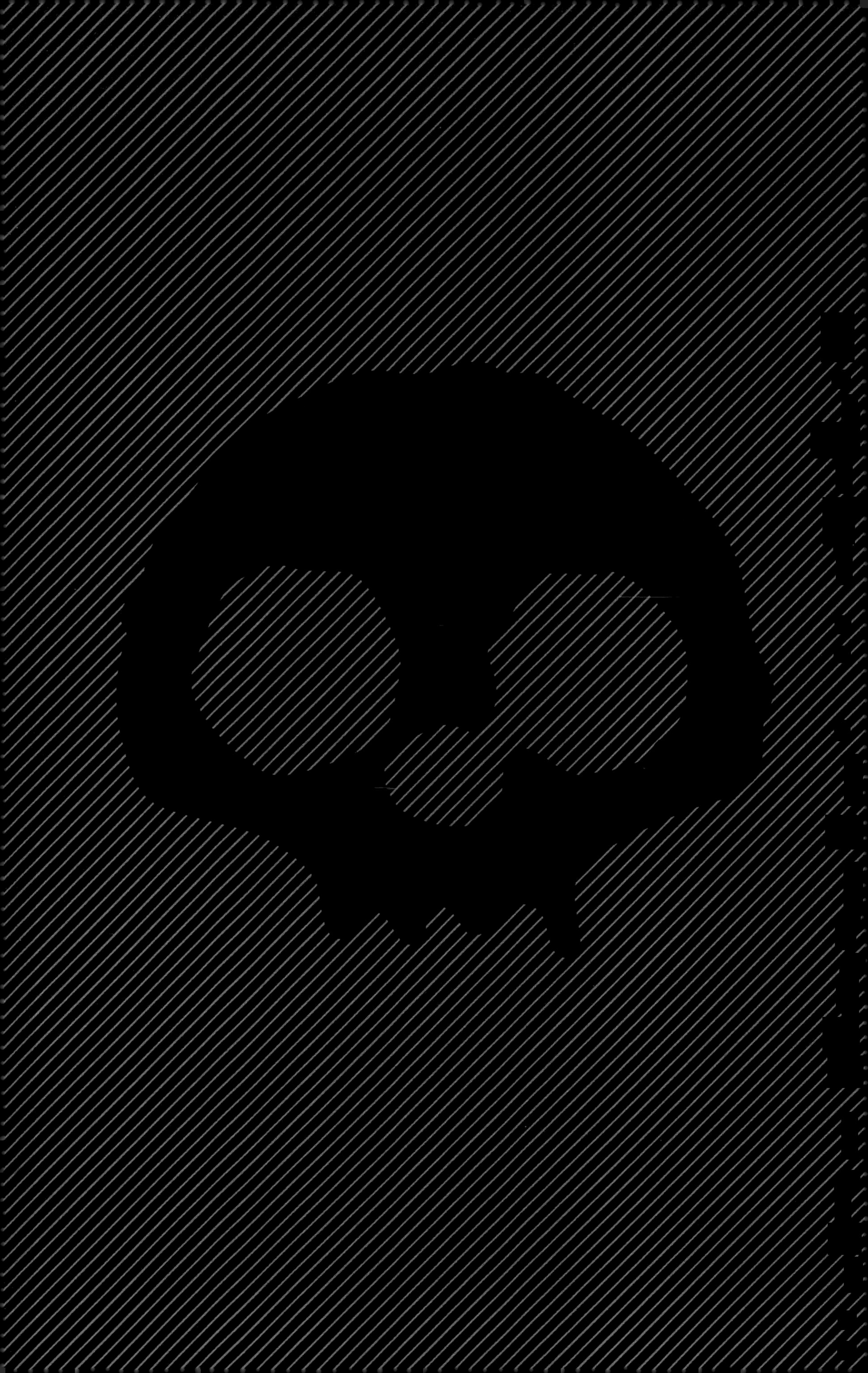

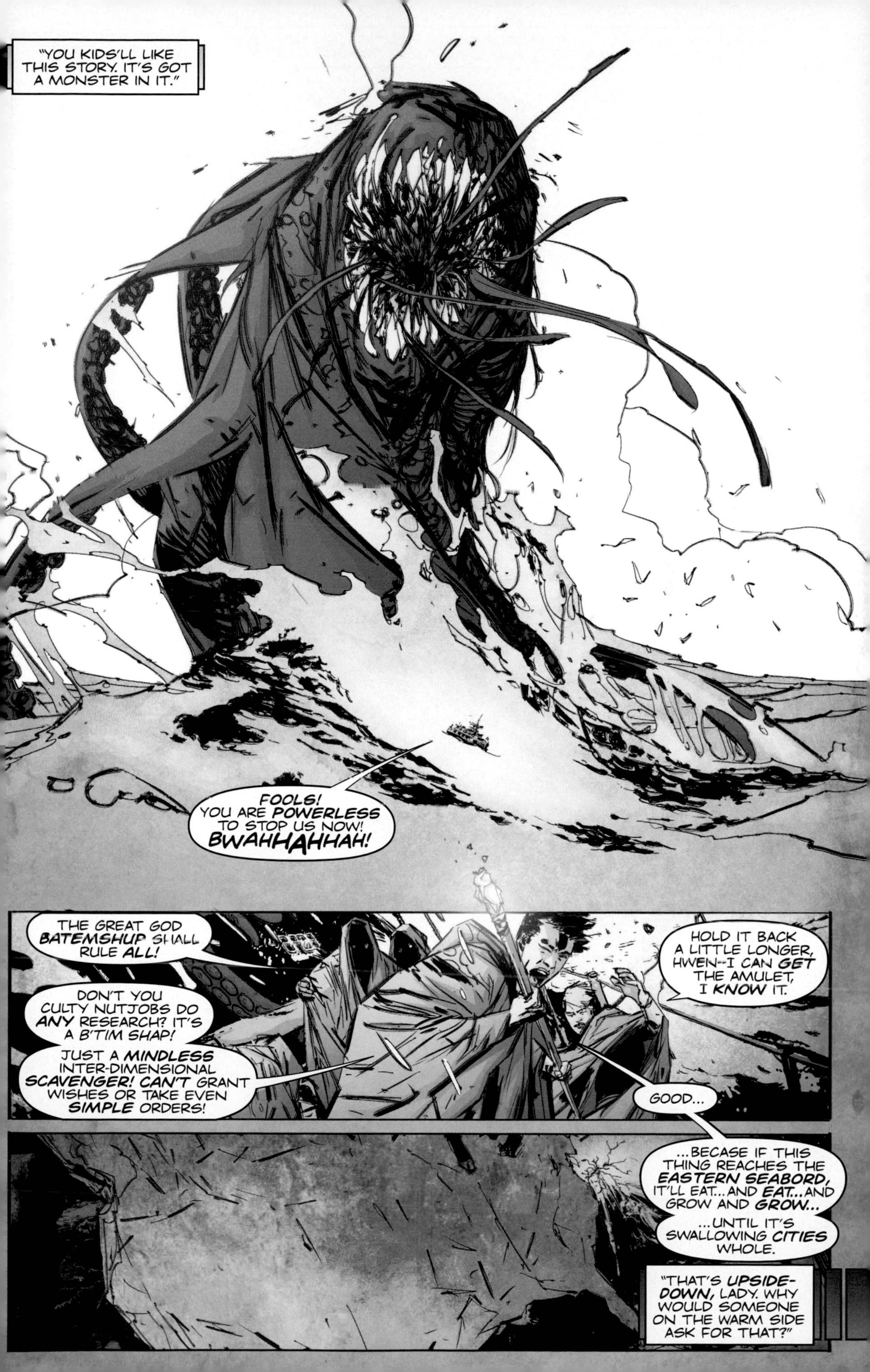
"YOU KIDS'LL LIKE THIS STORY. IT'S GOT A MONSTER IN IT."
FOOLS! YOU ARE POWERLESS TO STOP US NOW! BWAHHAHHAH!
THE GREAT GOD BATEMSHUP SHALL RULE ALL!
HOLD IT BACK A LITTLE LONGER, HWEN--I CAN GET THE AMULET, I KNOW IT.
DON'T YOU CULTY NUTJOBS DO ANY RESEARCH? IT'S A B'TIM SHAP!
JUST A MINDLESS INTER-DIMENSIONAL SCAVENGER! CAN'T GRANT WISHES OR TAKE EVEN SIMPLE ORDERS!
GOOD...
...BECASE IF THIS THING REACHES THE EASTERN SEABORD, IT'LL EAT...AND EAT...AND GROW AND GROW...
...UNTIL IT'S SWALLOWING CITIES WHOLE.
"THAT'S UPSIDE-DOWN, LADY. WHY WOULD SOMEONE ON THE WARM SIDE ASK FOR THAT?"

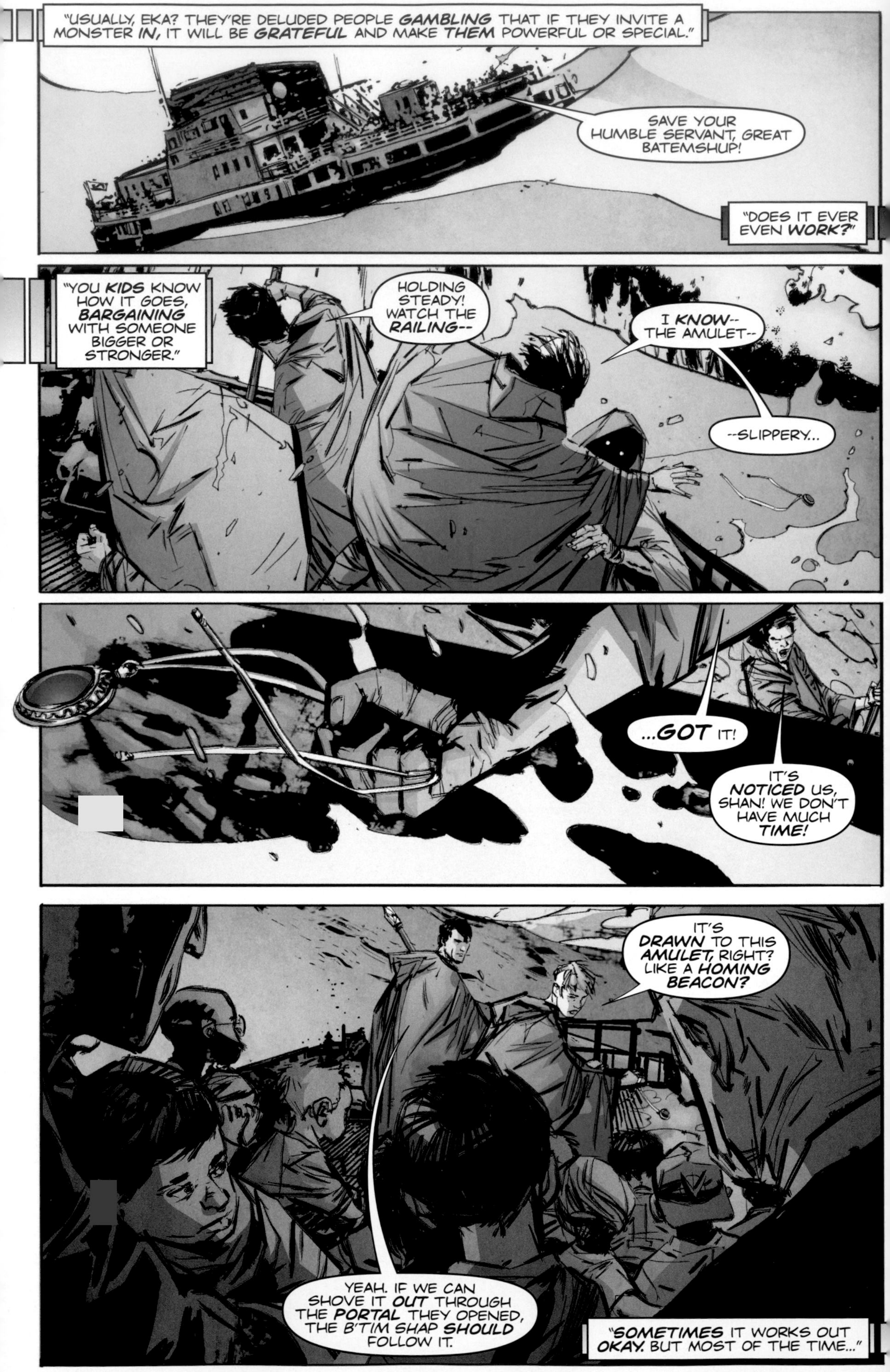
"USUALLY, EKA? THEY'RE DELUDED PEOPLE GAMBLING THAT IF THEY INVITE A MONSTER IN, IT WILL BE GRATEFUL AND MAKE THEM POWERFUL OR SPECIAL."
SAVE YOUR HUMBLE SERVANT, GREAT BATEMSHUP!
"DOES IT EVER EVEN WORK?"
"YOU KIDS KNOW HOW IT GOES, BARGAINING WITH SOMEONE BIGGER OR STRONGER."
HOLDING STEADY! WATCH THE RAILING--
I KNOW-- THE AMULET--
--SLIPPERY...
...GOT IT!
IT'S NOTICED US, SHAN! WE DON'T HAVE MUCH TIME!
IT'S DRAWN TO THIS AMULET, RIGHT? LIKE A HOMING BEACON?
YEAH. IF WE CAN SHOVE IT OUT THROUGH THE PORTAL THEY OPENED, THE B'TIM SHAP SHOULD FOLLOW IT.
"SOMETIMES IT WORKS OUT OKAY. BUT MOST OF THE TIME..."

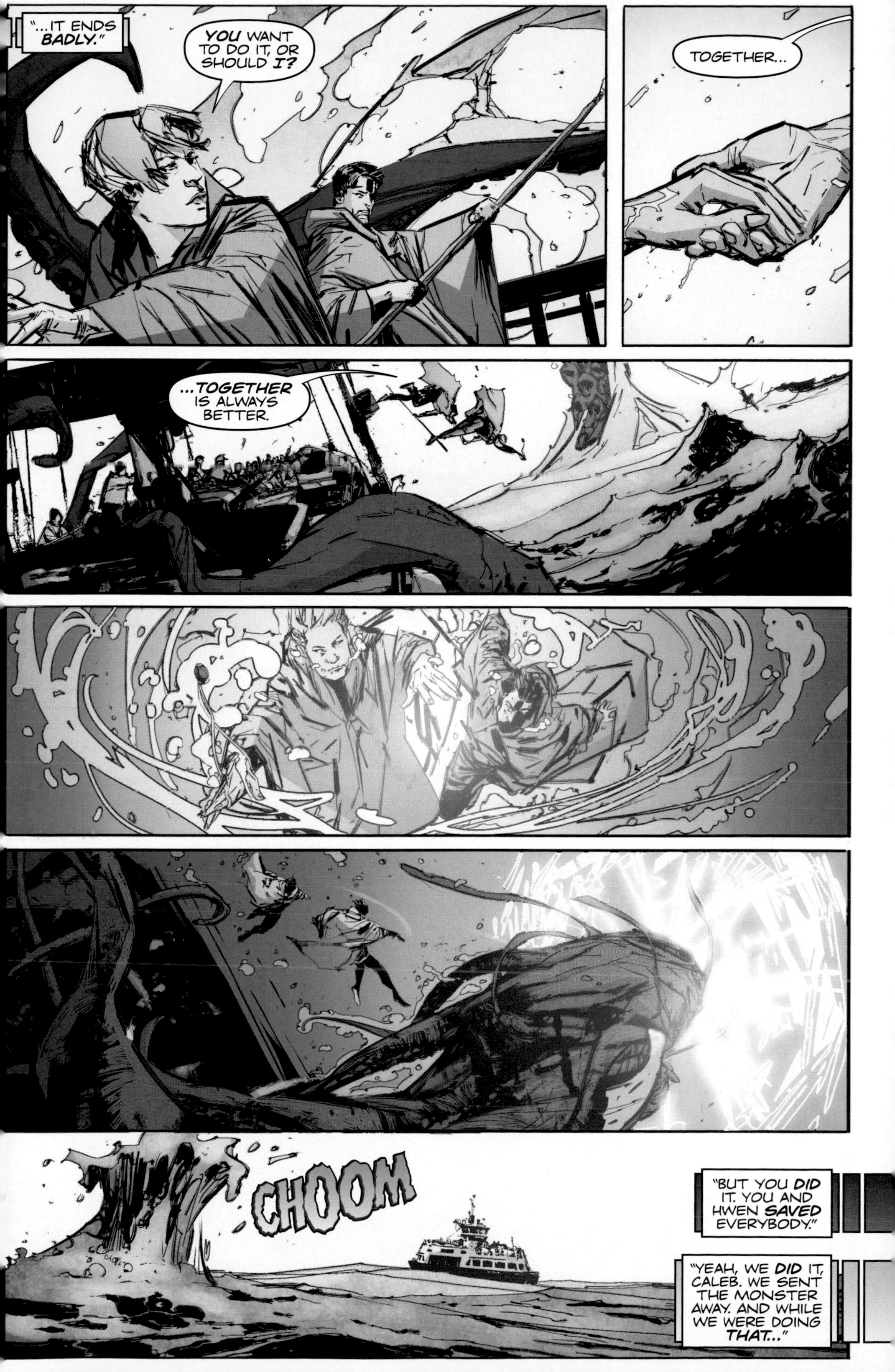
"...IT ENDS *BADLY.*"
YOU WANT TO DO IT, OR SHOULD *I?*
TOGETHER...
...*TOGETHER* IS ALWAYS BETTER.
CHOOM
"BUT YOU *DID* IT. YOU AND HWEN *SAVED* EVERYBODY."
"YEAH, WE *DID* IT, CALEB. WE SENT THE MONSTER AWAY. AND WHILE WE WERE DOING *THAT...*"

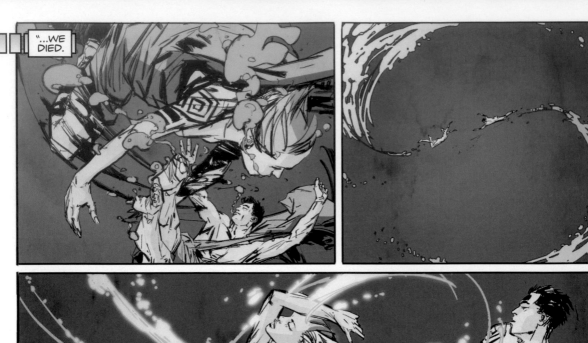

"...WE DIED.

"IT WAS PERFECT..."

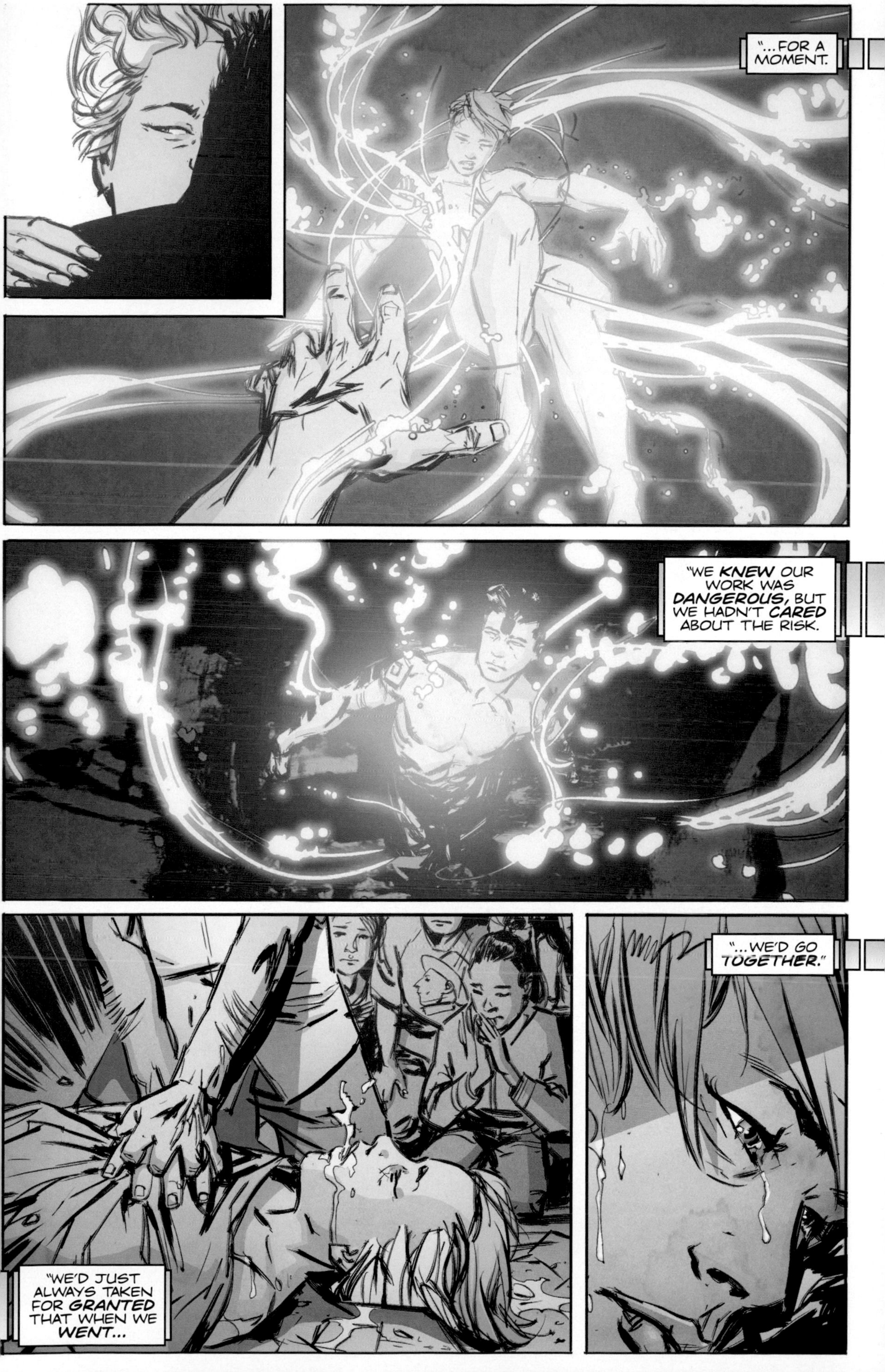
"...FOR A MOMENT.
"WE KNEW OUR WORK WAS DANGEROUS, BUT WE HADN'T CARED ABOUT THE RISK.
"WE'D JUST ALWAYS TAKEN FOR GRANTED THAT WHEN WE WENT...
"...WE'D GO TOGETHER."

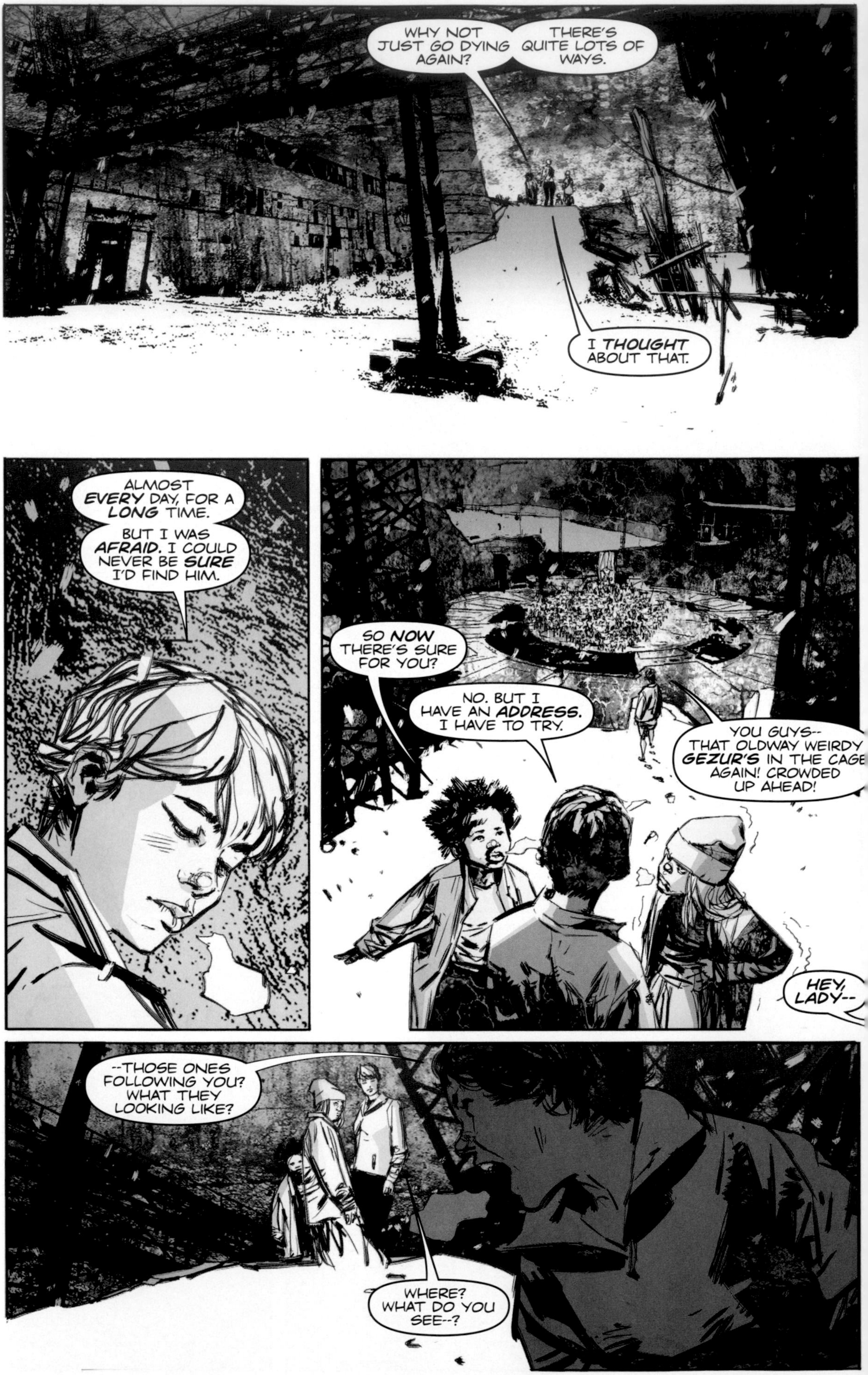

WHY NOT JUST GO DYING AGAIN?
THERE'S QUITE LOTS OF WAYS.
I *THOUGHT* ABOUT THAT.
ALMOST **EVERY** DAY, FOR A **LONG** TIME.
BUT I WAS **AFRAID.** I COULD NEVER BE **SURE** I'D FIND HIM.
SO **NOW** THERE'S SURE FOR YOU?
NO. BUT I HAVE AN **ADDRESS.** I HAVE TO TRY.
YOU GUYS-- THAT OLDWAY WEIRDY **GEZUR'S** IN THE CAGE AGAIN! CROWDED UP AHEAD!
HEY, LADY--
--THOSE ONES FOLLOWING YOU? WHAT THEY LOOKING LIKE?
WHERE? WHAT DO YOU SEE--?

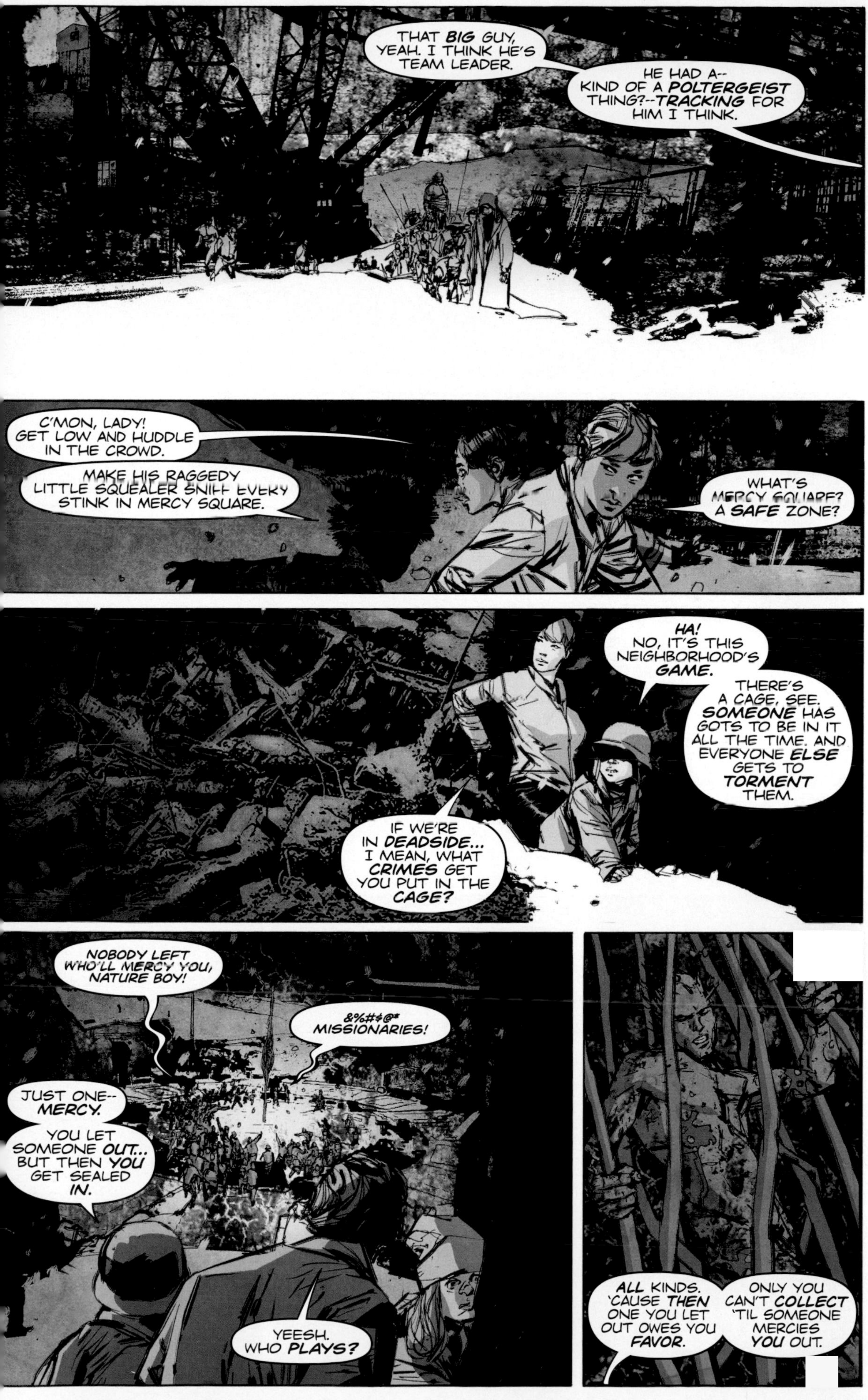
THAT BIG GUY, YEAH. I THINK HE'S TEAM LEADER.
HE HAD A-- KIND OF A POLTERGEIST THING?--TRACKING FOR HIM I THINK.
C'MON, LADY! GET LOW AND HUDDLE IN THE CROWD.
MAKE HIS RAGGEDY LITTLE SQUEALER SNIFF EVERY STINK IN MERCY SQUARE.
WHAT'S MERCY SQUARE? A SAFE ZONE?
HA! NO, IT'S THIS NEIGHBORHOOD'S GAME.
THERE'S A CAGE, SEE. SOMEONE HAS GOTS TO BE IN IT ALL THE TIME. AND EVERYONE ELSE GETS TO TORMENT THEM.
IF WE'RE IN DEADSIDE... I MEAN, WHAT CRIMES GET YOU PUT IN THE CAGE?
NOBODY LEFT WHO'LL MERCY YOU, NATURE BOY!
&%#$@* MISSIONARIES!
JUST ONE-- MERCY.
YOU LET SOMEONE OUT... BUT THEN YOU GET SEALED IN.
YEESH. WHO PLAYS?
ALL KINDS. 'CAUSE THEN ONE YOU LET OUT OWES YOU FAVOR.
ONLY YOU CAN'T COLLECT 'TIL SOMEONE MERCIES YOU OUT.

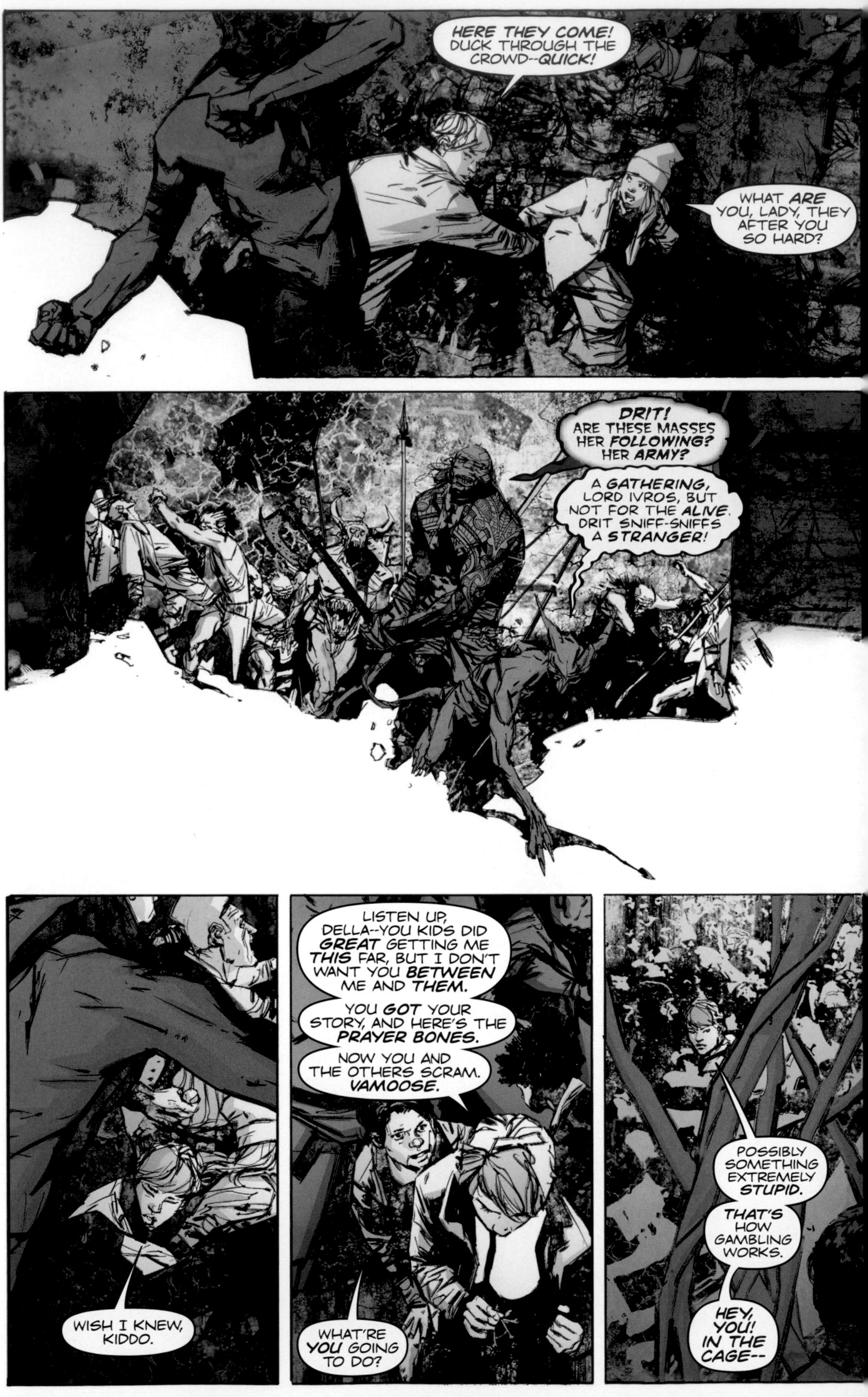
HERE THEY COME! DUCK THROUGH THE CROWD--QUICK!
WHAT ARE YOU, LADY, THEY AFTER YOU SO HARD?
DRIT! ARE THESE MASSES HER FOLLOWING? HER ARMY?
A GATHERING, LORD IVROS, BUT NOT FOR THE ALIVE. DRIT SNIFF-SNIFFS A STRANGER!
WISH I KNEW, KIDDO.
LISTEN UP, DELLA--YOU KIDS DID GREAT GETTING ME THIS FAR, BUT I DON'T WANT YOU BETWEEN ME AND THEM.
YOU GOT YOUR STORY, AND HERE'S THE PRAYER BONES.
NOW YOU AND THE OTHERS SCRAM. VAMOOSE.
WHAT'RE YOU GOING TO DO?
POSSIBLY SOMETHING EXTREMELY STUPID.
THAT'S HOW GAMBLING WORKS.
HEY, YOU! IN THE CAGE--

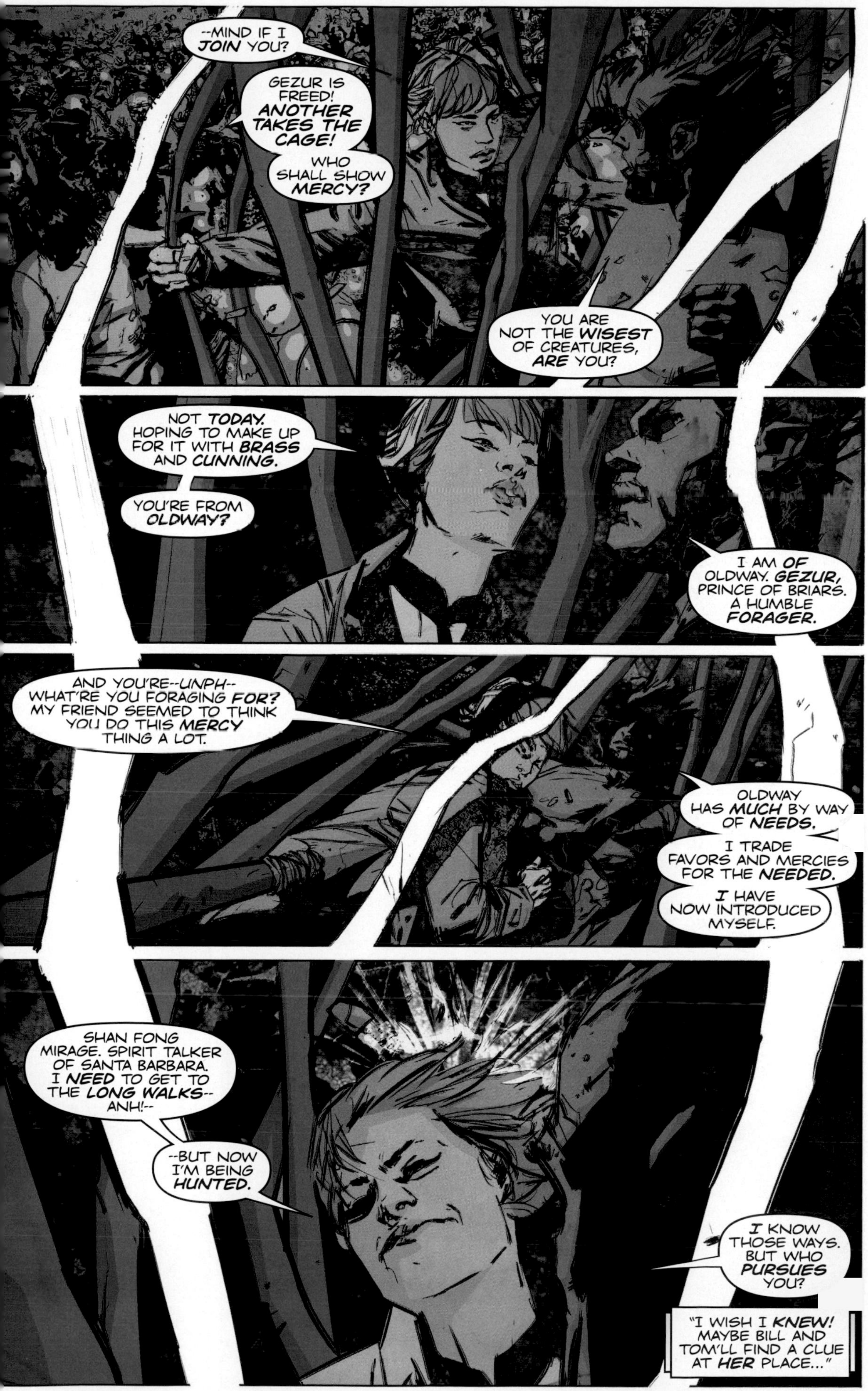
--MIND IF I JOIN YOU?
GEZUR IS FREED! ANOTHER TAKES THE CAGE!
WHO SHALL SHOW MERCY?
YOU ARE NOT THE WISEST OF CREATURES, ARE YOU?
NOT TODAY. HOPING TO MAKE UP FOR IT WITH BRASS AND CUNNING.
YOU'RE FROM OLDWAY?
I AM OF OLDWAY. GEZUR, PRINCE OF BRIARS. A HUMBLE FORAGER.
AND YOU'RE--UNPH-- WHAT'RE YOU FORAGING FOR? MY FRIEND SEEMED TO THINK YOU DO THIS MERCY THING A LOT.
OLDWAY HAS MUCH BY WAY OF NEEDS.
I TRADE FAVORS AND MERCIES FOR THE NEEDED.
I HAVE NOW INTRODUCED MYSELF.
SHAN FONG MIRAGE. SPIRIT TALKER OF SANTA BARBARA. I NEED TO GET TO THE LONG WALKS-- ANH!--
--BUT NOW I'M BEING HUNTED.
I KNOW THOSE WAYS. BUT WHO PURSUES YOU?
"I WISH I KNEW! MAYBE BILL AND TOM'LL FIND A CLUE AT HER PLACE..."

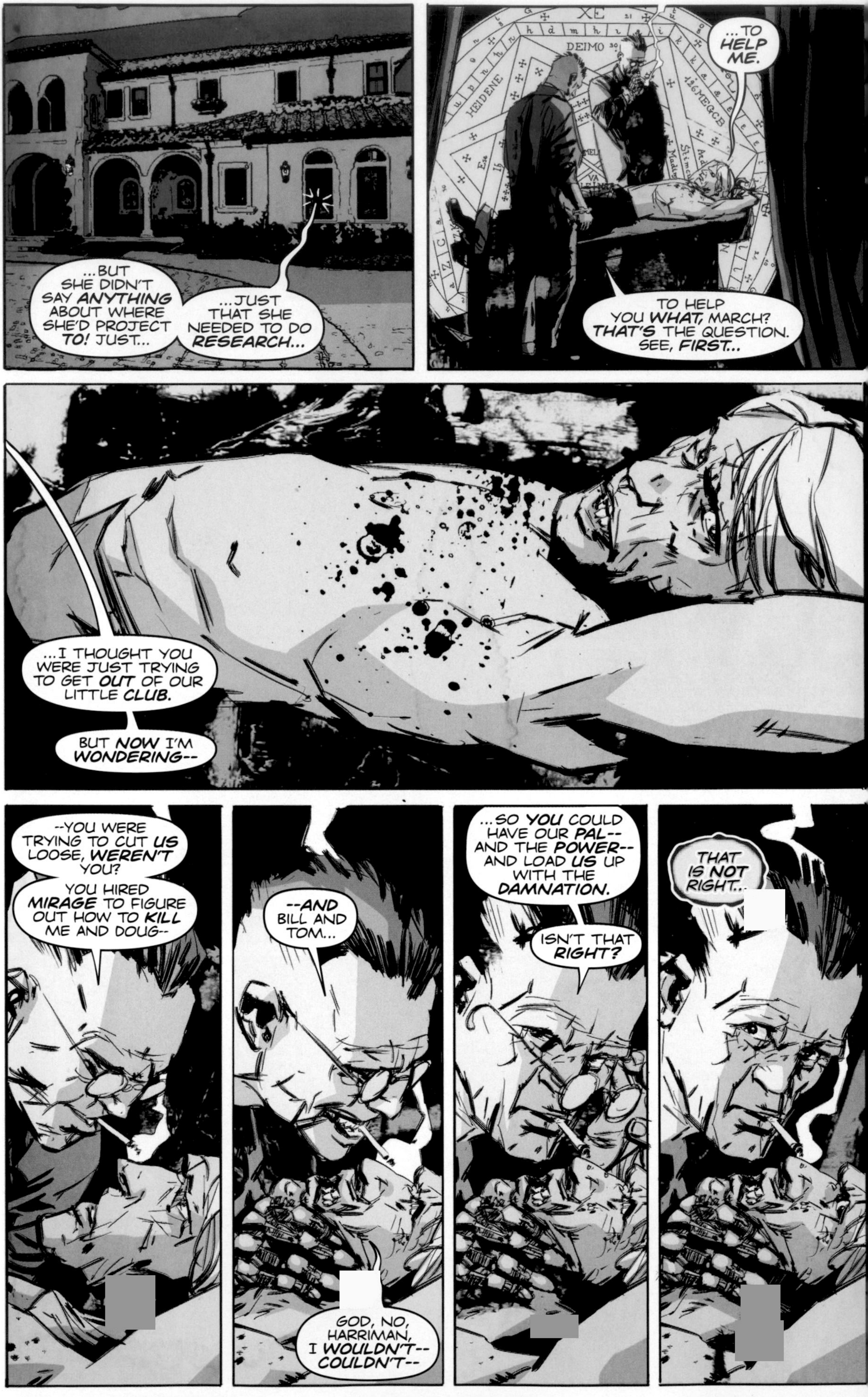
...BUT SHE DIDN'T SAY ANYTHING ABOUT WHERE SHE'D PROJECT TO! JUST...
...JUST THAT SHE NEEDED TO DO RESEARCH...
...TO HELP ME.
TO HELP YOU WHAT, MARCH? THAT'S THE QUESTION. SEE, FIRST...
...I THOUGHT YOU WERE JUST TRYING TO GET OUT OF OUR LITTLE CLUB.
BUT NOW I'M WONDERING--
--YOU WERE TRYING TO CUT US LOOSE, WEREN'T YOU?
YOU HIRED MIRAGE TO FIGURE OUT HOW TO KILL ME AND DOUG--
--AND BILL AND TOM...
GOD, NO, HARRIMAN, I WOULDN'T-- COULDN'T--
...SO YOU COULD HAVE OUR PAL-- AND THE POWER-- AND LOAD US UP WITH THE DAMNATION.
ISN'T THAT RIGHT?
THAT IS NOT RIGHT...

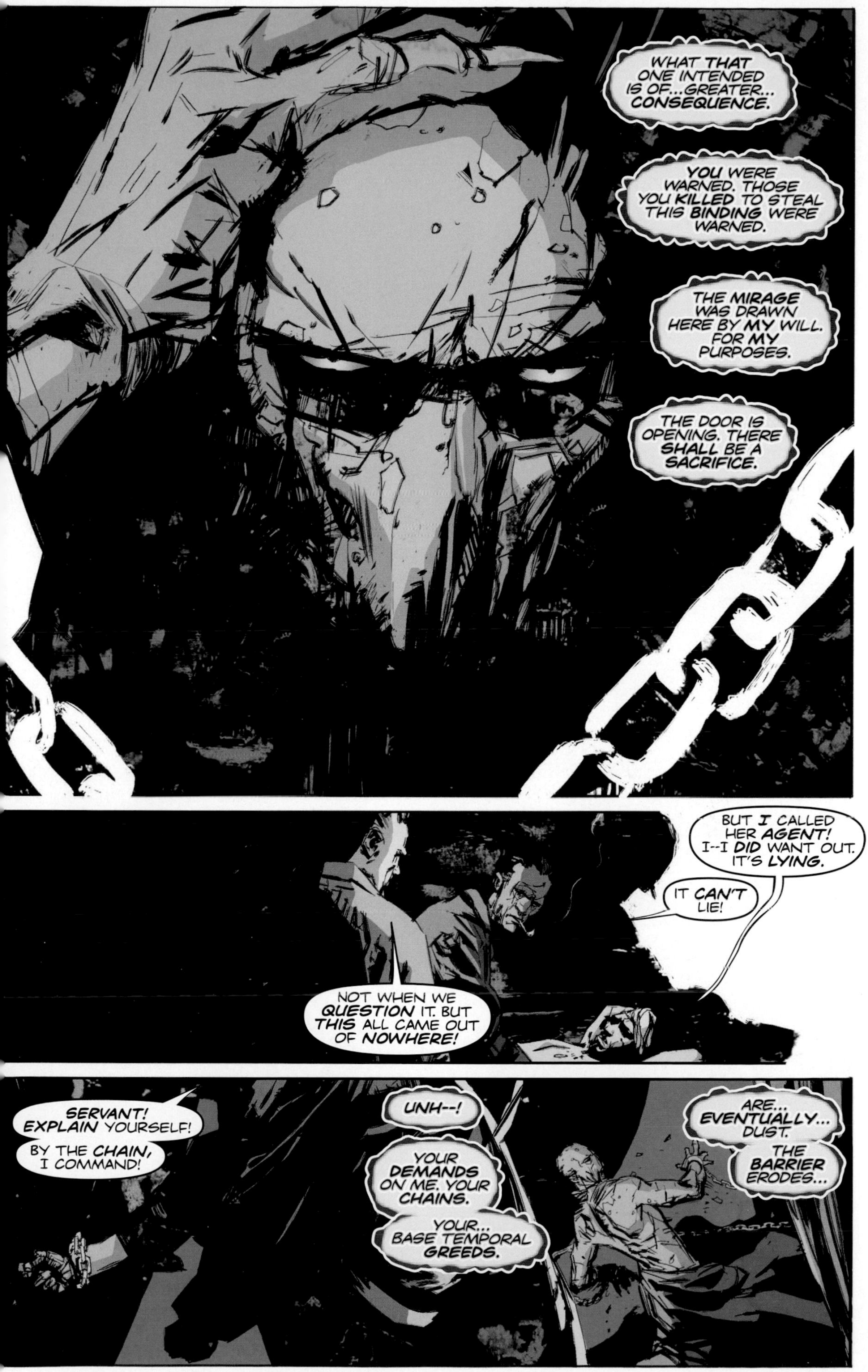

WHAT THAT ONE INTENDED IS OF...GREATER... CONSEQUENCE.
YOU WERE WARNED. THOSE YOU KILLED TO STEAL THIS BINDING WERE WARNED.
THE MIRAGE WAS DRAWN HERE BY MY WILL. FOR MY PURPOSES.
THE DOOR IS OPENING. THERE SHALL BE A SACRIFICE.
BUT I CALLED HER AGENT! I--I DID WANT OUT. IT'S LYING.
IT CAN'T LIE!
NOT WHEN WE QUESTION IT. BUT THIS ALL CAME OUT OF NOWHERE!
SERVANT! EXPLAIN YOURSELF!
BY THE CHAIN, I COMMAND!
UNH--!
YOUR DEMANDS ON ME. YOUR CHAINS.
YOUR... BASE TEMPORAL GREEDS.
ARE... EVENTUALLY... DUST.
THE BARRIER ERODES...

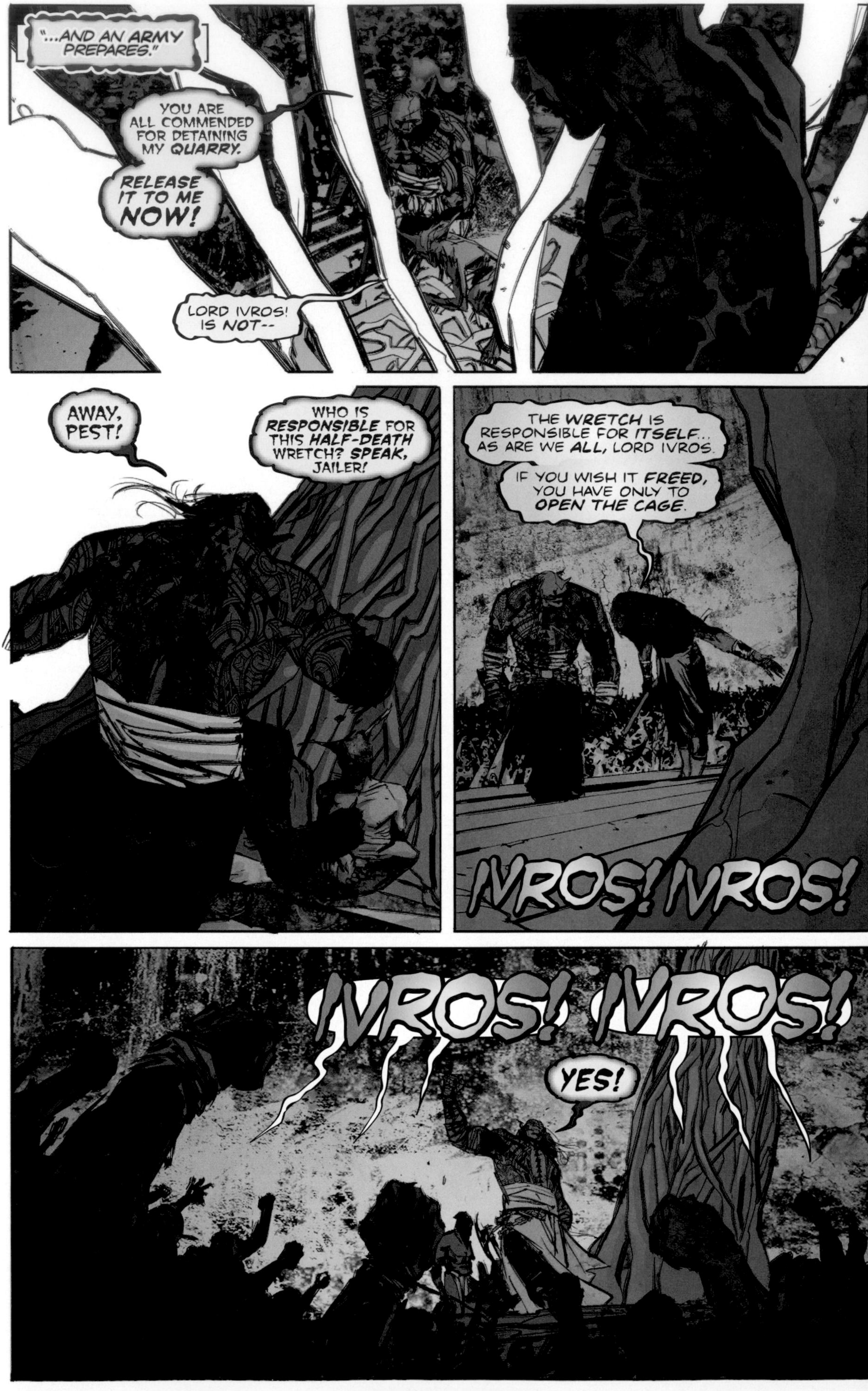
"...AND AN ARMY PREPARES."
YOU ARE ALL COMMENDED FOR DETAINING MY QUARRY.
RELEASE IT TO ME NOW!
LORD IVROS! IS NOT--
AWAY, PEST!
WHO IS RESPONSIBLE FOR THIS HALF-DEATH WRETCH? SPEAK, JAILER!
THE WRETCH IS RESPONSIBLE FOR ITSELF... AS ARE WE ALL, LORD IVROS.
IF YOU WISH IT FREED, YOU HAVE ONLY TO OPEN THE CAGE.
IVROS! IVROS!
IVROS! IVROS!
YES!

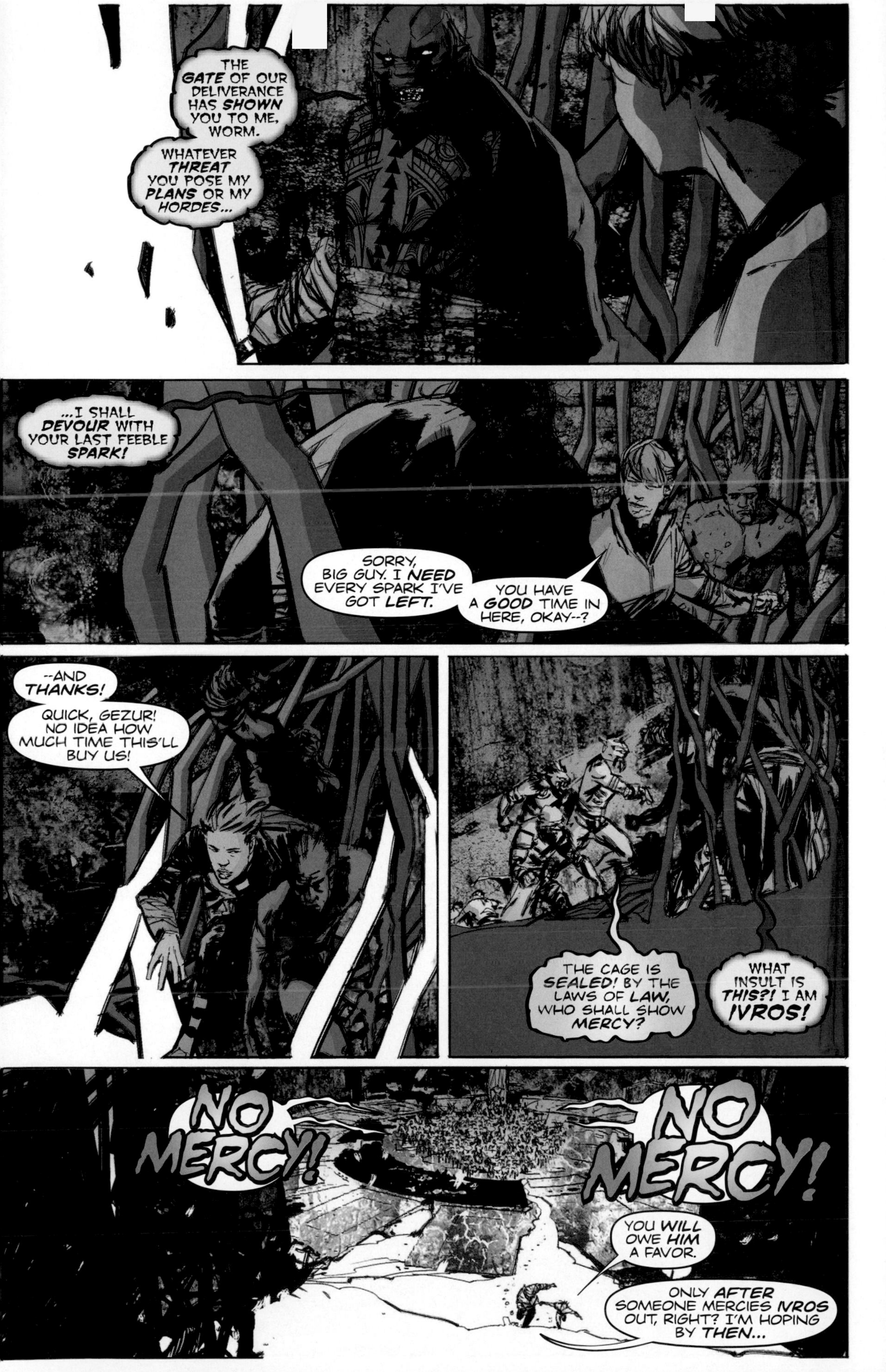
THE GATE OF OUR DELIVERANCE HAS SHOWN YOU TO ME, WORM.
WHATEVER THREAT YOU POSE MY PLANS OR MY HORDES...
...I SHALL DEVOUR WITH YOUR LAST FEEBLE SPARK!
SORRY, BIG GUY. I NEED EVERY SPARK I'VE GOT LEFT.
YOU HAVE A GOOD TIME IN HERE, OKAY--?
--AND THANKS!
QUICK, GEZUR! NO IDEA HOW MUCH TIME THIS'LL BUY US!
THE CAGE IS SEALED! BY THE LAWS OF LAW, WHO SHALL SHOW MERCY?
WHAT INSULT IS THIS?! I AM IVROS!
NO MERCY!
NO MERCY!
YOU WILL OWE HIM A FAVOR.
ONLY AFTER SOMEONE MERCIES IVROS OUT, RIGHT? I'M HOPING BY THEN...

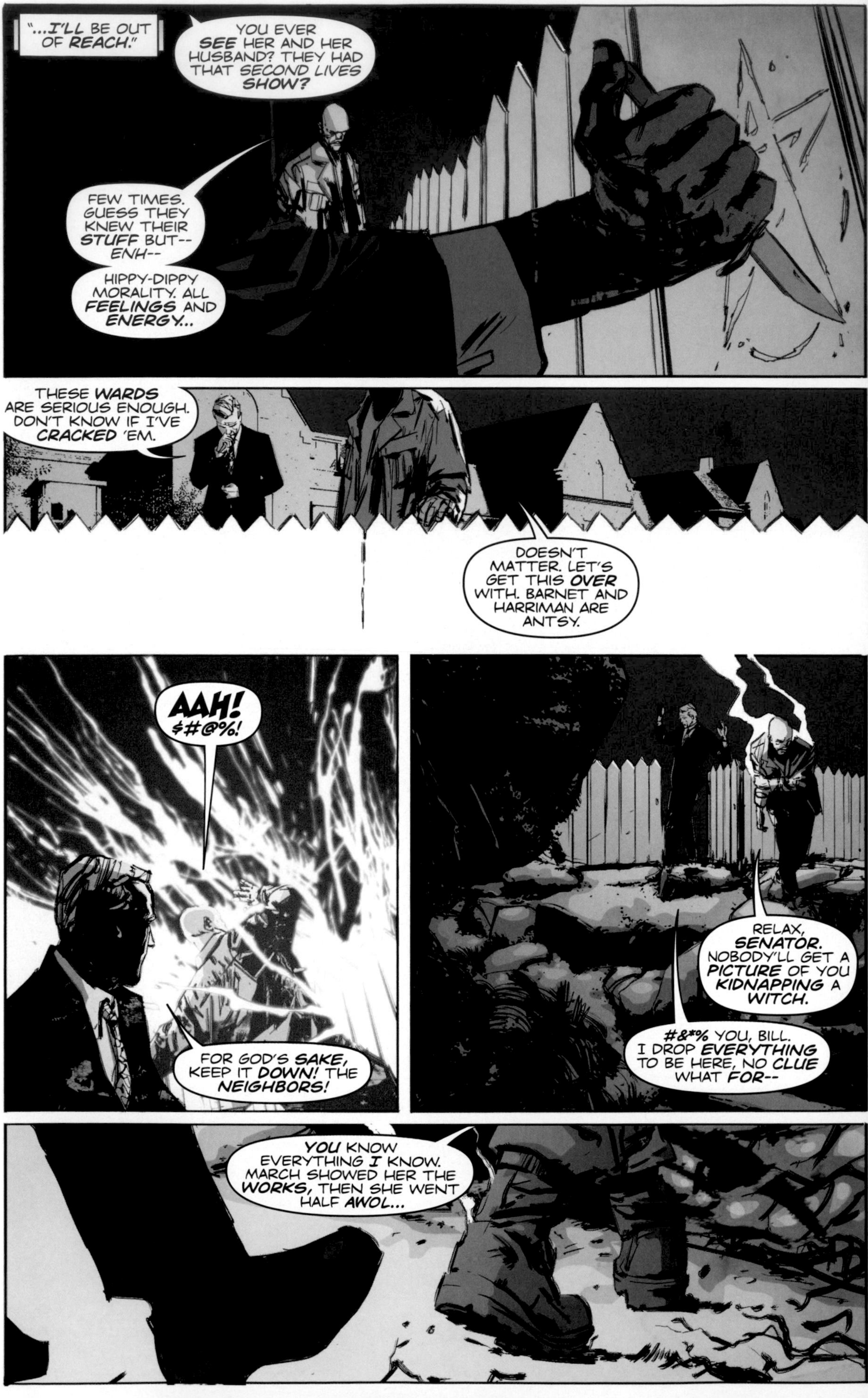
"...I'LL BE OUT OF REACH."
YOU EVER SEE HER AND HER HUSBAND? THEY HAD THAT SECOND LIVES SHOW?
FEW TIMES. GUESS THEY KNEW THEIR STUFF BUT-- ENH--
HIPPY-DIPPY MORALITY. ALL FEELINGS AND ENERGY...
THESE WARDS ARE SERIOUS ENOUGH. DON'T KNOW IF I'VE CRACKED 'EM.
DOESN'T MATTER. LET'S GET THIS OVER WITH. BARNET AND HARRIMAN ARE ANTSY.
AAH! $#@%!
FOR GOD'S SAKE, KEEP IT DOWN! THE NEIGHBORS!
RELAX, SENATOR. NOBODY'LL GET A PICTURE OF YOU KIDNAPPING A WITCH.
#&*% YOU, BILL. I DROP EVERYTHING TO BE HERE, NO CLUE WHAT FOR--
YOU KNOW EVERYTHING I KNOW. MARCH SHOWED HER THE WORKS, THEN SHE WENT HALF AWOL...

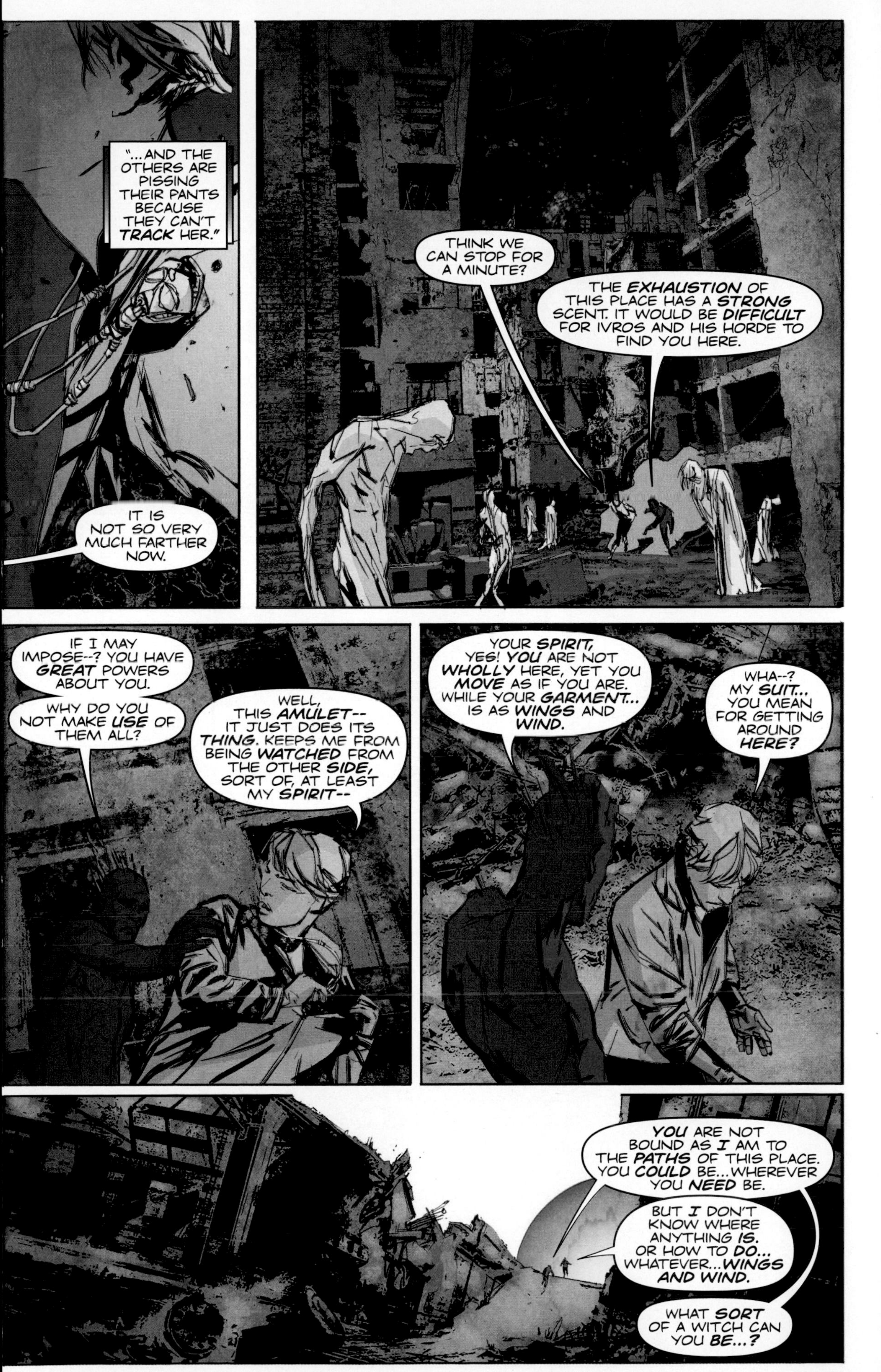
"...AND THE OTHERS ARE PISSING THEIR PANTS BECAUSE THEY CAN'T TRACK HER."
IT IS NOT SO VERY MUCH FARTHER NOW.
THINK WE CAN STOP FOR A MINUTE?
THE EXHAUSTION OF THIS PLACE HAS A STRONG SCENT. IT WOULD BE DIFFICULT FOR IVROS AND HIS HORDE TO FIND YOU HERE.
IF I MAY IMPOSE--? YOU HAVE GREAT POWERS ABOUT YOU.
WHY DO YOU NOT MAKE USE OF THEM ALL?
WELL, THIS AMULET-- IT JUST DOES ITS THING. KEEPS ME FROM BEING WATCHED FROM THE OTHER SIDE, SORT OF, AT LEAST MY SPIRIT--
YOUR SPIRIT, YES! YOU ARE NOT WHOLLY HERE, YET YOU MOVE AS IF YOU ARE. WHILE YOUR GARMENT... IS AS WINGS AND WIND.
WHA--? MY SUIT... YOU MEAN FOR GETTING AROUND HERE?
YOU ARE NOT BOUND AS I AM TO THE PATHS OF THIS PLACE. YOU COULD BE...WHEREVER YOU NEED BE.
BUT I DON'T KNOW WHERE ANYTHING IS. OR HOW TO DO... WHATEVER...WINGS AND WIND.
WHAT SORT OF A WITCH CAN YOU BE...?

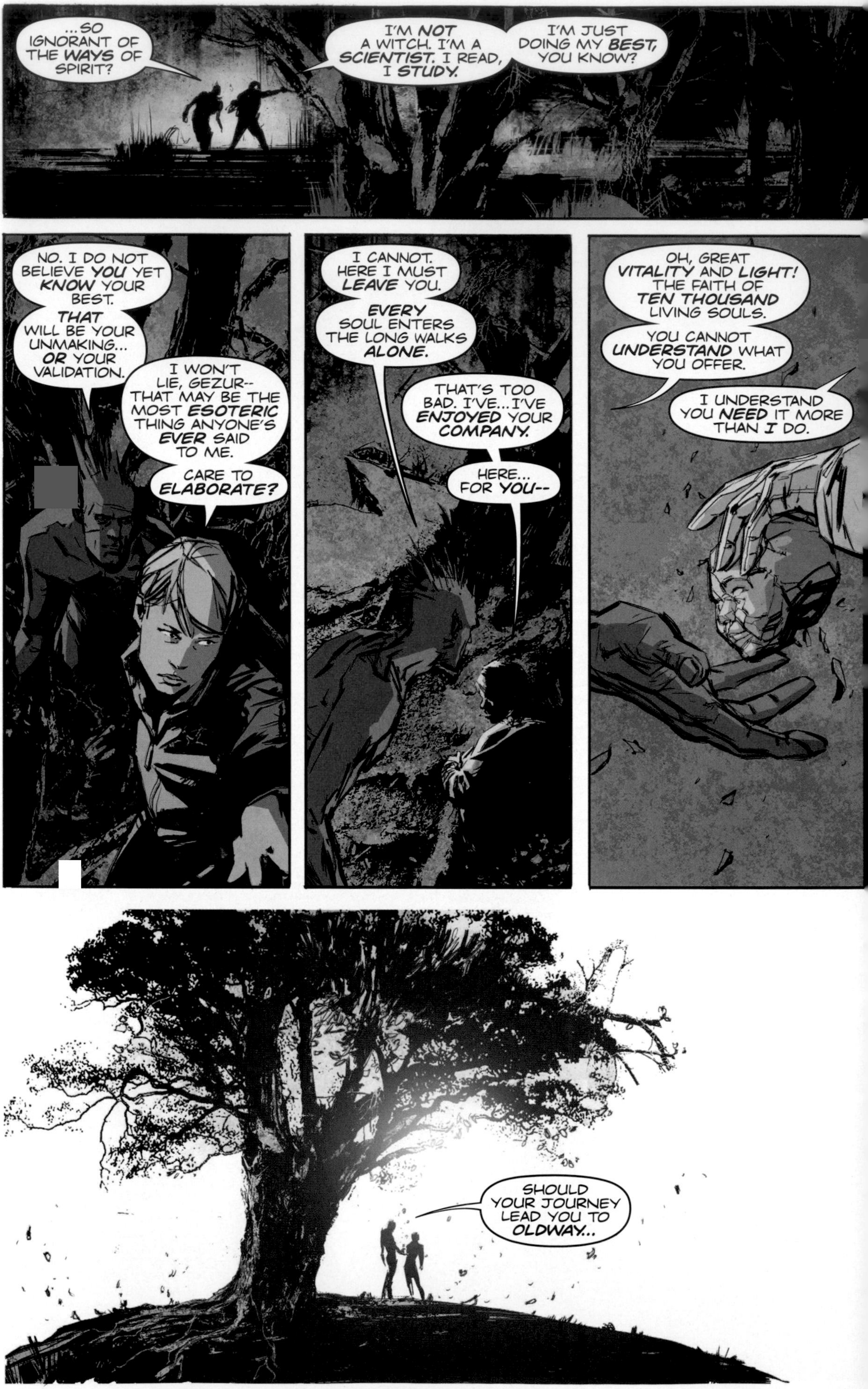
...SO IGNORANT OF THE WAYS OF SPIRIT?
I'M NOT A WITCH. I'M A SCIENTIST. I READ, I STUDY.
I'M JUST DOING MY BEST, YOU KNOW?
NO. I DO NOT BELIEVE YOU YET KNOW YOUR BEST.
THAT WILL BE YOUR UNMAKING... OR YOUR VALIDATION.
I WON'T LIE, GEZUR--THAT MAY BE THE MOST ESOTERIC THING ANYONE'S EVER SAID TO ME.
CARE TO ELABORATE?
I CANNOT. HERE I MUST LEAVE YOU.
EVERY SOUL ENTERS THE LONG WALKS ALONE.
THAT'S TOO BAD. I'VE...I'VE ENJOYED YOUR COMPANY.
HERE... FOR YOU--
OH, GREAT VITALITY AND LIGHT! THE FAITH OF TEN THOUSAND LIVING SOULS.
YOU CANNOT UNDERSTAND WHAT YOU OFFER.
I UNDERSTAND YOU NEED IT MORE THAN I DO.
SHOULD YOUR JOURNEY LEAD YOU TO OLDWAY...

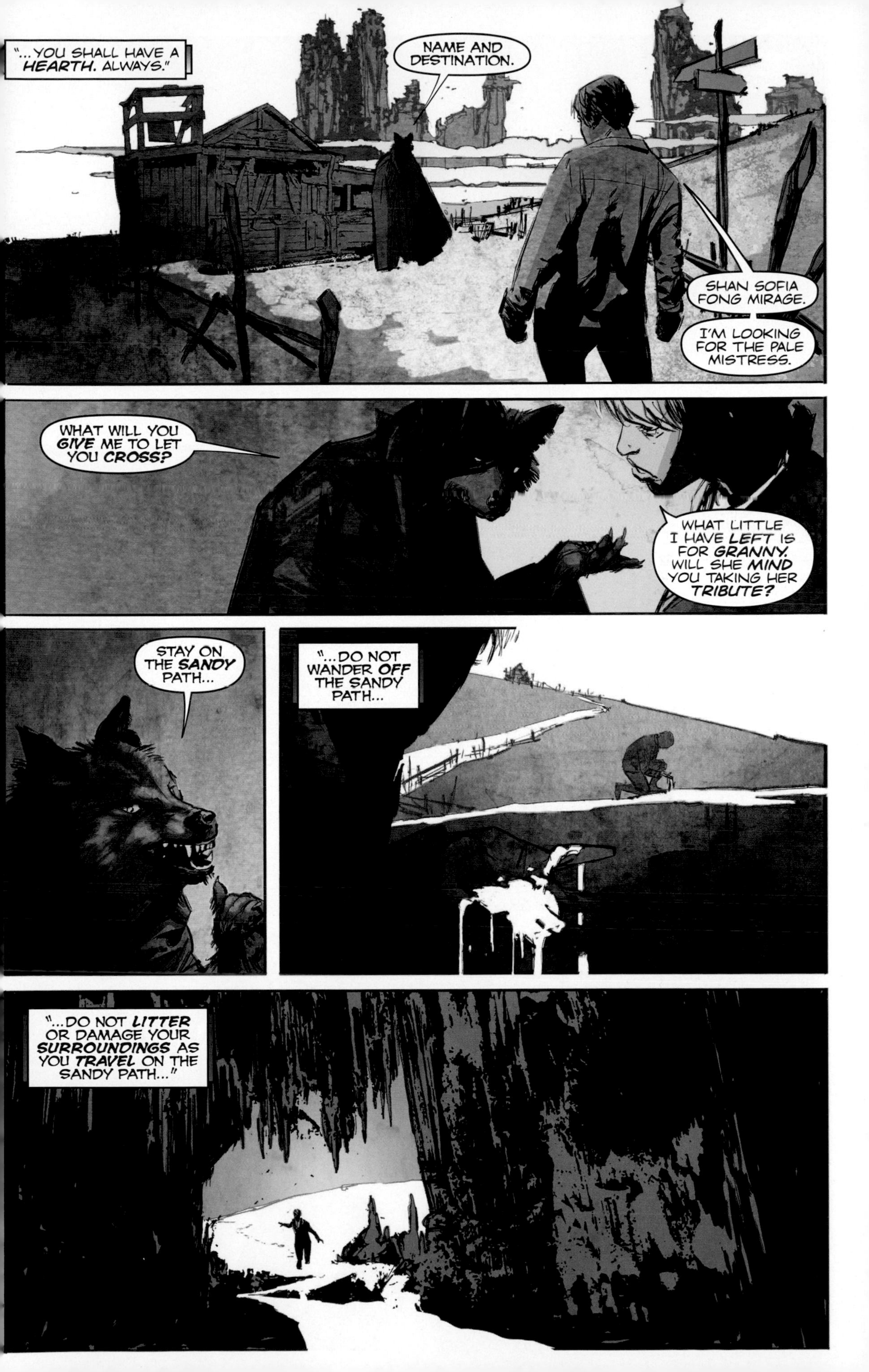
"...YOU SHALL HAVE A HEARTH. ALWAYS."
NAME AND DESTINATION.
SHAN SOFIA FONG MIRAGE.
I'M LOOKING FOR THE PALE MISTRESS.
WHAT WILL YOU GIVE ME TO LET YOU CROSS?
WHAT LITTLE I HAVE LEFT IS FOR GRANNY. WILL SHE MIND YOU TAKING HER TRIBUTE?
STAY ON THE SANDY PATH...
"...DO NOT WANDER OFF THE SANDY PATH...
"...DO NOT LITTER OR DAMAGE YOUR SURROUNDINGS AS YOU TRAVEL ON THE SANDY PATH..."

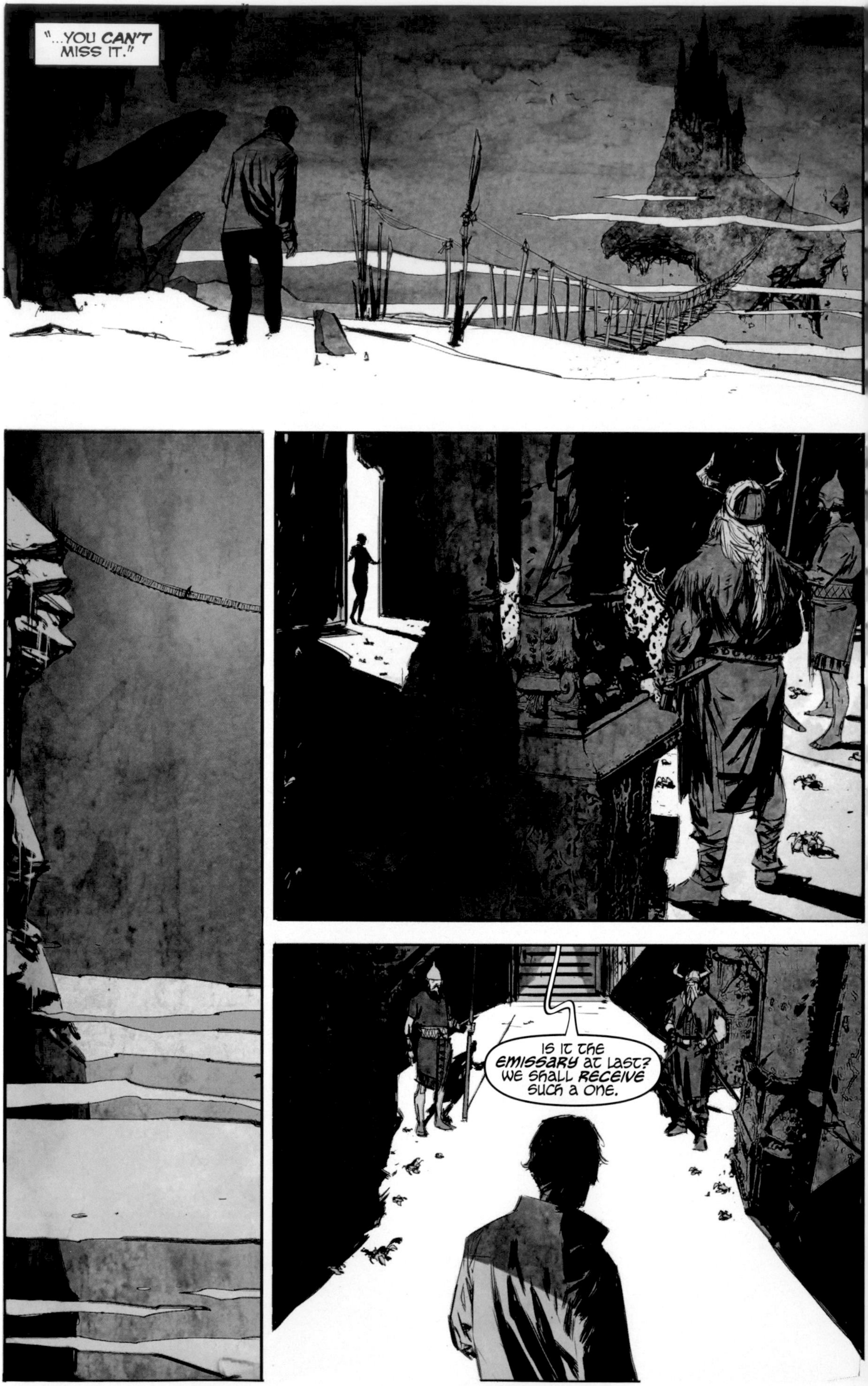
"...YOU CAN'T MISS IT."
IS IT THE EMISSARY AT LAST? WE SHALL RECEIVE SUCH A ONE.

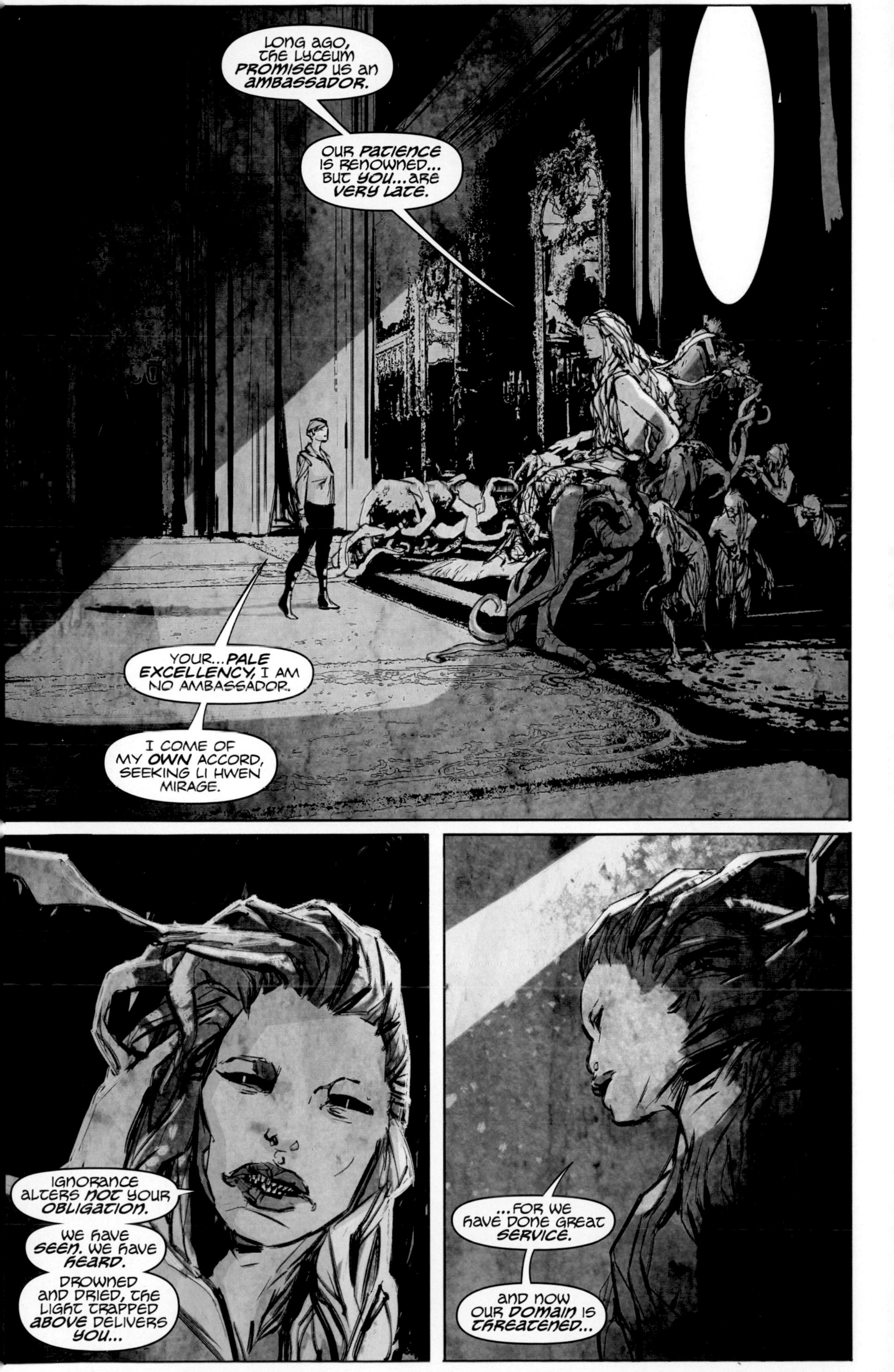
LONG AGO, THE LYCEUM PROMISED US AN AMBASSADOR.
OUR PATIENCE IS RENOWNED... BUT YOU...ARE VERY LATE.
YOUR...PALE EXCELLENCY, I AM NO AMBASSADOR.
I COME OF MY OWN ACCORD, SEEKING LI HWEN MIRAGE.
IGNORANCE ALTERS NOT YOUR OBLIGATION.
WE HAVE SEEN. WE HAVE HEARD.
DROWNED AND DRIED, THE LIGHT TRAPPED ABOVE DELIVERS YOU...
...FOR WE HAVE DONE GREAT SERVICE.
AND NOW OUR DOMAIN IS THREATENED...

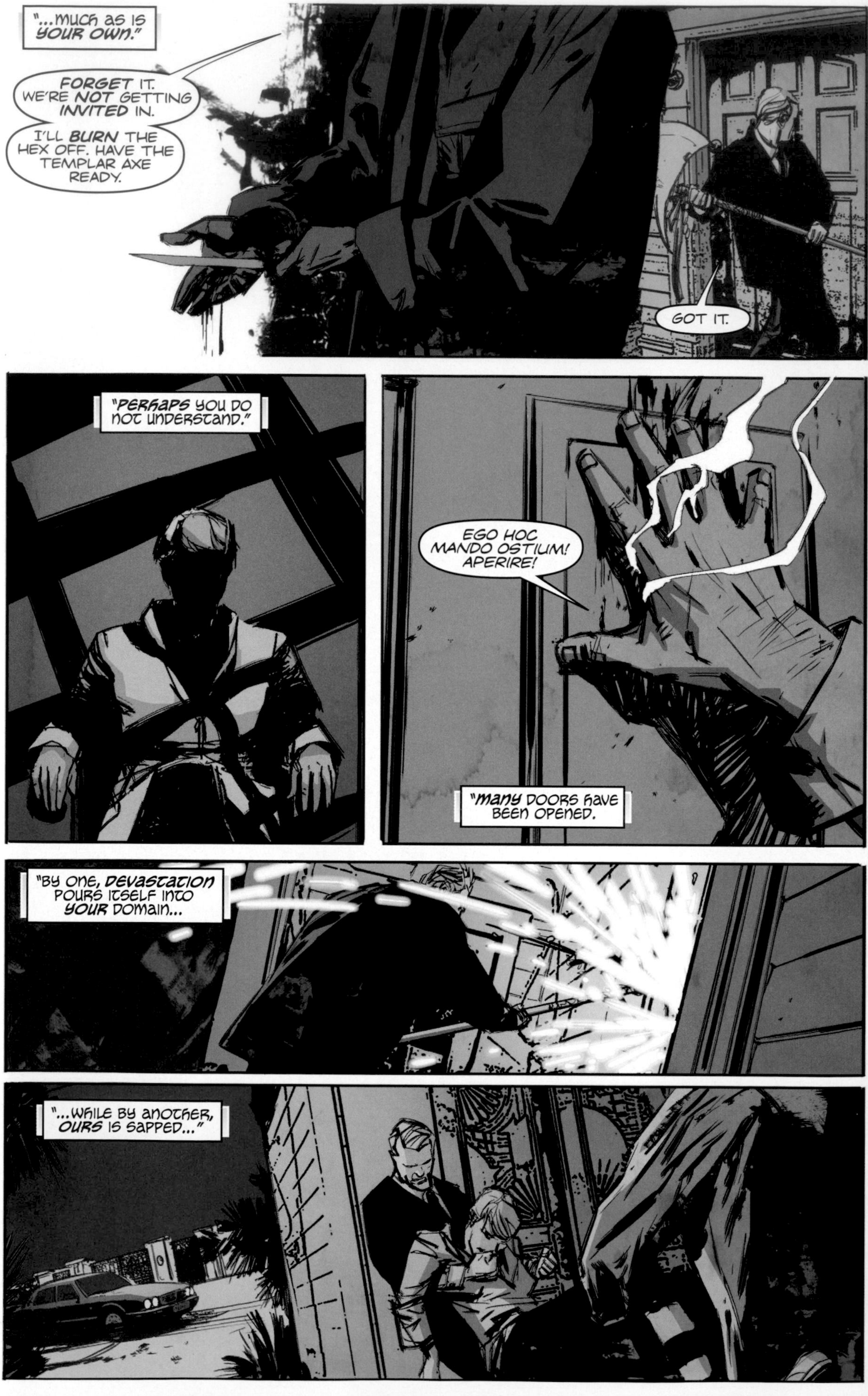
"...much as is your own."
Forget it. We're not getting invited in.
I'll burn the hex off. Have the Templar axe ready.
Got it.
"Perhaps you do not understand."
Ego hoc mando ostium! Aperire!
"Many doors have been opened.
"By one, devastation pours itself into your domain...
"...while by another, ours is sapped..."

...AND *THAT* BY *YOUR* HAND. THUS WE DEMAND *REDRESS.*

WHAT THE--? *NO!*

I DIDN'T-- I *CAME* BY A DOOR, BUT NOT TO *YOUR* DOMAIN. I DON'T--

I DON'T KNOW WHAT YOU'RE *TALKING* ABOUT, YOU KEEP *CHANGING* AND I-- MY *HEAD* HURTS.

I JUST WANT *HWEN.*

YOUR *TEMPORAL* FORM IS DISTURBED. THAT IS... UNFORTUNATE.

WE ARE AS THE FIRST AND LAST *SEAS,* CHANGING *AND* UNCHANGED.

AND WE CARE *LITTLE* FOR *YOUR* DESIRES. YOUR NEGLIGENCE *PARCHES* US--

MY *NEGLIGENCE?* WHAT DID I *DO?*

A *KEY* OF GREAT *POWER* LIES AT THE BOTTOM OF *YOUR* SEA...

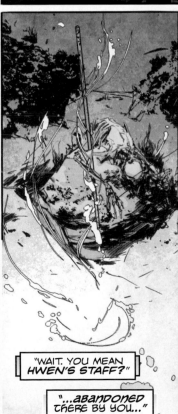

"WAIT. YOU MEAN *HWEN'S STAFF?*"

"...ABANDONED THERE BY YOU..."

...JUST AS YOU DID *THIS,* WHICH YOU NOW *CLAIM* TO *VALUE.*

SO.

YOU DO US *GRAVE* INJURY...

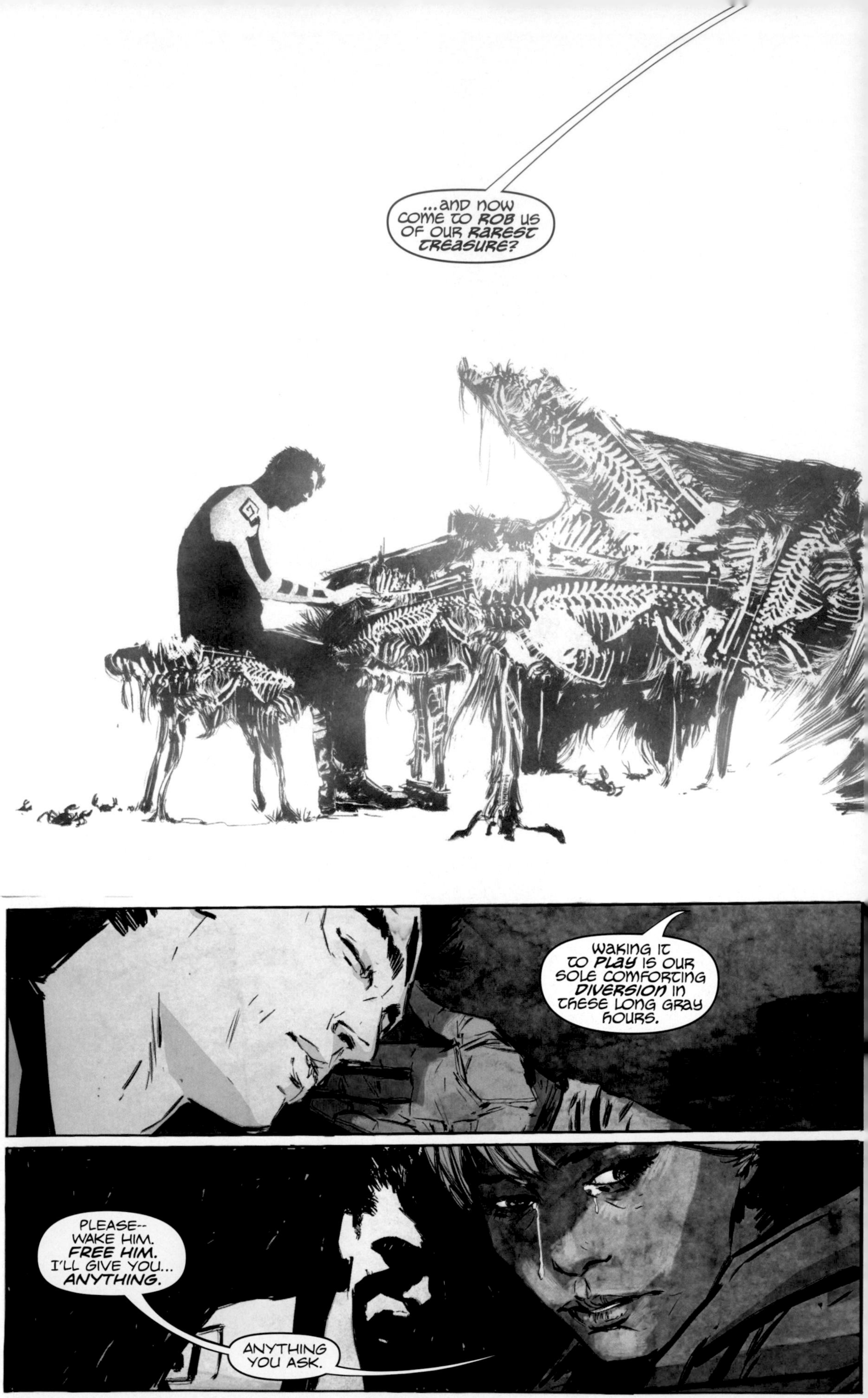
...and now come to ROB us of our RAREST TREASURE?
WAKING IT TO PLAY IS OUR SOLE COMFORTING DIVERSION IN THESE LONG GRAY HOURS.
PLEASE-- WAKE HIM. FREE HIM. I'LL GIVE YOU... ANYTHING.
ANYTHING YOU ASK.

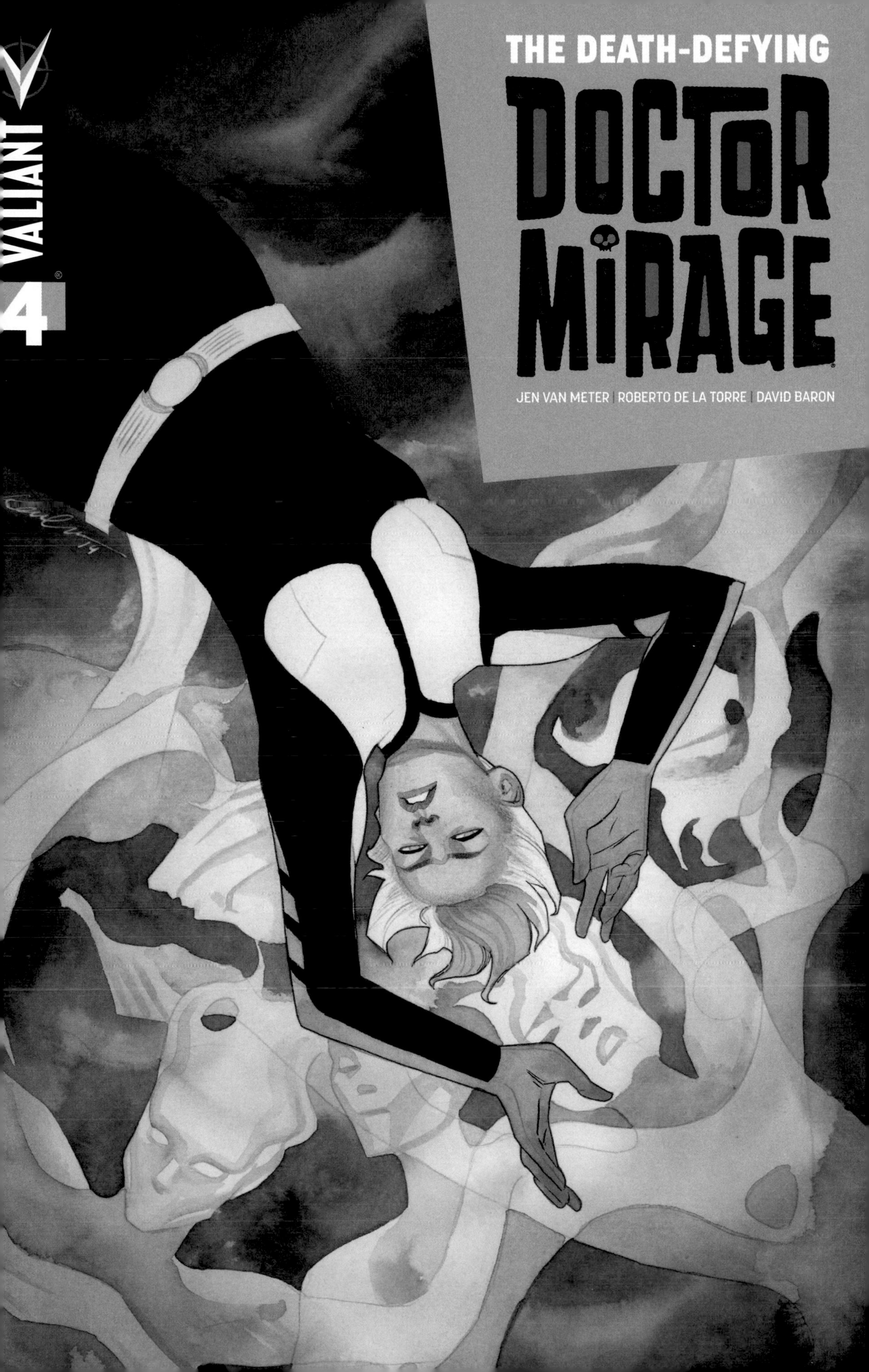
VALIANT
4
THE DEATH-DEFYING
DOCTOR MIRAGE
JEN VAN METER | ROBERTO DE LA TORRE | DAVID BARON

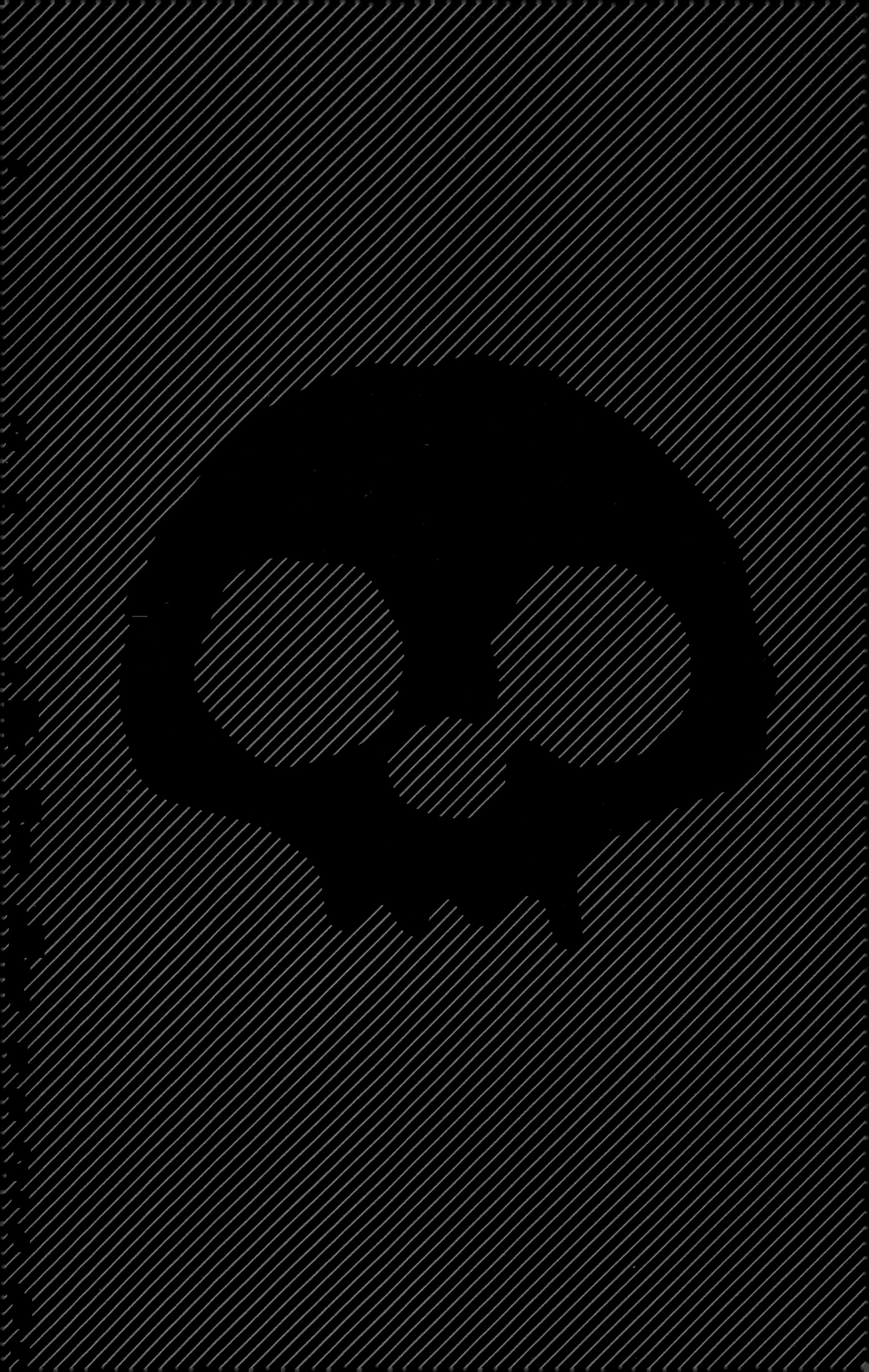

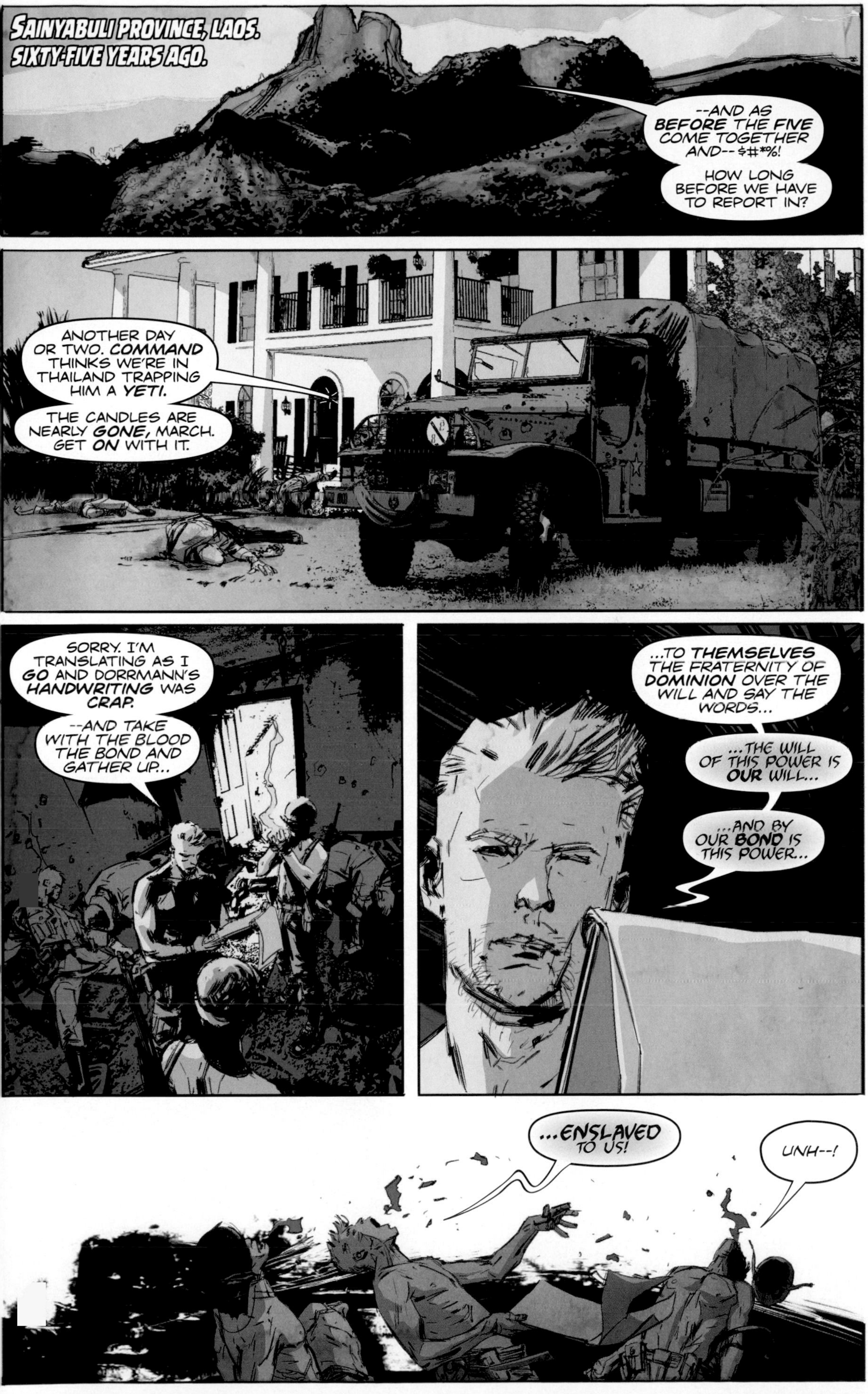
SAINYABULI PROVINCE, LAOS. SIXTY-FIVE YEARS AGO.
--AND AS BEFORE THE FIVE COME TOGETHER AND-- $#*%!
HOW LONG BEFORE WE HAVE TO REPORT IN?
ANOTHER DAY OR TWO. COMMAND THINKS WE'RE IN THAILAND TRAPPING HIM A YETI.
THE CANDLES ARE NEARLY GONE, MARCH. GET ON WITH IT.
SORRY. I'M TRANSLATING AS I GO AND DORRMANN'S HANDWRITING WAS CRAP.
--AND TAKE WITH THE BLOOD THE BOND AND GATHER UP...
...TO THEMSELVES THE FRATERNITY OF DOMINION OVER THE WILL AND SAY THE WORDS...
...THE WILL OF THIS POWER IS OUR WILL...
...AND BY OUR BOND IS THIS POWER...
...ENSLAVED TO US!
UNH--!

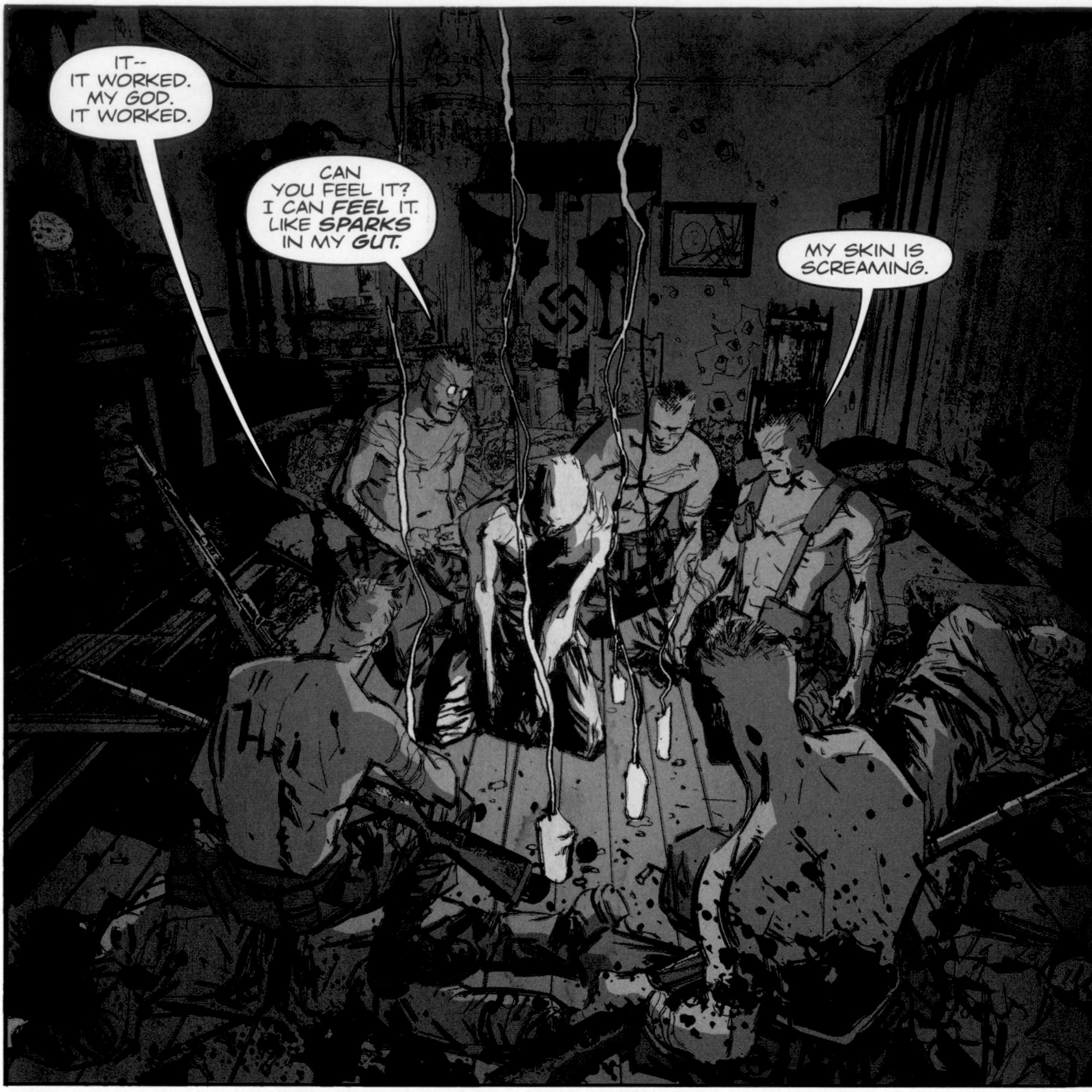
IT--
IT WORKED.
MY GOD.
IT WORKED.
CAN YOU FEEL IT? I CAN FEEL IT. LIKE SPARKS IN MY GUT.
MY SKIN IS SCREAMING.

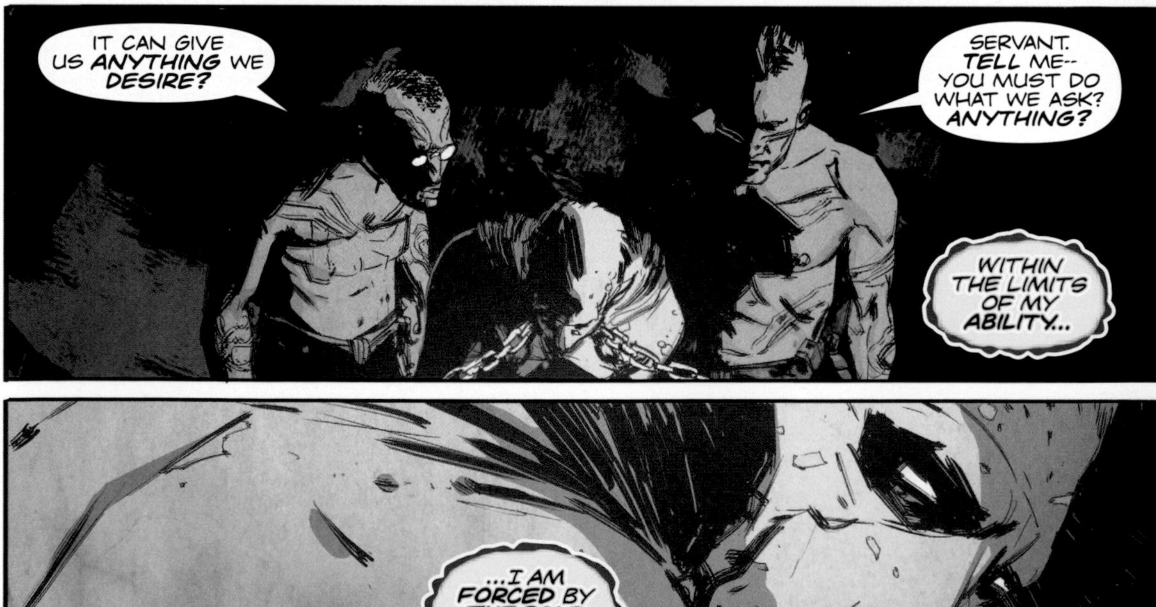
IT CAN GIVE US ANYTHING WE DESIRE?
SERVANT. TELL ME-- YOU MUST DO WHAT WE ASK? ANYTHING?
WITHIN THE LIMITS OF MY ABILITY...

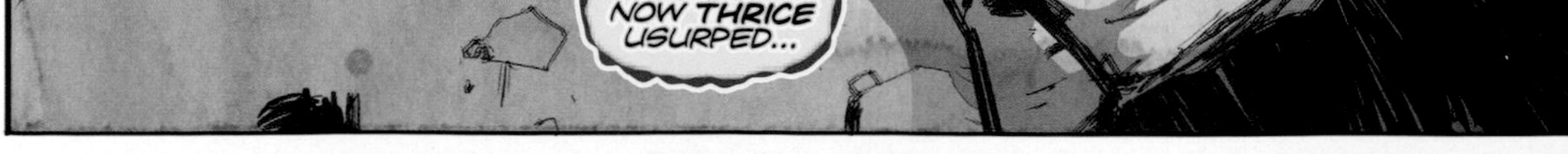
...I AM FORCED BY THE BOND NOW THRICE USURPED...

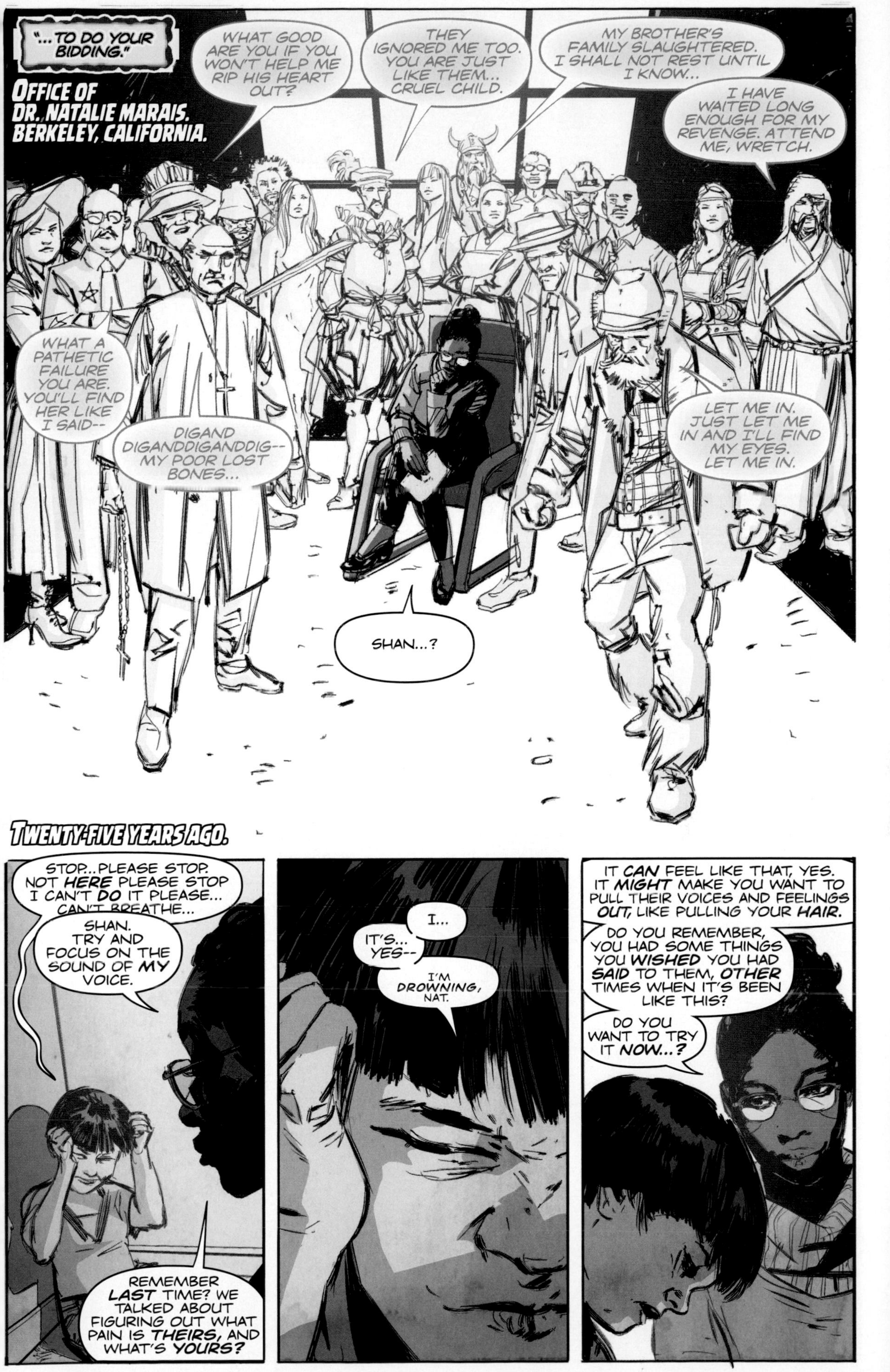
"...TO DO YOUR BIDDING."
OFFICE OF DR. NATALIE MARAIS. BERKELEY, CALIFORNIA.
WHAT GOOD ARE YOU IF YOU WON'T HELP ME RIP HIS HEART OUT?
THEY IGNORED ME TOO. YOU ARE JUST LIKE THEM... CRUEL CHILD.
MY BROTHER'S FAMILY SLAUGHTERED. I SHALL NOT REST UNTIL I KNOW...
I HAVE WAITED LONG ENOUGH FOR MY REVENGE. ATTEND ME, WRETCH.
WHAT A PATHETIC FAILURE YOU ARE. YOU'LL FIND HER LIKE I SAID--
DIGAND DIGANDDIGANDDIG-- MY POOR LOST BONES...
LET ME IN. JUST LET ME IN AND I'LL FIND MY EYES. LET ME IN.
SHAN...?
TWENTY-FIVE YEARS AGO.
STOP...PLEASE STOP. NOT HERE PLEASE STOP I CAN'T DO IT PLEASE... CAN'T BREATHE...
SHAN. TRY AND FOCUS ON THE SOUND OF MY VOICE.
REMEMBER LAST TIME? WE TALKED ABOUT FIGURING OUT WHAT PAIN IS THEIRS, AND WHAT'S YOURS?
I...
IT'S... YES--
I'M DROWNING, NAT.
IT CAN FEEL LIKE THAT, YES. IT MIGHT MAKE YOU WANT TO PULL THEIR VOICES AND FEELINGS OUT, LIKE PULLING YOUR HAIR.
DO YOU REMEMBER, YOU HAD SOME THINGS YOU WISHED YOU HAD SAID TO THEM, OTHER TIMES WHEN IT'S BEEN LIKE THIS?
DO YOU WANT TO TRY IT NOW...?

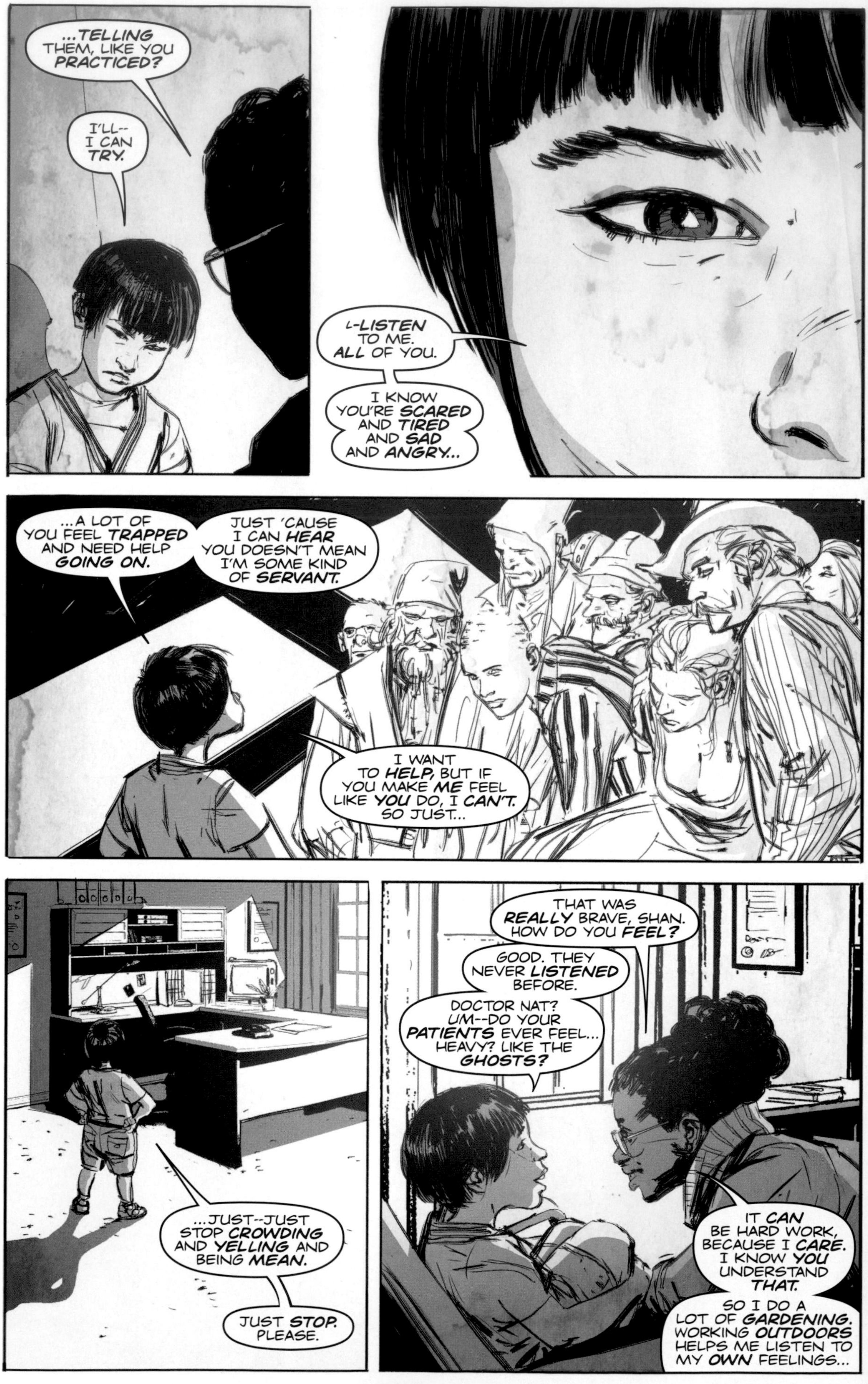
...TELLING THEM, LIKE YOU PRACTICED?
I'LL-- I CAN TRY.
L-LISTEN TO ME. ALL OF YOU.
I KNOW YOU'RE SCARED AND TIRED AND SAD AND ANGRY...
...A LOT OF YOU FEEL TRAPPED AND NEED HELP GOING ON.
JUST 'CAUSE I CAN HEAR YOU DOESN'T MEAN I'M SOME KIND OF SERVANT.
I WANT TO HELP, BUT IF YOU MAKE ME FEEL LIKE YOU DO, I CAN'T. SO JUST...
...JUST--JUST STOP CROWDING AND YELLING AND BEING MEAN.
JUST STOP. PLEASE.
THAT WAS REALLY BRAVE, SHAN. HOW DO YOU FEEL?
GOOD. THEY NEVER LISTENED BEFORE.
DOCTOR NAT? UM--DO YOUR PATIENTS EVER FEEL... HEAVY? LIKE THE GHOSTS?
IT CAN BE HARD WORK, BECAUSE I CARE. I KNOW YOU UNDERSTAND THAT.
SO I DO A LOT OF GARDENING. WORKING OUTDOORS HELPS ME LISTEN TO MY OWN FEELINGS...

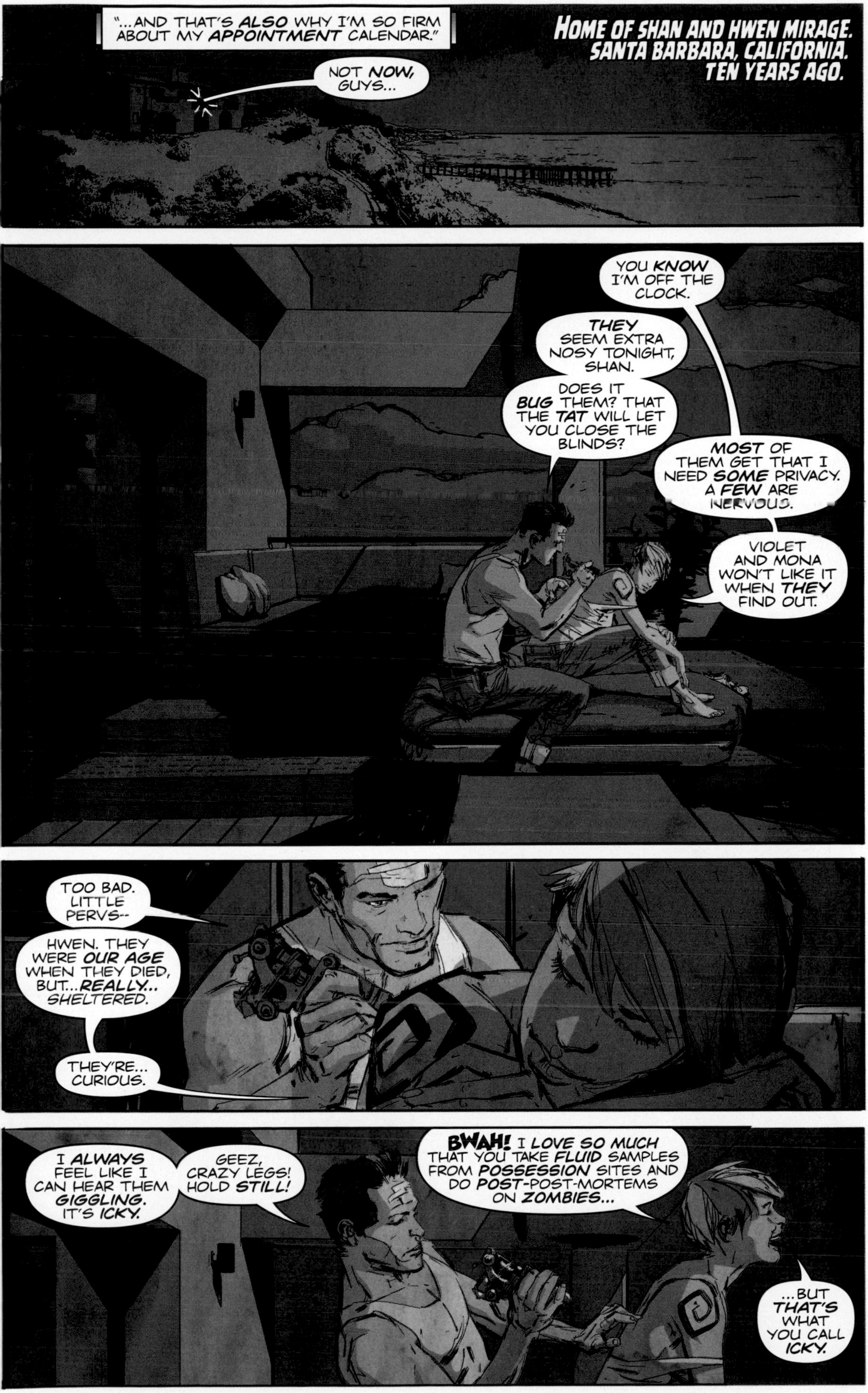
"...AND THAT'S ALSO WHY I'M SO FIRM ABOUT MY APPOINTMENT CALENDAR."
HOME OF SHAN AND HWEN MIRAGE. SANTA BARBARA, CALIFORNIA. TEN YEARS AGO.
NOT NOW, GUYS...
YOU KNOW I'M OFF THE CLOCK.
THEY SEEM EXTRA NOSY TONIGHT, SHAN.
DOES IT BUG THEM? THAT THE TAT WILL LET YOU CLOSE THE BLINDS?
MOST OF THEM GET THAT I NEED SOME PRIVACY. A FEW ARE NERVOUS.
VIOLET AND MONA WON'T LIKE IT WHEN THEY FIND OUT.
TOO BAD. LITTLE PERVS--
HWEN. THEY WERE OUR AGE WHEN THEY DIED, BUT...REALLY... SHELTERED.
THEY'RE... CURIOUS.
I ALWAYS FEEL LIKE I CAN HEAR THEM GIGGLING. IT'S ICKY.
GEEZ, CRAZY LEGS! HOLD STILL!
BWAH! I LOVE SO MUCH THAT YOU TAKE FLUID SAMPLES FROM POSSESSION SITES AND DO POST-POST-MORTEMS ON ZOMBIES...
...BUT THAT'S WHAT YOU CALL ICKY.

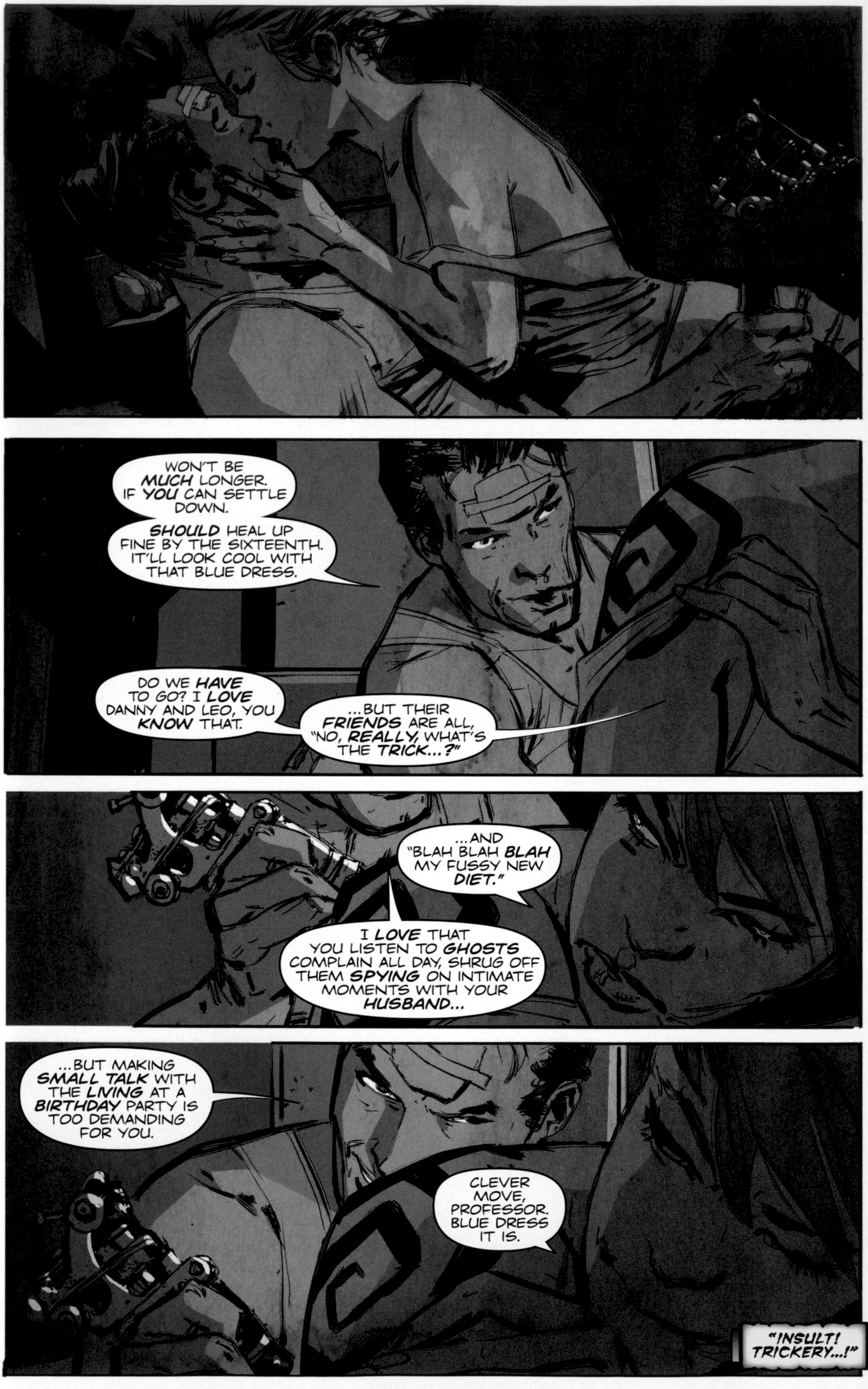
WON'T BE MUCH LONGER. IF YOU CAN SETTLE DOWN.
SHOULD HEAL UP FINE BY THE SIXTEENTH. IT'LL LOOK COOL WITH THAT BLUE DRESS.
DO WE HAVE TO GO? I LOVE DANNY AND LEO, YOU KNOW THAT.
...BUT THEIR FRIENDS ARE ALL, "NO, REALLY, WHAT'S THE TRICK...?"
...AND "BLAH BLAH BLAH MY FUSSY NEW DIET."
I LOVE THAT YOU LISTEN TO GHOSTS COMPLAIN ALL DAY, SHRUG OFF THEM SPYING ON INTIMATE MOMENTS WITH YOUR HUSBAND...
...BUT MAKING SMALL TALK WITH THE LIVING AT A BIRTHDAY PARTY IS TOO DEMANDING FOR YOU.
CLEVER MOVE, PROFESSOR. BLUE DRESS IT IS.
"INSULT! TRICKERY...!"

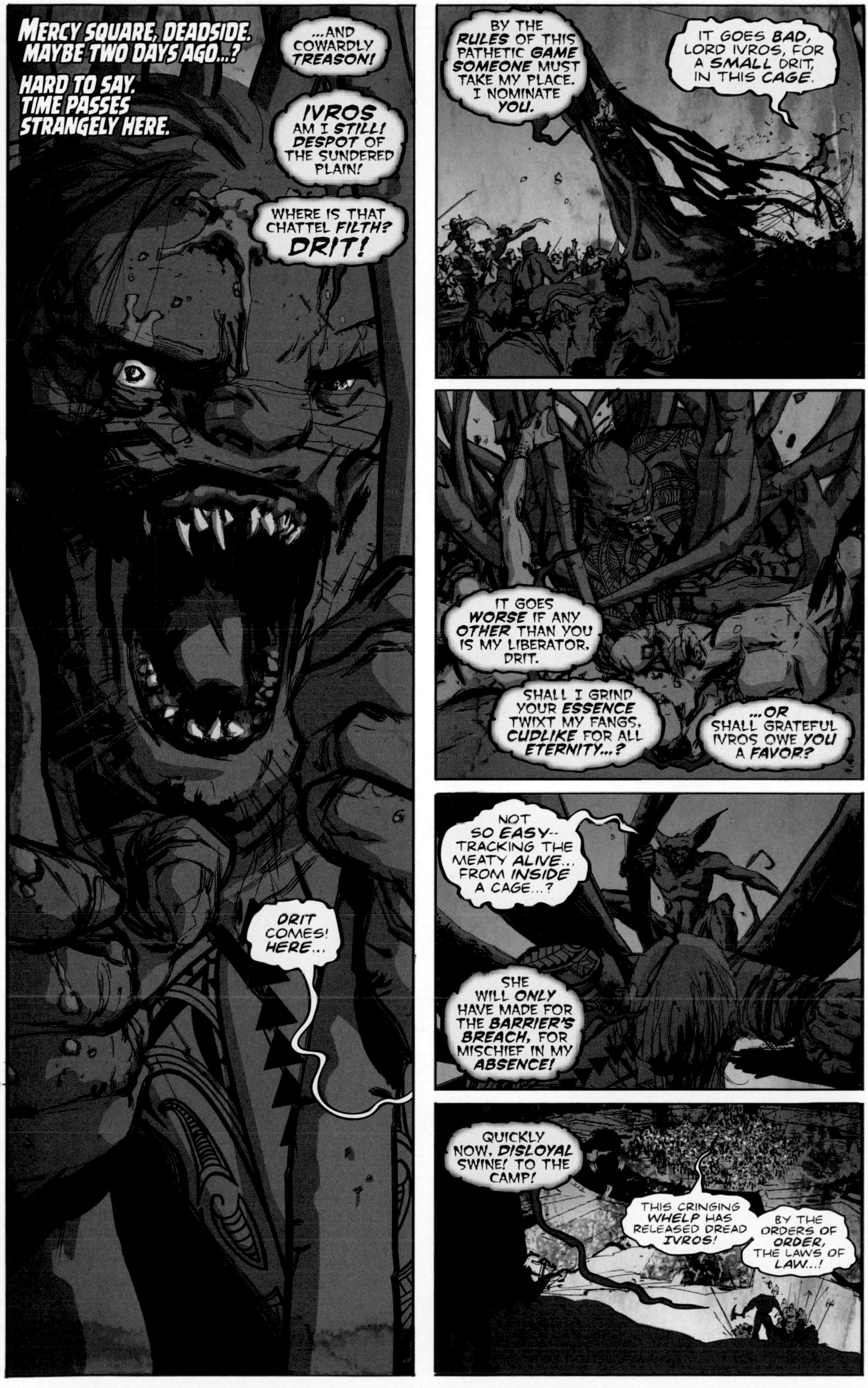
MERCY SQUARE, DEADSIDE. MAYBE TWO DAYS AGO...?
HARD TO SAY. TIME PASSES STRANGELY HERE.
...AND COWARDLY TREASON!
IVROS AM I STILL! DESPOT OF THE SUNDERED PLAIN!
WHERE IS THAT CHATTEL FILTH? DRIT!
DRIT COMES! HERE...
BY THE RULES OF THIS PATHETIC GAME SOMEONE MUST TAKE MY PLACE. I NOMINATE YOU.
IT GOES BAD, LORD IVROS, FOR A SMALL DRIT, IN THIS CAGE.
IT GOES WORSE IF ANY OTHER THAN YOU IS MY LIBERATOR, DRIT.
SHALL I GRIND YOUR ESSENCE TWIXT MY FANGS, CUDLIKE FOR ALL ETERNITY...?
...OR SHALL GRATEFUL IVROS OWE YOU A FAVOR?
NOT SO EASY-- TRACKING THE MEATY ALIVE... FROM INSIDE A CAGE...?
SHE WILL ONLY HAVE MADE FOR THE BARRIER'S BREACH, FOR MISCHIEF IN MY ABSENCE!
QUICKLY NOW, DISLOYAL SWINE! TO THE CAMP!
THIS CRINGING WHELP HAS RELEASED DREAD IVROS!
BY THE ORDERS OF ORDER, THE LAWS OF LAW...!

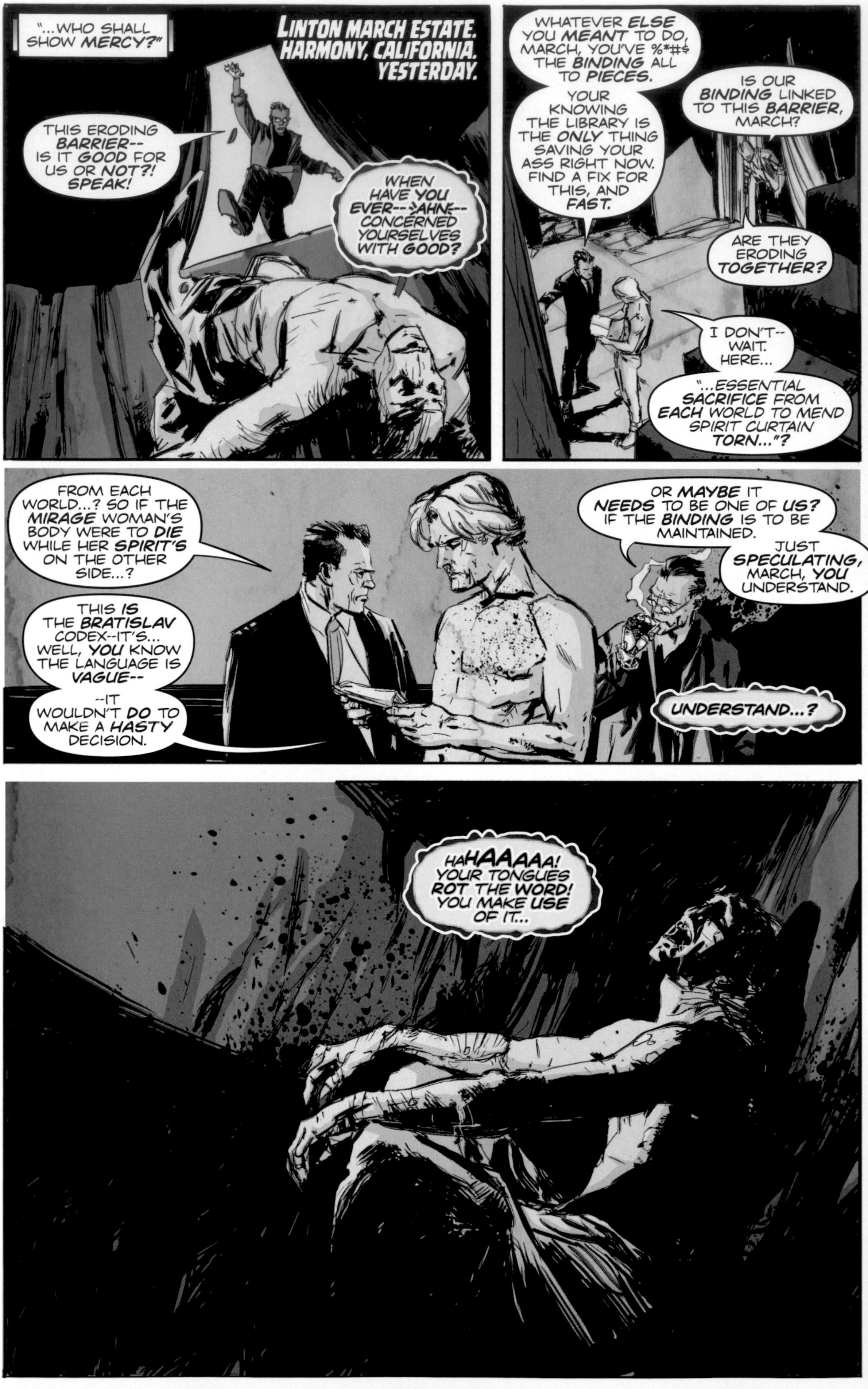
"...WHO SHALL SHOW MERCY?"
LINTON MARCH ESTATE. HARMONY, CALIFORNIA. YESTERDAY.
THIS ERODING BARRIER-- IS IT GOOD FOR US OR NOT?! SPEAK!
WHEN HAVE YOU EVER--AHN--CONCERNED YOURSELVES WITH GOOD?
WHATEVER ELSE YOU MEANT TO DO, MARCH, YOU'VE %*#$ THE BINDING ALL TO PIECES.
YOUR KNOWING THE LIBRARY IS THE ONLY THING SAVING YOUR ASS RIGHT NOW. FIND A FIX FOR THIS, AND FAST.
IS OUR BINDING LINKED TO THIS BARRIER, MARCH?
ARE THEY ERODING TOGETHER?
I DON'T-- WAIT. HERE...
"...ESSENTIAL SACRIFICE FROM EACH WORLD TO MEND SPIRIT CURTAIN TORN..."?
FROM EACH WORLD...? SO IF THE MIRAGE WOMAN'S BODY WERE TO DIE WHILE HER SPIRIT'S ON THE OTHER SIDE...?
THIS IS THE BRATISLAV CODEX--IT'S... WELL, YOU KNOW THE LANGUAGE IS VAGUE--
--IT WOULDN'T DO TO MAKE A HASTY DECISION.
OR MAYBE IT NEEDS TO BE ONE OF US? IF THE BINDING IS TO BE MAINTAINED.
JUST SPECULATING, MARCH, YOU UNDERSTAND.
UNDERSTAND...?
HAHAAAAA! YOUR TONGUES ROT THE WORD! YOU MAKE USE OF IT...

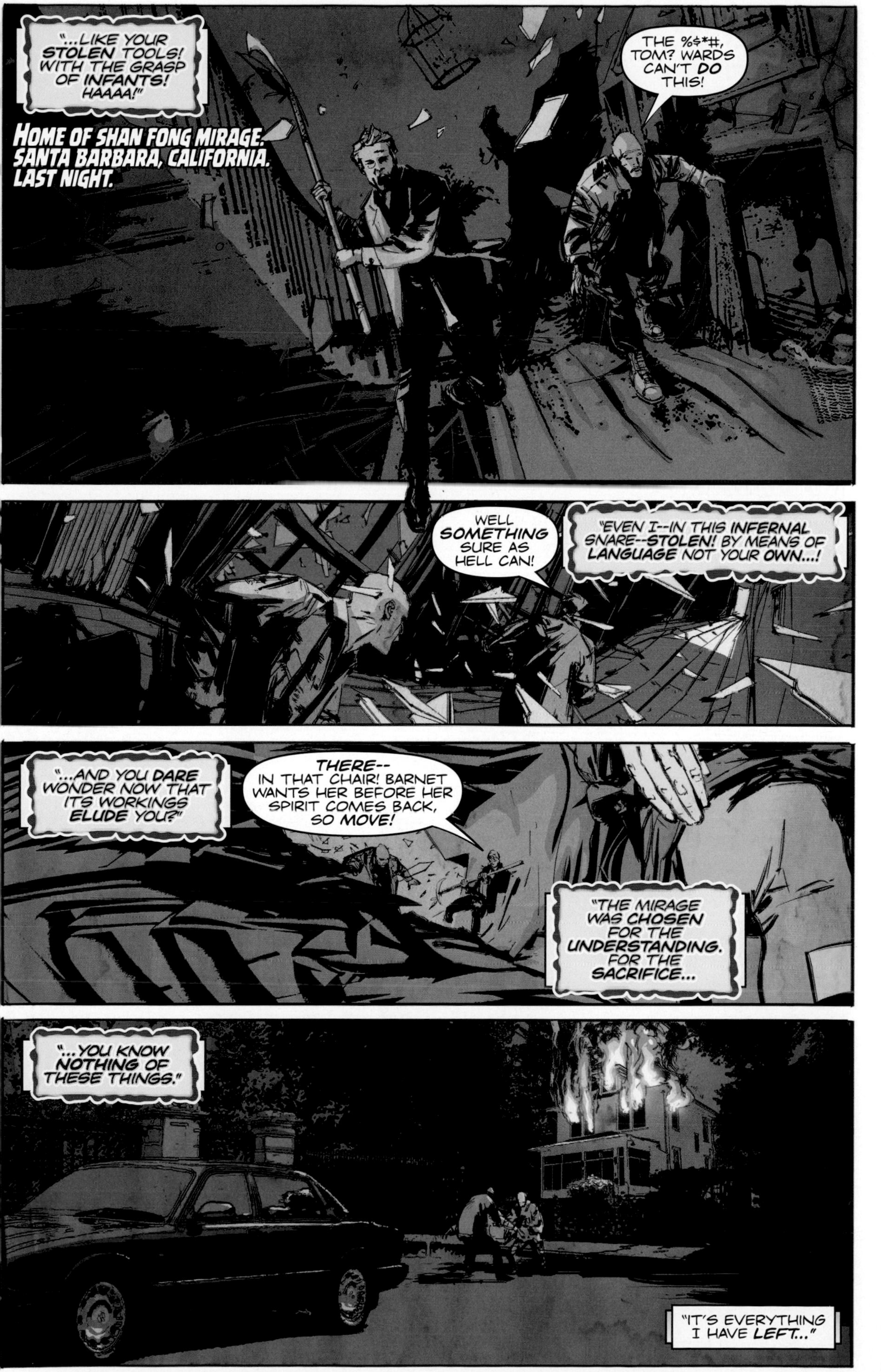
"...LIKE YOUR STOLEN TOOLS! WITH THE GRASP OF INFANTS! HAAAA!"
HOME OF SHAN FONG MIRAGE. SANTA BARBARA, CALIFORNIA. LAST NIGHT.
THE %$*#, TOM? WARDS CAN'T DO THIS!
WELL SOMETHING SURE AS HELL CAN!
"EVEN I--IN THIS INFERNAL SNARE--STOLEN! BY MEANS OF LANGUAGE NOT YOUR OWN...!
"...AND YOU DARE WONDER NOW THAT ITS WORKINGS ELUDE YOU?"
THERE-- IN THAT CHAIR! BARNET WANTS HER BEFORE HER SPIRIT COMES BACK, SO MOVE!
"THE MIRAGE WAS CHOSEN FOR THE UNDERSTANDING. FOR THE SACRIFICE...
"...YOU KNOW NOTHING OF THESE THINGS."
"IT'S EVERYTHING I HAVE LEFT..."

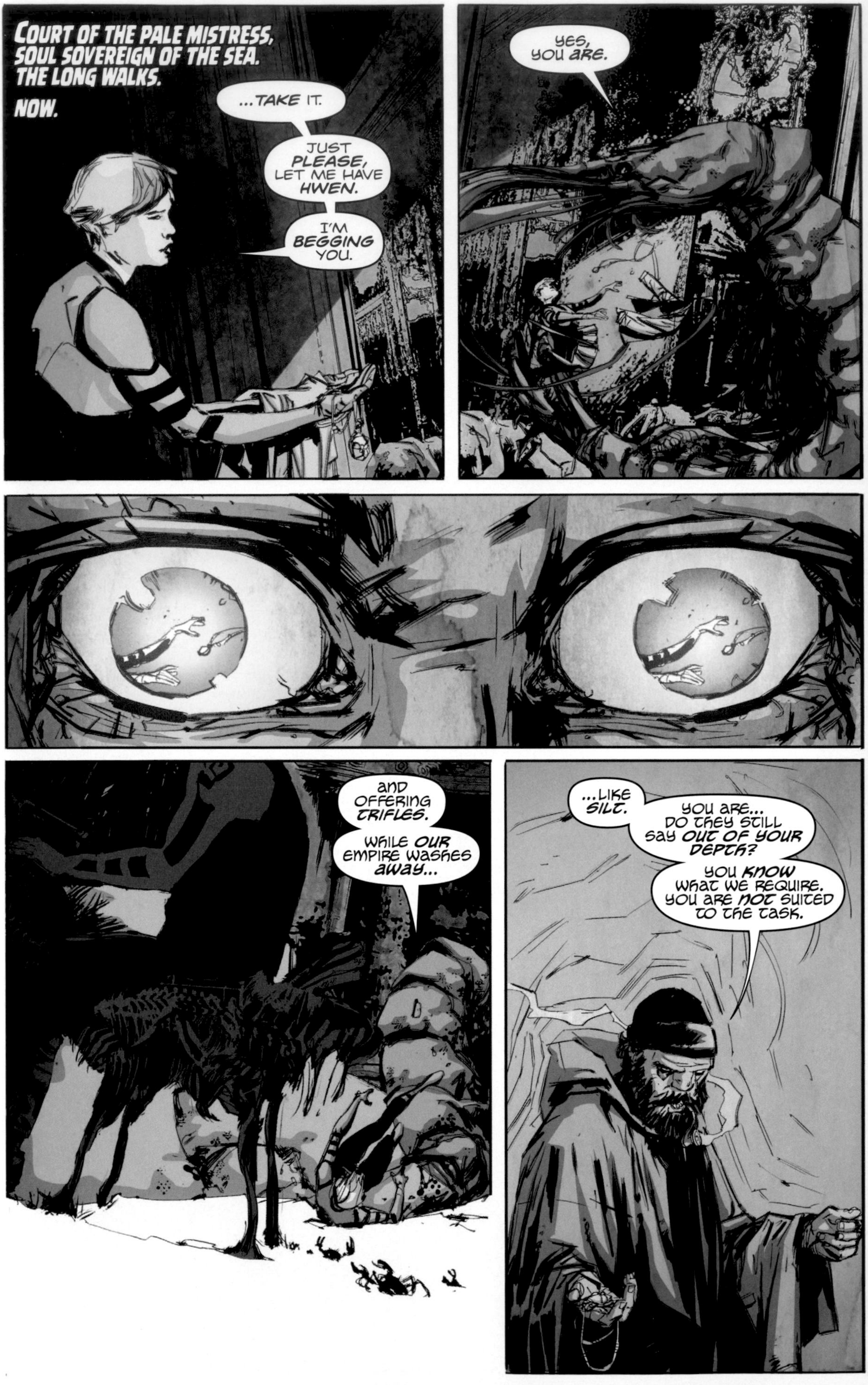
COURT OF THE PALE MISTRESS, SOUL SOVEREIGN OF THE SEA. THE LONG WALKS.
NOW.
...TAKE IT.
JUST PLEASE, LET ME HAVE HWEN.
I'M BEGGING YOU.
YES, YOU ARE.
AND OFFERING TRIFLES.
WHILE OUR EMPIRE WASHES AWAY...
...LIKE SILT.
YOU ARE... DO THEY STILL SAY OUT OF YOUR DEPTH?
YOU KNOW WHAT WE REQUIRE. YOU ARE NOT SUITED TO THE TASK.

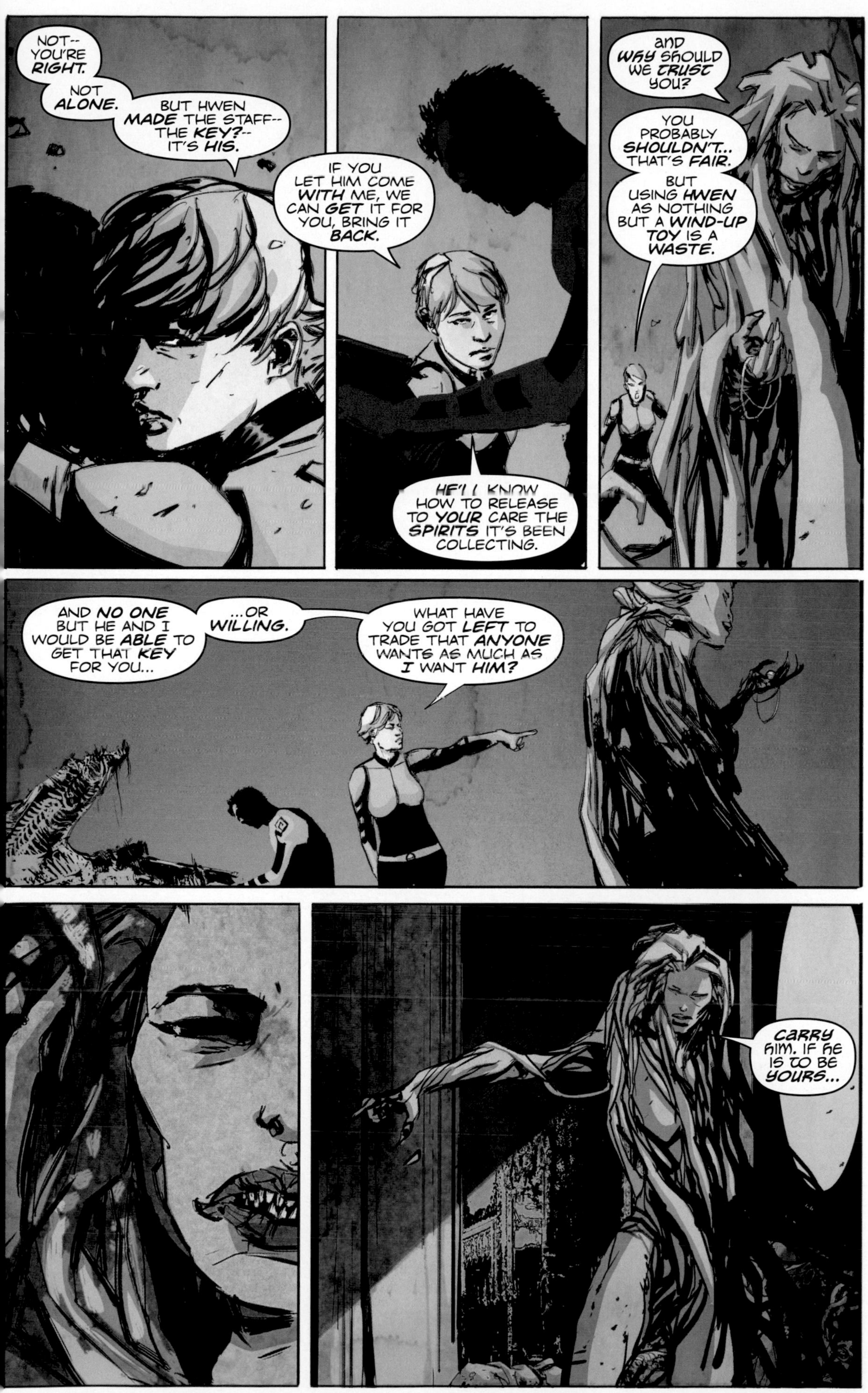
NOT-- YOU'RE RIGHT.
NOT ALONE.
BUT HWEN MADE THE STAFF-- THE KEY?-- IT'S HIS.
IF YOU LET HIM COME WITH ME, WE CAN GET IT FOR YOU, BRING IT BACK.
HE'LL KNOW HOW TO RELEASE TO YOUR CARE THE SPIRITS IT'S BEEN COLLECTING.
AND WHY SHOULD WE TRUST YOU?
YOU PROBABLY SHOULDN'T... THAT'S FAIR.
BUT USING HWEN AS NOTHING BUT A WIND-UP TOY IS A WASTE.
AND NO ONE BUT HE AND I WOULD BE ABLE TO GET THAT KEY FOR YOU...
...OR WILLING.
WHAT HAVE YOU GOT LEFT TO TRADE THAT ANYONE WANTS AS MUCH AS I WANT HIM?
CARRY HIM. IF HE IS TO BE YOURS...

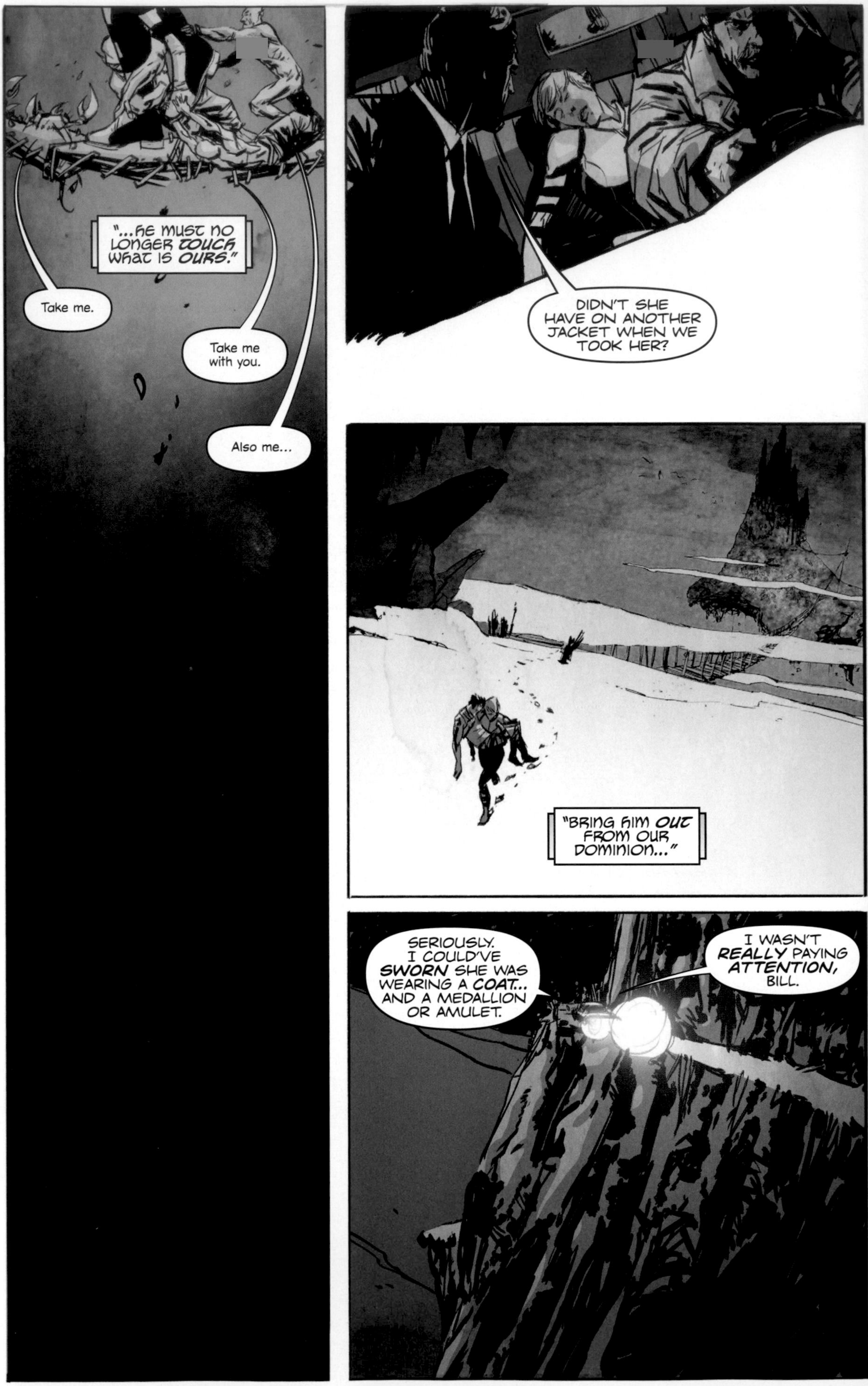
"...HE MUST NO LONGER *TOUCH* WHAT IS *OURS*."
Take me.
Take me with you.
Also me...
DIDN'T SHE HAVE ON ANOTHER JACKET WHEN WE TOOK HER?
"BRING HIM *OUT* FROM OUR DOMINION..."
SERIOUSLY. I COULD'VE *SWORN* SHE WAS WEARING A *COAT*... AND A MEDALLION OR AMULET.
I WASN'T *REALLY* PAYING *ATTENTION*, BILL.

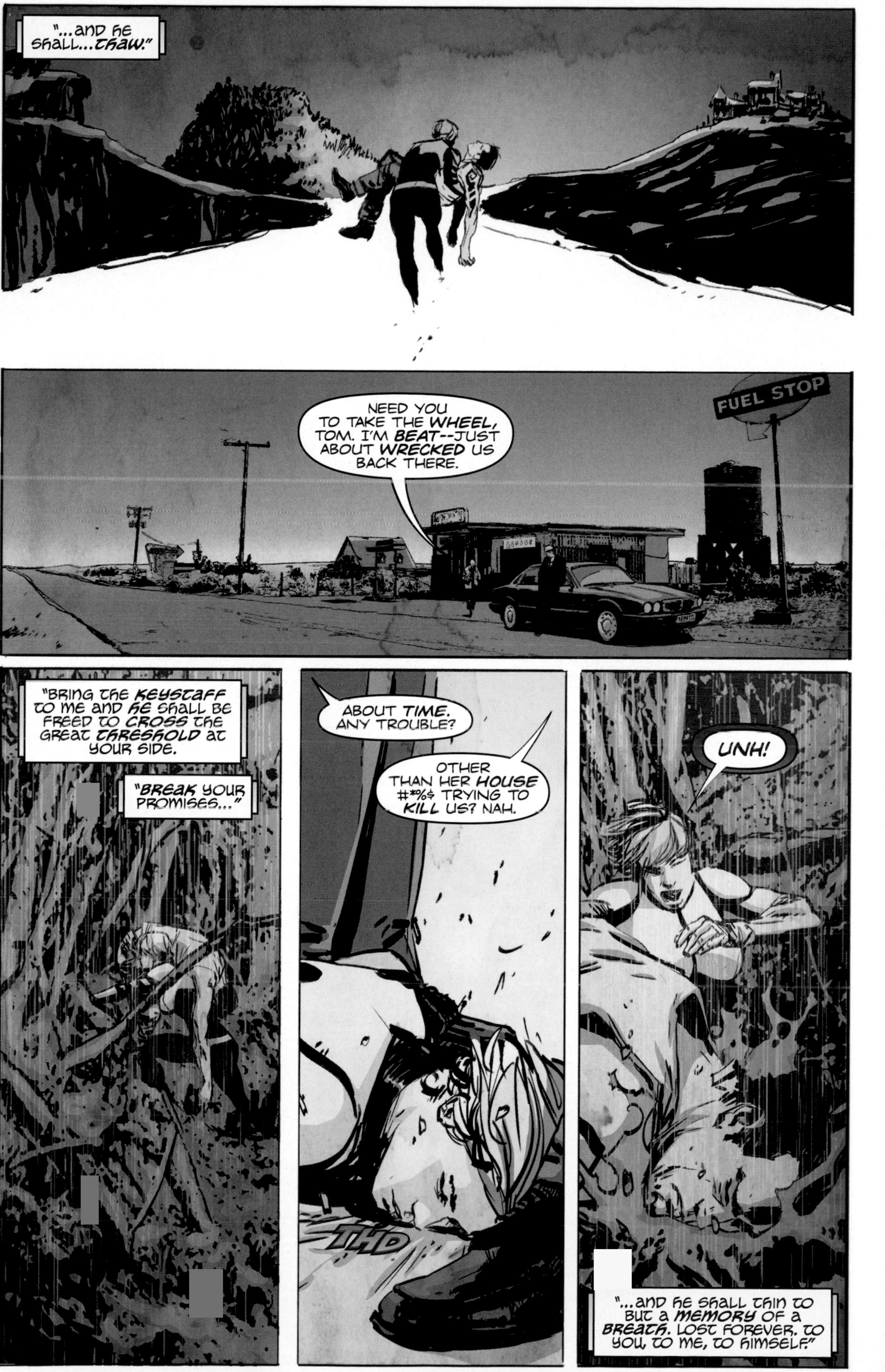
"...and he shall...thaw."
FUEL STOP
NEED YOU TO TAKE THE WHEEL, TOM. I'M BEAT--JUST ABOUT WRECKED US BACK THERE.
"Bring the keystaff to me and he shall be freed to cross the great threshold at your side.
"Break your promises..."
ABOUT TIME. ANY TROUBLE?
OTHER THAN HER HOUSE #*%$ TRYING TO KILL US? NAH.
THD
UNH!
"...and he shall thin to but a memory of a breath. Lost forever. To you, to me, to himself."

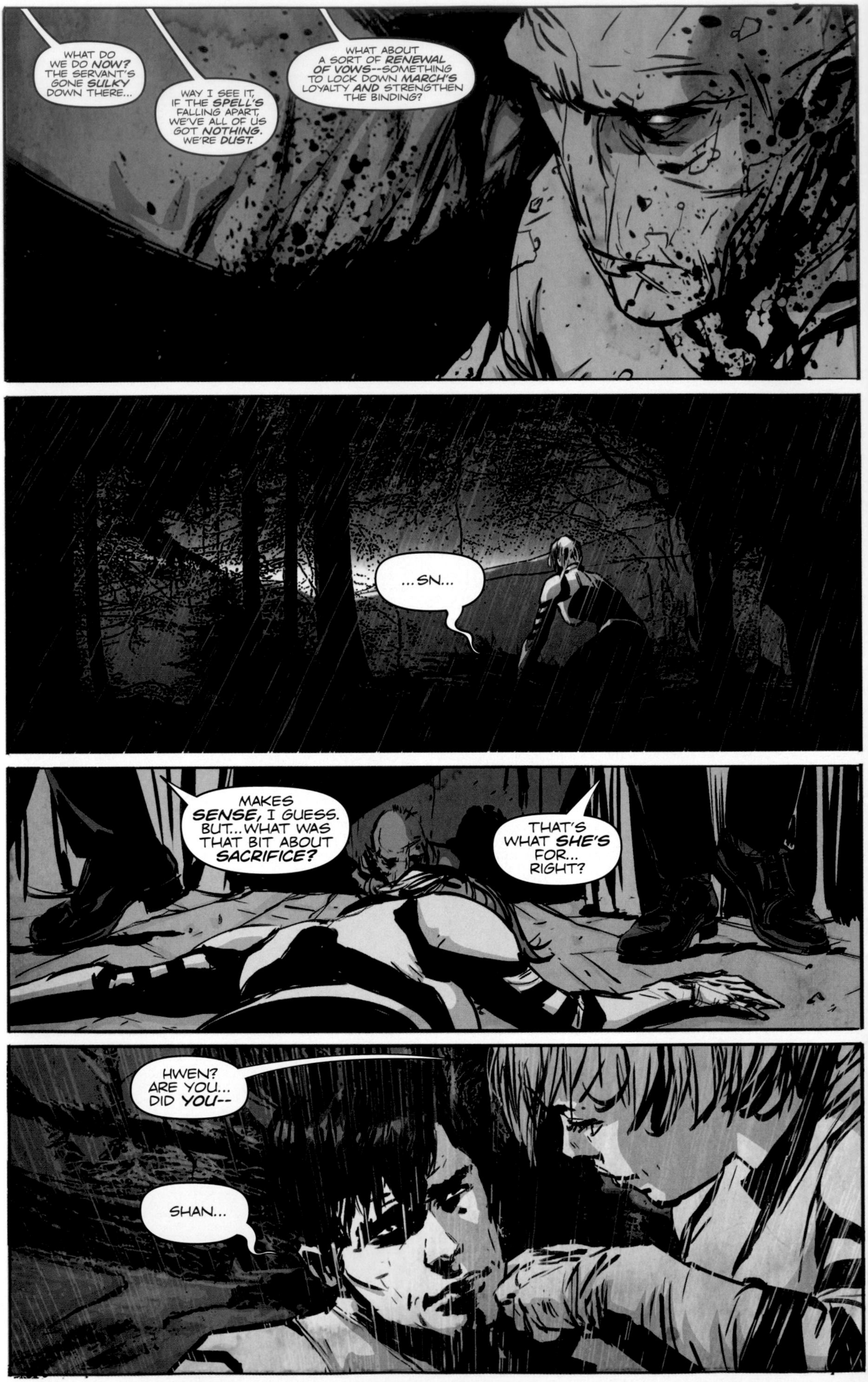
WHAT DO WE DO NOW? THE SERVANT'S GONE SULKY DOWN THERE...
WAY I SEE IT, IF THE SPELL'S FALLING APART, WE'VE ALL OF US GOT NOTHING. WE'RE DUST.
WHAT ABOUT A SORT OF RENEWAL OF VOWS--SOMETHING TO LOCK DOWN MARCH'S LOYALTY AND STRENGTHEN THE BINDING?
...SN...
MAKES SENSE, I GUESS. BUT...WHAT WAS THAT BIT ABOUT SACRIFICE?
THAT'S WHAT SHE'S FOR... RIGHT?
HWEN? ARE YOU... DID YOU--
SHAN...

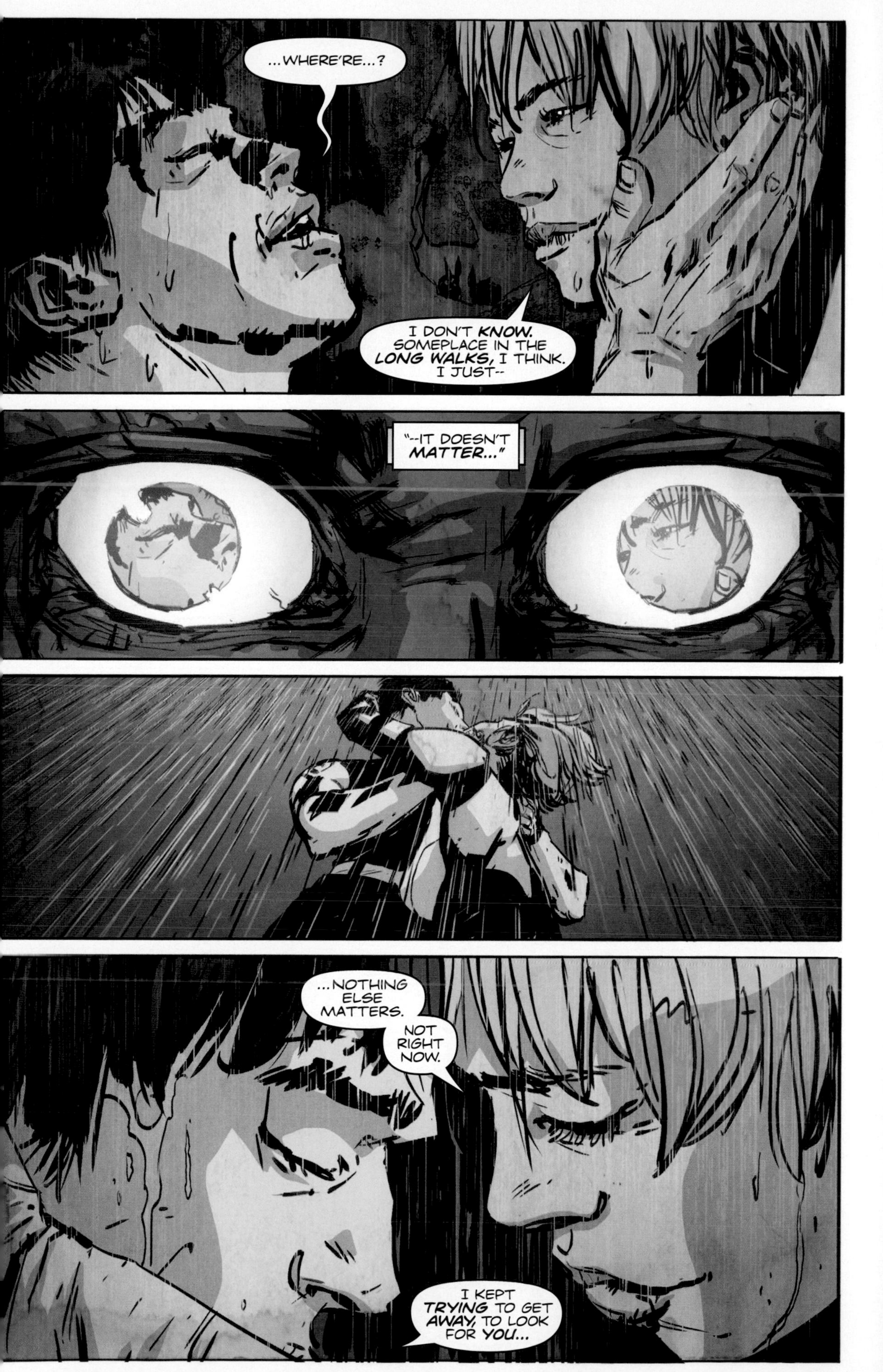

...WHERE'RE...?
I DON'T **KNOW.** SOMEPLACE IN THE ***LONG WALKS,*** I THINK. I JUST--
"--IT DOESN'T ***MATTER...***"
...NOTHING ELSE MATTERS.
NOT RIGHT NOW.
I KEPT ***TRYING*** TO GET ***AWAY,*** TO LOOK FOR ***YOU...***

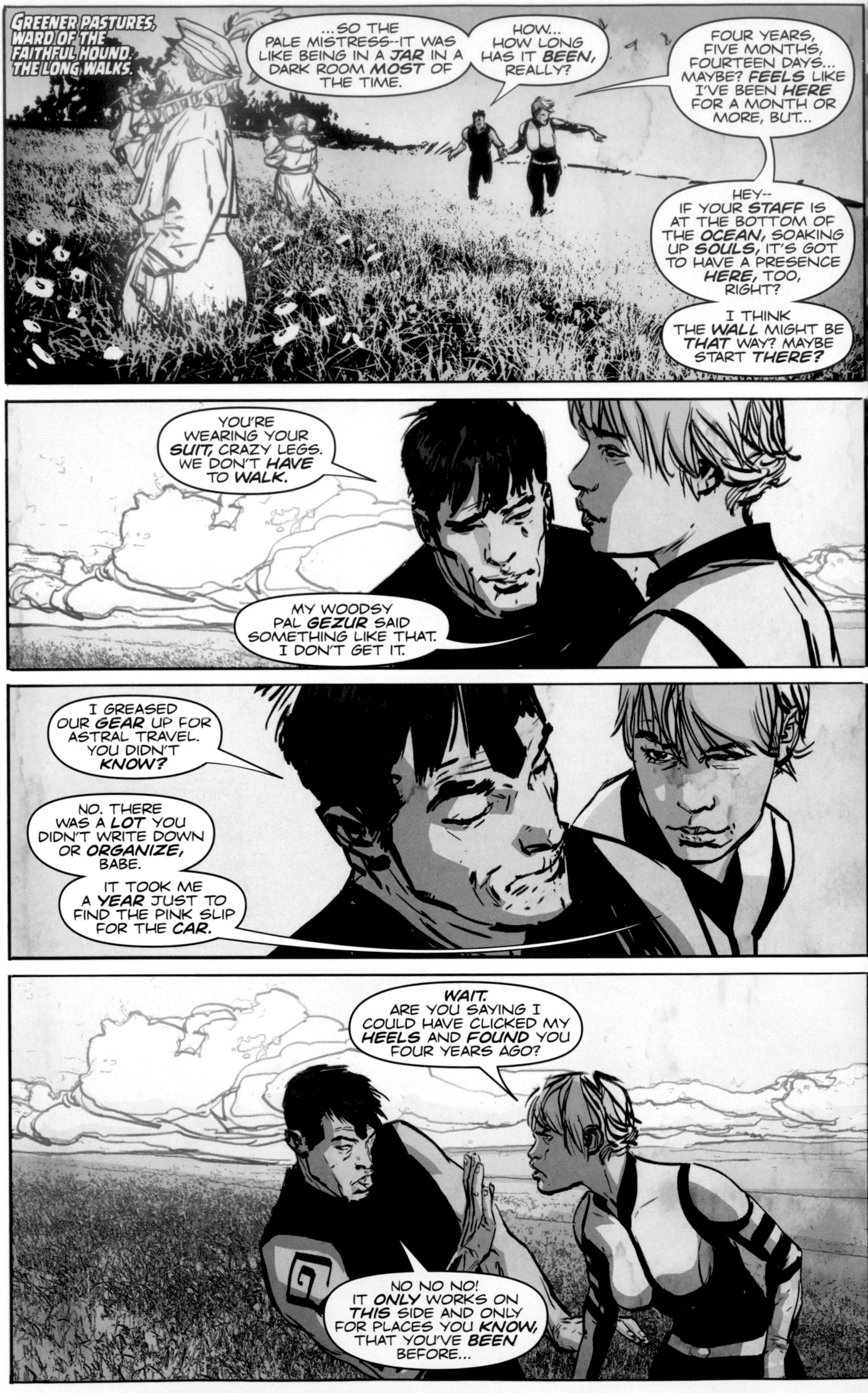
GREENER PASTURES, WARD OF THE FAITHFUL HOUND. THE LONG WALKS.
...SO THE PALE MISTRESS--IT WAS LIKE BEING IN A JAR IN A DARK ROOM MOST OF THE TIME.
HOW... HOW LONG HAS IT BEEN, REALLY?
FOUR YEARS, FIVE MONTHS, FOURTEEN DAYS... MAYBE? FEELS LIKE I'VE BEEN HERE FOR A MONTH OR MORE, BUT...
HEY-- IF YOUR STAFF IS AT THE BOTTOM OF THE OCEAN, SOAKING UP SOULS, IT'S GOT TO HAVE A PRESENCE HERE, TOO, RIGHT?
I THINK THE WALL MIGHT BE THAT WAY? MAYBE START THERE?
YOU'RE WEARING YOUR SUIT, CRAZY LEGS. WE DON'T HAVE TO WALK.
MY WOODSY PAL GEZUR SAID SOMETHING LIKE THAT. I DON'T GET IT.
I GREASED OUR GEAR UP FOR ASTRAL TRAVEL. YOU DIDN'T KNOW?
NO. THERE WAS A LOT YOU DIDN'T WRITE DOWN OR ORGANIZE, BABE.
IT TOOK ME A YEAR JUST TO FIND THE PINK SLIP FOR THE CAR.
WAIT. ARE YOU SAYING I COULD HAVE CLICKED MY HEELS AND FOUND YOU FOUR YEARS AGO?
NO NO NO! IT ONLY WORKS ON THIS SIDE AND ONLY FOR PLACES YOU KNOW, THAT YOU'VE BEEN BEFORE...

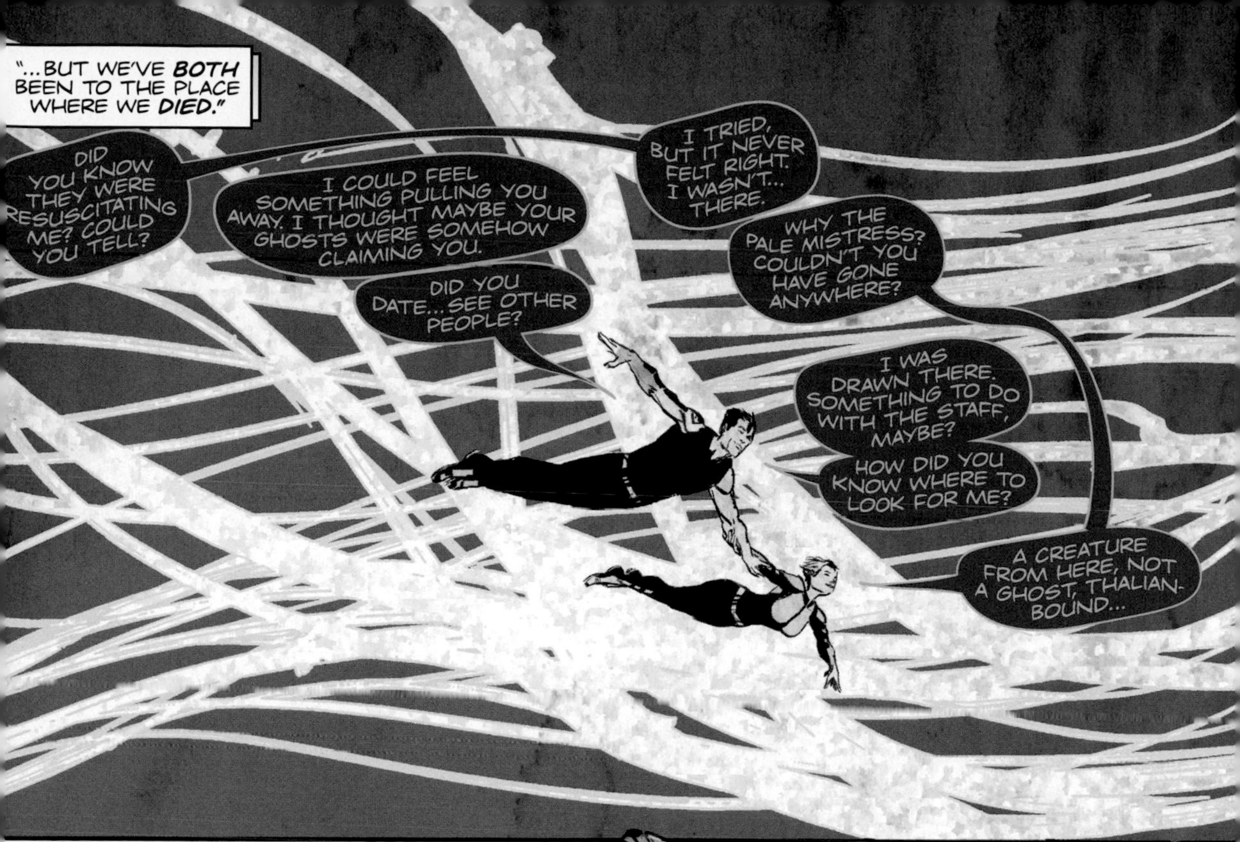
"...BUT WE'VE BOTH BEEN TO THE PLACE WHERE WE DIED."
DID YOU KNOW THEY WERE RESUSCITATING ME? COULD YOU TELL?
I COULD FEEL SOMETHING PULLING YOU AWAY. I THOUGHT MAYBE YOUR GHOSTS WERE SOMEHOW CLAIMING YOU.
I TRIED, BUT IT NEVER FELT RIGHT. I WASN'T... THERE.
DID YOU DATE...SEE OTHER PEOPLE?
WHY THE PALE MISTRESS? COULDN'T YOU HAVE GONE ANYWHERE?
I WAS DRAWN THERE. SOMETHING TO DO WITH THE STAFF, MAYBE?
HOW DID YOU KNOW WHERE TO LOOK FOR ME?
A CREATURE FROM HERE, NOT A GHOST, THALIAN-BOUND...

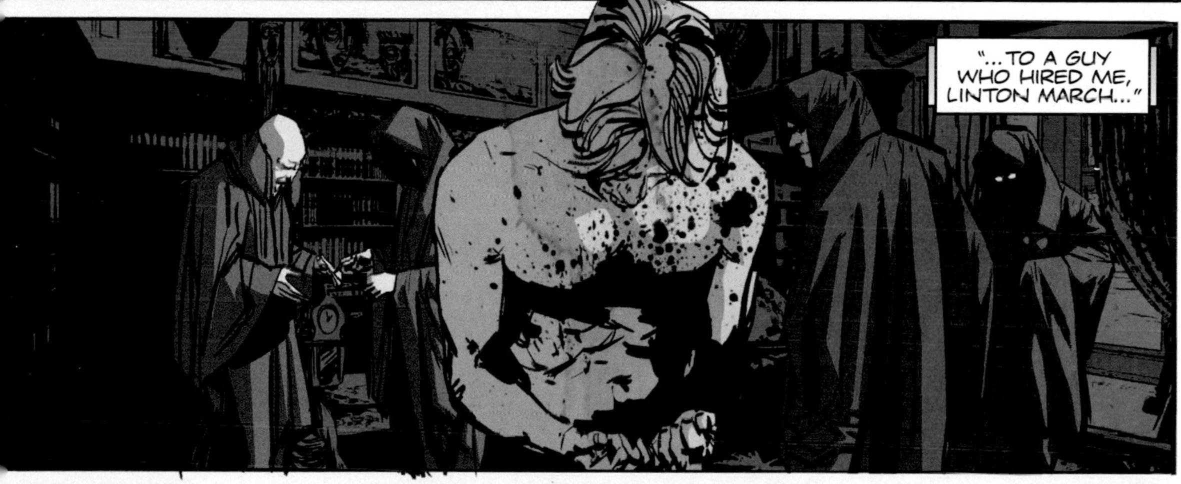
"...TO A GUY WHO HIRED ME, LINTON MARCH..."

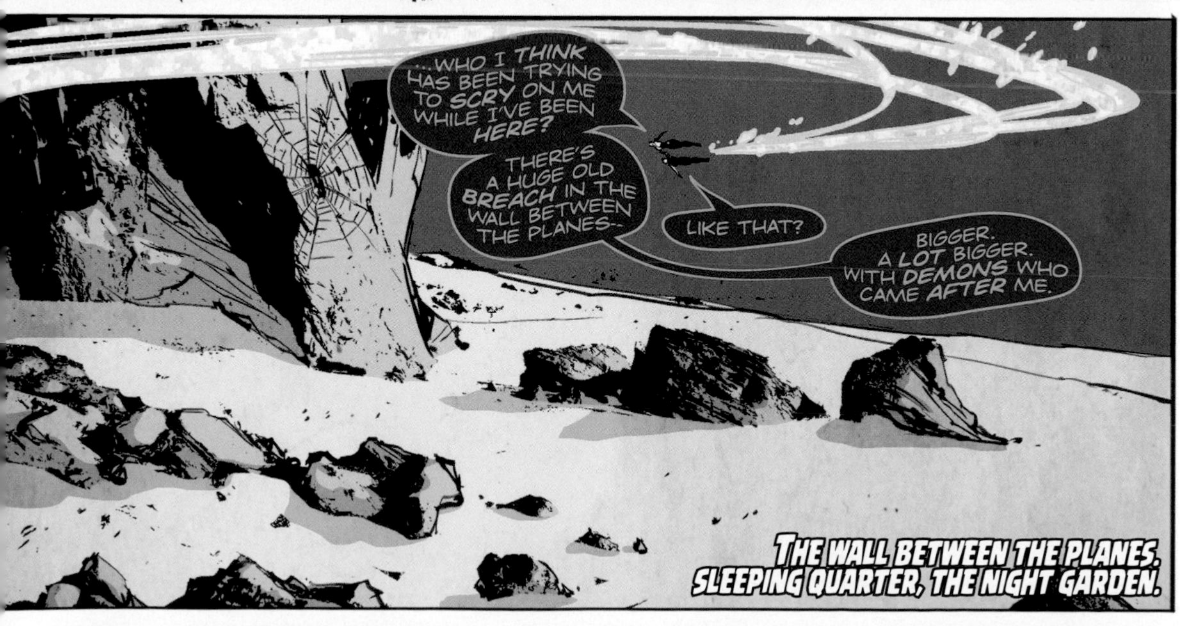
...WHO I THINK HAS BEEN TRYING TO SCRY ON ME WHILE I'VE BEEN HERE?
THERE'S A HUGE OLD BREACH IN THE WALL BETWEEN THE PLANES--
LIKE THAT?
BIGGER. A LOT BIGGER. WITH DEMONS WHO CAME AFTER ME.
THE WALL BETWEEN THE PLANES. SLEEPING QUARTER, THE NIGHT GARDEN.

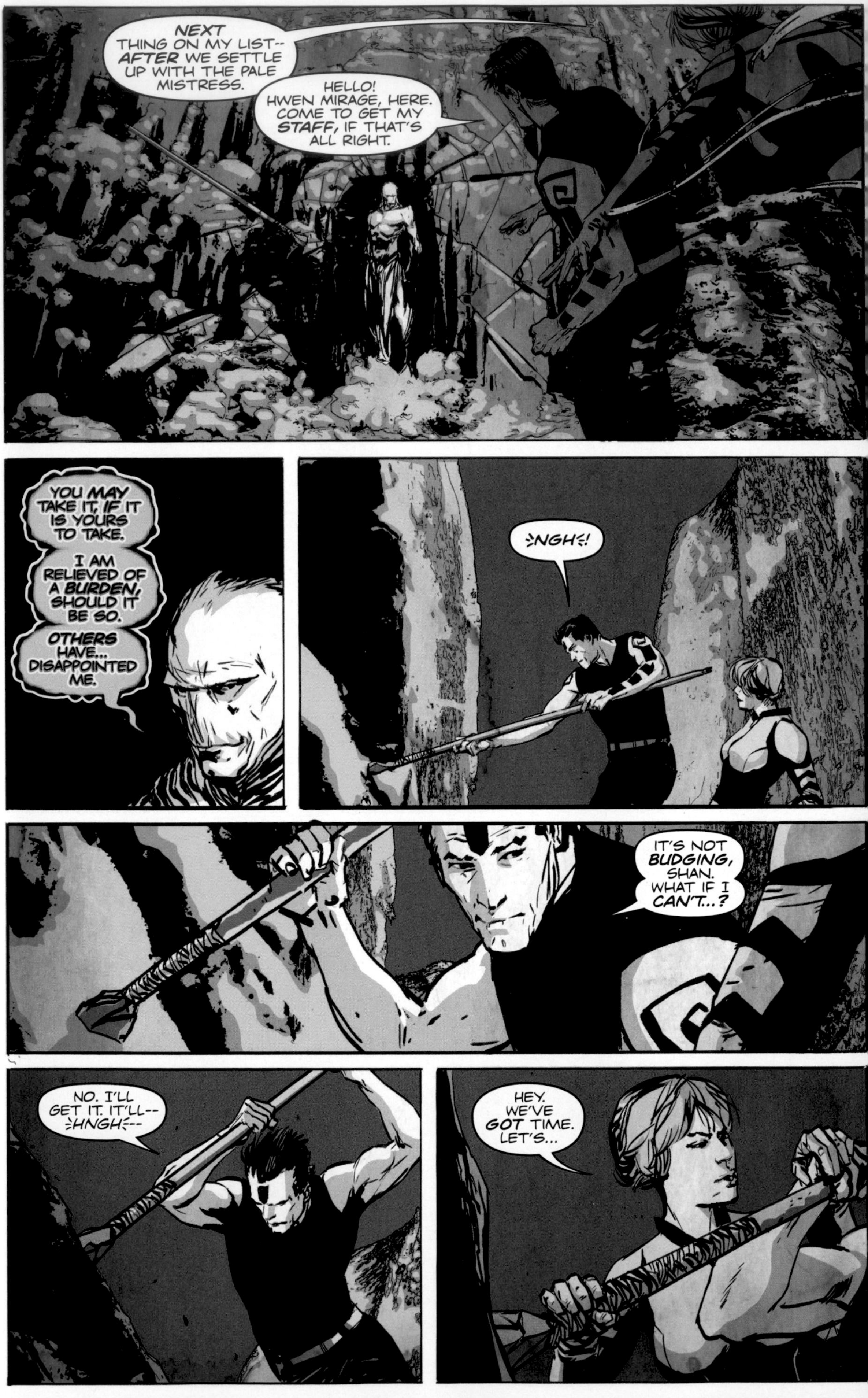
NEXT THING ON MY LIST-- AFTER WE SETTLE UP WITH THE PALE MISTRESS.
HELLO! HWEN MIRAGE, HERE. COME TO GET MY STAFF, IF THAT'S ALL RIGHT.
YOU MAY TAKE IT, IF IT IS YOURS TO TAKE.
I AM RELIEVED OF A BURDEN, SHOULD IT BE SO.
OTHERS HAVE... DISAPPOINTED ME.
NGH!
IT'S NOT BUDGING, SHAN. WHAT IF I CAN'T...?
NO. I'LL GET IT. IT'LL-- HNGH--
HEY. WE'VE GOT TIME. LET'S...

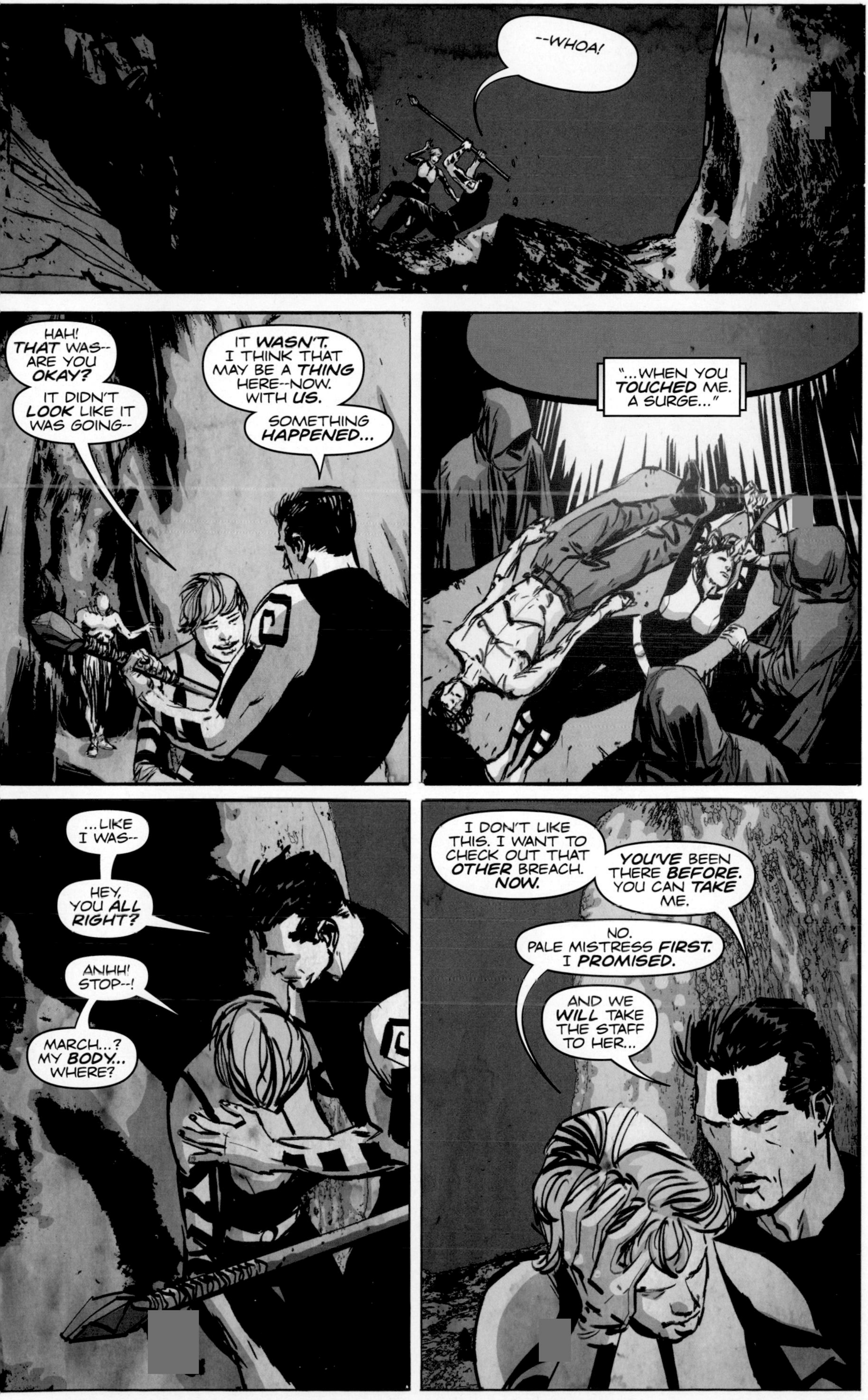
--WHOA!
HAH! THAT WAS-- ARE YOU OKAY?
IT DIDN'T LOOK LIKE IT WAS GOING--
IT WASN'T. I THINK THAT MAY BE A THING HERE--NOW. WITH US.
SOMETHING HAPPENED...
"...WHEN YOU TOUCHED ME. A SURGE..."
...LIKE I WAS--
HEY, YOU ALL RIGHT?
ANHH! STOP--!
MARCH...? MY BODY... WHERE?
I DON'T LIKE THIS. I WANT TO CHECK OUT THAT OTHER BREACH. NOW.
YOU'VE BEEN THERE BEFORE. YOU CAN TAKE ME.
NO. PALE MISTRESS FIRST. I PROMISED.
AND WE WILL TAKE THE STAFF TO HER...

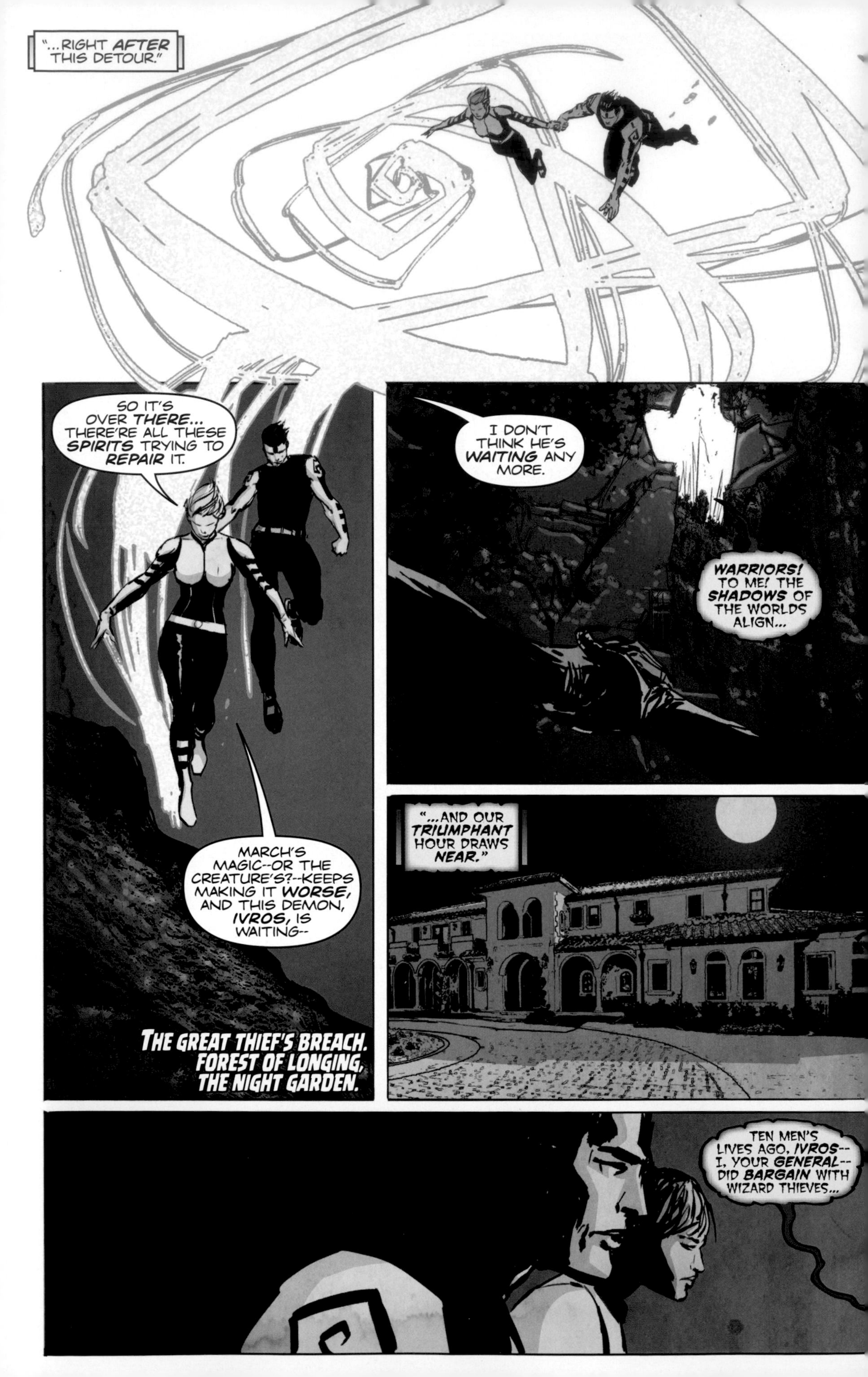
"...RIGHT *AFTER* THIS DETOUR."
SO IT'S OVER *THERE...* THERE'RE ALL THESE *SPIRITS* TRYING TO *REPAIR* IT.
MARCH'S MAGIC--OR THE CREATURE'S?--KEEPS MAKING IT *WORSE,* AND THIS DEMON, *IVROS,* IS WAITING--
THE GREAT THIEF'S BREACH. FOREST OF LONGING, THE NIGHT GARDEN.
I DON'T THINK HE'S *WAITING* ANY MORE.
WARRIORS! TO ME! THE *SHADOWS* OF THE WORLDS ALIGN...
"...AND OUR *TRIUMPHANT* HOUR DRAWS *NEAR.*"
TEN MEN'S LIVES AGO, *IVROS*-- I, YOUR *GENERAL*-- DID *BARGAIN* WITH WIZARD THIEVES...

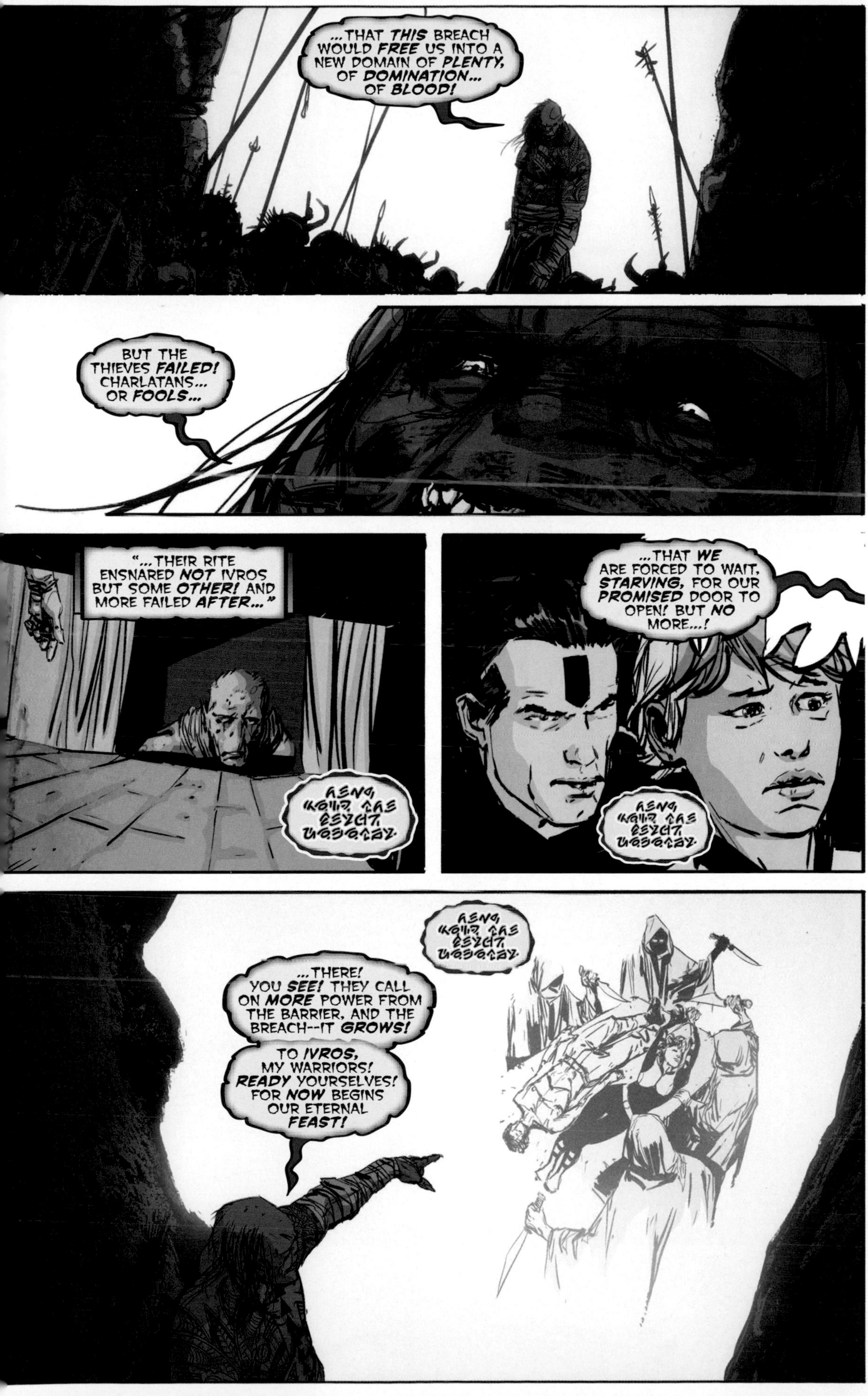
...THAT THIS BREACH WOULD FREE US INTO A NEW DOMAIN OF PLENTY, OF DOMINATION... OF BLOOD!
BUT THE THIEVES FAILED! CHARLATANS... OR FOOLS...
"...THEIR RITE ENSNARED NOT IVROS BUT SOME OTHER! AND MORE FAILED AFTER..."
...THAT WE ARE FORCED TO WAIT, STARVING, FOR OUR PROMISED DOOR TO OPEN! BUT NO MORE...!
...THERE! YOU SEE! THEY CALL ON MORE POWER FROM THE BARRIER, AND THE BREACH--IT GROWS!
TO IVROS, MY WARRIORS! READY YOURSELVES! FOR NOW BEGINS OUR ETERNAL FEAST!

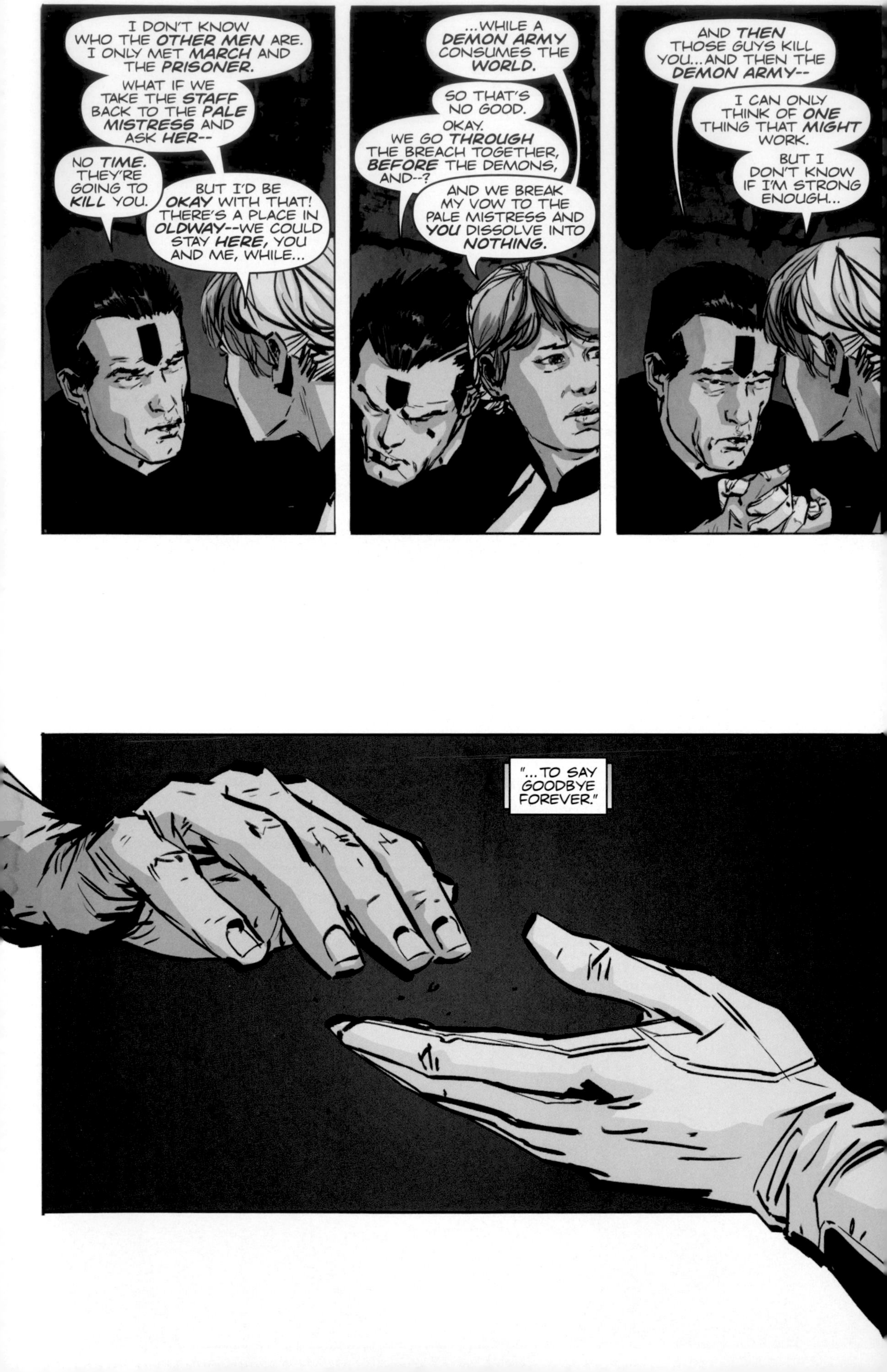
I DON'T KNOW WHO THE OTHER MEN ARE. I ONLY MET MARCH AND THE PRISONER.
WHAT IF WE TAKE THE STAFF BACK TO THE PALE MISTRESS AND ASK HER--
NO TIME. THEY'RE GOING TO KILL YOU.
BUT I'D BE OKAY WITH THAT! THERE'S A PLACE IN OLDWAY--WE COULD STAY HERE, YOU AND ME, WHILE...
...WHILE A DEMON ARMY CONSUMES THE WORLD.
SO THAT'S NO GOOD.
OKAY. WE GO THROUGH THE BREACH TOGETHER, BEFORE THE DEMONS, AND--?
AND WE BREAK MY VOW TO THE PALE MISTRESS AND YOU DISSOLVE INTO NOTHING.
AND THEN THOSE GUYS KILL YOU...AND THEN THE DEMON ARMY--
I CAN ONLY THINK OF ONE THING THAT MIGHT WORK.
BUT I DON'T KNOW IF I'M STRONG ENOUGH...
"...TO SAY GOODBYE FOREVER."

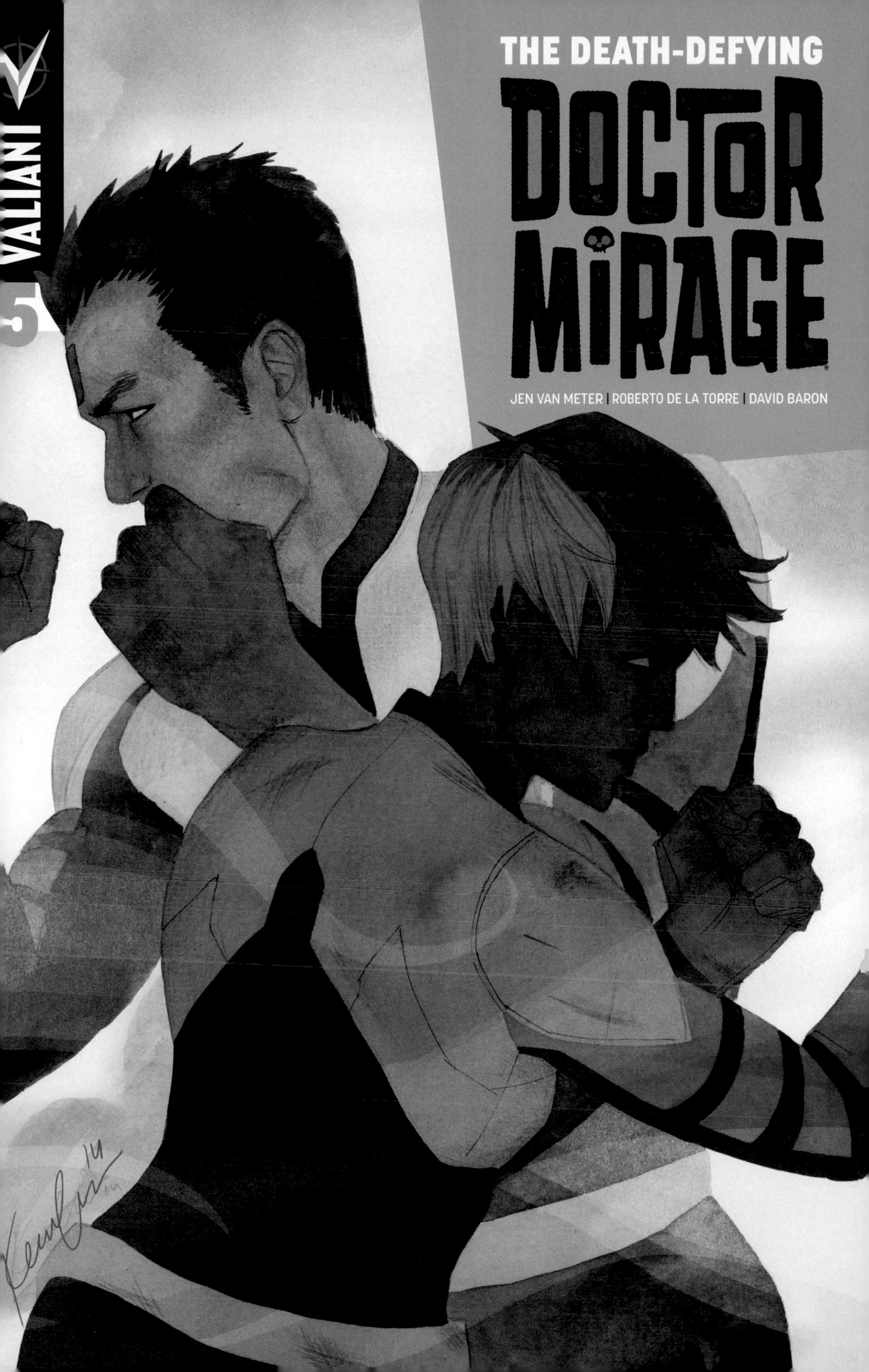
VALIANT
5
THE DEATH-DEFYING
DOCTOR MIRAGE
JEN VAN METER | ROBERTO DE LA TORRE | DAVID BARON

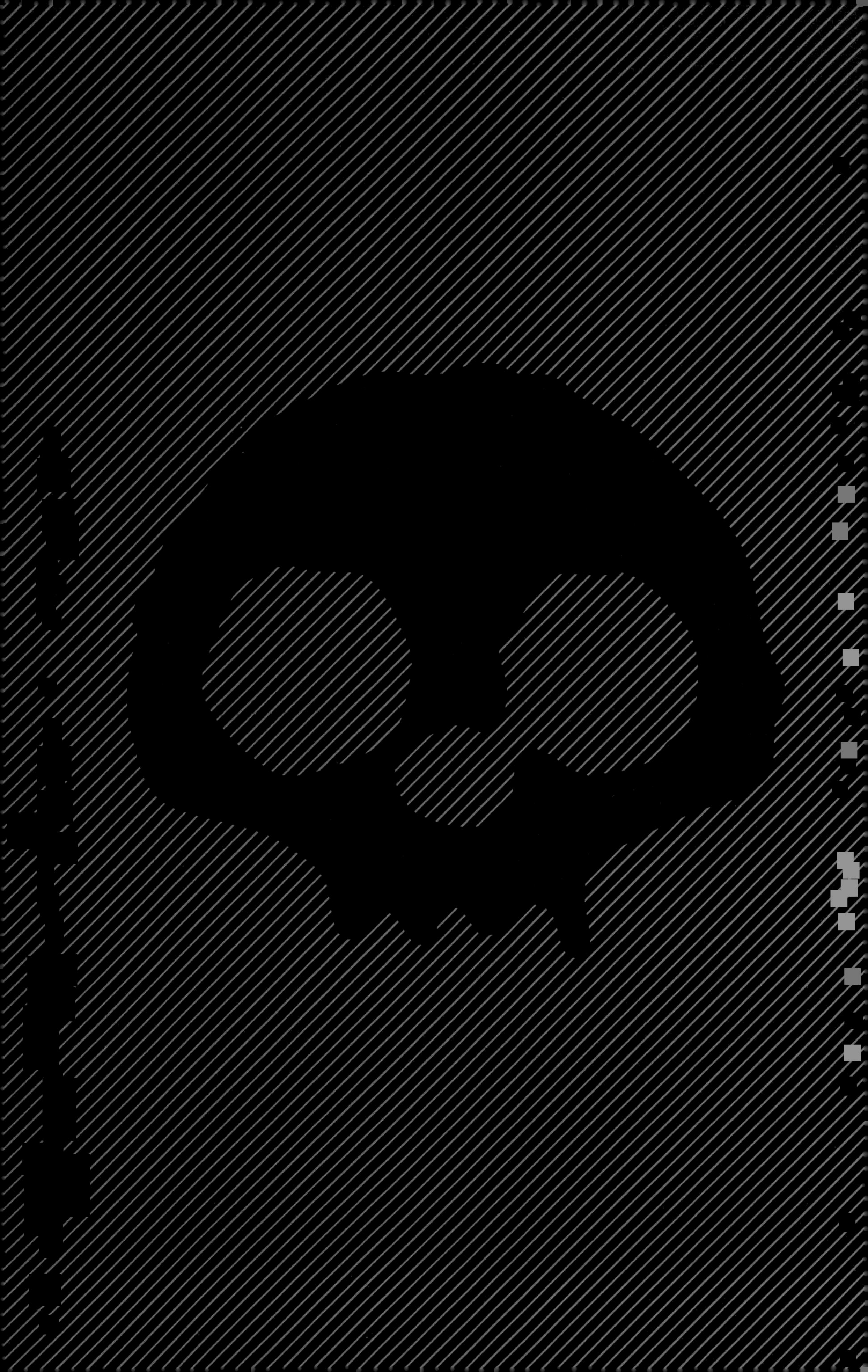

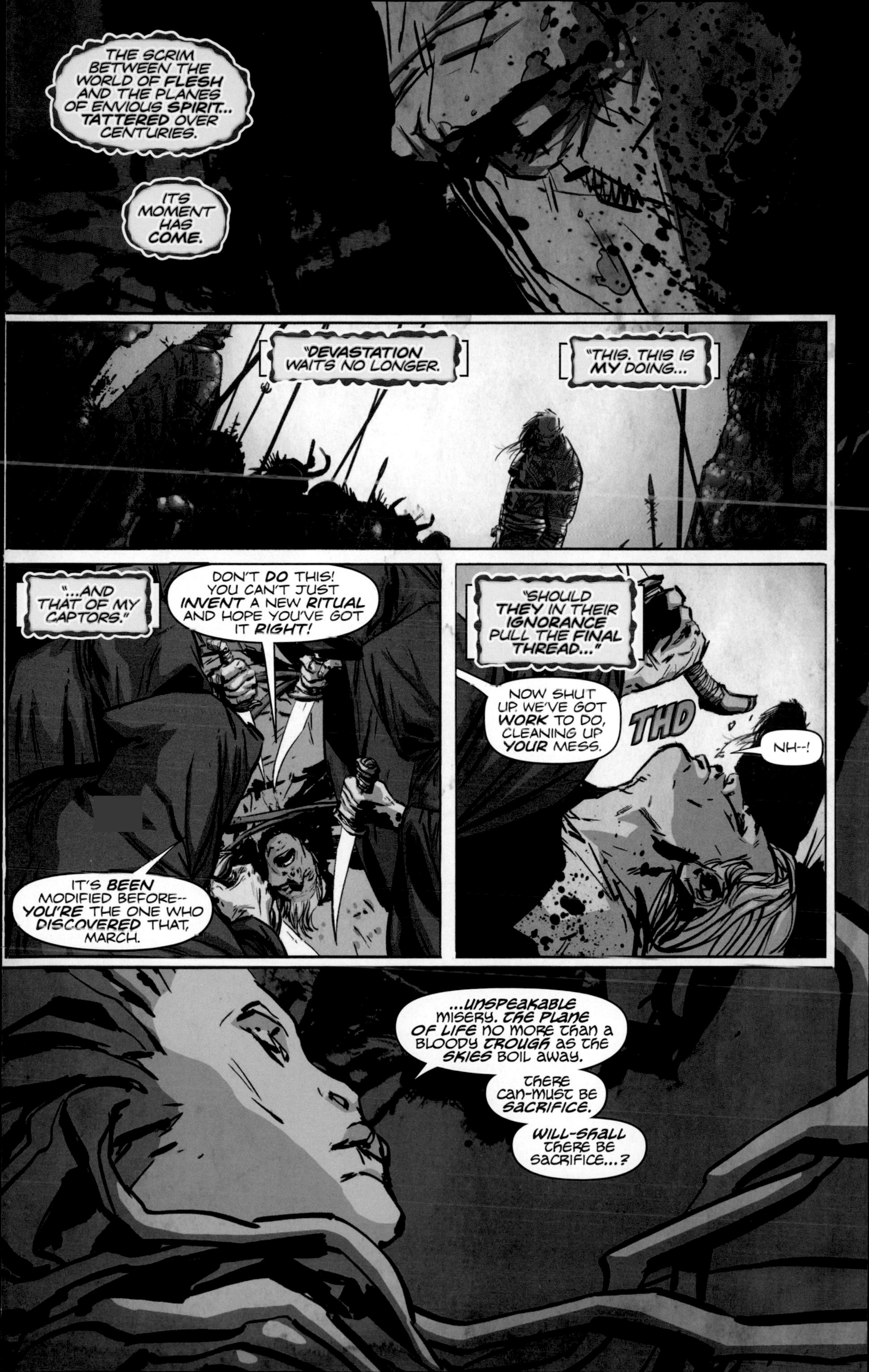
THE SCRIM BETWEEN THE WORLD OF FLESH AND THE PLANES OF ENVIOUS SPIRIT... TATTERED OVER CENTURIES.
ITS MOMENT HAS COME.
"DEVASTATION WAITS NO LONGER.
"THIS. THIS IS MY DOING...
"...AND THAT OF MY CAPTORS."
DON'T DO THIS! YOU CAN'T JUST INVENT A NEW RITUAL AND HOPE YOU'VE GOT IT RIGHT!
IT'S BEEN MODIFIED BEFORE-- YOU'RE THE ONE WHO DISCOVERED THAT, MARCH.
"SHOULD THEY IN THEIR IGNORANCE PULL THE FINAL THREAD..."
NOW SHUT UP. WE'VE GOT WORK TO DO, CLEANING UP YOUR MESS.
THD
NH--!
...UNSPEAKABLE MISERY. THE PLANE OF LIFE NO MORE THAN A BLOODY TROUGH AS THE SKIES BOIL AWAY.
THERE CAN-MUST BE SACRIFICE.
WILL-SHALL THERE BE SACRIFICE...?

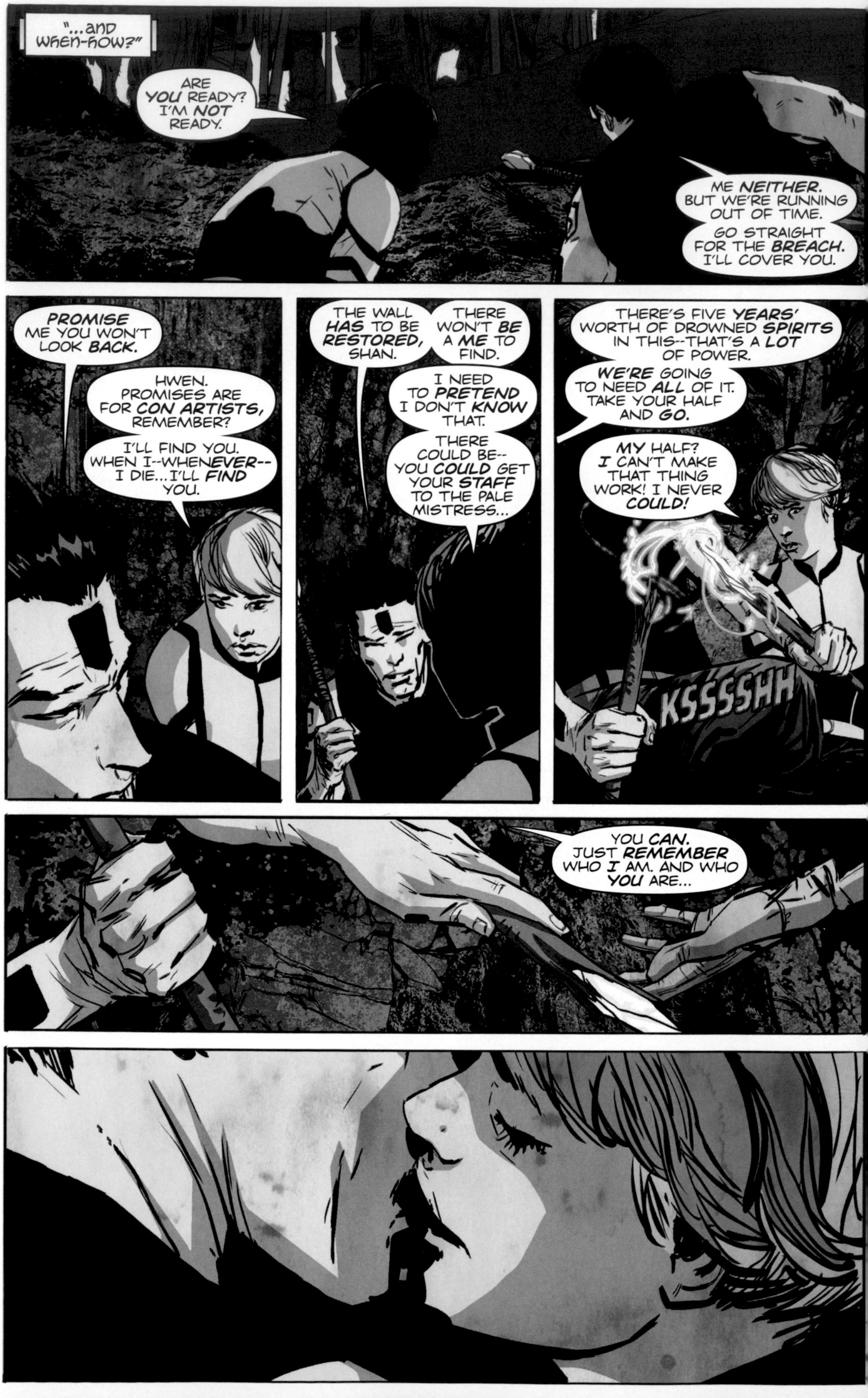
"...and when-how?"
ARE YOU READY? I'M NOT READY.
ME NEITHER. BUT WE'RE RUNNING OUT OF TIME.
GO STRAIGHT FOR THE BREACH. I'LL COVER YOU.
PROMISE ME YOU WON'T LOOK BACK.
HWEN. PROMISES ARE FOR CON ARTISTS, REMEMBER?
I'LL FIND YOU. WHEN I--WHENEVER--I DIE...I'LL FIND YOU.
THE WALL HAS TO BE RESTORED, SHAN.
THERE WON'T BE A ME TO FIND.
I NEED TO PRETEND I DON'T KNOW THAT.
THERE COULD BE--YOU COULD GET YOUR STAFF TO THE PALE MISTRESS...
THERE'S FIVE YEARS' WORTH OF DROWNED SPIRITS IN THIS--THAT'S A LOT OF POWER.
WE'RE GOING TO NEED ALL OF IT. TAKE YOUR HALF AND GO.
MY HALF? I CAN'T MAKE THAT THING WORK! I NEVER COULD!
KSSSSHH
YOU CAN. JUST REMEMBER WHO I AM. AND WHO YOU ARE...

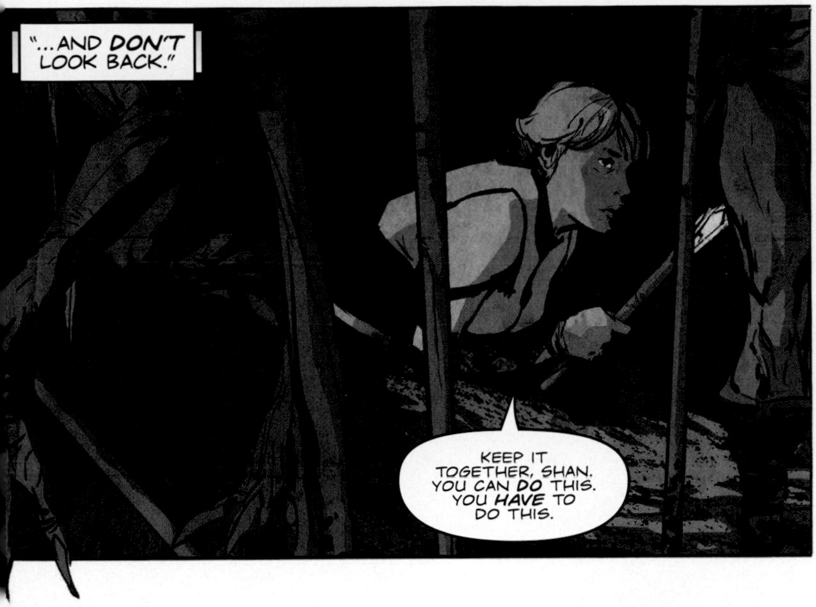
"...AND DON'T LOOK BACK."
KEEP IT TOGETHER, SHAN. YOU CAN DO THIS. YOU HAVE TO DO THIS.

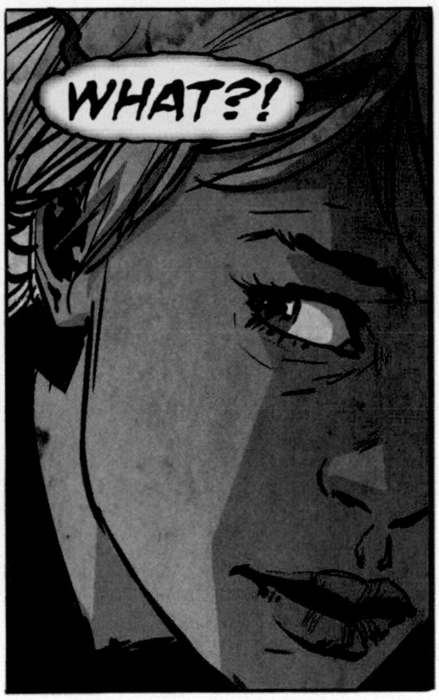
WHAT?!

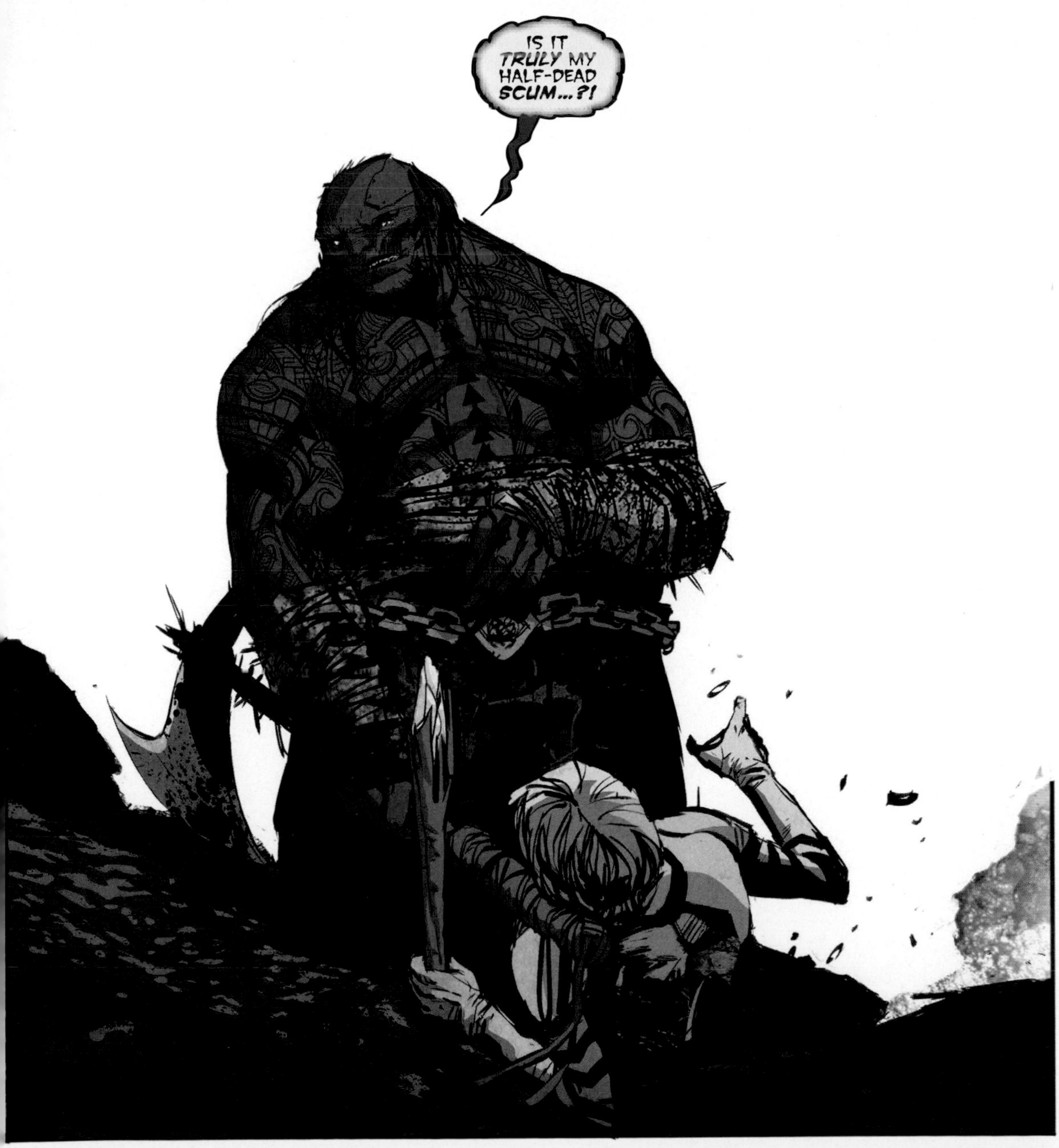
IS IT TRULY MY HALF-DEAD SCUM...?!

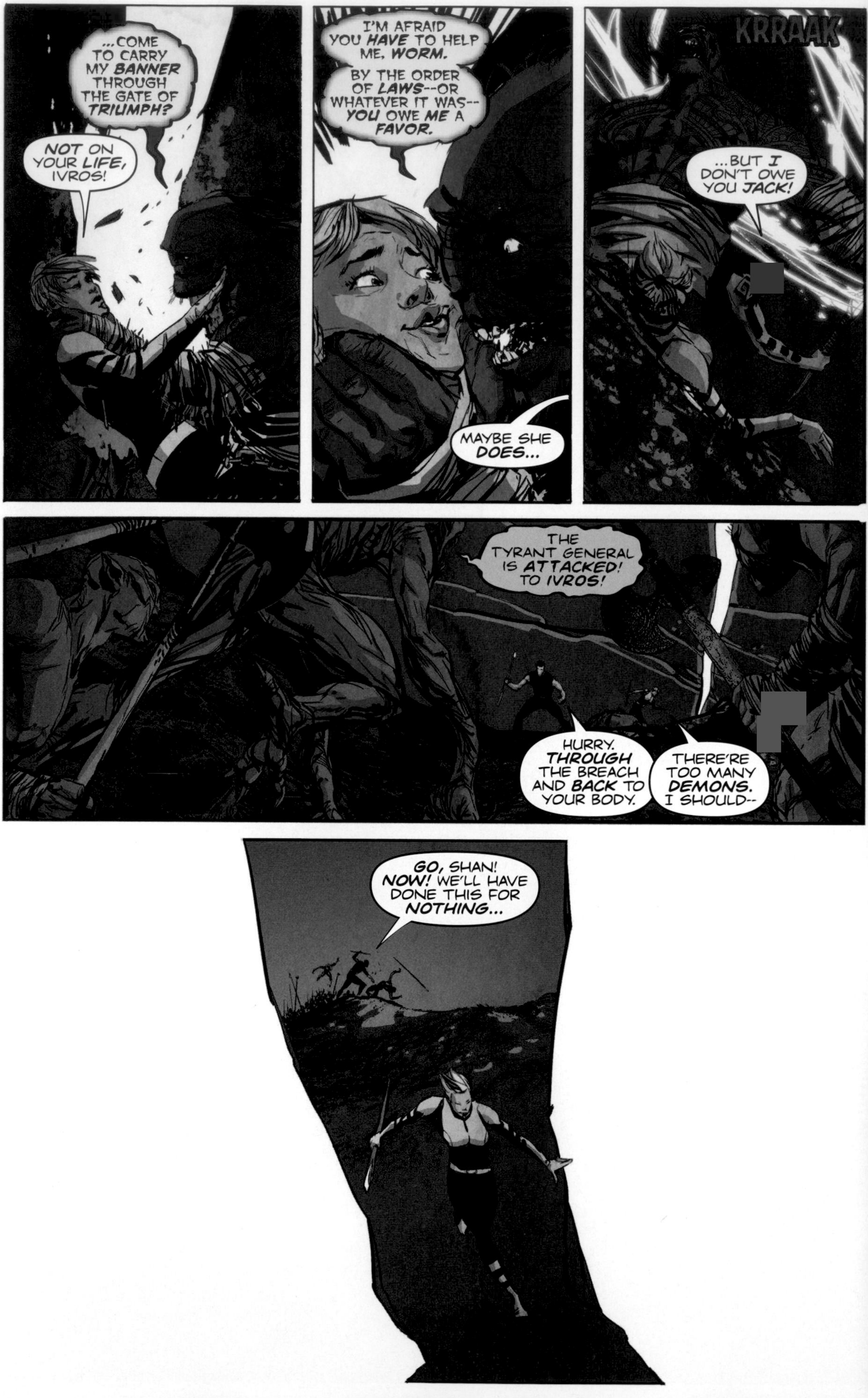

...COME TO CARRY MY BANNER THROUGH THE GATE OF TRIUMPH?
NOT ON YOUR LIFE, IVROS!
I'M AFRAID YOU HAVE TO HELP ME, WORM.
BY THE ORDER OF LAWS--OR WHATEVER IT WAS--YOU OWE ME A FAVOR.
MAYBE SHE DOES...
KRRAAK
...BUT I DON'T OWE YOU JACK!
THE TYRANT GENERAL IS ATTACKED! TO IVROS!
HURRY. THROUGH THE BREACH AND BACK TO YOUR BODY.
THERE'RE TOO MANY DEMONS. I SHOULD--
GO, SHAN! NOW! WE'LL HAVE DONE THIS FOR NOTHING...

"...IF MARCH'S COHORT *KILLS* YOU."

THESE SAME *FIVE* TOGETHER IN DOMINION OVER THE POWER BOUND...

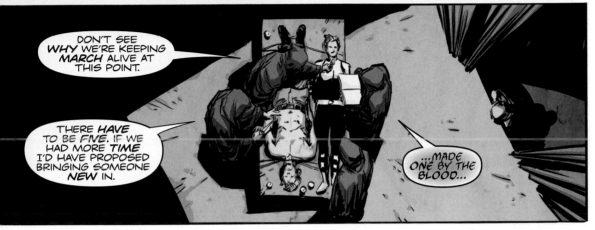

DON'T SEE *WHY* WE'RE KEEPING *MARCH* ALIVE AT THIS POINT.

THERE *HAVE* TO BE *FIVE*. IF WE HAD MORE *TIME* I'D HAVE PROPOSED BRINGING SOMEONE *NEW* IN.

...MADE *ONE* BY THE *BLOOD*...

...SPILT OF OUR *BROTHER*...

...DO SEVER THIS VESSEL, COMMITTING IT TO OUR PURPOSE...

...HN...

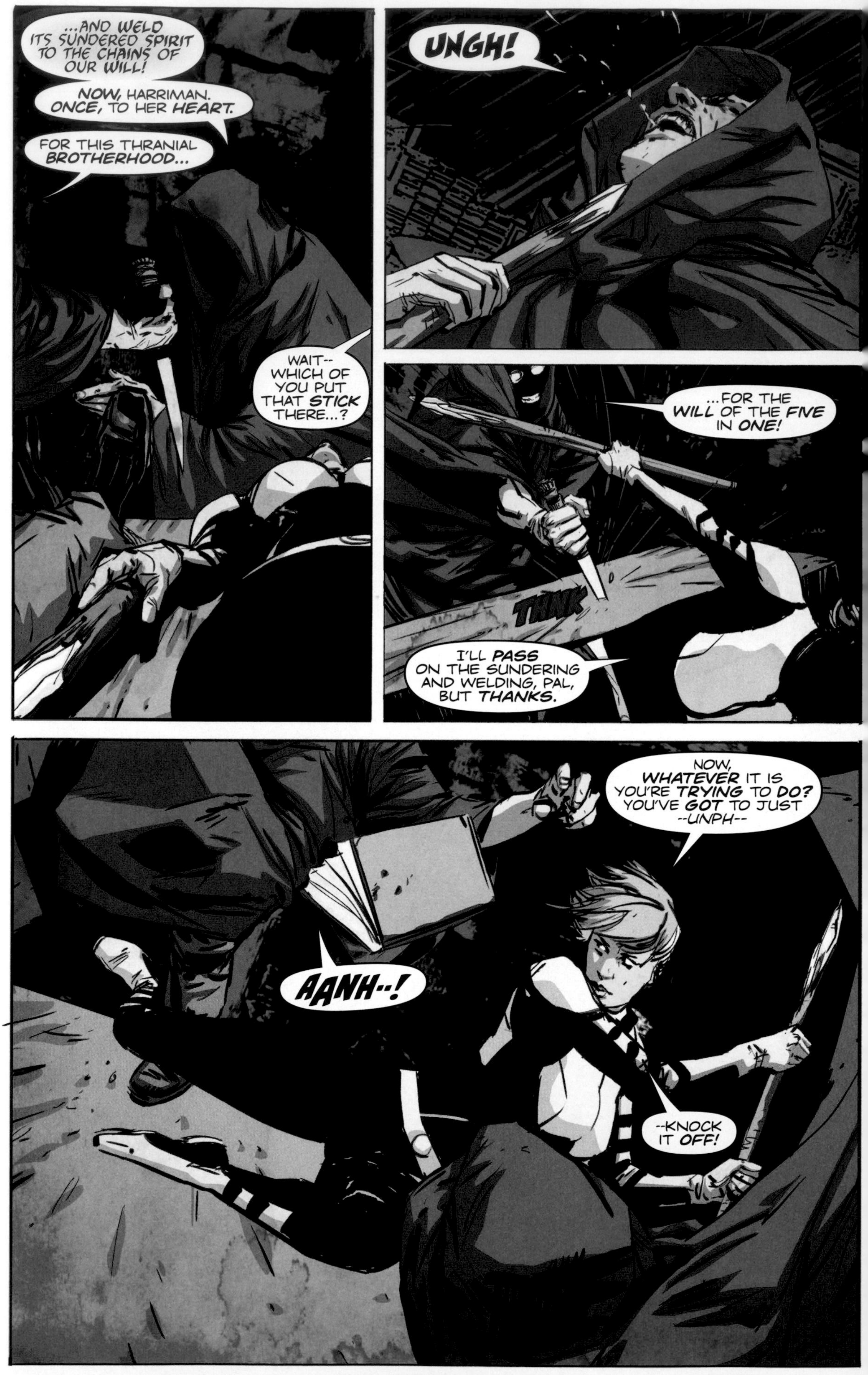
...AND WELD ITS SUNDERED SPIRIT TO THE CHAINS OF OUR WILL!
NOW, HARRIMAN. ONCE, TO HER HEART.
FOR THIS THRANIAL BROTHERHOOD...
WAIT-- WHICH OF YOU PUT THAT STICK THERE...?
UNGH!
...FOR THE WILL OF THE FIVE IN ONE!
THNK
I'LL PASS ON THE SUNDERING AND WELDING, PAL, BUT THANKS.
NOW, WHATEVER IT IS YOU'RE TRYING TO DO? YOU'VE GOT TO JUST --UNPH--
AANH--!
--KNOCK IT OFF!

LISTEN, HONEY. MARCH HAD **NO** BUSINESS BRINGING YOU **INTO** THIS. IT'S A **SHAME**, BUT WE'VE GOT TO--

NO! THE **WALL**-- THE WALL THAT KEEPS THE **BAD** STUFF OUT? YOUR **MAGIC'S** BEEN **WRECKING** IT! THIS ISN'T **ABOUT** MARCH!

SO...

...YOU WON'T **MIND** IF I TAKE HIM OUT OF THE **EQUATION**...?

THAT WOULD BE A **REALLY** BAD IDEA!

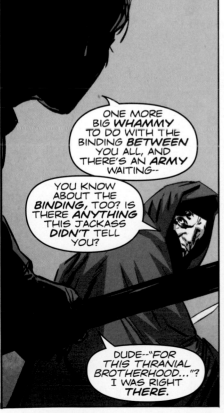

ONE MORE BIG **WHAMMY** TO DO WITH THE BINDING **BETWEEN** YOU ALL, AND THERE'S AN **ARMY** WAITING--

YOU KNOW ABOUT THE **BINDING**, TOO? IS THERE **ANYTHING** THIS JACKASS **DIDN'T** TELL YOU?

DUDE--"FOR THIS THRANIAL BROTHERHOOD..."? I WAS RIGHT **THERE**.

--ANH!

ARMY...?!

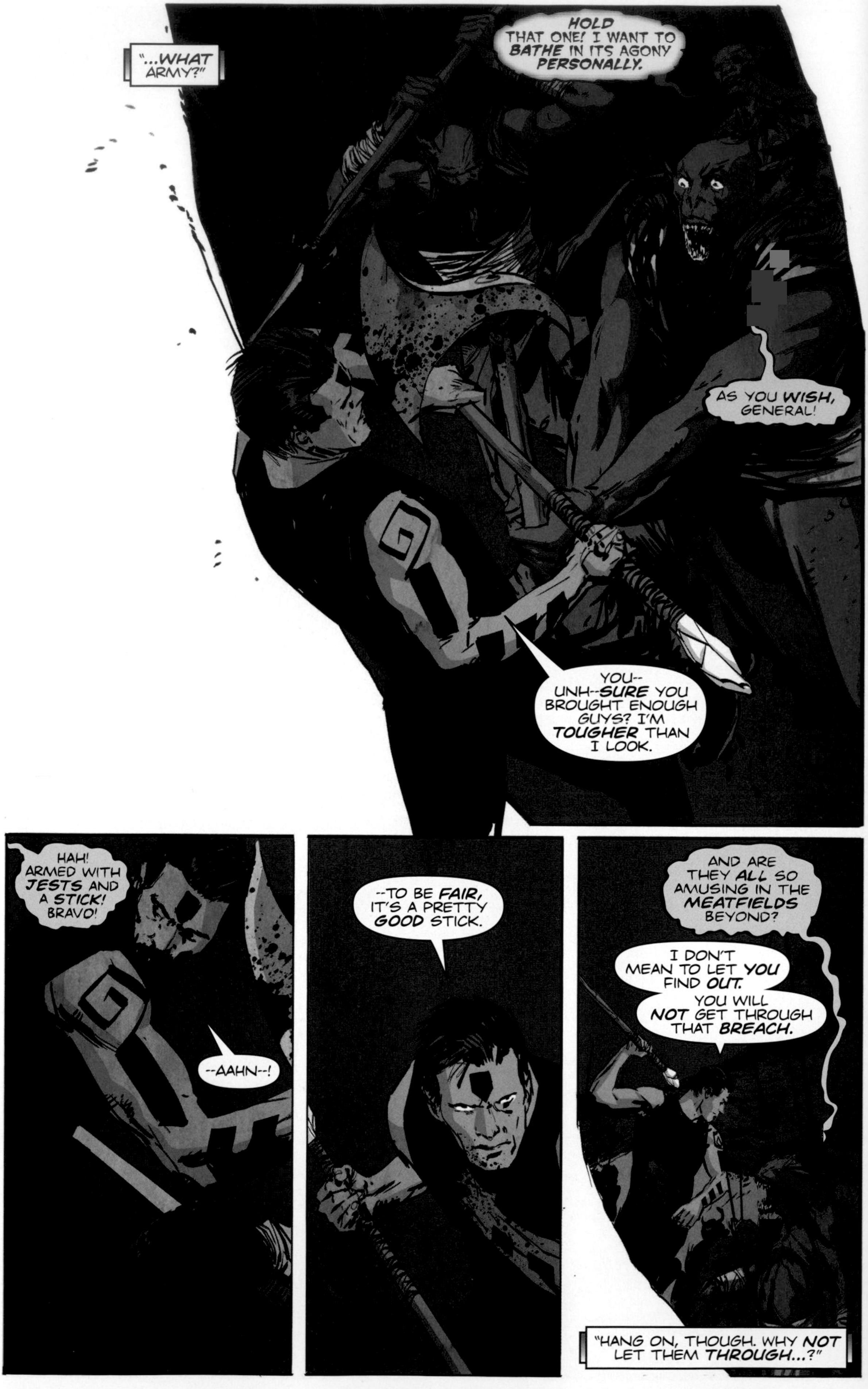
"...WHAT ARMY?"
HOLD THAT ONE! I WANT TO BATHE IN ITS AGONY PERSONALLY.
AS YOU WISH, GENERAL!
YOU-- UNH--SURE YOU BROUGHT ENOUGH GUYS? I'M TOUGHER THAN I LOOK.
HAH! ARMED WITH JESTS AND A STICK! BRAVO!
--AAHN--!
--TO BE FAIR, IT'S A PRETTY GOOD STICK.
AND ARE THEY ALL SO AMUSING IN THE MEATFIELDS BEYOND?
I DON'T MEAN TO LET YOU FIND OUT.
YOU WILL NOT GET THROUGH THAT BREACH.
"HANG ON, THOUGH. WHY NOT LET THEM THROUGH...?"

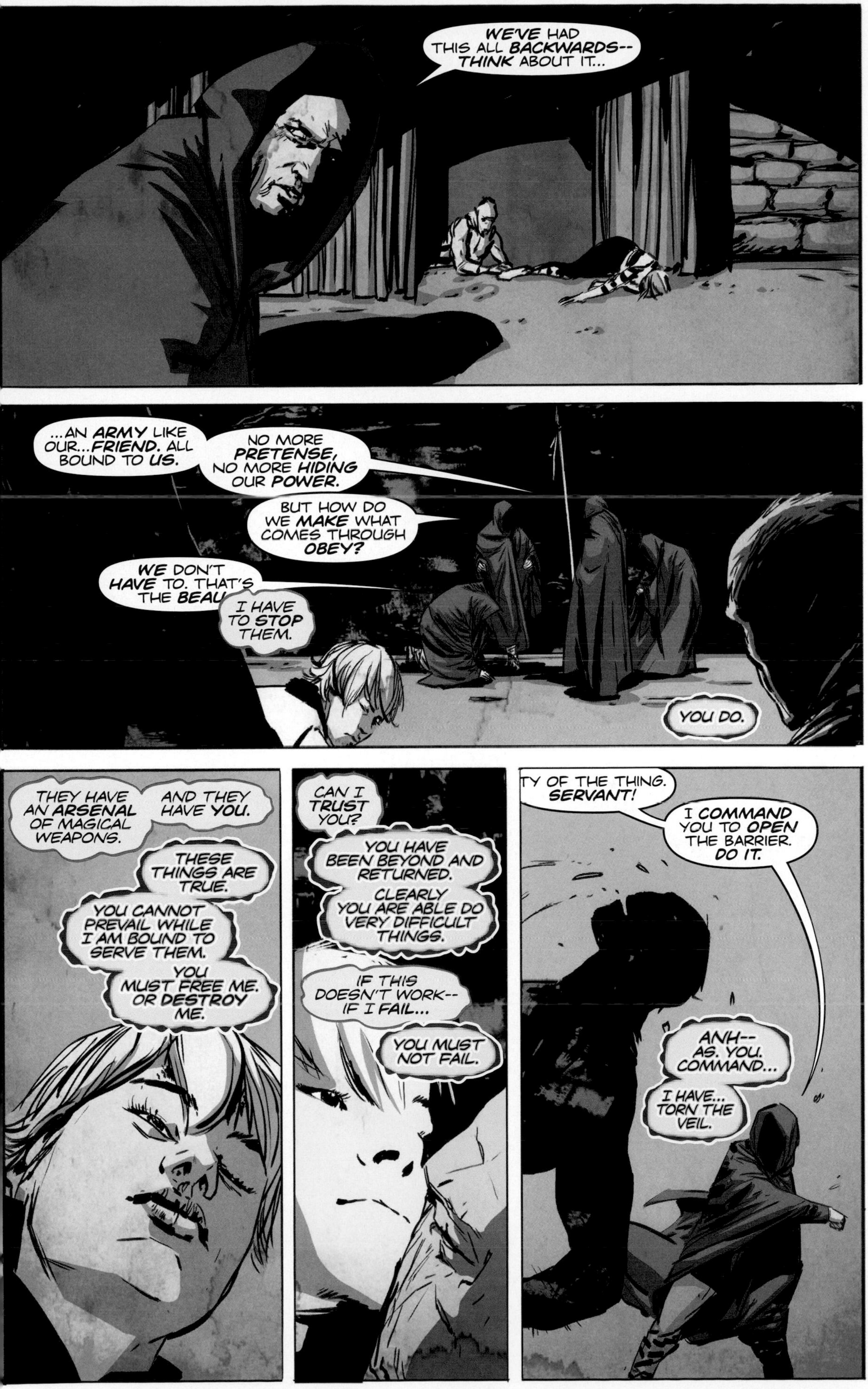
WE'VE HAD THIS ALL BACKWARDS-- THINK ABOUT IT...
...AN ARMY LIKE OUR...FRIEND. ALL BOUND TO US.
NO MORE PRETENSE, NO MORE HIDING OUR POWER.
BUT HOW DO WE MAKE WHAT COMES THROUGH OBEY?
WE DON'T HAVE TO. THAT'S THE BEAU
I HAVE TO STOP THEM.
YOU DO.
THEY HAVE AN ARSENAL OF MAGICAL WEAPONS.
AND THEY HAVE YOU.
THESE THINGS ARE TRUE.
YOU CANNOT PREVAIL WHILE I AM BOUND TO SERVE THEM.
YOU MUST FREE ME. OR DESTROY ME.
CAN I TRUST YOU?
YOU HAVE BEEN BEYOND AND RETURNED.
CLEARLY YOU ARE ABLE DO VERY DIFFICULT THINGS.
IF THIS DOESN'T WORK-- IF I FAIL...
YOU MUST NOT FAIL.
TY OF THE THING. SERVANT!
I COMMAND YOU TO OPEN THE BARRIER. DO IT.
ANH-- AS. YOU. COMMAND...
I HAVE... TORN THE VEIL.

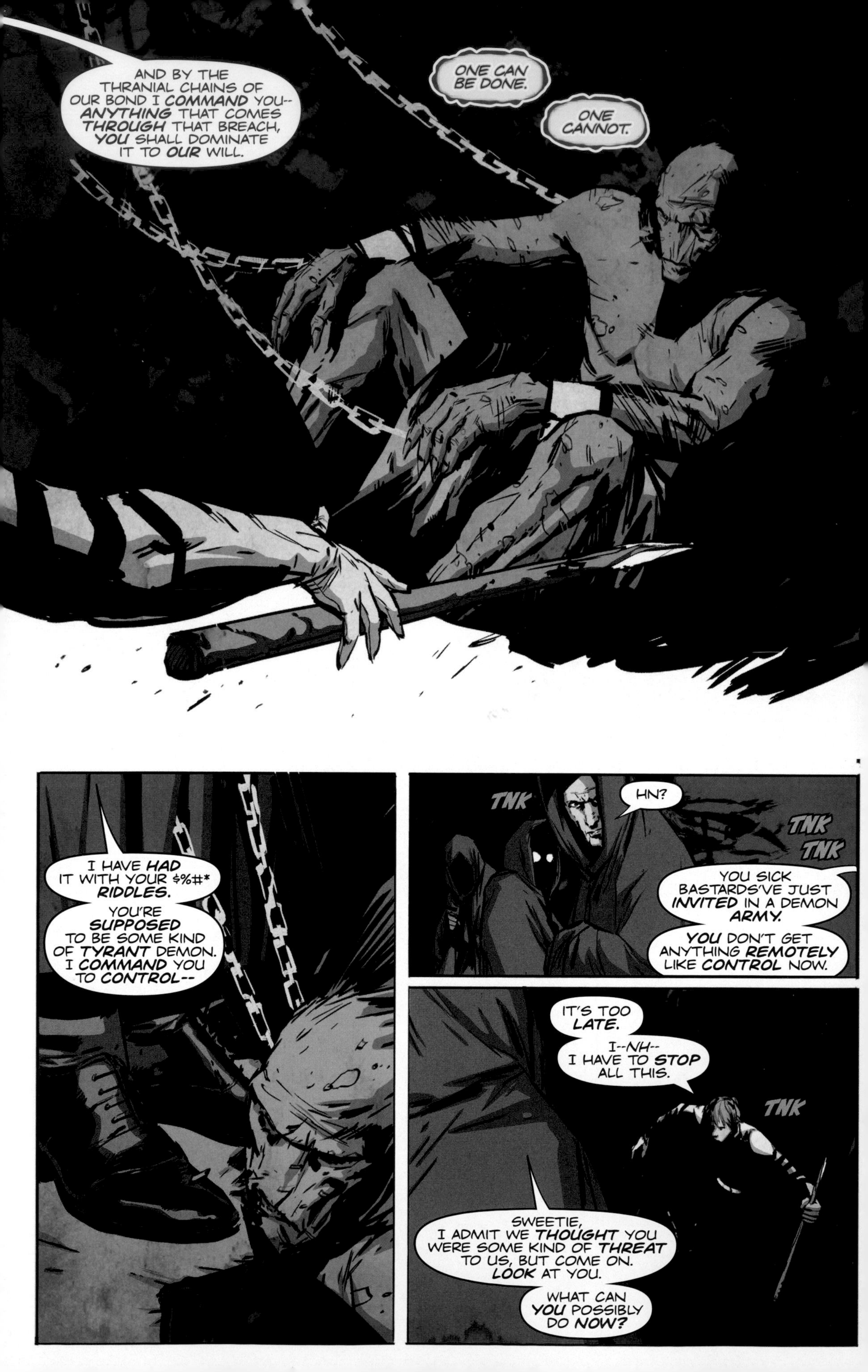

AND BY THE THRANIAL CHAINS OF OUR BOND I COMMAND YOU-- ANYTHING THAT COMES THROUGH THAT BREACH, YOU SHALL DOMINATE IT TO OUR WILL.
ONE CAN BE DONE.
ONE CANNOT.
I HAVE HAD IT WITH YOUR $%#* RIDDLES.
YOU'RE SUPPOSED TO BE SOME KIND OF TYRANT DEMON. I COMMAND YOU TO CONTROL--
TNK
HN?
TNK
TNK
YOU SICK BASTARDS'VE JUST INVITED IN A DEMON ARMY.
YOU DON'T GET ANYTHING REMOTELY LIKE CONTROL NOW.
IT'S TOO LATE.
I--NH-- I HAVE TO STOP ALL THIS.
TNK
SWEETIE, I ADMIT WE THOUGHT YOU WERE SOME KIND OF THREAT TO US, BUT COME ON. LOOK AT YOU.
WHAT CAN YOU POSSIBLY DO NOW?

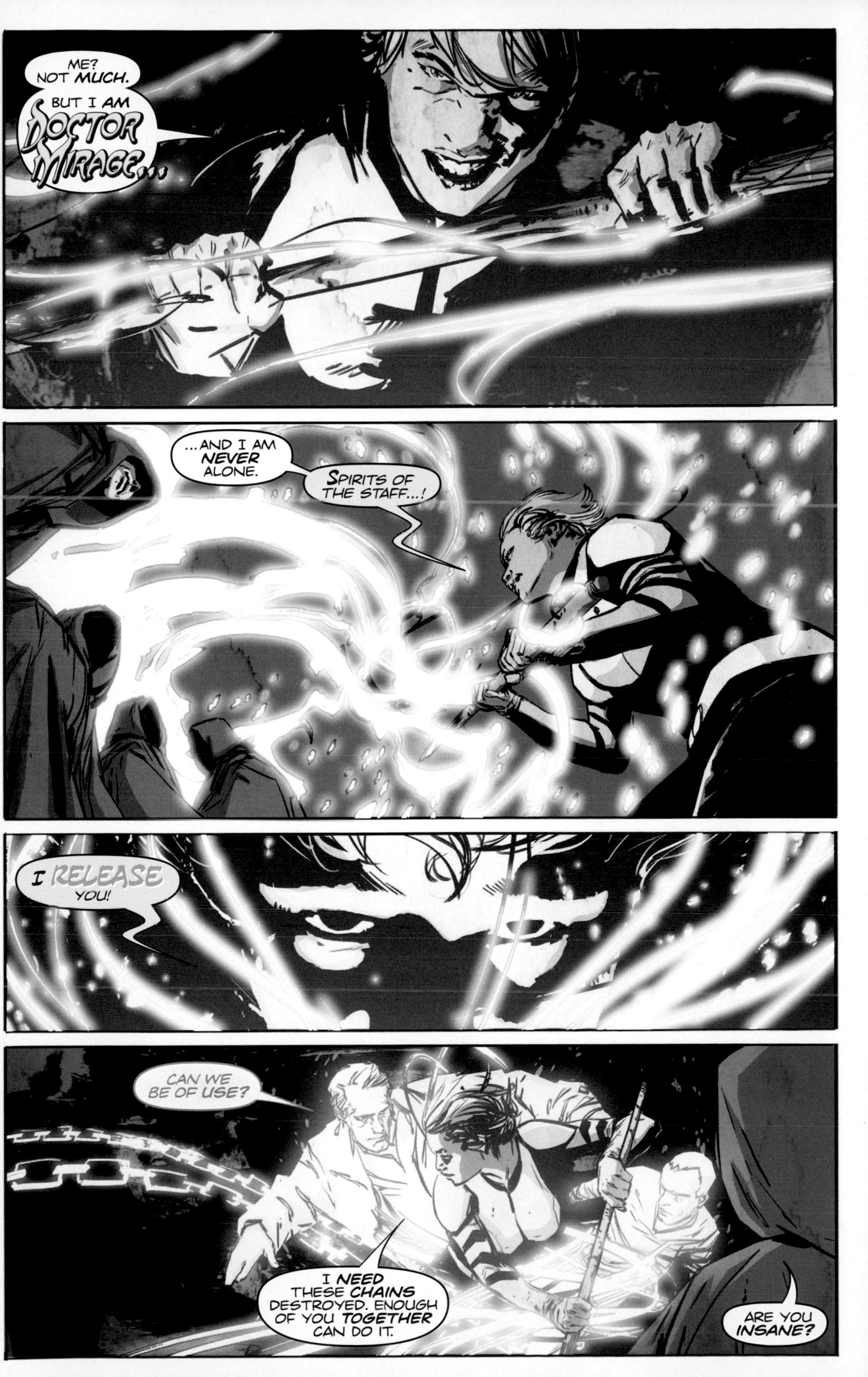
ME? NOT MUCH.
BUT I AM DOCTOR MIRAGE...
...AND I AM NEVER ALONE.
SPIRITS OF THE STAFF...!
I RELEASE YOU!
CAN WE BE OF USE?
I NEED THESE CHAINS DESTROYED. ENOUGH OF YOU TOGETHER CAN DO IT.
ARE YOU INSANE?

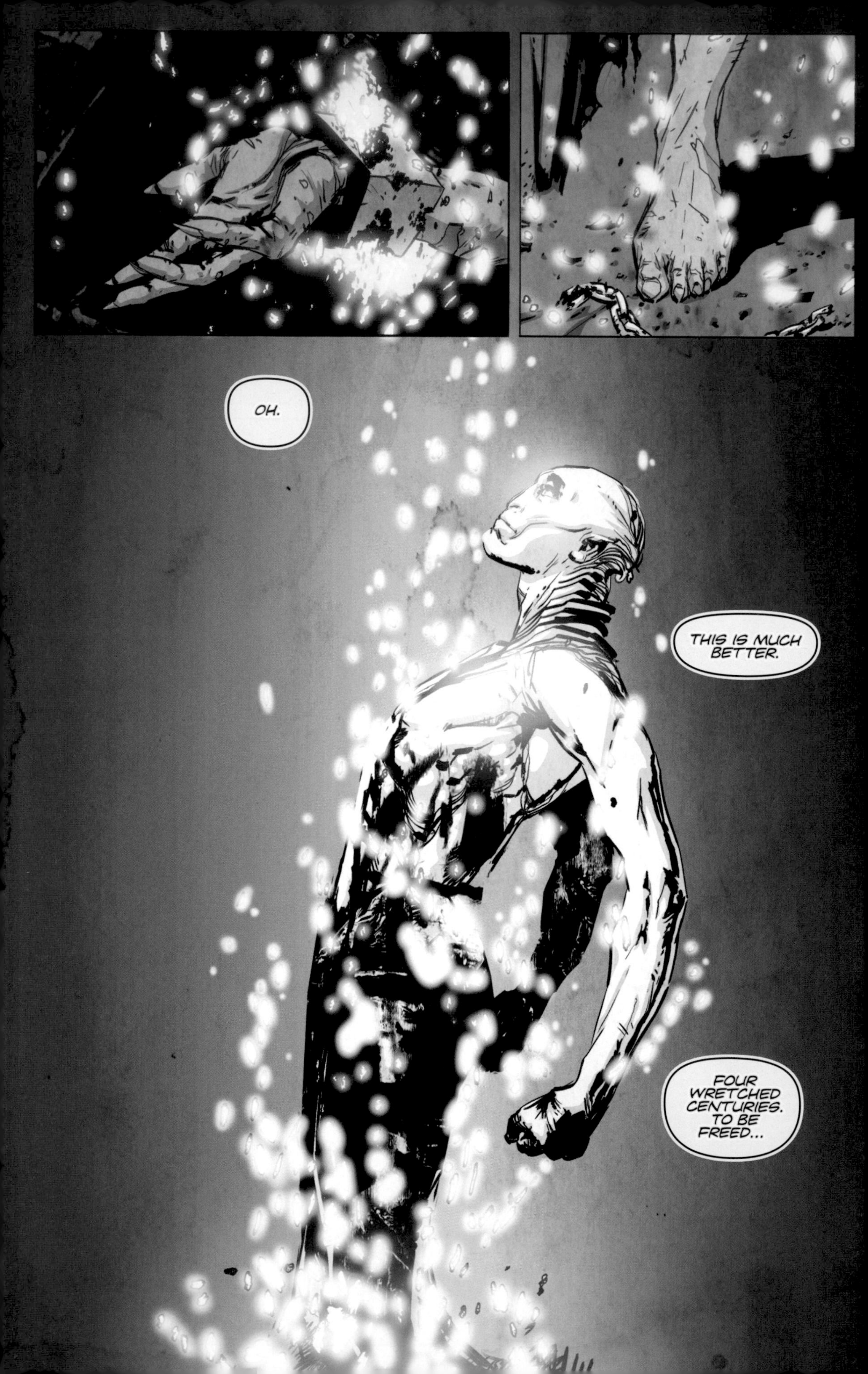
OH.
THIS IS MUCH BETTER.
FOUR WRETCHED CENTURIES. TO BE FREED...

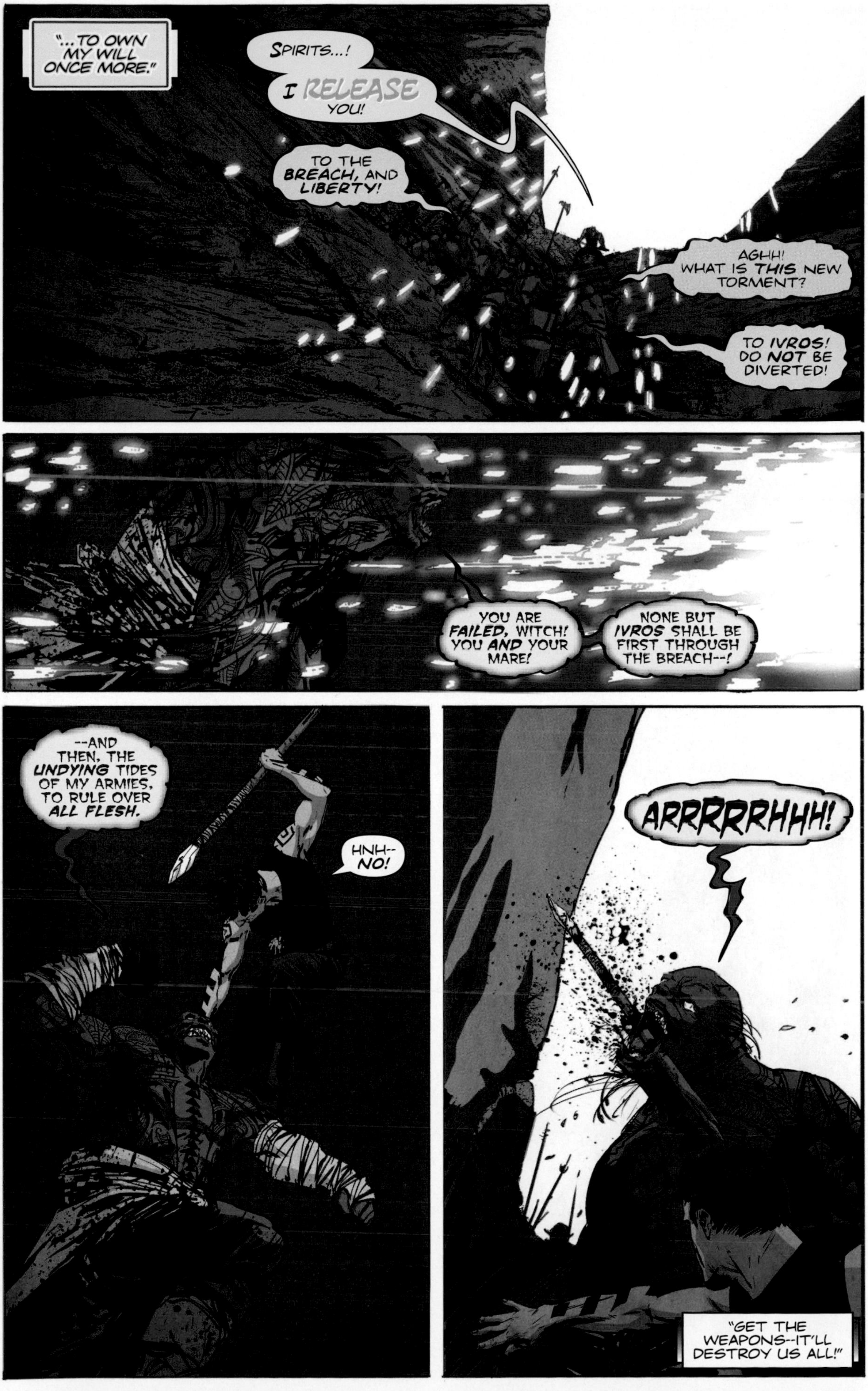
"...TO OWN MY WILL ONCE MORE."
SPIRITS...!
I RELEASE YOU!
TO THE BREACH, AND LIBERTY!
AGHH! WHAT IS THIS NEW TORMENT?
TO IVROS! DO NOT BE DIVERTED!
YOU ARE FAILED, WITCH! YOU AND YOUR MARE!
NONE BUT IVROS SHALL BE FIRST THROUGH THE BREACH--!
--AND THEN, THE UNDYING TIDES OF MY ARMIES, TO RULE OVER ALL FLESH.
HNH-- NO!
ARRRRRHHH!
"GET THE WEAPONS--IT'LL DESTROY US ALL!"

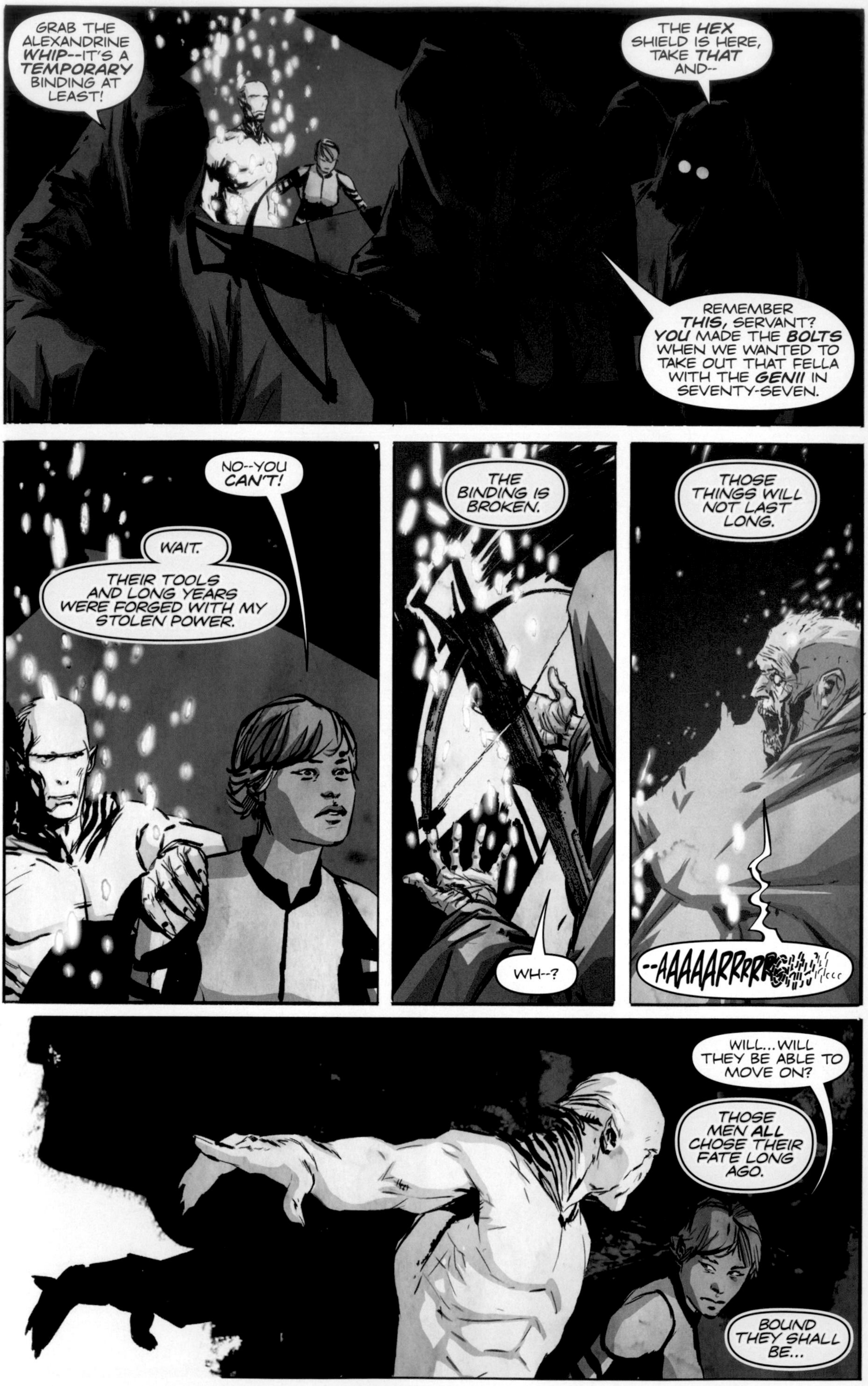
GRAB THE ALEXANDRINE WHIP--IT'S A TEMPORARY BINDING AT LEAST!
THE HEX SHIELD IS HERE, TAKE THAT AND--
REMEMBER THIS, SERVANT? YOU MADE THE BOLTS WHEN WE WANTED TO TAKE OUT THAT FELLA WITH THE GENII IN SEVENTY-SEVEN.
NO--YOU CAN'T!
WAIT.
THEIR TOOLS AND LONG YEARS WERE FORGED WITH MY STOLEN POWER.
THE BINDING IS BROKEN.
WH--?
THOSE THINGS WILL NOT LAST LONG.
--AAAAARRRR
WILL...WILL THEY BE ABLE TO MOVE ON?
THOSE MEN ALL CHOSE THEIR FATE LONG AGO.
BOUND THEY SHALL BE...

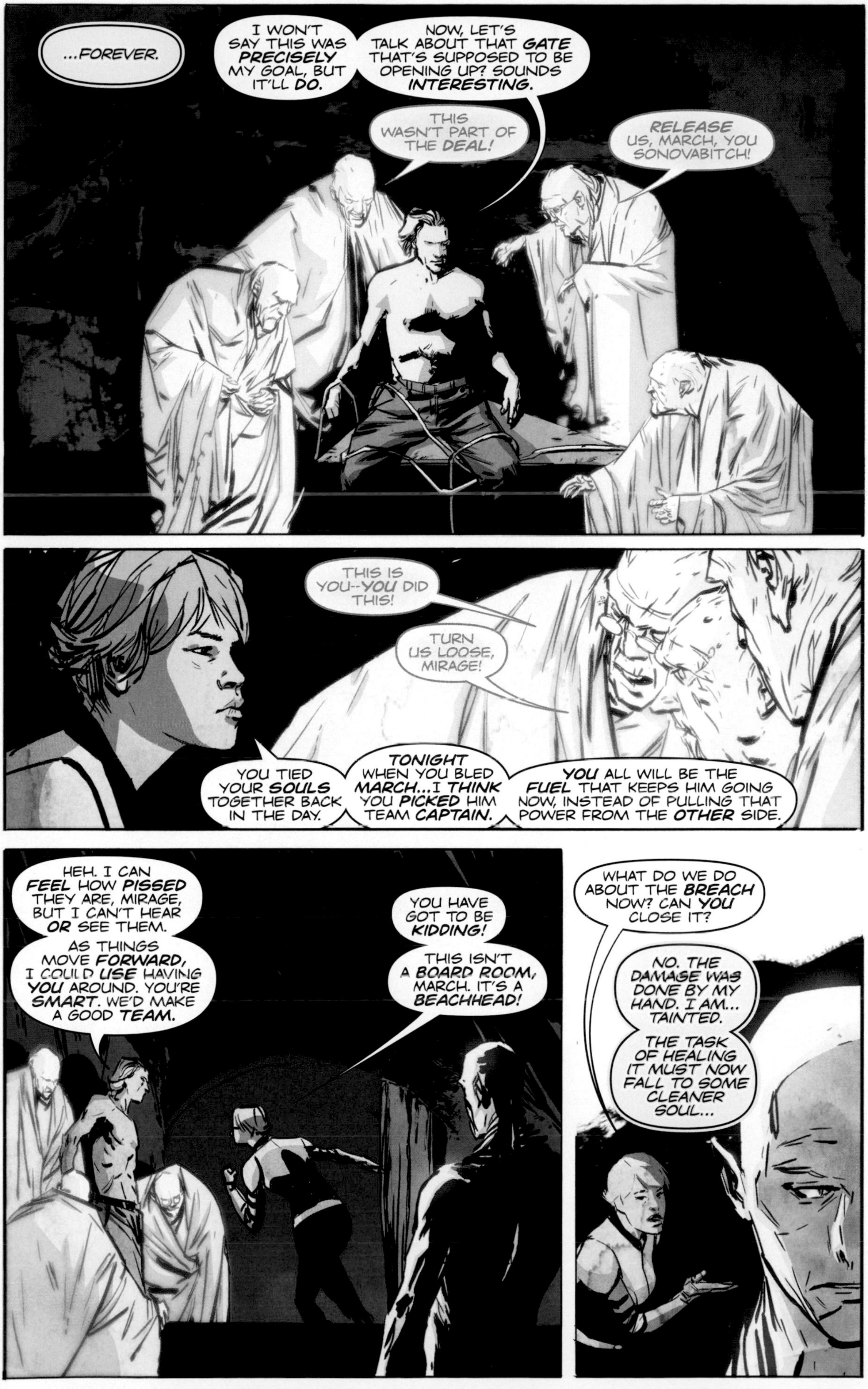
...FOREVER.
I WON'T SAY THIS WAS PRECISELY MY GOAL, BUT IT'LL DO.
NOW, LET'S TALK ABOUT THAT GATE THAT'S SUPPOSED TO BE OPENING UP? SOUNDS INTERESTING.
THIS WASN'T PART OF THE DEAL!
RELEASE US, MARCH, YOU SONOVABITCH!
THIS IS YOU--YOU DID THIS!
TURN US LOOSE, MIRAGE!
YOU TIED YOUR SOULS TOGETHER BACK IN THE DAY.
TONIGHT WHEN YOU BLED MARCH...I THINK YOU PICKED HIM TEAM CAPTAIN.
YOU ALL WILL BE THE FUEL THAT KEEPS HIM GOING NOW, INSTEAD OF PULLING THAT POWER FROM THE OTHER SIDE.
HEH. I CAN FEEL HOW PISSED THEY ARE, MIRAGE, BUT I CAN'T HEAR OR SEE THEM.
AS THINGS MOVE FORWARD, I COULD USE HAVING YOU AROUND. YOU'RE SMART. WE'D MAKE A GOOD TEAM.
YOU HAVE GOT TO BE KIDDING!
THIS ISN'T A BOARD ROOM, MARCH. IT'S A BEACHHEAD!
WHAT DO WE DO ABOUT THE BREACH NOW? CAN YOU CLOSE IT?
NO. THE DAMAGE WAS DONE BY MY HAND. I AM... TAINTED.
THE TASK OF HEALING IT MUST NOW FALL TO SOME CLEANER SOUL...

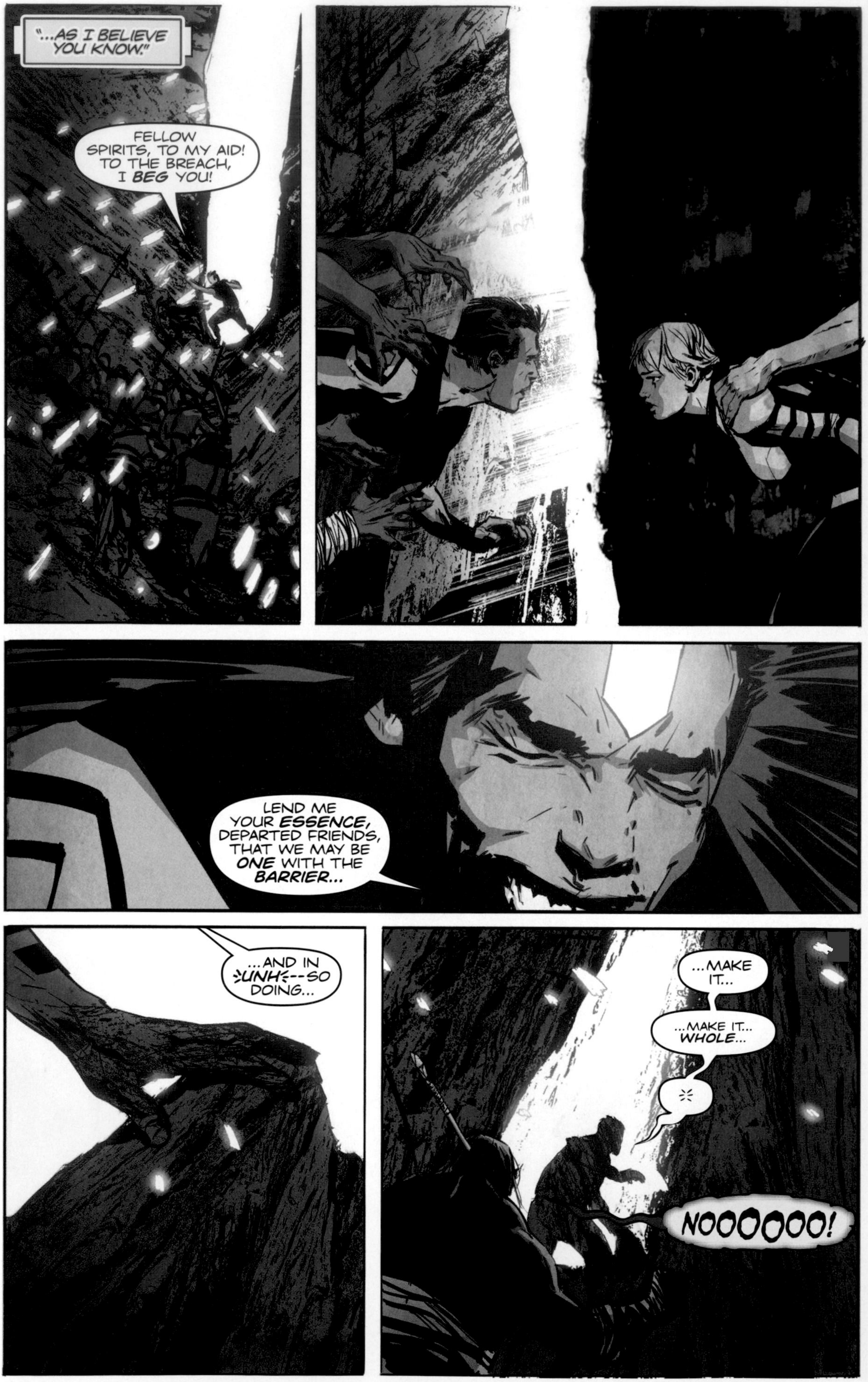
"...AS I BELIEVE YOU KNOW."
FELLOW SPIRITS, TO MY AID! TO THE BREACH, I BEG YOU!
LEND ME YOUR ESSENCE, DEPARTED FRIENDS, THAT WE MAY BE ONE WITH THE BARRIER...
...AND IN UNH--SO DOING...
...MAKE IT...
...MAKE IT... WHOLE...
NOOOOOO!

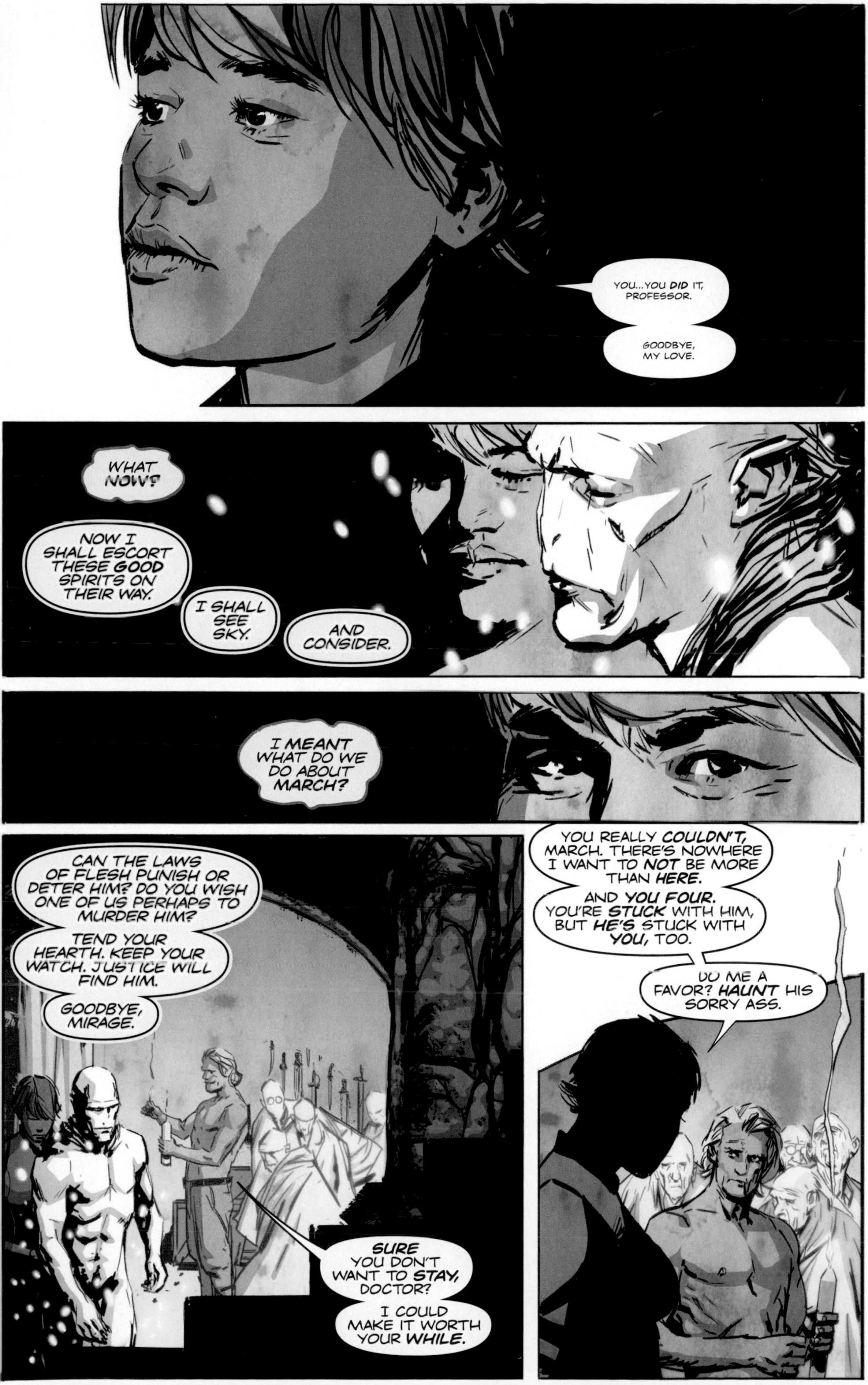
YOU...YOU DID IT, PROFESSOR.
GOODBYE, MY LOVE.
WHAT NOW?
NOW I SHALL ESCORT THESE GOOD SPIRITS ON THEIR WAY.
I SHALL SEE SKY.
AND CONSIDER.
I MEANT WHAT DO WE DO ABOUT MARCH?
CAN THE LAWS OF FLESH PUNISH OR DETER HIM? DO YOU WISH ONE OF US PERHAPS TO MURDER HIM?
TEND YOUR HEARTH. KEEP YOUR WATCH. JUSTICE WILL FIND HIM.
GOODBYE, MIRAGE.
SURE YOU DON'T WANT TO STAY, DOCTOR?
I COULD MAKE IT WORTH YOUR WHILE.
YOU REALLY COULDN'T, MARCH. THERE'S NOWHERE I WANT TO NOT BE MORE THAN HERE.
AND YOU FOUR. YOU'RE STUCK WITH HIM, BUT HE'S STUCK WITH YOU, TOO.
DO ME A FAVOR? HAUNT HIS SORRY ASS.

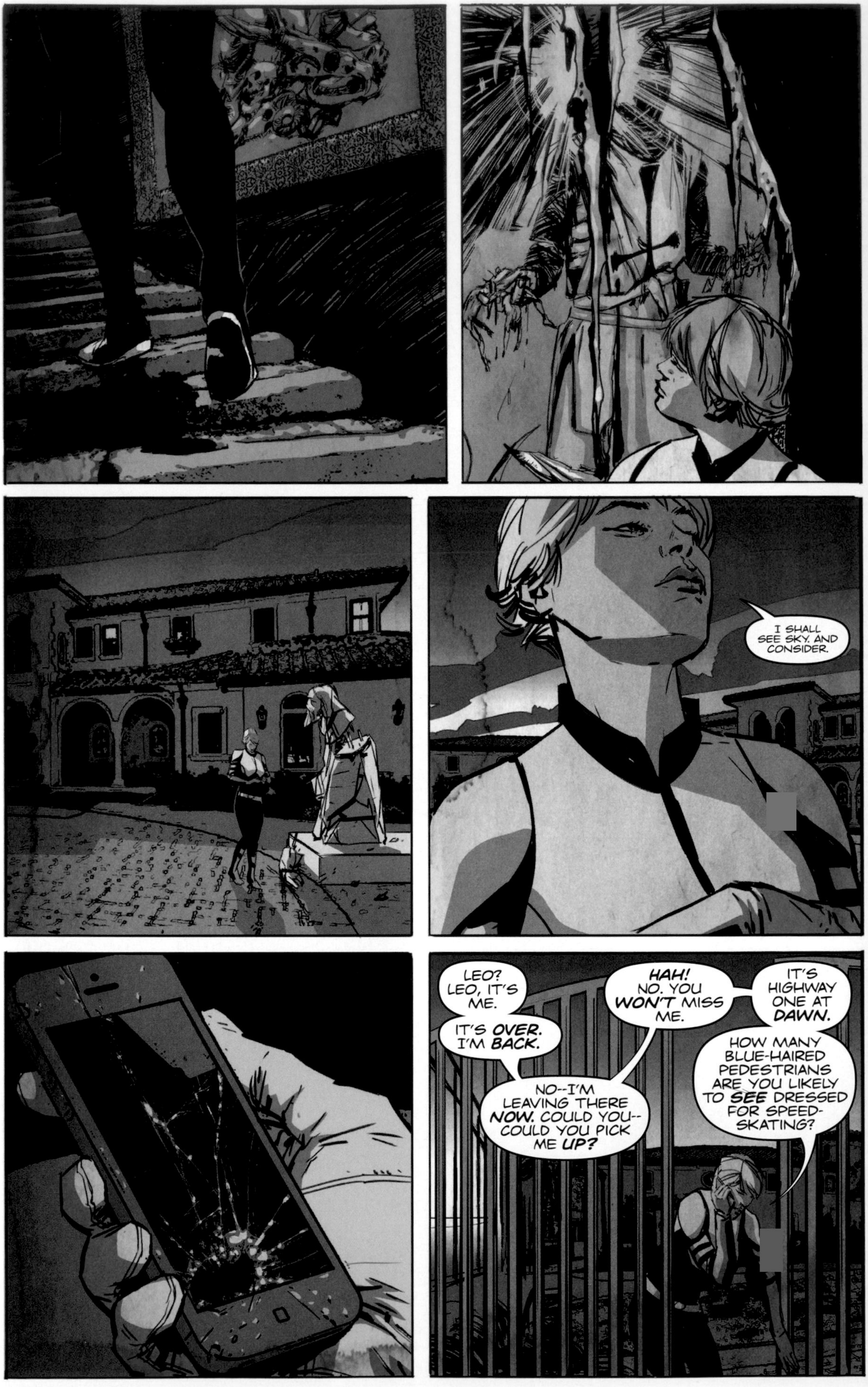
I SHALL SEE SKY. AND CONSIDER.
LEO? LEO, IT'S ME.
IT'S OVER. I'M BACK.
HAH! NO. YOU WON'T MISS ME.
NO--I'M LEAVING THERE NOW. COULD YOU-- COULD YOU PICK ME UP?
IT'S HIGHWAY ONE AT DAWN.
HOW MANY BLUE-HAIRED PEDESTRIANS ARE YOU LIKELY TO SEE DRESSED FOR SPEED-SKATING?

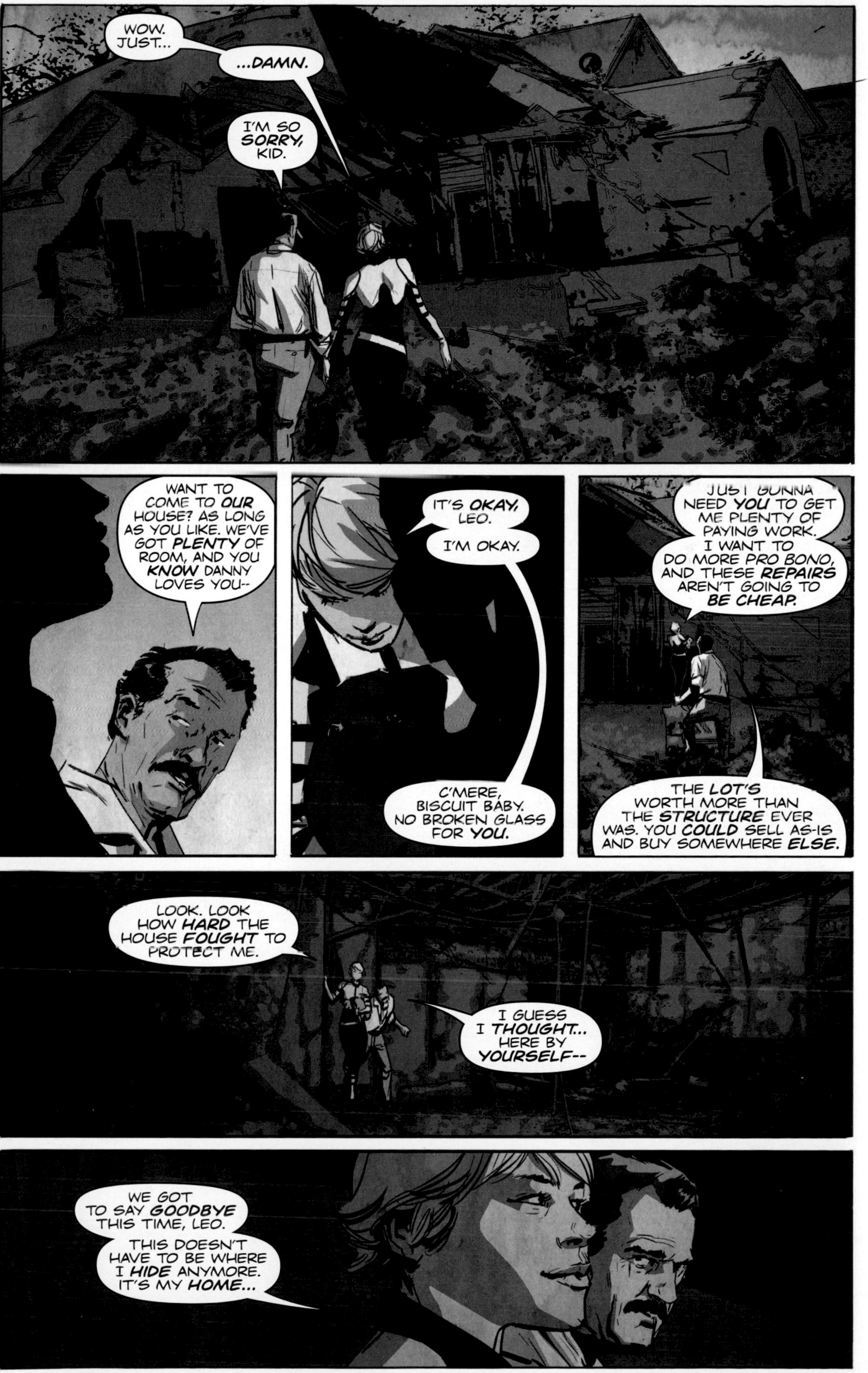
WOW. JUST...
...DAMN.
I'M SO SORRY, KID.
WANT TO COME TO OUR HOUSE? AS LONG AS YOU LIKE. WE'VE GOT PLENTY OF ROOM, AND YOU KNOW DANNY LOVES YOU--
IT'S OKAY, LEO.
I'M OKAY.
C'MERE, BISCUIT BABY. NO BROKEN GLASS FOR YOU.
JUST GONNA NEED YOU TO GET ME PLENTY OF PAYING WORK. I WANT TO DO MORE PRO BONO, AND THESE REPAIRS AREN'T GOING TO BE CHEAP.
THE LOT'S WORTH MORE THAN THE STRUCTURE EVER WAS. YOU COULD SELL AS-IS AND BUY SOMEWHERE ELSE.
LOOK. LOOK HOW HARD THE HOUSE FOUGHT TO PROTECT ME.
I GUESS I THOUGHT... HERE BY YOURSELF--
WE GOT TO SAY GOODBYE THIS TIME, LEO.
THIS DOESN'T HAVE TO BE WHERE I HIDE ANYMORE. IT'S MY HOME...

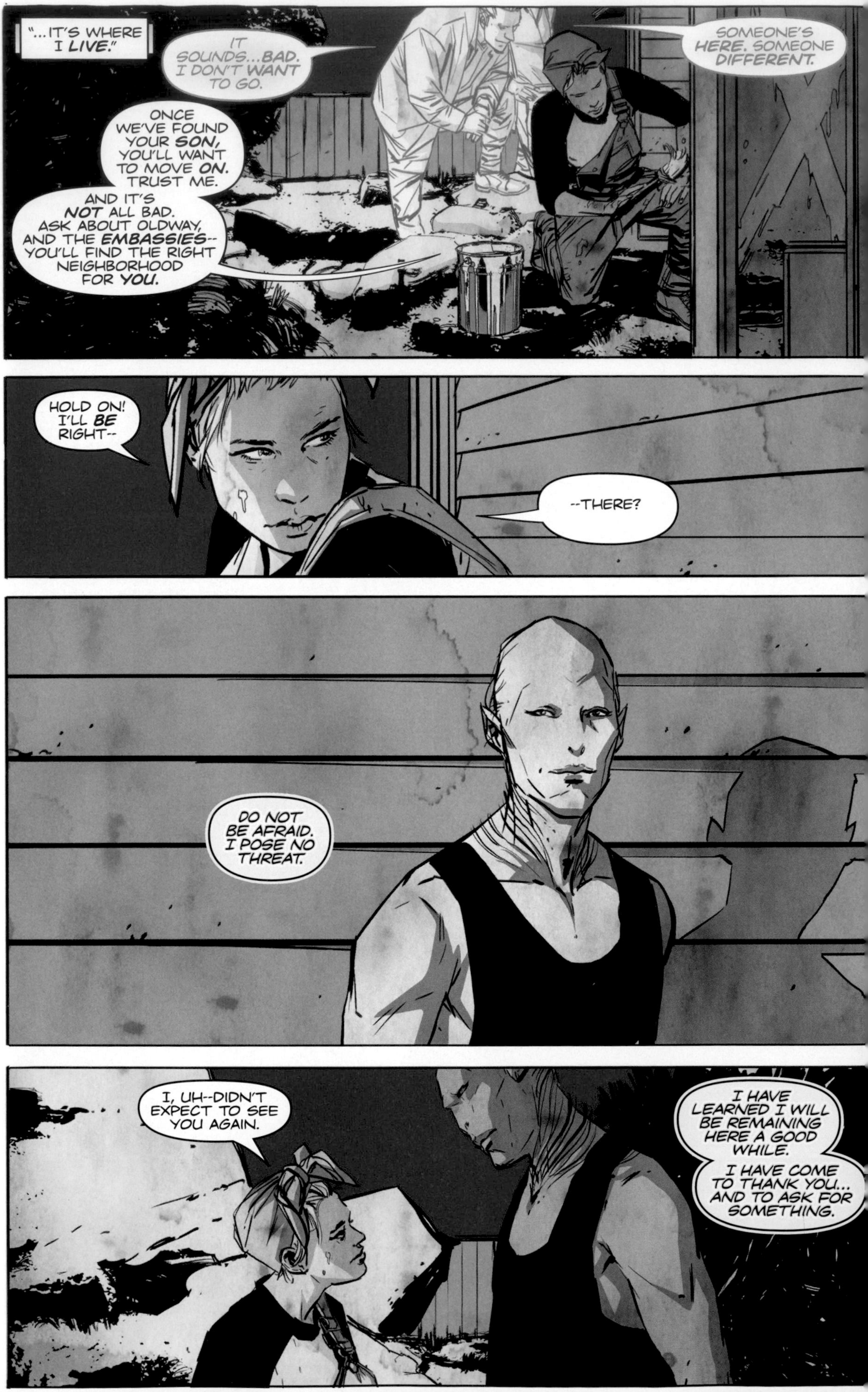
"...IT'S WHERE I LIVE."
IT SOUNDS...BAD. I DON'T WANT TO GO.
SOMEONE'S HERE. SOMEONE DIFFERENT.
ONCE WE'VE FOUND YOUR SON, YOU'LL WANT TO MOVE ON. TRUST ME.
AND IT'S NOT ALL BAD. ASK ABOUT OLDWAY, AND THE EMBASSIES-- YOU'LL FIND THE RIGHT NEIGHBORHOOD FOR YOU.
HOLD ON! I'LL BE RIGHT--
--THERE?
DO NOT BE AFRAID. I POSE NO THREAT.
I, UH--DIDN'T EXPECT TO SEE YOU AGAIN.
I HAVE LEARNED I WILL BE REMAINING HERE A GOOD WHILE.
I HAVE COME TO THANK YOU... AND TO ASK FOR SOMETHING.

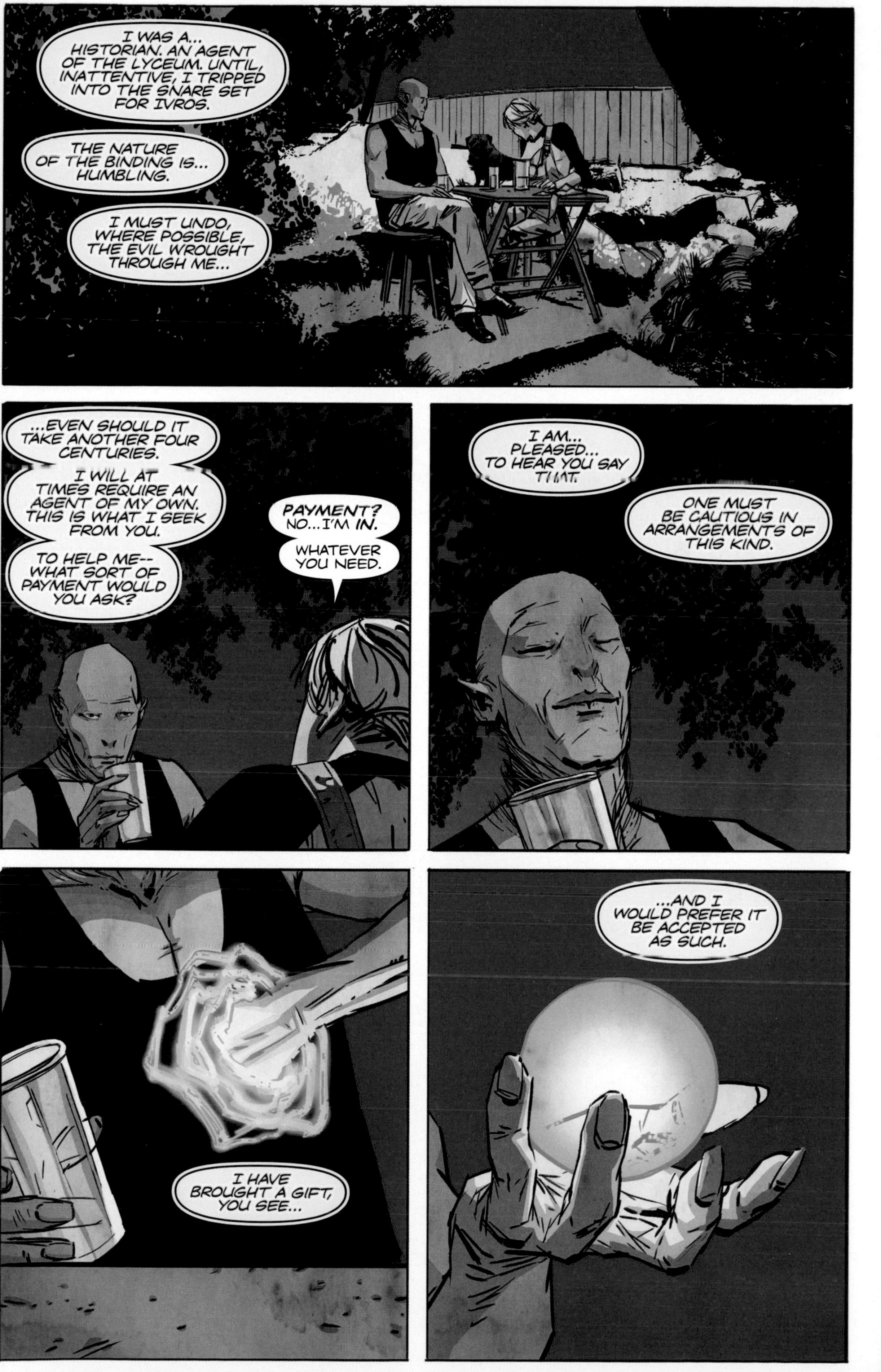
I WAS A... HISTORIAN. AN AGENT OF THE LYCEUM. UNTIL, INATTENTIVE, I TRIPPED INTO THE SNARE SET FOR IVROS.
THE NATURE OF THE BINDING IS... HUMBLING.
I MUST UNDO, WHERE POSSIBLE, THE EVIL WROUGHT THROUGH ME...
...EVEN SHOULD IT TAKE ANOTHER FOUR CENTURIES.
I WILL AT TIMES REQUIRE AN AGENT OF MY OWN. THIS IS WHAT I SEEK FROM YOU.
TO HELP ME-- WHAT SORT OF PAYMENT WOULD YOU ASK?
PAYMENT? NO...I'M IN.
WHATEVER YOU NEED.
I AM... PLEASED... TO HEAR YOU SAY THAT.
ONE MUST BE CAUTIOUS IN ARRANGEMENTS OF THIS KIND.
I HAVE BROUGHT A GIFT, YOU SEE...
...AND I WOULD PREFER IT BE ACCEPTED AS SUCH.

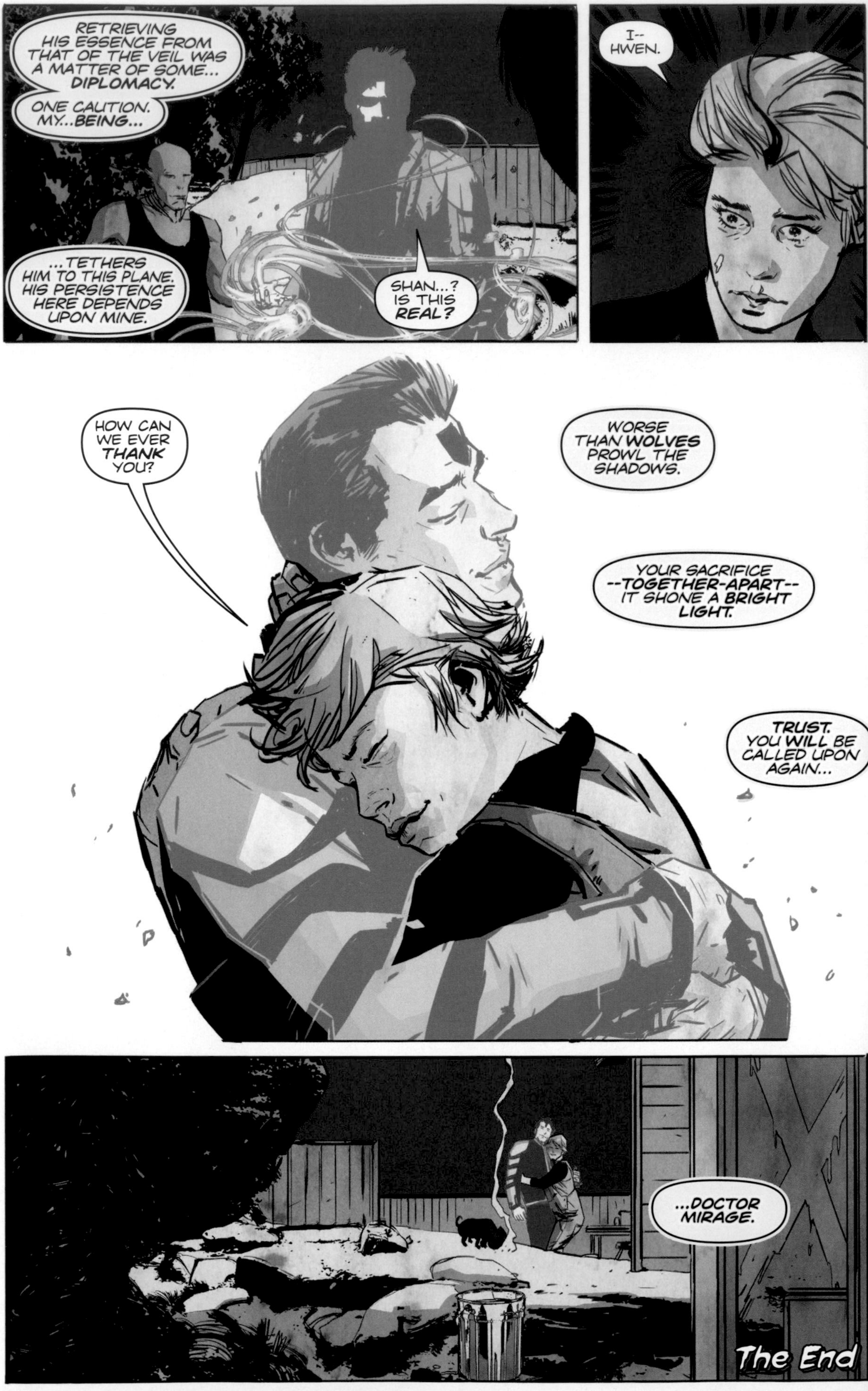
RETRIEVING HIS ESSENCE FROM THAT OF THE VEIL WAS A MATTER OF SOME... DIPLOMACY.
ONE CAUTION. MY...BEING...
...TETHERS HIM TO THIS PLANE. HIS PERSISTENCE HERE DEPENDS UPON MINE.
SHAN...? IS THIS REAL?
I-- HWEN.
HOW CAN WE EVER THANK YOU?
WORSE THAN WOLVES PROWL THE SHADOWS.
YOUR SACRIFICE --TOGETHER-APART-- IT SHONE A BRIGHT LIGHT.
TRUST. YOU WILL BE CALLED UPON AGAIN...
...DOCTOR MIRAGE.
The End

BONUS: DOCTOR MIRAGE'S FIRST APPEARANCE

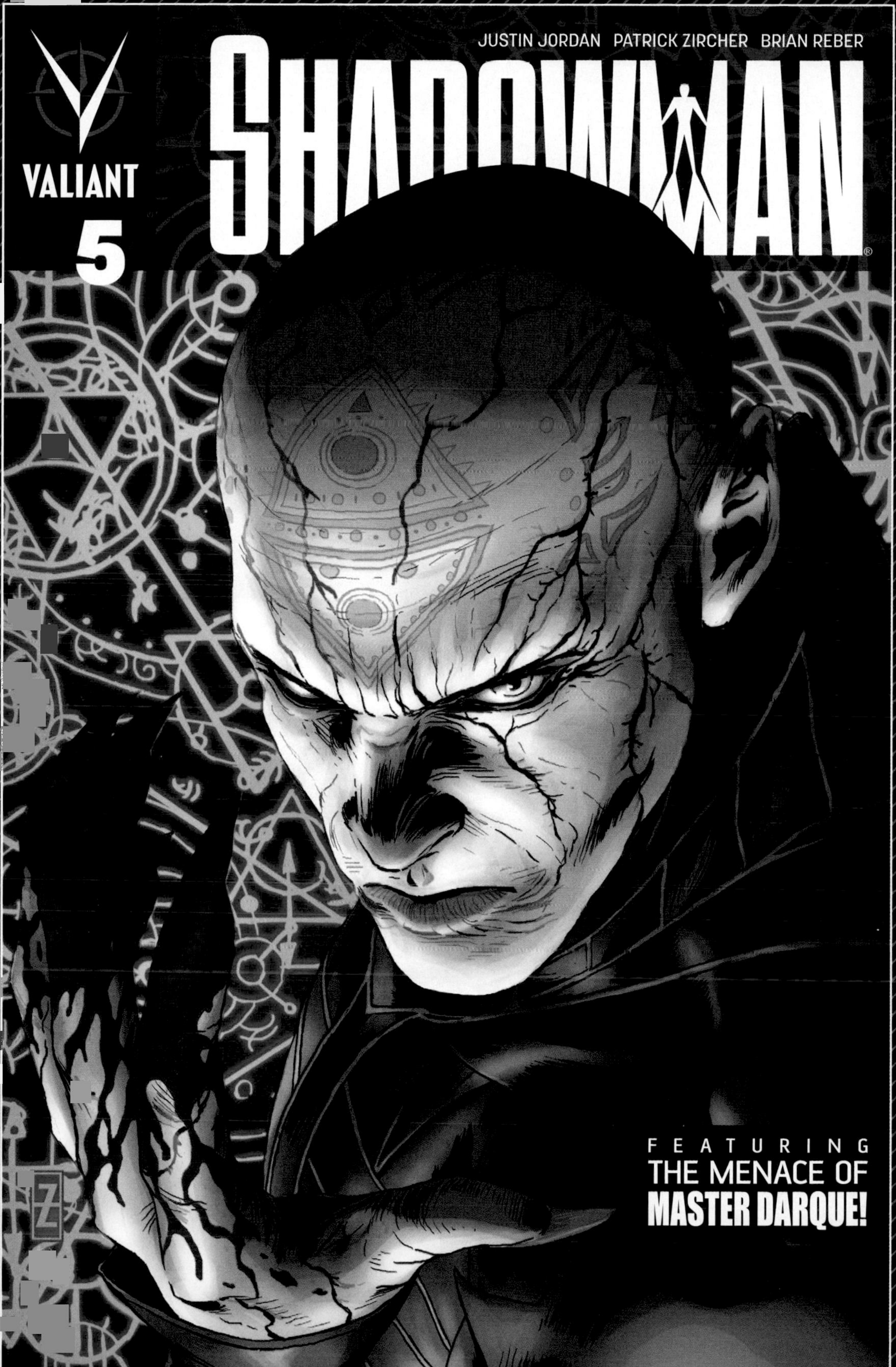
VALIANT
5
JUSTIN JORDAN PATRICK ZIRCHER BRIAN REBER
SHADOWMAN
FEATURING
THE MENACE OF
MASTER DARQUE!

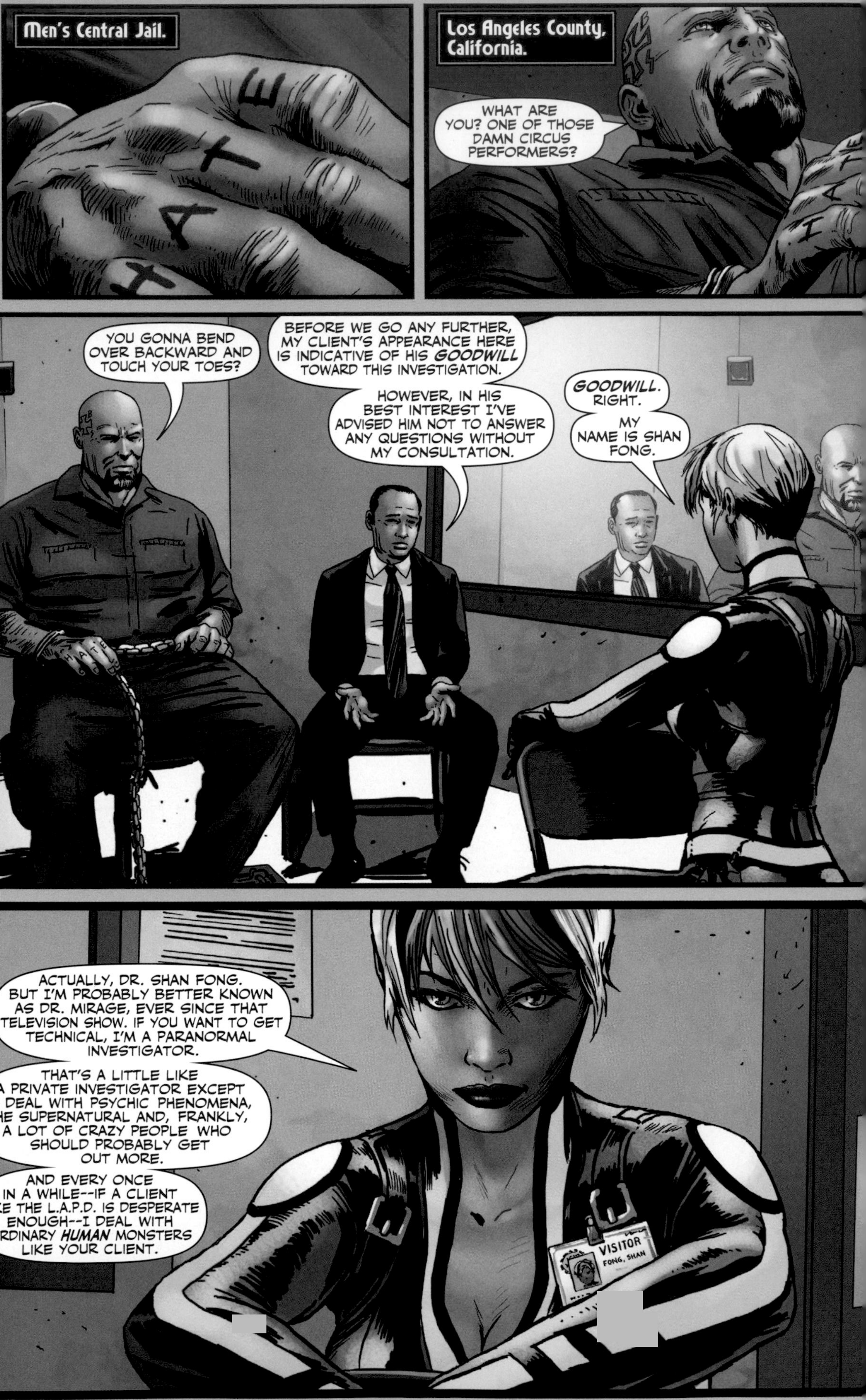
Men's Central Jail.
Los Angeles County, California.
WHAT ARE YOU? ONE OF THOSE DAMN CIRCUS PERFORMERS?
YOU GONNA BEND OVER BACKWARD AND TOUCH YOUR TOES?
BEFORE WE GO ANY FURTHER, MY CLIENT'S APPEARANCE HERE IS INDICATIVE OF HIS *GOODWILL* TOWARD THIS INVESTIGATION.
HOWEVER, IN HIS BEST INTEREST I'VE ADVISED HIM NOT TO ANSWER ANY QUESTIONS WITHOUT MY CONSULTATION.
GOODWILL. RIGHT.
MY NAME IS SHAN FONG.
ACTUALLY, DR. SHAN FONG. BUT I'M PROBABLY BETTER KNOWN AS DR. MIRAGE, EVER SINCE THAT TELEVISION SHOW. IF YOU WANT TO GET TECHNICAL, I'M A PARANORMAL INVESTIGATOR.
THAT'S A LITTLE LIKE A PRIVATE INVESTIGATOR EXCEPT I DEAL WITH PSYCHIC PHENOMENA, THE SUPERNATURAL AND, FRANKLY, A LOT OF CRAZY PEOPLE WHO SHOULD PROBABLY GET OUT MORE.
AND EVERY ONCE IN A WHILE--IF A CLIENT LIKE THE L.A.P.D. IS DESPERATE ENOUGH--I DEAL WITH ORDINARY *HUMAN* MONSTERS LIKE YOUR CLIENT.
VISITOR
FONG, SHAN

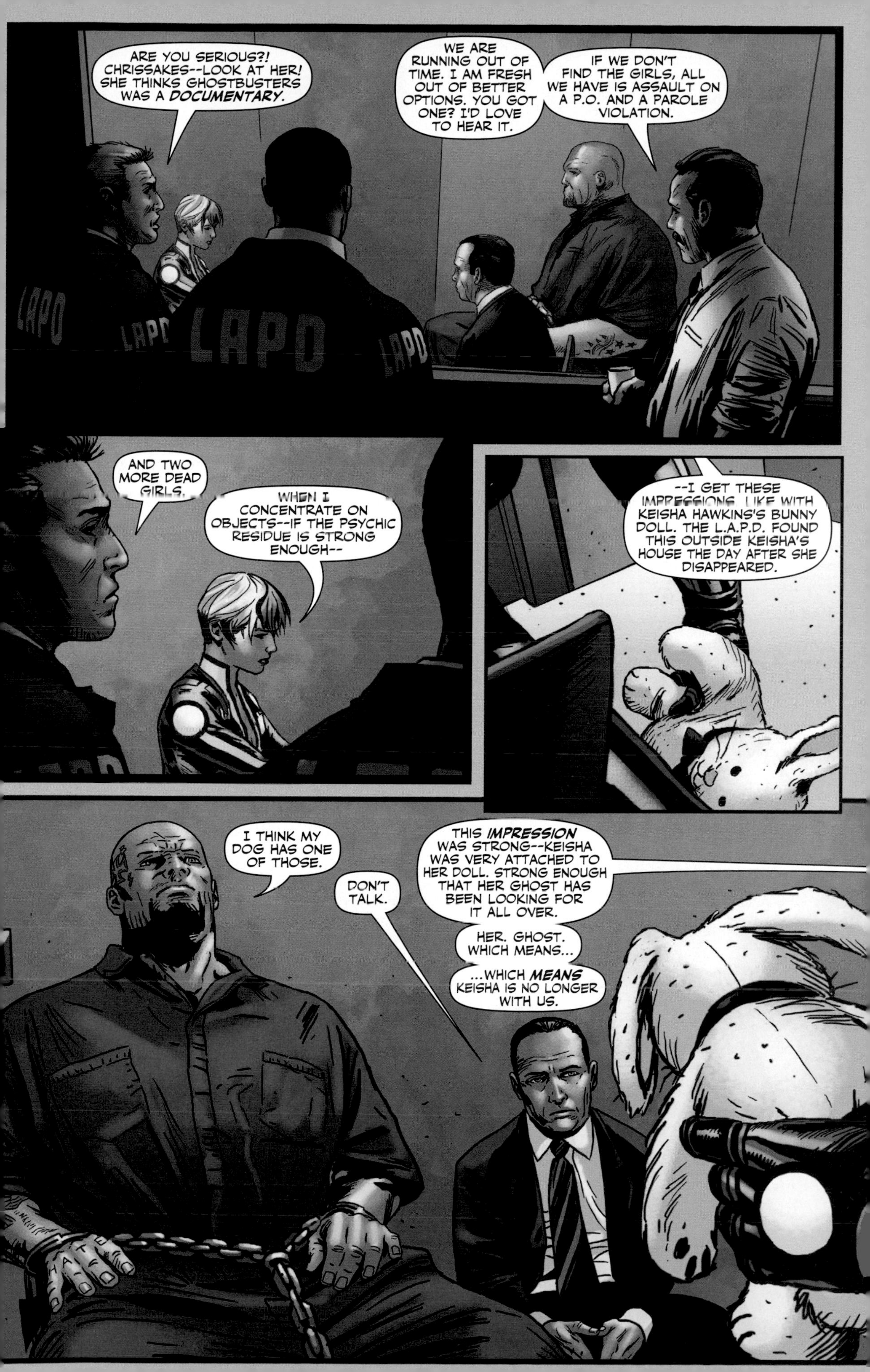
ARE YOU SERIOUS?! CHRISSAKES--LOOK AT HER! SHE THINKS GHOSTBUSTERS WAS A DOCUMENTARY.
WE ARE RUNNING OUT OF TIME. I AM FRESH OUT OF BETTER OPTIONS. YOU GOT ONE? I'D LOVE TO HEAR IT.
IF WE DON'T FIND THE GIRLS, ALL WE HAVE IS ASSAULT ON A P.O. AND A PAROLE VIOLATION.
LAPD
AND TWO MORE DEAD GIRLS.
WHEN I CONCENTRATE ON OBJECTS--IF THE PSYCHIC RESIDUE IS STRONG ENOUGH--
--I GET THESE IMPRESSIONS. LIKE WITH KEISHA HAWKINS'S BUNNY DOLL. THE L.A.P.D. FOUND THIS OUTSIDE KEISHA'S HOUSE THE DAY AFTER SHE DISAPPEARED.
I THINK MY DOG HAS ONE OF THOSE.
DON'T TALK.
THIS IMPRESSION WAS STRONG--KEISHA WAS VERY ATTACHED TO HER DOLL. STRONG ENOUGH THAT HER GHOST HAS BEEN LOOKING FOR IT ALL OVER.
HER. GHOST. WHICH MEANS...
...WHICH MEANS KEISHA IS NO LONGER WITH US.

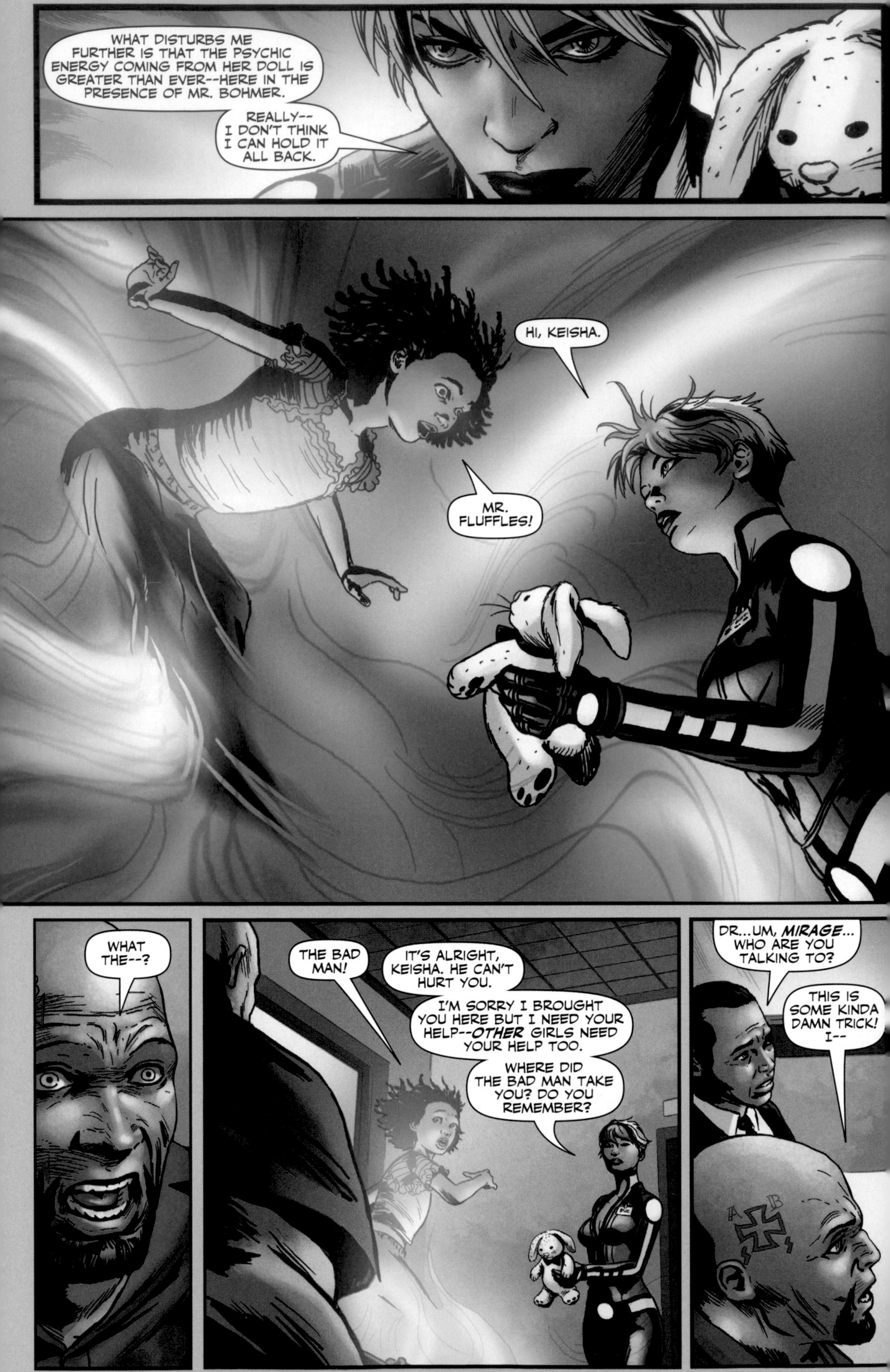
WHAT DISTURBS ME FURTHER IS THAT THE PSYCHIC ENERGY COMING FROM HER DOLL IS GREATER THAN EVER--HERE IN THE PRESENCE OF MR. BOHMER.
REALLY-- I DON'T THINK I CAN HOLD IT ALL BACK.
HI, KEISHA.
MR. FLUFFLES!
WHAT THE--?
THE BAD MAN!
IT'S ALRIGHT, KEISHA. HE CAN'T HURT YOU.
I'M SORRY I BROUGHT YOU HERE BUT I NEED YOUR HELP--OTHER GIRLS NEED YOUR HELP TOO.
WHERE DID THE BAD MAN TAKE YOU? DO YOU REMEMBER?
DR...UM, MIRAGE... WHO ARE YOU TALKING TO?
THIS IS SOME KINDA DAMN TRICK! I--

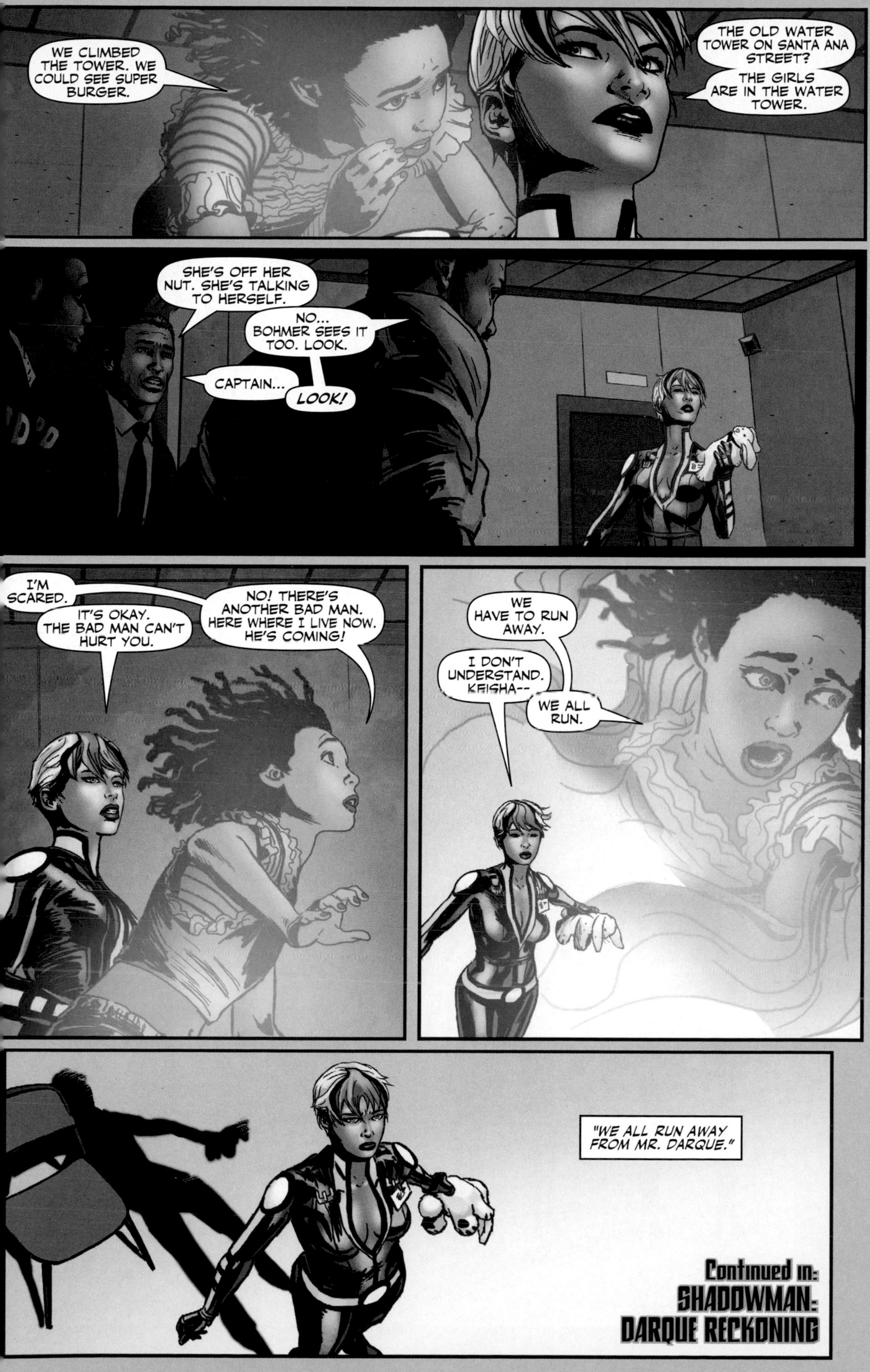
WE CLIMBED THE TOWER. WE COULD SEE SUPER BURGER.
THE OLD WATER TOWER ON SANTA ANA STREET?
THE GIRLS ARE IN THE WATER TOWER.
SHE'S OFF HER NUT. SHE'S TALKING TO HERSELF.
NO... BOHMER SEES IT TOO. LOOK.
CAPTAIN...
LOOK!
I'M SCARED.
IT'S OKAY. THE BAD MAN CAN'T HURT YOU.
NO! THERE'S ANOTHER BAD MAN. HERE WHERE I LIVE NOW. HE'S COMING!
WE HAVE TO RUN AWAY.
I DON'T UNDERSTAND. KEISHA--
WE ALL RUN.
"WE ALL RUN AWAY FROM MR. DARQUE."
Continued in:
SHADOWMAN:
DARQUE RECKONING

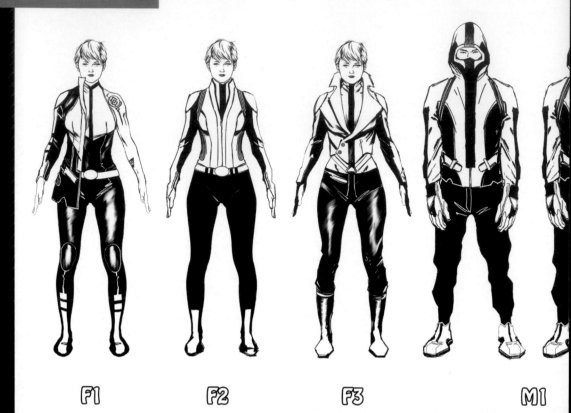

F1   F2   F3   M1

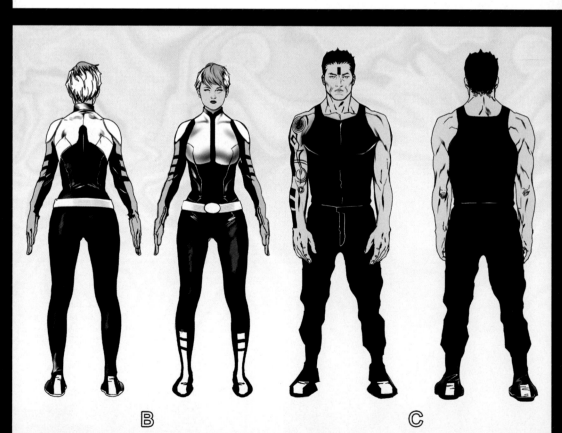

B   C

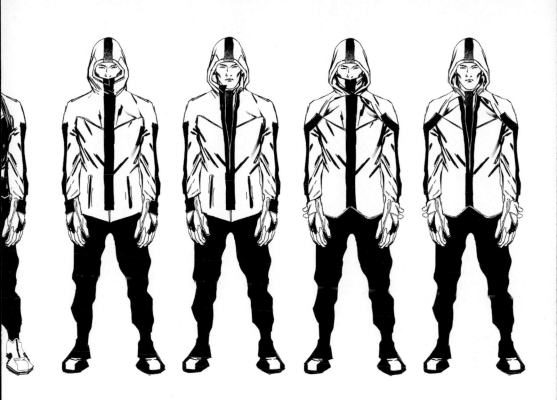

M2

M3

THE DEATH-DEFYING DOCTOR MIRAGE MINISERIES PROPOSAL

Series pitch (excerpt) by Jen Van Meter • Character designs by Khari Evans

Shan Fong (Doctor Mirage) has little interest in the living or the dead, if she's honest. In the years since Hwen – her husband and fellow paranormal investigator – died, she's been going through the motions, making ends meet and wondering why he is the one departed spirit she can't seem to reach. She tries to put a good face on it, but she really hasn't felt complete without him. When a wealthy but repugnant client's case presents her with the possibility of finding Hwen, Shan is drawn into the sordid results of cold-war era occult experiments and a string of dangerous bargains with otherworldly forces. She thought she was done with this world, but when forced to choose between her personal quest and the safety of the living, Doctor Mirage will discover loyalties and talents she didn't know she had.

We meet Shan reluctantly working with a widows' support group and establish her money troubles, her reluctance to engage with the world of the living, her commitment to the house she and Hwen built, and her relationship with Leo, who, despite his brassy agent's veneer, is intensely loyal to her.

Leo's excited about a great new gig: reclusive billionaire Linton March claims to be burdened with evil spirits, debris from his involvement with the CIA's efforts to beat the Soviets in an occult/paranormal space race. March is willing to pay handsomely for Doctor Mirage's help, but she knows he's withholding information and she really doesn't like him. Shan is prepared to walk when she discovers one of the things he's hiding – a bound "demon" that tells her Hwen is "with the Pale Mistress" and implies it will help her get him back in exchange for its freedom. Shan tells March she's taking the job but has to return home to do research.

A flashback lets us see what Shan and Hwen's life together was like: sexy, fun, action-magic couple, feeling good about the people they helped and the monsters they vanquished. His sudden and mundane death caught her completely off-guard. We get background about her costume and their house.

Shan determines to go to the Pale Mistress – a powerful spirit associated with water and drowning victims – "just to see" if there's any truth in what the imprisoned entity has told her. Such creatures can be deceptive, and she's not willing to let it loose only to find it's lying.

While Shan's bizarre trip to this aspect of the underworld begins, other members of March's cabal discover that he's shared some of their secrets with an outsider; as they confront him and the imprisoned creature, we learn a little more about their pact with one another and with the forces that have maintained their wealth and power. [It's a little like a

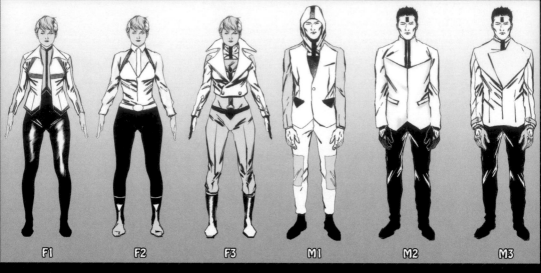

F1 F2 F3 M1 M2 M3

spiritual tontine – the last man standing will amass the arcane power of the others, but also be host to their spirits. What March <u>really</u> wanted was for Shan to help him break the pact in such a way that he gets all the power for himself and cuts the other guys' spirits loose.]

Shan meets spirit guards/secretaries on the path to the dwelling of the Pale Mistress – confirms she's going the right way but sets up dangers ahead: "she will take everything you have."

<u>COSTUME NOTES</u>: Occult practitioners have specialized clothes for a lot of different reasons, but charmed, warded, or blessed clothes – however they <u>look</u> – can function a little like armor when, say, fighting evil spirits. Hwen, who was great at ritual, designed outfits for himself and Shan that were meant to:
    1) protect the wearer – they are like teflon in the spirit world, can't be stained or possessed by the spirits that touch them, so you don't bring back gross psychic residue and have to burn them.
    2) not evoke or appropriate the identity of any specific religious or cultural occult practice since that wasn't his and Shan's way of doing things
    3) inspire confidence in the frightened living by looking specialized – he was thinking of scientists and mechanics
The outfit Shan wears is the only piece she has left that Hwen warded – that's why she wears it all the time.

<u>THE HOUSE</u>: Ghosts and spirits don't knock, and they don't much care how late you were up last night or whether you feel like dealing with them. And when you have powerful magical items, all manner of crackpots try to bust into your place to take them. When Hwen was alive, he and Shan carefully remodeled a sweet little beach cottage into the perfect haven for themselves. Every opening is triple-warded, every lock and key is magicked like crazy, the garden is full of useful herbs and the library is carefully organized (or was, before Hwen died). The whole property is a powerful arcane safe house; it's the one place where Shan can be assured of getting a good night's sleep, and it's the place where she feels closest to her late husband.

And even though it's tiny, they got crazy lucky with location; the property taxes alone are killing her.

<u>RELIGIOUS/CULTURAL INTERPRETATION & THE WORLD OF SPIRIT</u>: All the spirit-world stuff is one big soup of powers and forces. Practitioners among the living come to it through various cultural or religious traditions that color what they see when encountering entities of Spirit. An exorcist may see a powerful evil spirit as a horned and tailed "demon," but a Taoist practitioner right next to her might see a child with a dog's head and a four-foot tongue of fire. They might use very different rituals to summon the creature as well, but to the spirit, both sound and "feel" the same. For someone like Shan, who approaches this world from a polyglot background, an encounter with the spirit world is one of fluid perceptions – she may see the Pale Mistress, for instance, as a Naiad, a queen made of pearls and coral, Neptune, a drowned corpse, a talking monstrous octopus and then as a phosphorescent child with angler-fish teeth, all in quick succession, but she knows she's seeing the same entity.

The trick when dealing with the spirits of the recently dead, in particular, is that they are often still playing by the rules as they understood them in life – you have to know what they believed in order to engage them, because they are waiting for you to speak their specific language, whereas older, more powerful spirits, or those that were never bound to this plane, can understand almost any cultural language you might care to speak, but are waiting for you to observe the customs or laws they care about.

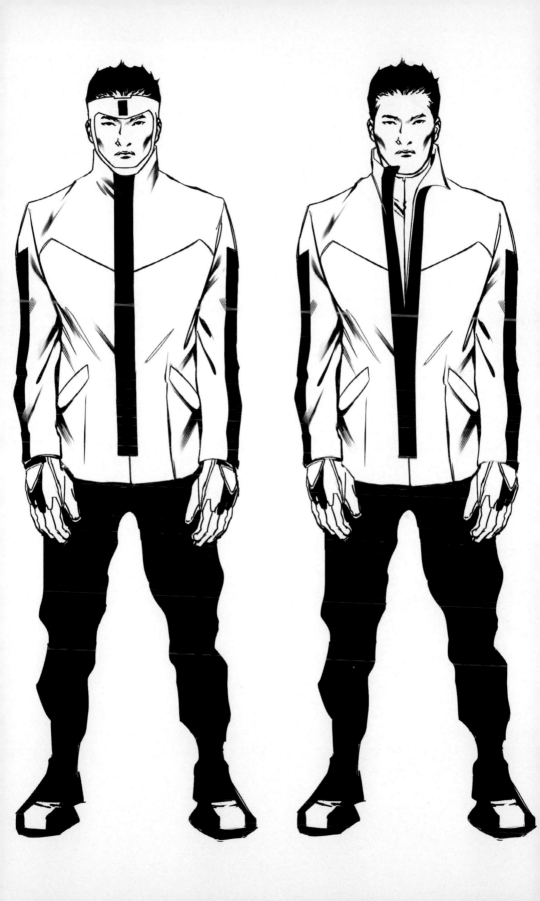

DOCTOR MIRAGE COLORING PROCESS

Commentary by colorist David Baron and artist Roberto de la Torre.

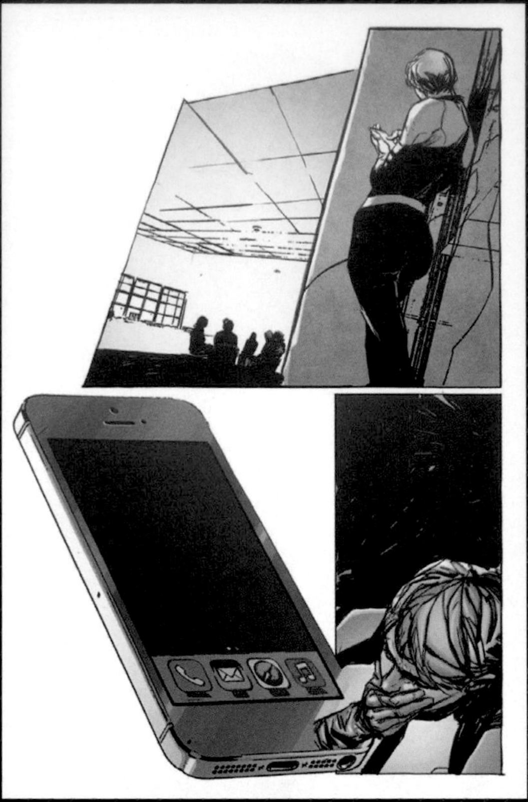

DAVID BARON

My original thought was to render Roberto's art, giving him a different look. Something that was more rendered than my previous work with him. My [initial] attempt did not fit the art or the feel of the book, and after talking with Roberto, I started moving in the right direction. We wanted to keep things to a minimum, focusing on certain aspects of the art, keeping away from overdoing anything.

For the first five pages, I did four to five versions each. The pages [that ran] in the preview were version three of my trial-and-error process as I was finding my voice for the project. [(*What's shown here is an intermediate step on the way to the final color.*)] Roberto's guidance was key to merging his vision with mine. He provided color-contrast samples, texture files, and shadow concepts [(*some of which are featured here*)] to help me visualize the process. I took all that and ran with it.

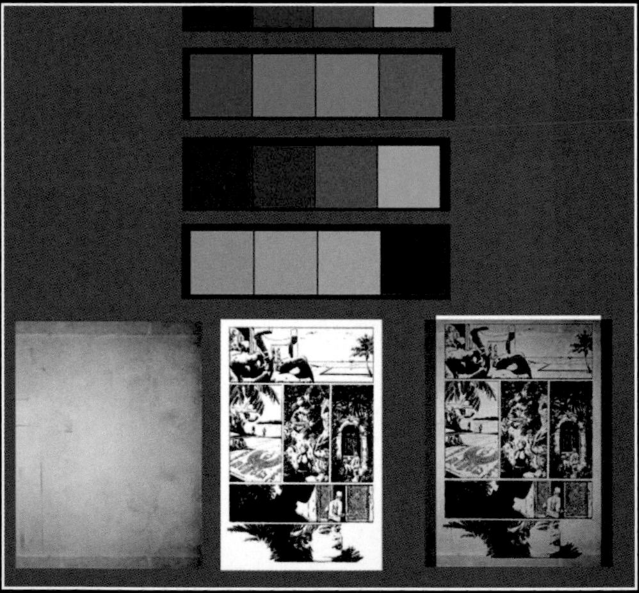

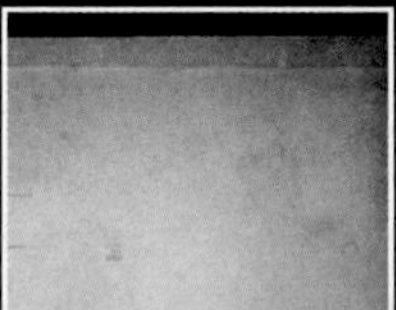

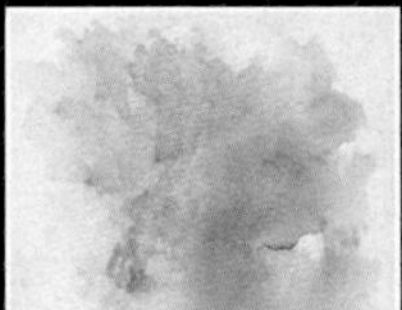

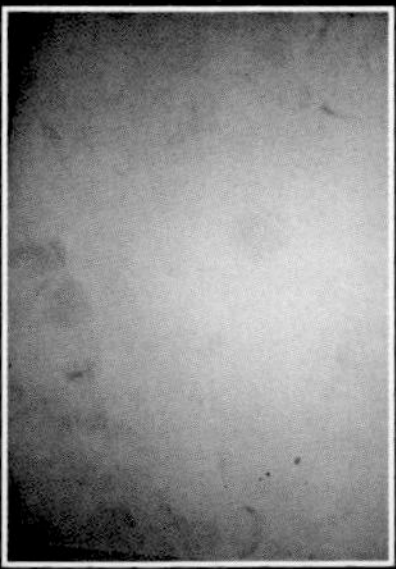

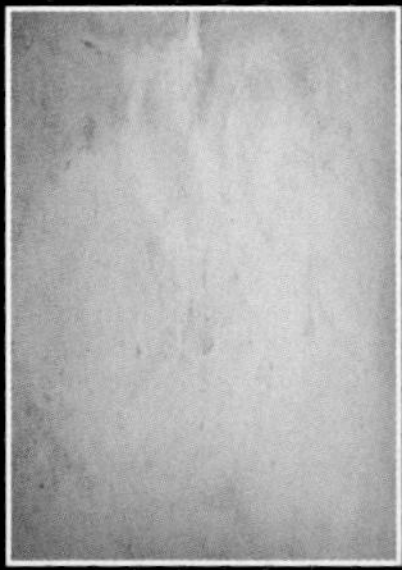

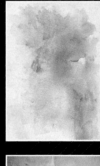

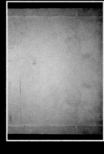

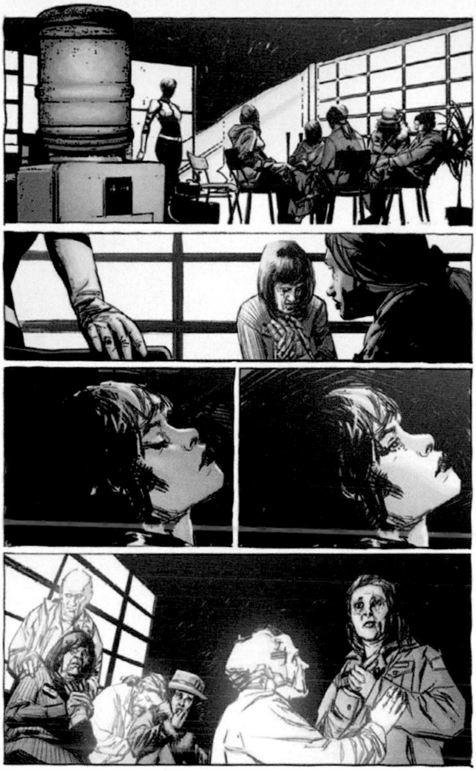

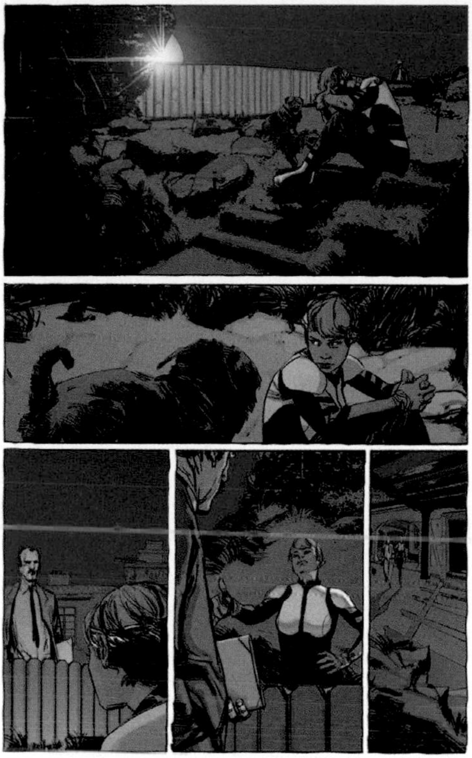

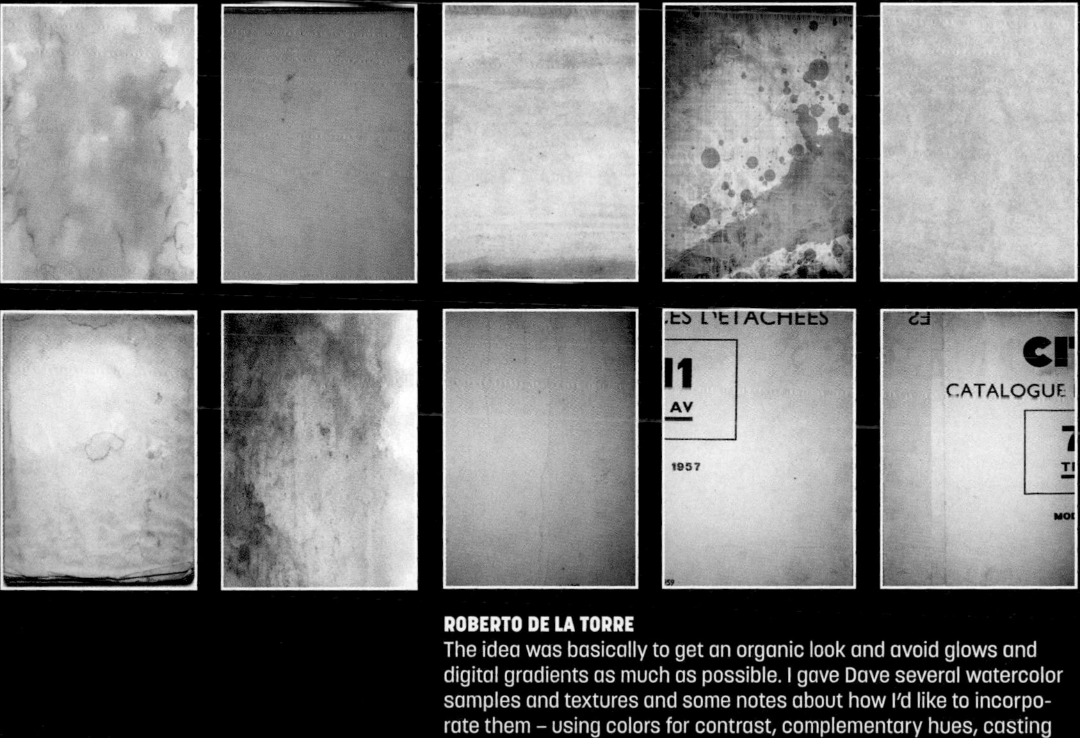
11
AV
1957
CATALOGUE

ROBERTO DE LA TORRE

The idea was basically to get an organic look and avoid glows and digital gradients as much as possible. I gave Dave several watercolor samples and textures and some notes about how I'd like to incorporate them – using colors for contrast, complementary hues, casting

DOCTOR MIRAGE LETTERING PROCESS

Commentary by letterer David Lanphear.

This series stretched me, from recreating smartphone graphics to the creation of a cohesive style for a host of demonic magical characters. Let's dig in!

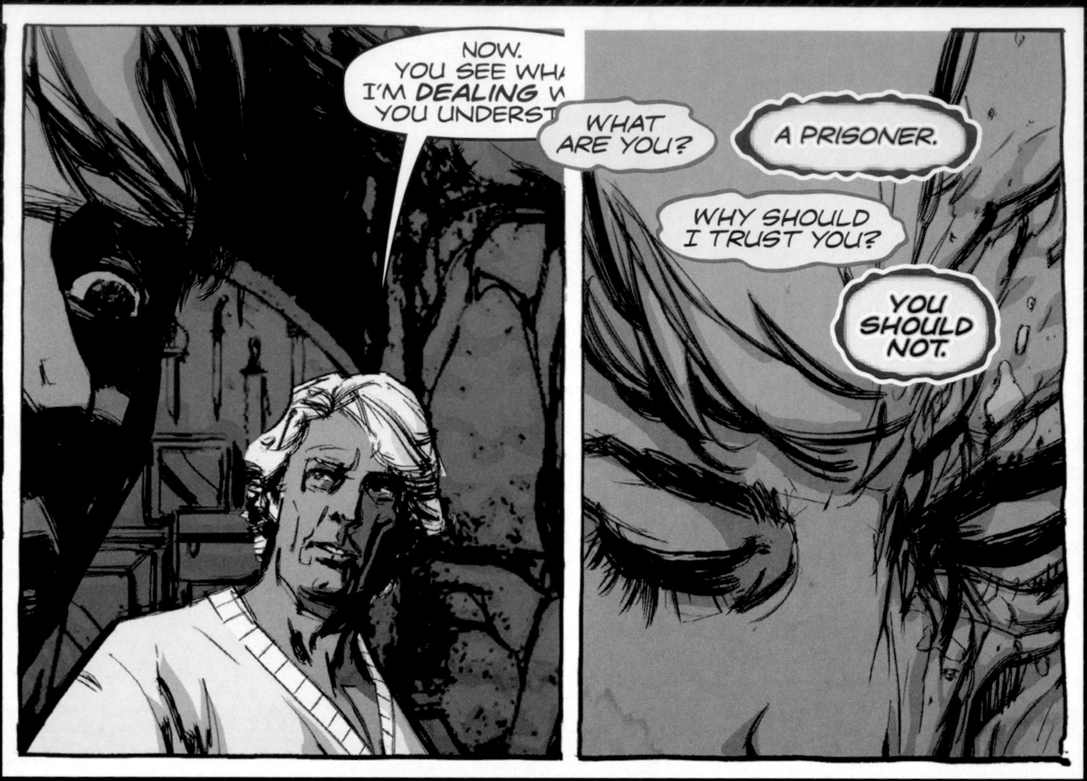
NOW. YOU SEE WHA I'M DEALING W YOU UNDERST
WHAT ARE YOU?
A PRISONER.
WHY SHOULD I TRUST YOU?
YOU SHOULD NOT.

ISSUE 1, PAGE 14, PANELS 3-4 / PAGE 15, PANEL 2
From Jen Van Meter's script:

PANEL 3: We're back here with MARCH, who shows no sign of hearing anything, but looks pleased that Shan seems to have changed her mind...

2 MARCH: Now. You see what I'm dealing with, you under...

PANEL 4: SHAN experiences a mental communion with the PRISONER.

I drafted my lettering to illustrate Linton March's dialogue interrupted by the panel frame. He's not trailing off, but Shan's stopped hearing him because she's suddenly mentally somewhere else. Since the last panel is a metaphoric shot of Shan and the Prisoner communing, I could get away with having their dialogue overlap Linton's, too. Those panel gutters are slices in between moments, and I enjoyed the physical effect of this particular one, slicing right through one reality to show another.

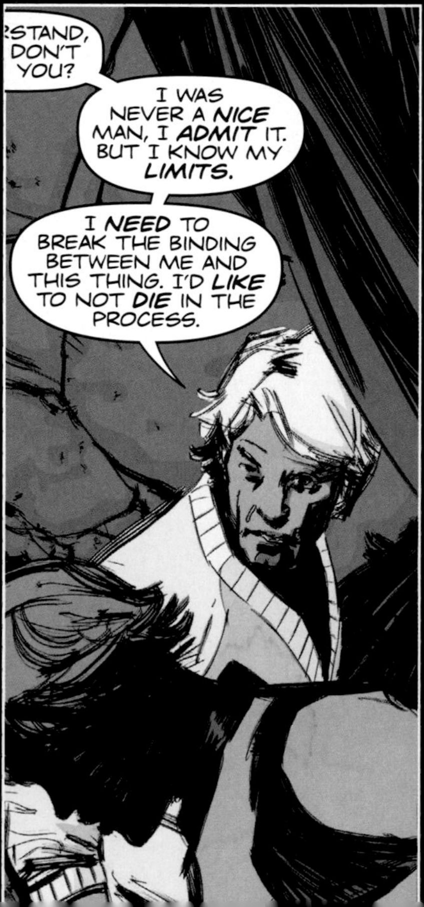
RSTAND, DON'T YOU?
I WAS NEVER A NICE MAN, I ADMIT IT. BUT I KNOW MY LIMITS.
I NEED TO BREAK THE BINDING BETWEEN ME AND THIS THING. I'D LIKE TO NOT DIE IN THE PROCESS.

SSUE 3, PAGES 11 AND 12

DEMON BALLOONS!
There are some squishy, wobbly balloons all over these pages. The look is consistent overall to each, because they're all otherworldly demons. They're styled to the individual attitude of the characters, though. The Prisoner's balloons are substantial with heavy borders. But they're also calm, whispering, soft-toned, illustrated by the slight blur on the borders and his words. Ivros, on the other hand... his font is big, craggy, dark, no blur, which suits his dominant character as a conqueror and warrior. This brute talks in gravelly shouts. His sibilant lackeys like Drit all have a snaky look to their balloons and lettering because they're inferior to Ivros and don't dare raise their voices to him!

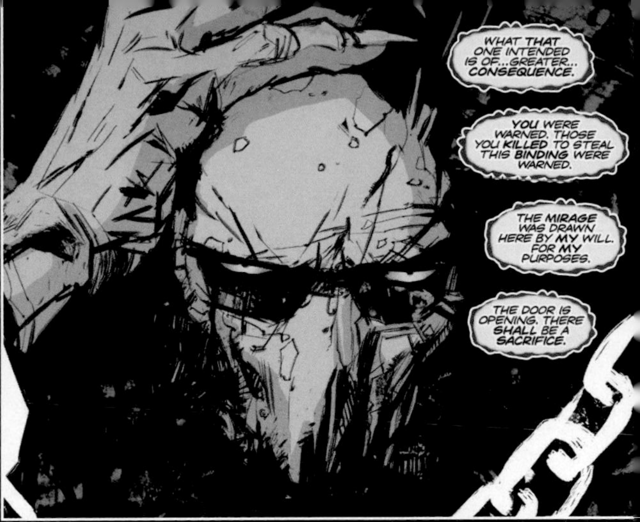
WHAT THAT ONE INTENDED IS OF...GREATER... CONSEQUENCE.
YOU WERE WARNED. THOSE YOU KILLED TO STEAL THIS BINDING WERE WARNED.
THE MIRAGE WAS DRAWN HERE BY MY WILL. FOR MY PURPOSES.
THE DOOR IS OPENING. THERE SHALL BE A SACRIFICE.

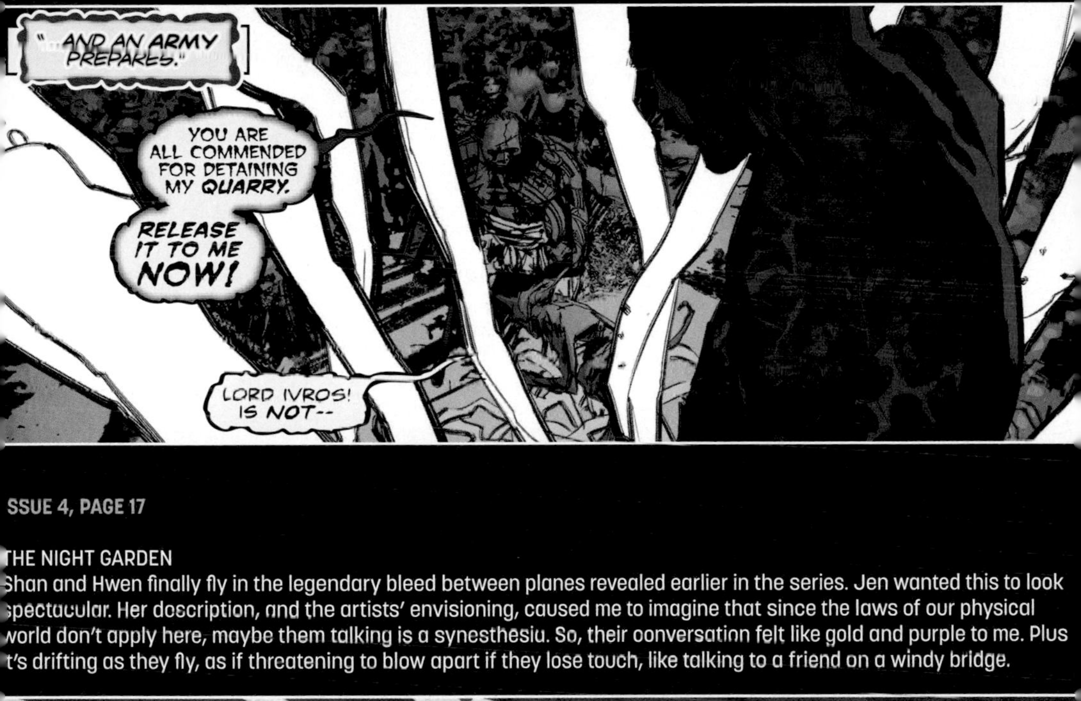
"...AND AN ARMY PREPARES."
YOU ARE ALL COMMENDED FOR DETAINING MY QUARRY.
RELEASE IT TO ME NOW!
LORD IVROS! IS NOT--

SSUE 4, PAGE 17

THE NIGHT GARDEN
Shan and Hwen finally fly in the legendary bleed between planes revealed earlier in the series. Jen wanted this to look spectacular. Her description, and the artists' envisioning, caused me to imagine that since the laws of our physical world don't apply here, maybe them talking is a synesthesia. So, their conversation felt like gold and purple to me. Plus it's drifting as they fly, as if threatening to blow apart if they lose touch, like talking to a friend on a windy bridge.

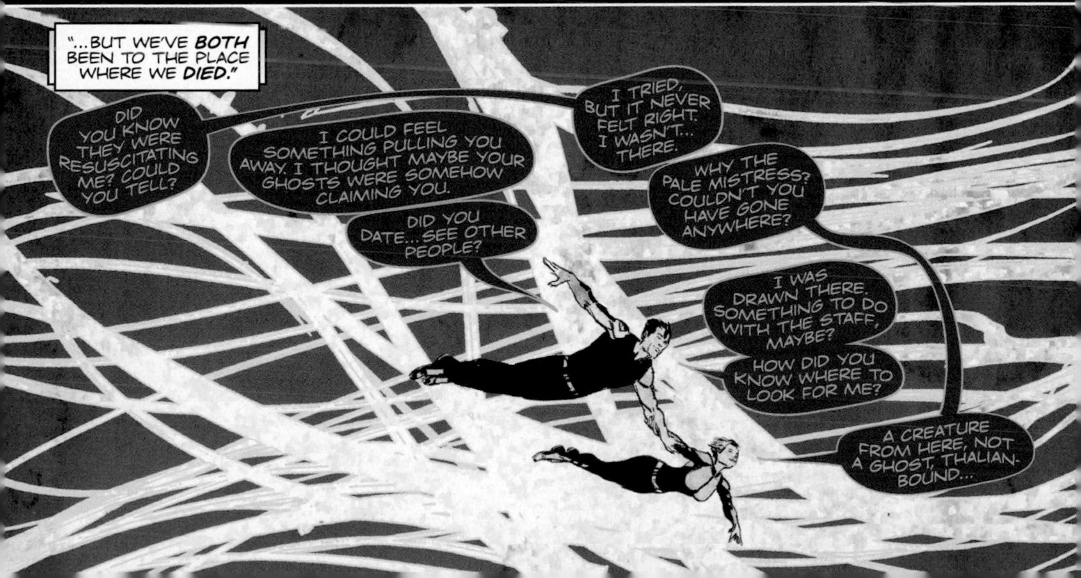
"...BUT WE'VE BOTH BEEN TO THE PLACE WHERE WE DIED."
DID YOU KNOW THEY WERE RESUSCITATING ME? COULD YOU TELL?
I COULD FEEL SOMETHING PULLING YOU AWAY. I THOUGHT MAYBE YOUR GHOSTS WERE SOMEHOW CLAIMING YOU.
I TRIED, BUT IT NEVER FELT RIGHT. I WASN'T... THERE.
DID YOU DATE... SEE OTHER PEOPLE?
WHY THE PALE MISTRESS? COULDN'T YOU HAVE GONE ANYWHERE?
I WAS DRAWN THERE. SOMETHING TO DO WITH THE STAFF, MAYBE?
HOW DID YOU KNOW WHERE TO LOOK FOR ME?
A CREATURE FROM HERE, NOT A GHOST, THALIAN-BOUND...

THE DEATH-DEFYING DOCTOR MIRAGE #1 PAGE FOURTEEN

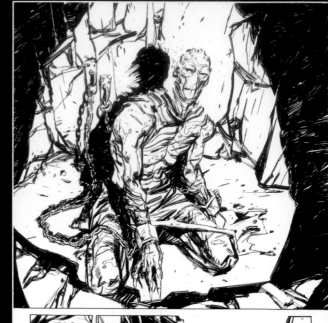

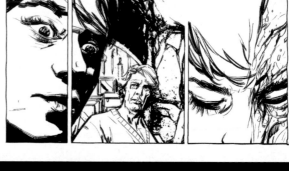

PANEL 1: Big. We're looking down into a shallow pit, maybe two feet deep, in which THE PRISONER crouches, withdrawn. Once an amazing androgynous creature of pure light, beauty and knowledge, just going about its business in the realm of Spirit, it was mistaken for a demon, kidnapped to this plane and bound by chains it cannot break. A hundred years of torture, squalor and slavery have rendered it unrecognizable; desiccated, extremely long, withered limbs, dirty rags, a withdrawn crouch, matted hair, scars, claw-like hands and feet. <<I think we should avoid wings.>> Its majesty would have once inspired awe, but in this degraded state, it can only sicken and horrify. But those eyes. It's staring right at us with big eyes that burn as if the skull of this creature were a furnace. We can see that it is shackled with chains that look like the one on March's wrist.

1 PRISONER/EFFECT:
Li Hwen Mirage abides with the Pale Mistress.

PANEL 2: Small. Inset on 1? SHAN's EYES reflect the fire.

NO COPY

PANEL 3: We're back here with MARCH, who shows no sign of hearing anything, but looks pleased that Shan seems to have changed her mind. SHAN looks into the opening of the alcove where the prisoner is kept, steadying herself against the stone wall.

2 MARCH:
Now. You see what I'm <u>dealing</u> with, you under...

PANEL 4: SHAN experiences a mental communion with the PRISONER. Is it just them, falling together through blackness? Is it a face-to-face image, grounded against that same crazy eye-fire?

3 SHAN/TAILLESS:
What are you?

4 PRISONER/TAILLESS:
A prisoner.

5 SHAN/TAILLESS:
Why should I trust you?

6 PRISONER/TAILLESS:
<u>You should not.</u>

THE DEATH-DEFYING DOCTOR MIRAGE #1, p. 14
Written by JEN VAN METER
Art by ROBERTO DE LA TORRE
Color by DAVID BARON

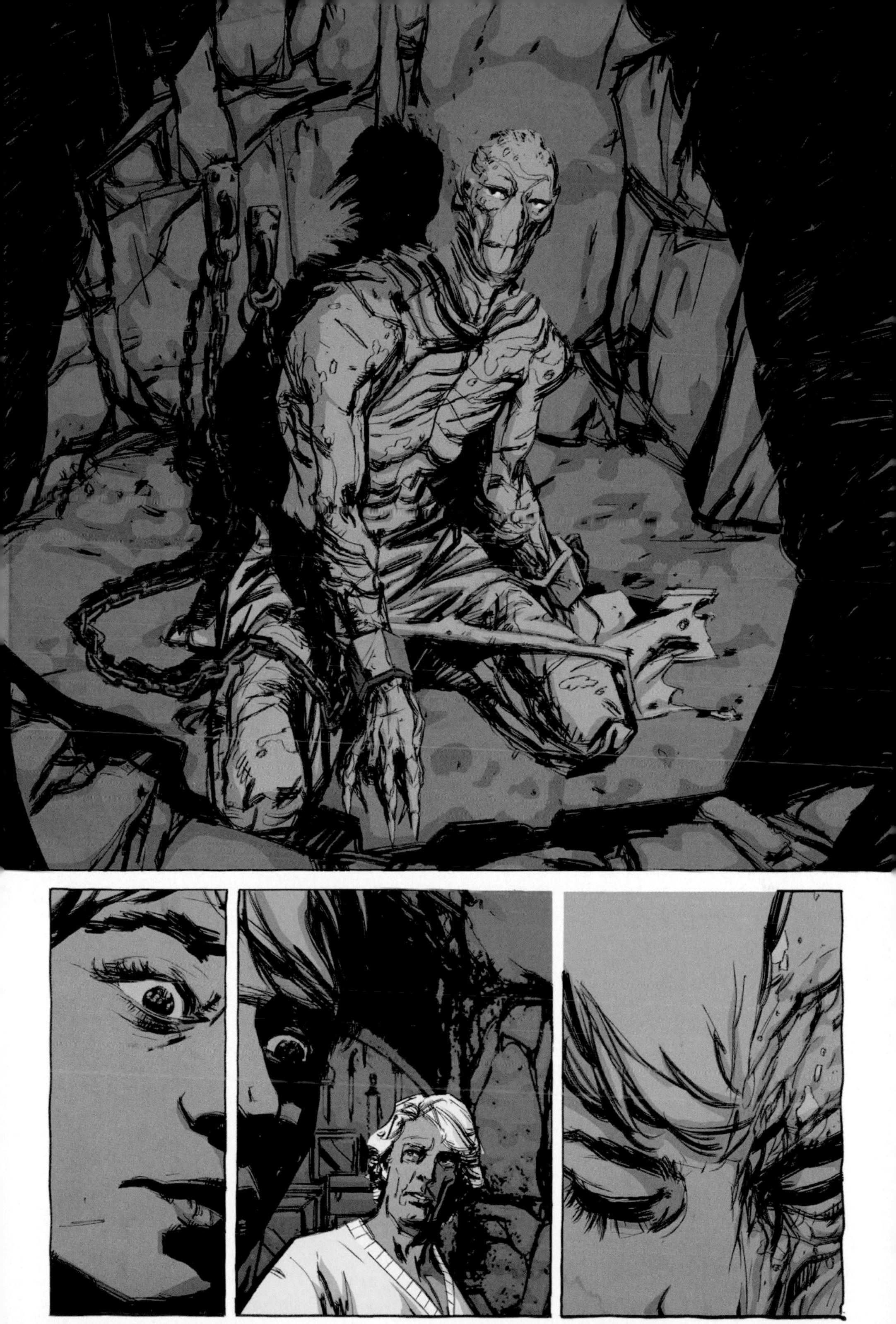

THE DEATH-DEFYING DOCTOR MIRAGE #1 PAGE FIFTEEN

PANEL 1: So this could be broken down into three panels, or just be big and splashy. The main thing is that Shan, while unharmed, is not "safe" – this experience is raw, elemental, vast and scary. It's neither gory nor sexy – this creature is basically an angel – but nothing about the experience should tell Shan "it's cool, this is one of the good guys," either.

1 SHAN/TAILLESS:
What do you want?

2 PRISONER/TAILLESS:
What does any Prisoner want?

3 PRISONER/TAILLESS:
I ask nothing. You will do as you will.

4 SHAN/TAILLESS
I don't want to work for him.

5 PRISONER/TAILLESS:
This is your path, not his.

6 PRISONER/TAILLESS:
Still he will give you things you need.

PANEL 2: Almost identical to Page 14, Panel 3, as if only a second has passed. SHAN has turned toward MARCH, away from the prisoner, bringing a hand up to push hair out her face, baffled.

7 MARCH:
...stand, don't you? I was never a nice man, I admit it. But I know my limits.

8 MARCH/link:
I need to know how to cut it loose. I'd like to not die in the process.

PANEL 3: Tighter on SHAN – pushing her hair back, thinking.

9 SHAN:
I'm going to need to do some homework. I'll have to borrow some stuff.

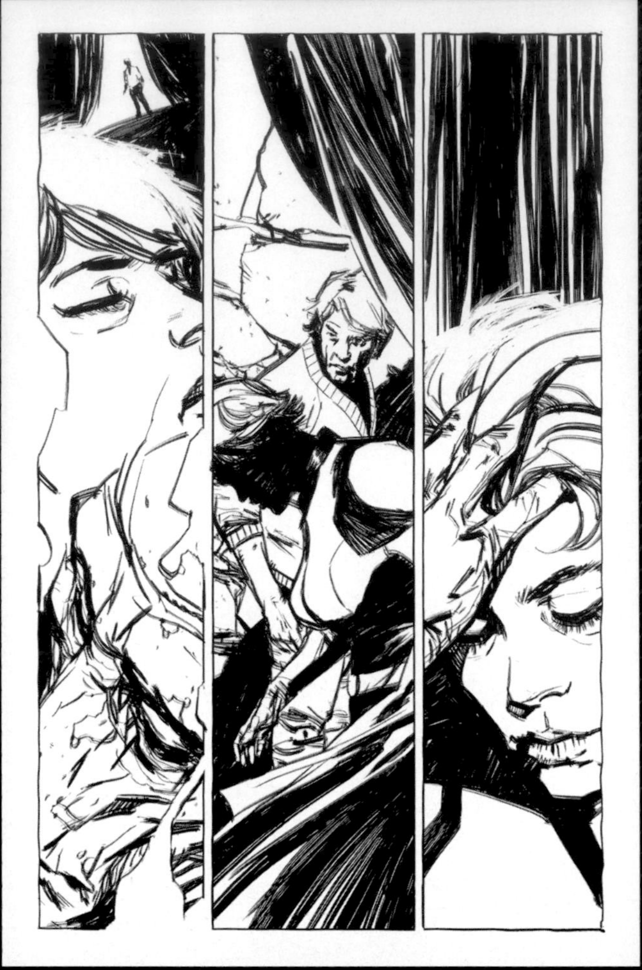

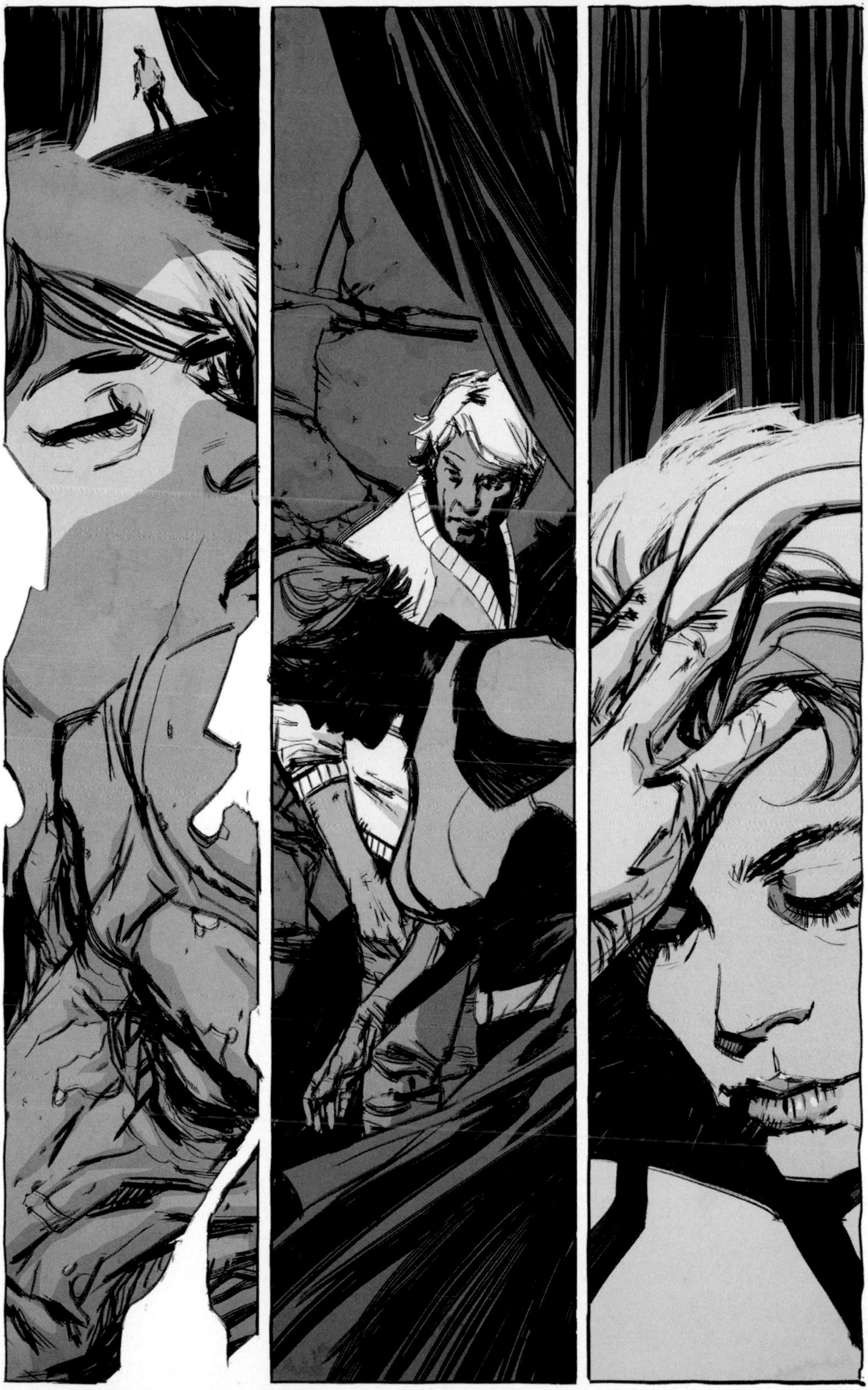

THE DEATH-DEFYING DOCTOR MIRAGE #1

PAGE SIXTEEN

PANEL 1: From a shelf full of small objects, Shan's hand choosing a little bundle of dark/black bones bound together with a ragged scrap of cloth.

NO COPY

PANEL 2: SHAN has taken the stopper out of a little ceramic bottle, sniffing the stinky contents.

NO COPY

PANEL 3: An amulet hanging from a hook with several other pendants and such. Shan's hand has pulled this one out from amongst the others: a cat-like eye framed by leaf shapes, bronze with maybe a jewel for part of the eye?

NO COPY

PANEL 4: Amongst the many knives arranged and displayed here, there's a <u>very</u> old one, Iron Age workmanship; small, fat blade like a punch dagger, only where the handle should be is shaped like the bowl of a spoon or ladle – hard to imagine how one would hold it easily to use either end.

NO COPY

PANEL 5: They've gone back up to the library level; colors are a little brighter, a little more light here and over the next panels. Shan's hand removes a small book from a shelf – a few thick pages bound between carved wooden covers – the carvings represent a sort of elaborate stylized tree, or maybe a river and tributaries?

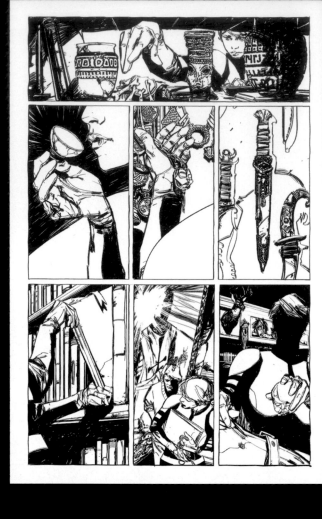

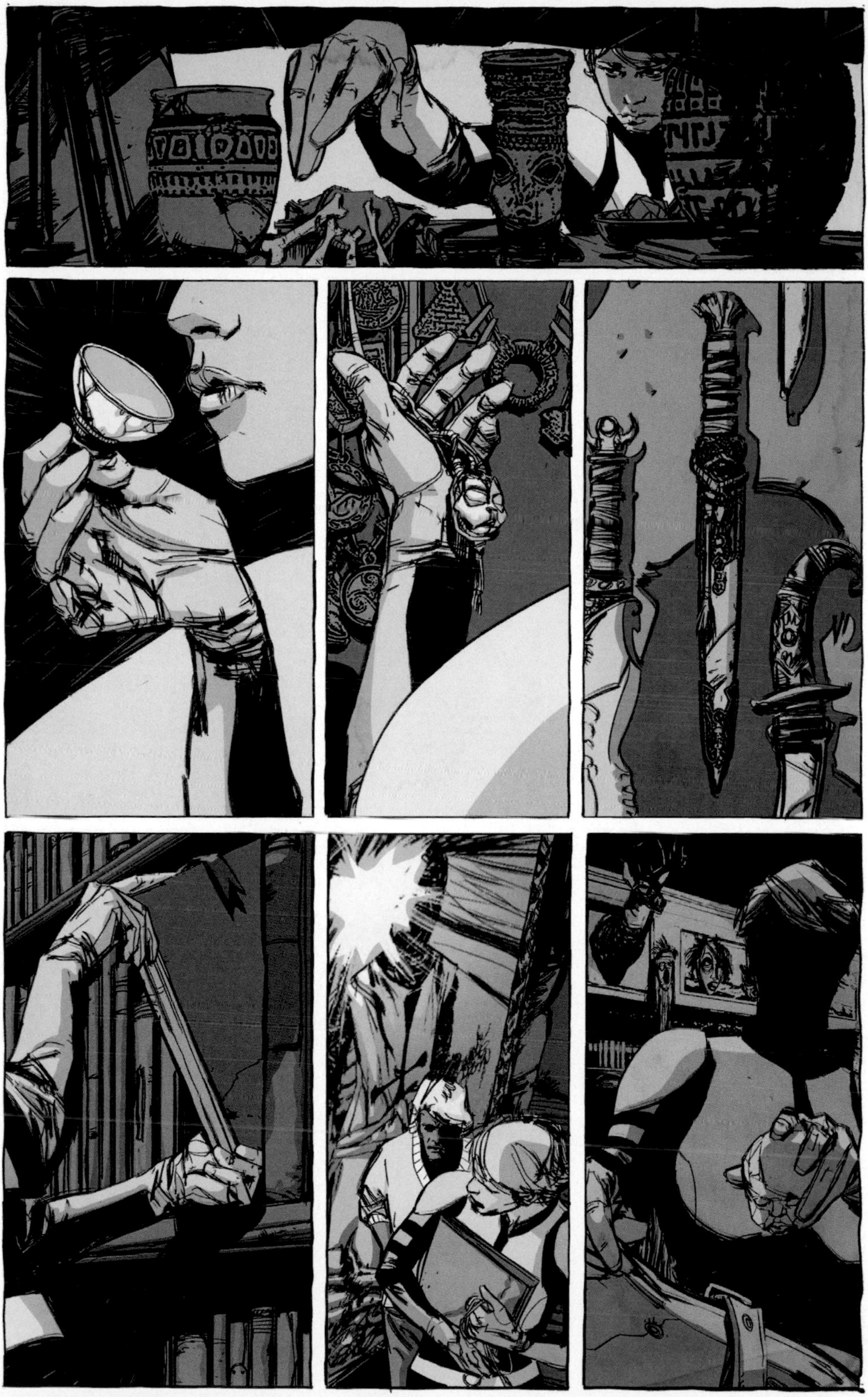

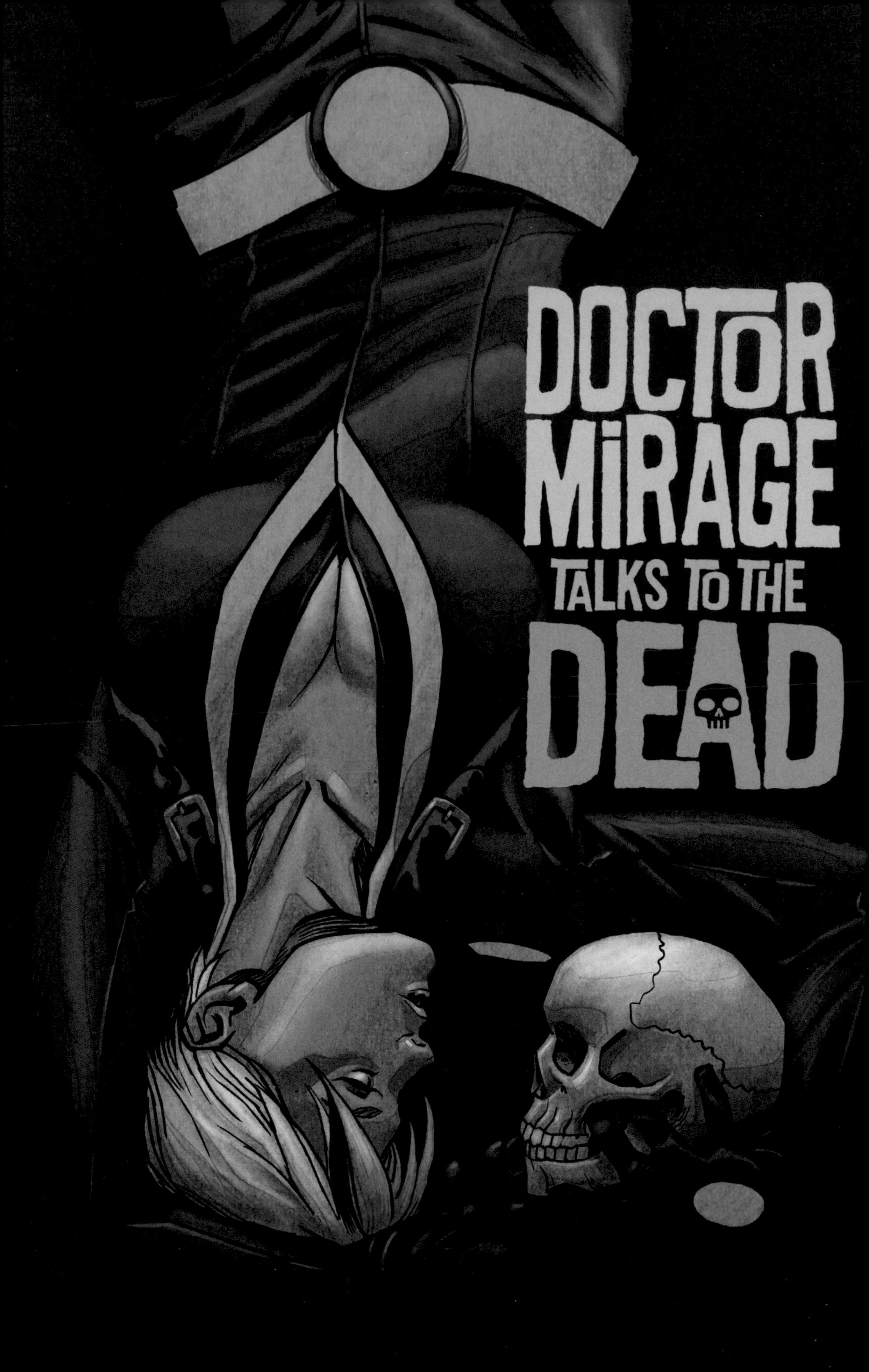
DOCTOR MIRAGE
TALKS TO THE
DEAD

SHADOWMAN #7 VARIANT COVER (facing)
Art by DAVE JOHNSON

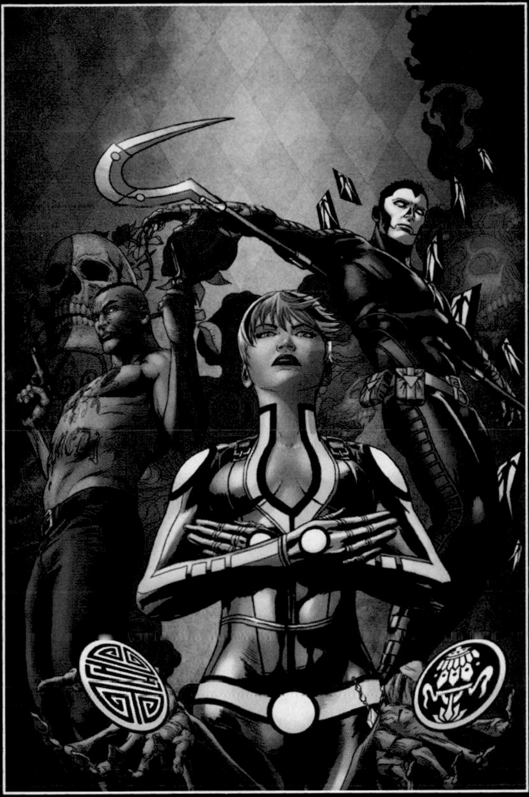

SHADOWMAN #7 COVER
Art by PATRICK ZIRCHER with BRIAN REBER

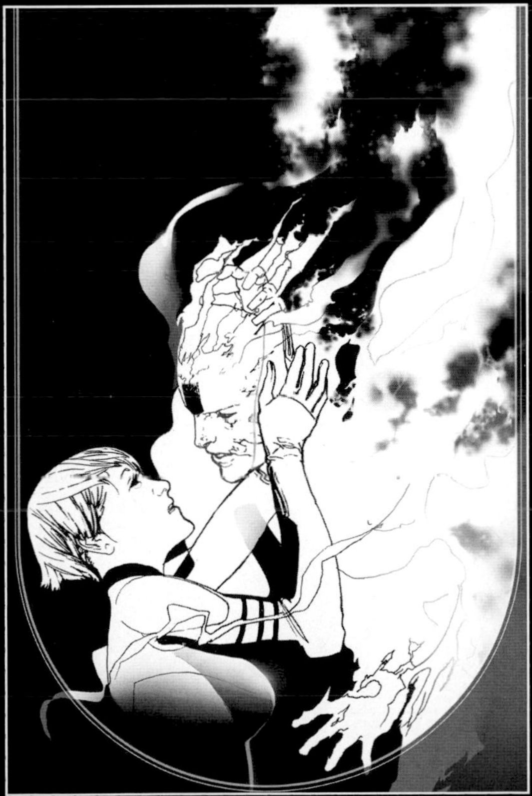

THE DEATH-DEFYING DOCTOR MIRAGE #1 COVER
Art by TRAVEL FOREMAN

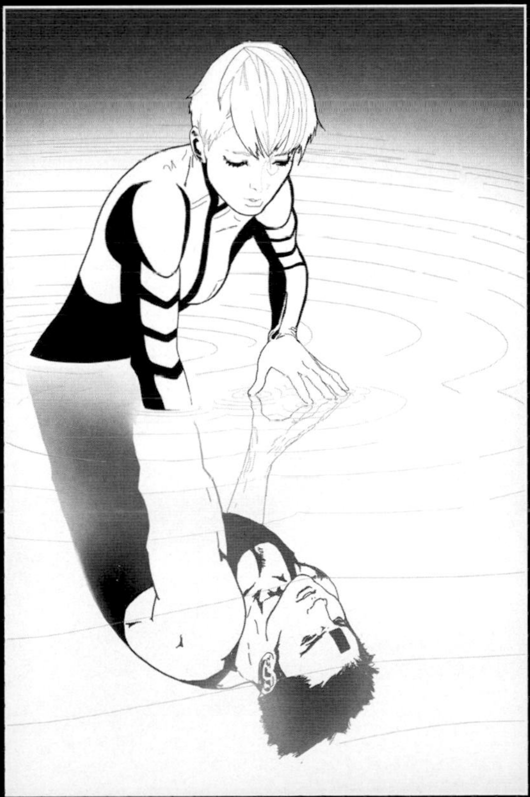

THE DEATH-DEFYING DOCTOR MIRAGE #2 COVER
Art by TRAVEL FOREMAN

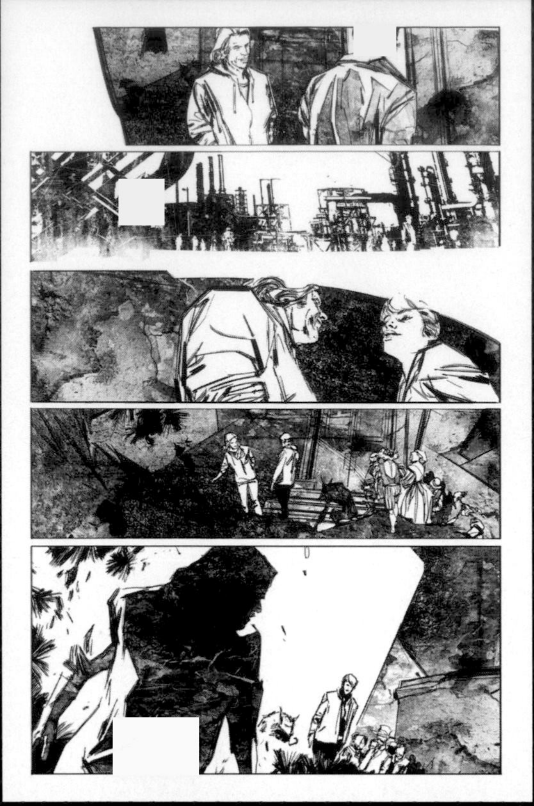

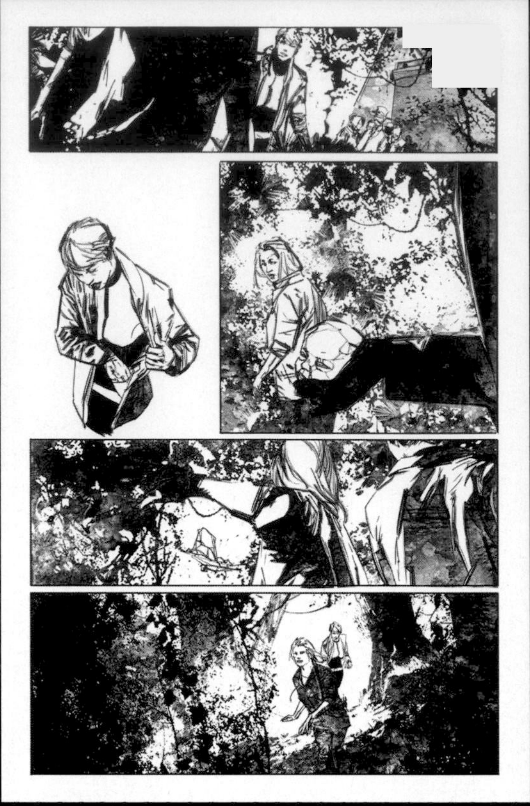

THE DEATH-DEFYING DOCTOR MIRAGE #2,
pages 7, 8, 12, and (facing) 13
Art by ROBERTO DE LA TORRE

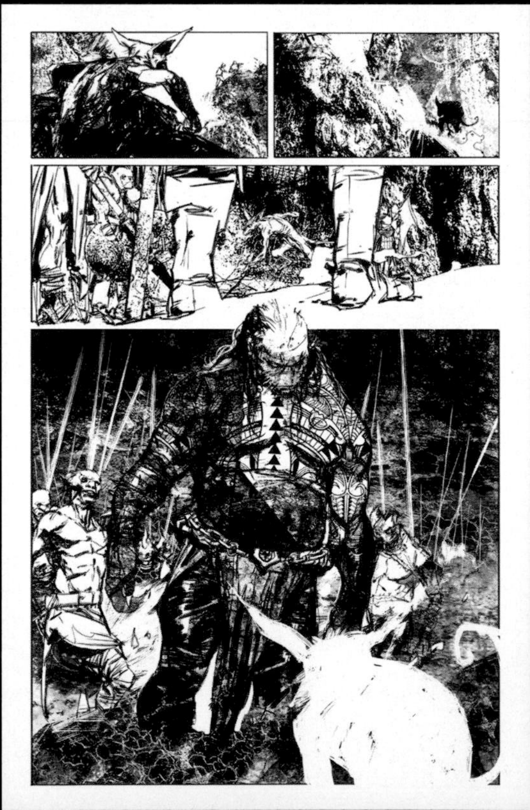

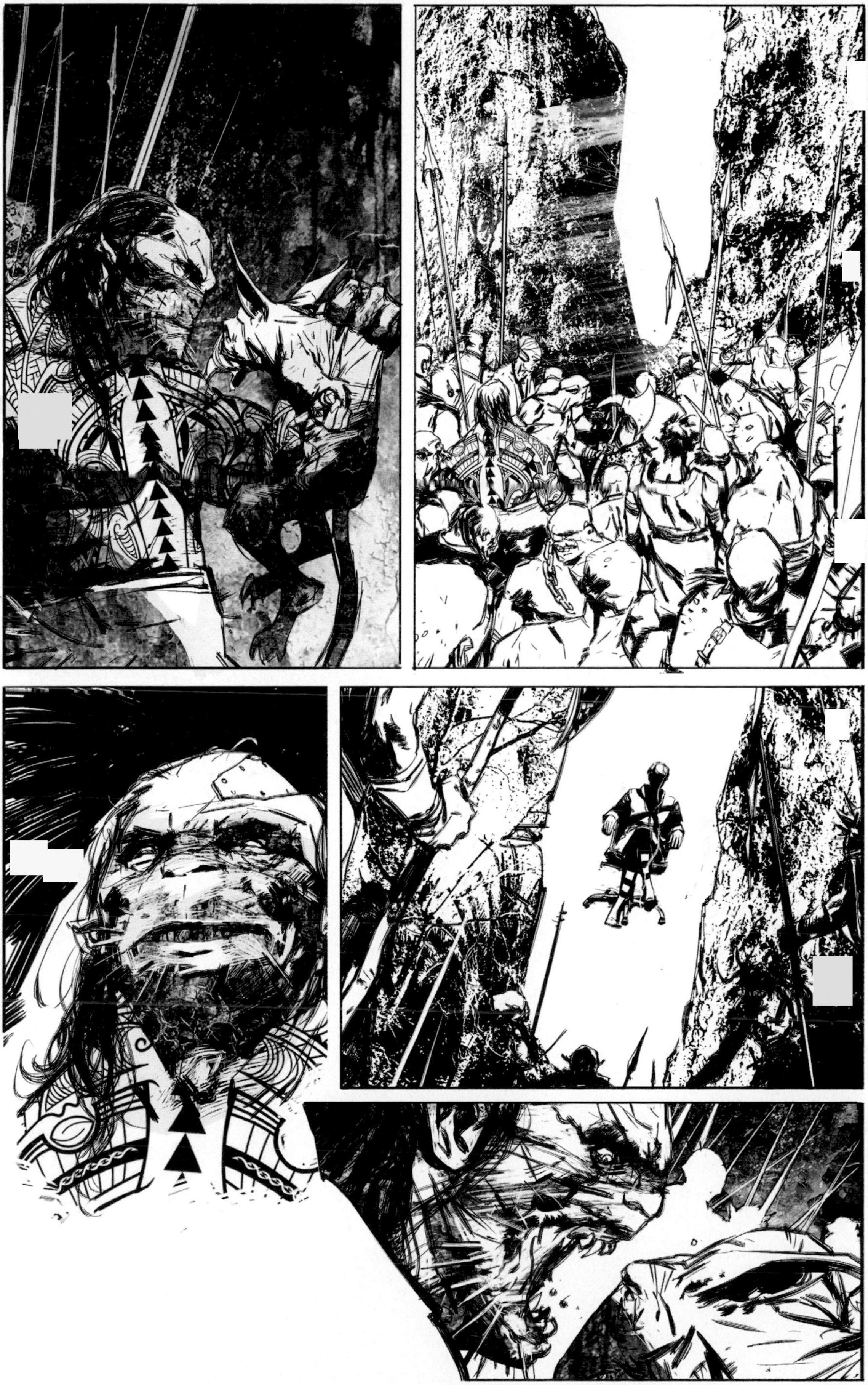

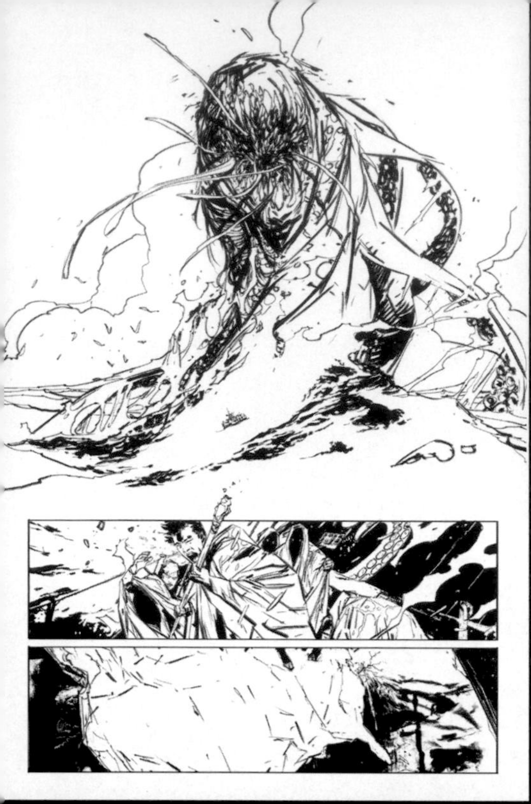

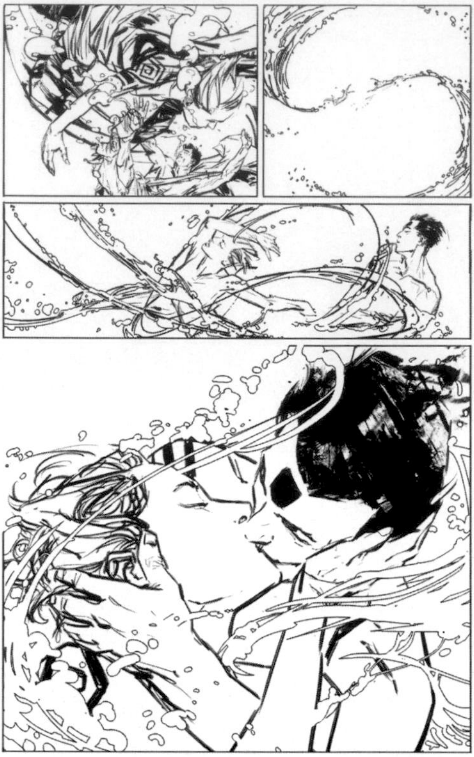

THE DEATH-DEFYING DOCTOR MIRAGE #3,
pages 1, 4, 5, and (facing) 22
Art by ROBERTO DE LA TORRE

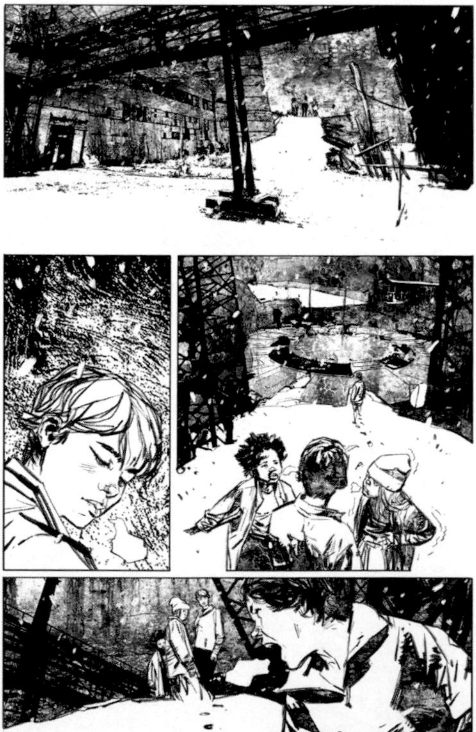

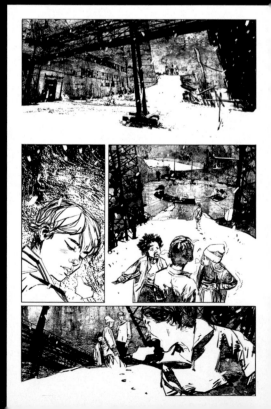

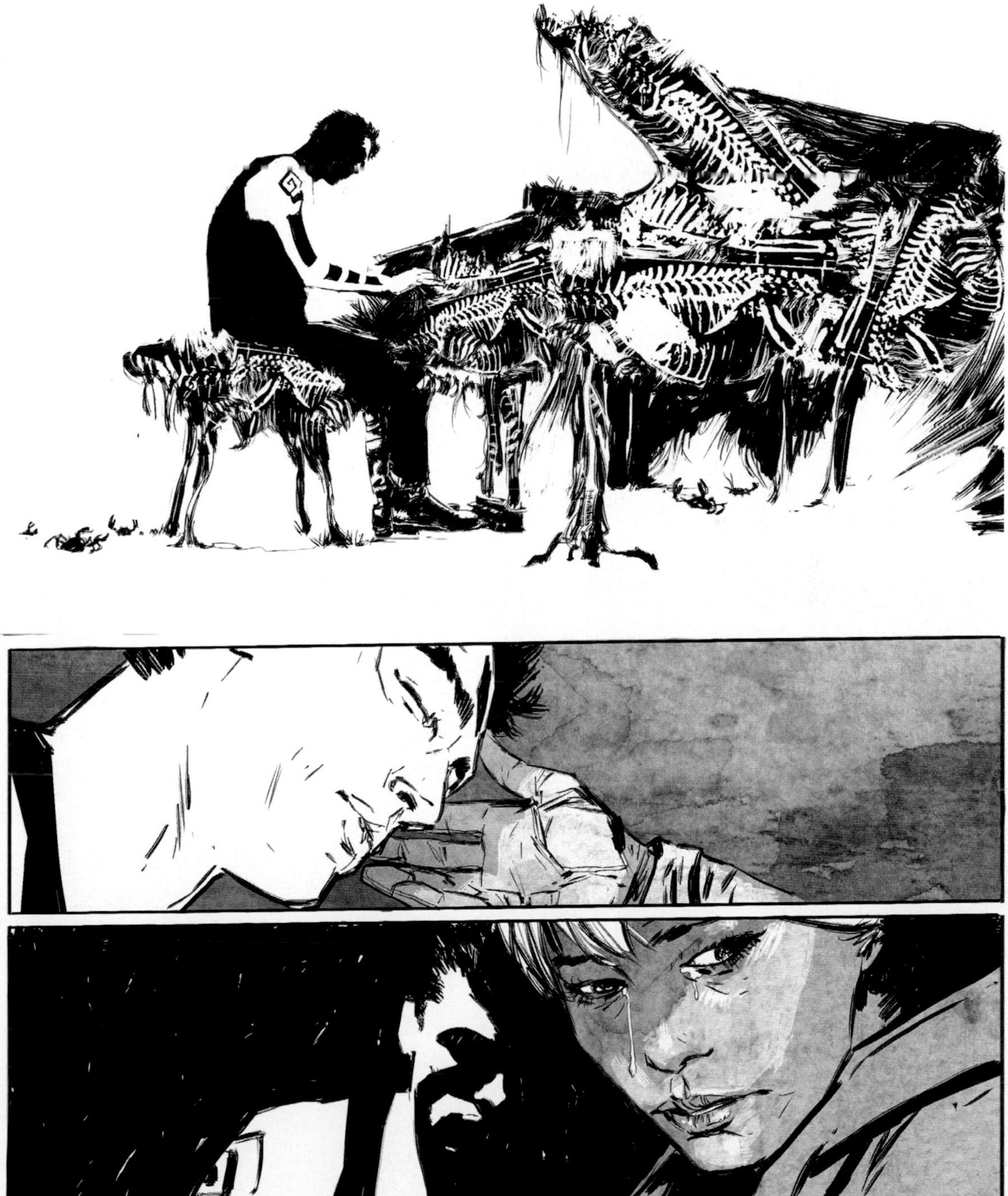

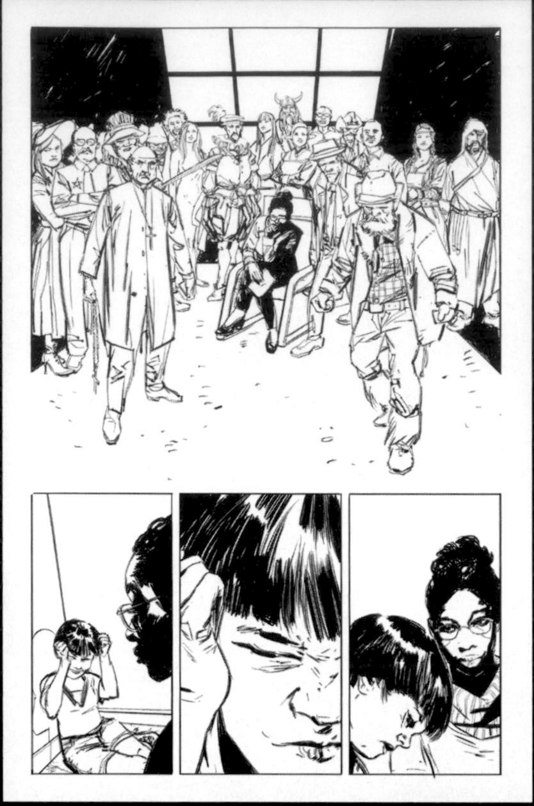

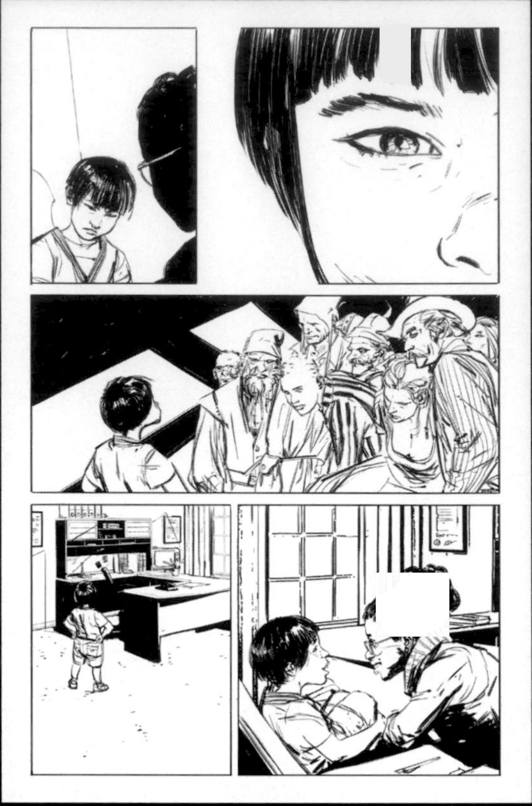

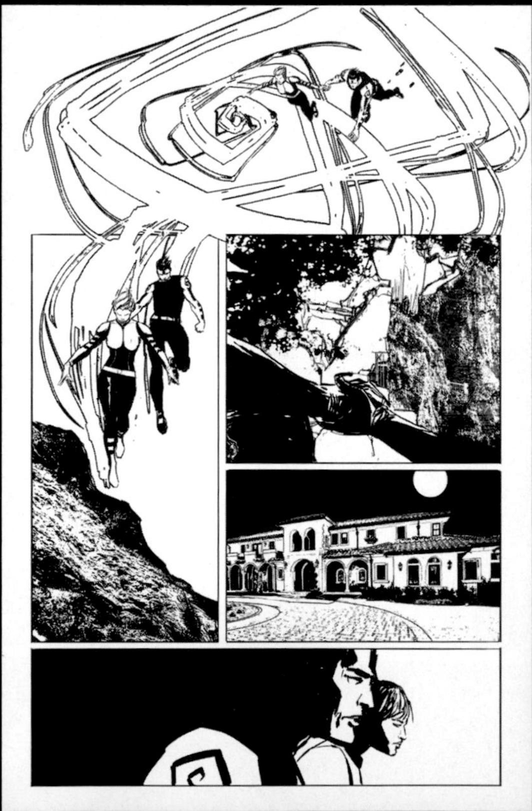

THE DEATH-DEFYING DOCTOR MIRAGE #4,
pages 3, 4, 20, and (facing) 21
Art by ROBERTO DE LA TORRE

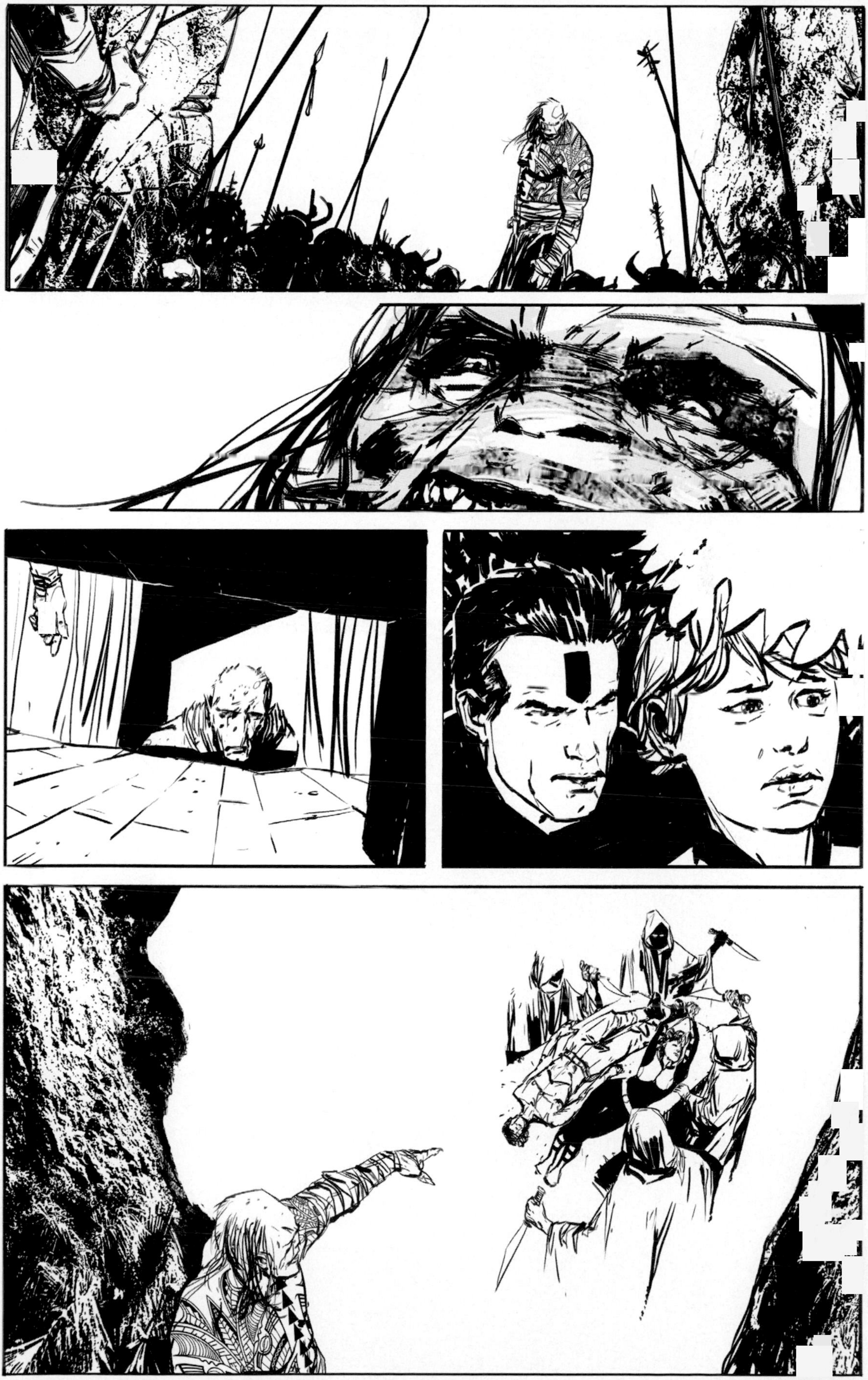

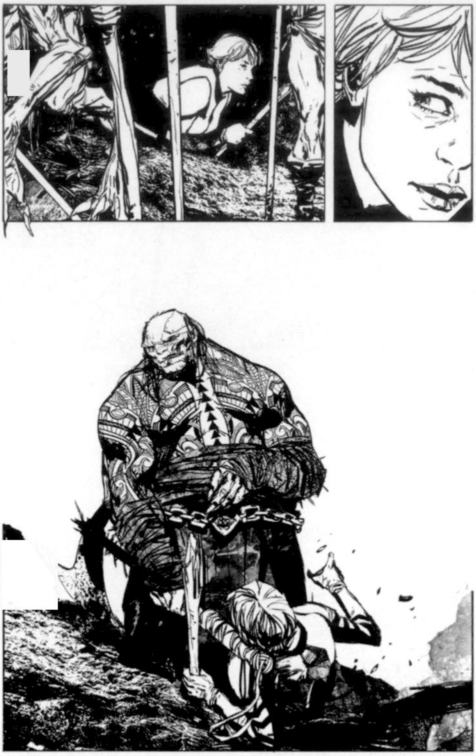

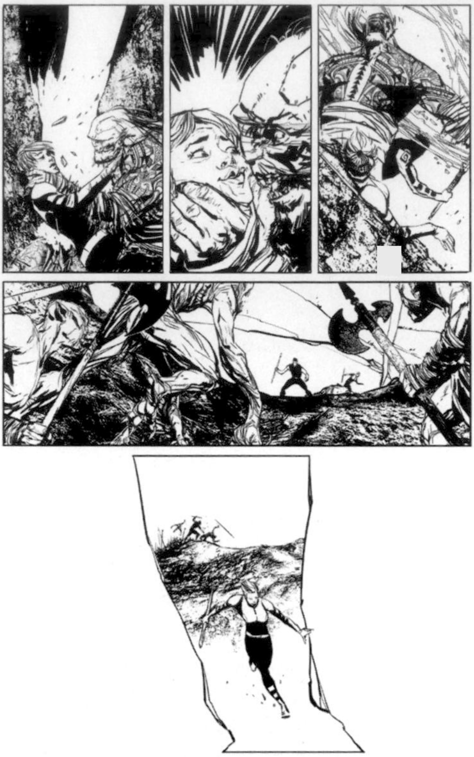

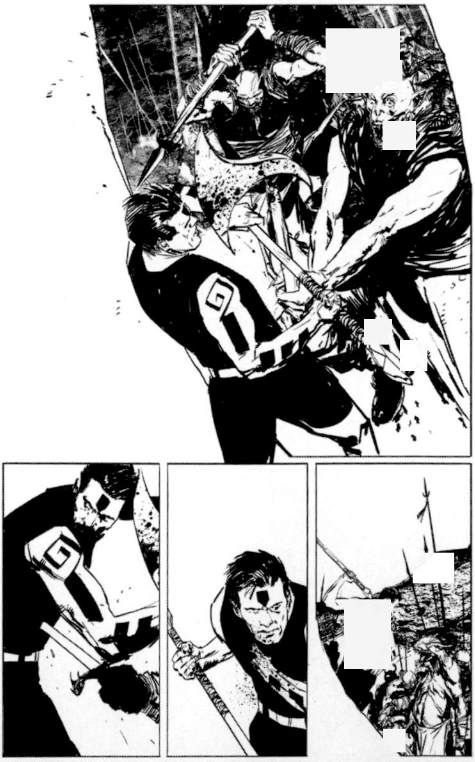

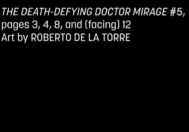

THE DEATH-DEFYING DOCTOR MIRAGE #5,
pages 3, 4, 8, and (facing) 12
Art by ROBERTO DE LA TORRE

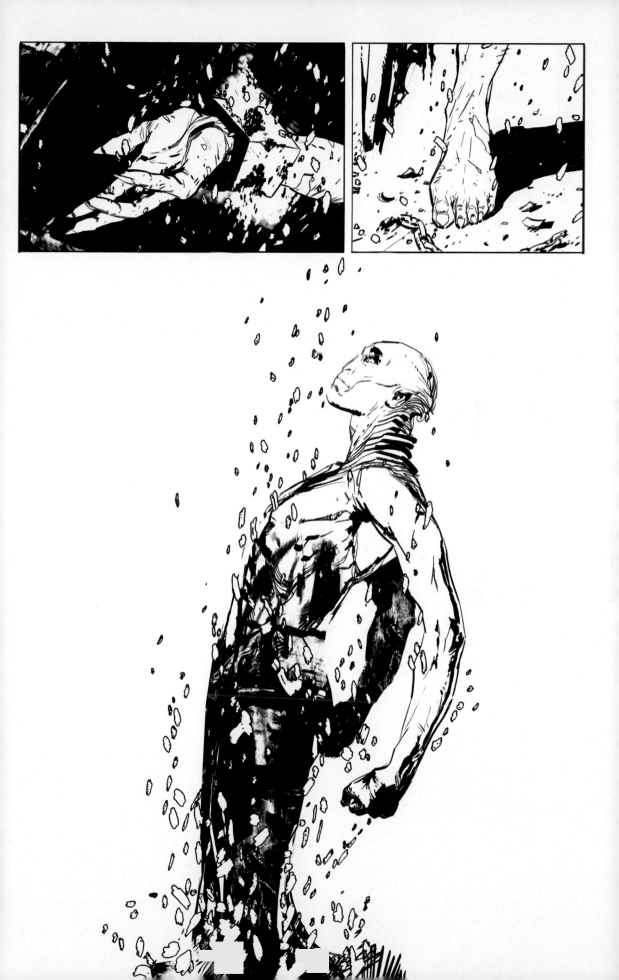

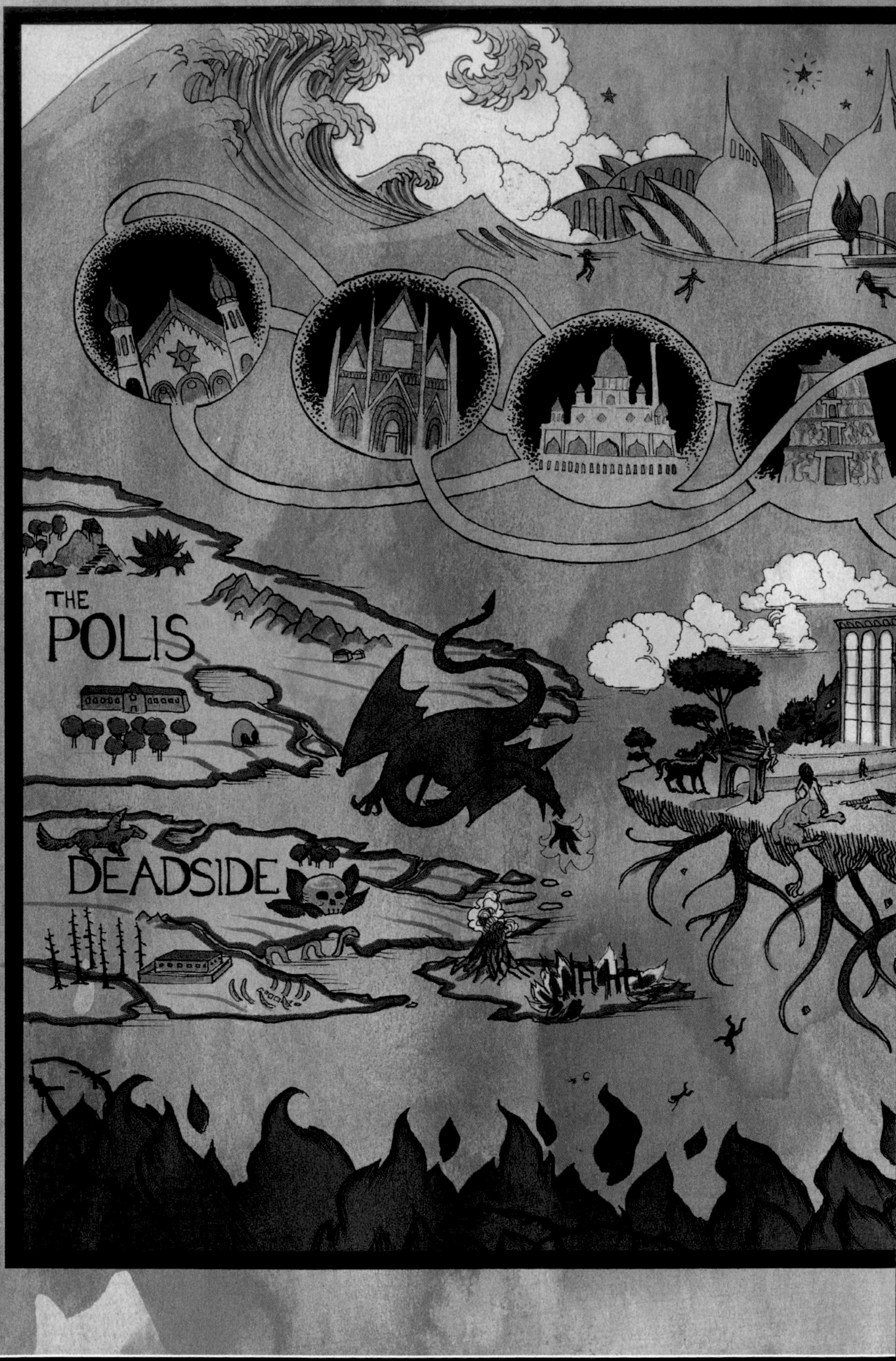
THE
POLIS
DEADSIDE

MAP OF WORLDS (previously unpublished)
By STEPHANIE HANS
Based on notes by JEN VAN METER

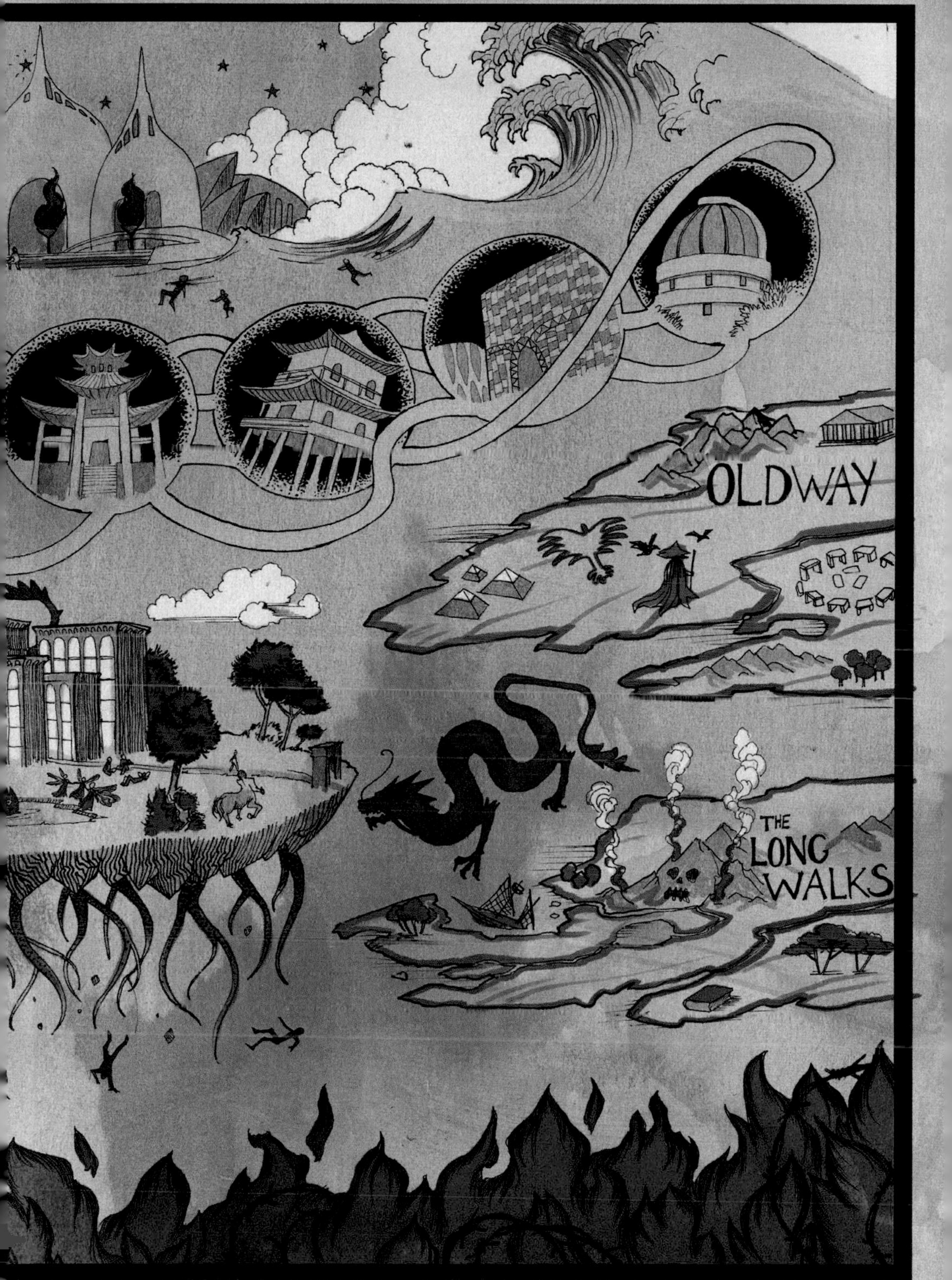
OLDWAY
THE LONG WALKS

EXPLORE THE VALIANT UNIVERSE

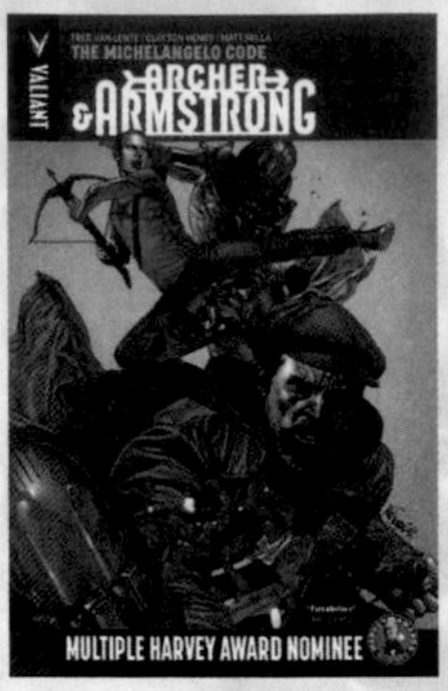
THE MICHELANGELO CODE
ARCHER & ARMSTRONG
MULTIPLE HARVEY AWARD NOMINEE
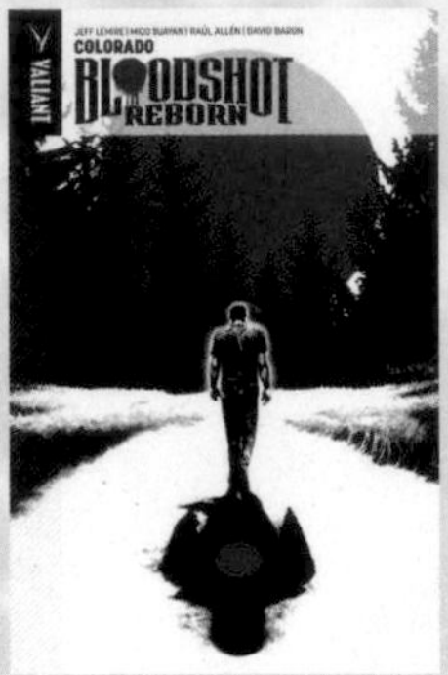
COLORADO
BLOODSHOT REBORN
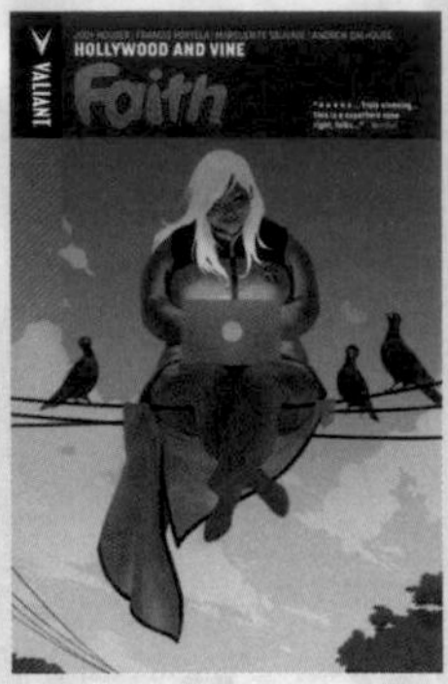
HOLLYWOOD AND VINE
Faith
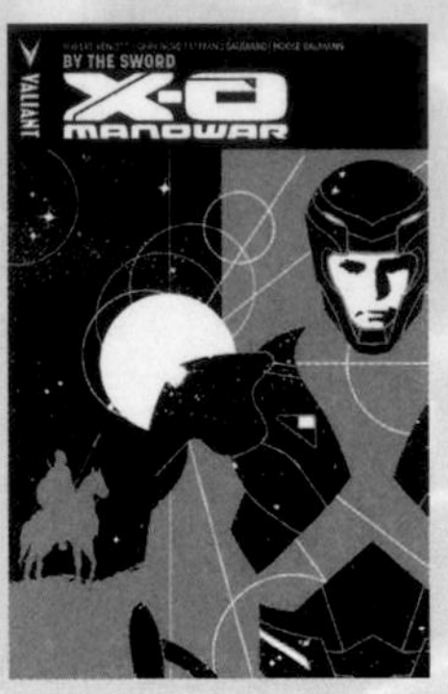
BY THE SWORD
X-O MANOWAR
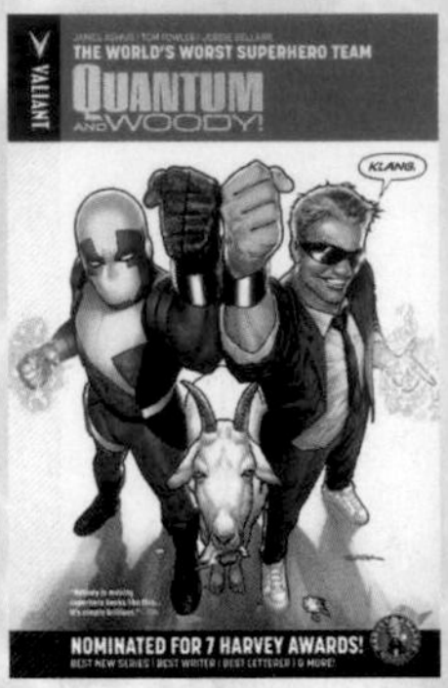
THE WORLD'S WORST SUPERHERO TEAM
QUANTUM AND WOODY!
KLANG
NOMINATED FOR 7 HARVEY AWARDS!

A&A: THE ADVENTURES OF ARCHER AND ARMSTRONG

Volume 1: In the Bag
ISBN: 9781682151495

ARCHER & ARMSTRONG

Volume 1: The Michelangelo Code
ISBN: 9780979640988

Volume 2: Wrath of the Eternal Warrior
ISBN: 9781939346049

Volume 3: Far Faraway
ISBN: 9781939346148

Volume 4: Sect Civil War
ISBN: 9781939346254

Volume 5: Mission: Improbable
ISBN: 9781939346353

Volume 6: American Wasteland
ISBN: 9781939346421

Volume 7: The One Percent and Other Tales
ISBN: 9781939346537

ARMOR HUNTERS

Armor Hunters
ISBN: 9781939346452

Armor Hunters: Bloodshot
ISBN: 9781939346469

Armor Hunters: Harbinger
ISBN: 9781939346506

Unity Vol. 3: Armor Hunters
ISBN: 9781939346445

X-O Manowar Vol. 7: Armor Hunters
ISBN: 9781939346476

BLOODSHOT

Volume 1: Setting the World on Fire
ISBN: 9780979640964

Volume 2: The Rise and the Fall
ISBN: 9781939346032

Volume 3: Harbinger Wars
ISBN: 9781939346124

Volume 4: H.A.R.D. Corps
ISBN: 9781939346193

Volume 5: Get Some!
ISBN: 9781939346315

Volume 6: The Glitch and Other Tales
ISBN: 9781939346711

BLOODSHOT REBORN

Volume 1: Colorado
ISBN: 9781939346674

Volume 2: The Hunt
ISBN: 9781939346827

Volume 3: The Analog Man
ISBN: 9781682151334

BOOK OF DEATH

Book of Death
ISBN: 9781939346971

Book of Death: The Fall of the Valiant Universe
ISBN: 9781939346988

DEAD DROP

ISBN: 9781939346858

THE DEATH-DEFYING DOCTOR MIRAGE

Volume 1
ISBN: 9781939346490

Volume 2: Second Lives
ISBN: 9781682151297

THE DELINQUENTS

ISBN: 9781939346513

DIVINITY

Volume 1
ISBN: 9781939346766

Volume 2
ISBN: 9781682151518

ETERNAL WARRIOR

Volume 1: Sword of the Wild
ISBN: 9781939346209

Volume 2: Eternal Emperor
ISBN: 9781939346292

Volume 3: Days of Steel
ISBN: 9781939346742

WRATH OF THE ETERNAL WARRIOR

Volume 1: Risen
ISBN: 9781682151235

HARBINGER

Volume 1: Omega Rising
ISBN: 9780979640957

Volume 2: Renegades
ISBN: 9781939346025

Volume 3: Harbinger Wars
ISBN: 9781939346117

Volume 4: Perfect Day
ISBN: 9781939346155

Volume 5: Death of a Renegade
ISBN: 9781939346339

Volume 6: Omegas
ISBN: 9781939346384

HARBINGER WARS

Harbinger Wars
ISBN: 9781939346094

Bloodshot Vol. 3: Harbinger Wars
ISBN: 9781939346124

Harbinger Vol. 3: Harbinger Wars
ISBN: 9781939346117

EXPLORE THE VALIANT UNIVERSE

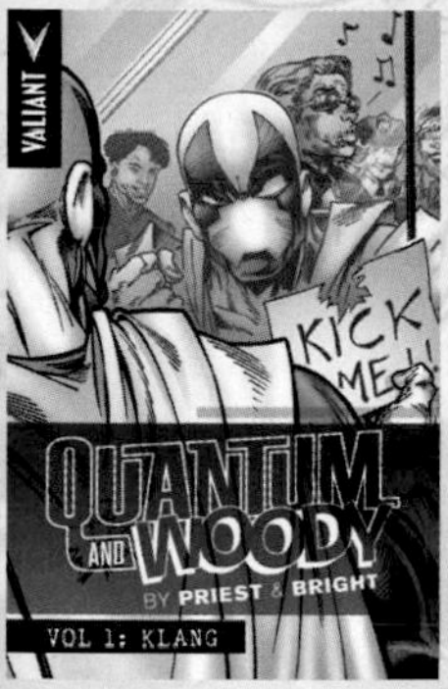
VALIANT
KICK ME
QUANTUM AND WOODY
BY PRIEST & BRIGHT
VOL 1: KLANG

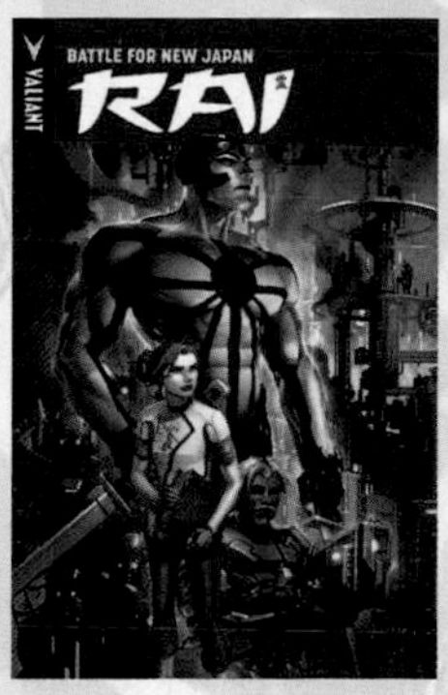
VALIANT
BATTLE FOR NEW JAPAN
RAI

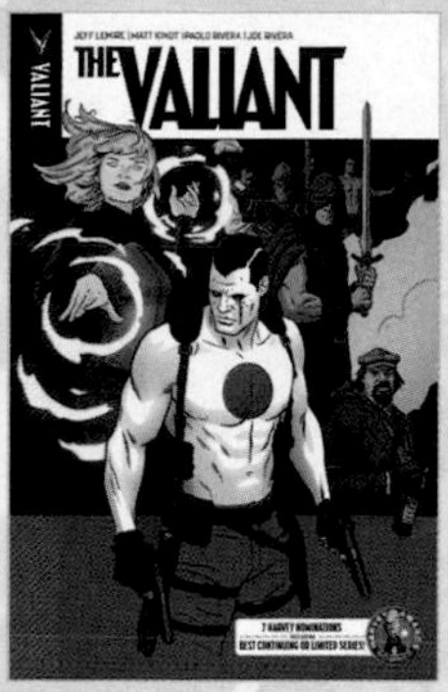
VALIANT
THE VALIANT

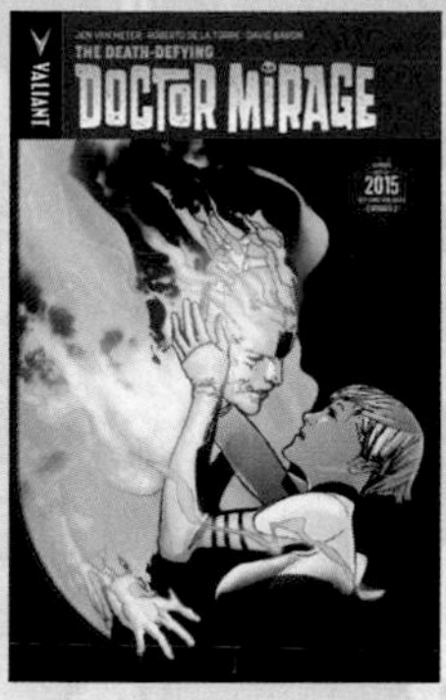
VALIANT
THE DEATH-DEFYING
DOCTOR MIRAGE

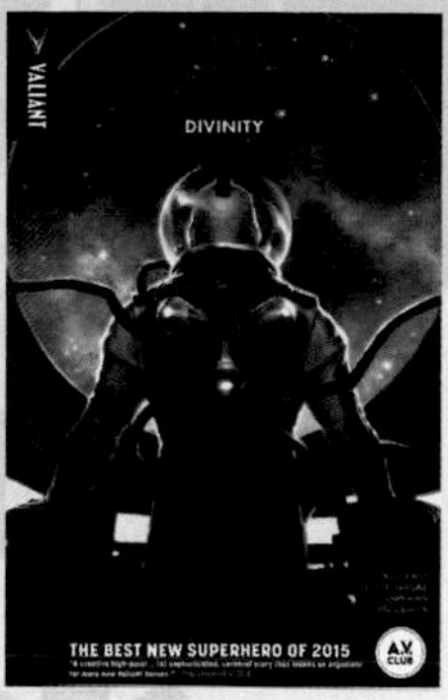
VALIANT
DIVINITY
THE BEST NEW SUPERHERO OF 2015

IMPERIUM

Volume 1: Collecting Monsters
ISBN: 9781939346759

Volume 2: Broken Angels
ISBN: 9781939346896

Volume 3: The Vine Imperative
ISBN: 9781682151112

Volume 4: Stormbreak
ISBN: 9781682151372

NINJAK

Volume 1: Weaponeer
ISBN: 9781939346667

Volume 2: The Shadow Wars
ISBN: 9781939346940

Volume 3: Operation: Deadside
ISBN: 9781682151259

Volume 4: The Siege of King's Castle
ISBN: 9781682151617

QUANTUM AND WOODY

Volume 1: The World's Worst Superhero Team
ISBN: 9781939346186

Volume 2: In Security
ISBN: 9781939346230

Volume 3: Crooked Pasts, Present Tense
ISBN: 9781939346391

Volume 4: Quantum and Woody Must Die!
ISBN: 9781939346629

QUANTUM AND WOODY BY PRIEST & BRIGHT

Volume 1: Klang
ISBN: 9781939346780

Volume 2: Switch
ISBN: 9781939346803

Volume 3: And So...
ISBN: 9781939346865

Volume 4: Q2 - The Return
ISBN: 9781682151099

RAI

Volume 1: Welcome to New Japan
ISBN: 9781939346414

Volume 2: Battle for New Japan
ISBN: 9781939346612

Volume 3: The Orphan
ISBN: 9781939346841

SHADOWMAN

Volume 1: Birth Rites
ISBN: 9781939346001

Volume 2: Darque Reckoning
ISBN: 9781939346056

Volume 3: Deadside Blues
ISBN: 9781939346162

Volume 4: Fear, Blood, And Shadows
ISBN: 9781939346278

Volume 5: End Times
ISBN: 9781939346377

SHADOWMAN BY ENNIS & WOOD

ISBN: 9781682151358

IVAR, TIMEWALKER

Volume 1: Making History
ISBN: 9781939346636

Volume 2: Breaking History
ISBN: 9781939346834

Volume 3: Ending History
ISBN: 9781939346995

UNITY

Volume 1: To Kill a King
ISBN: 9781939346261

Volume 2: Trapped by Webnet
ISBN: 9781939346346

Volume 3: Armor Hunters
ISBN: 9781939346445

Volume 4: The United
ISBN: 9781939346544

Volume 5: Homefront
ISBN: 9781939346797

Volume 6: The War-Monger
ISBN: 9781939346902

Volume 7: Revenge of the Armor Hunters
ISBN: 9781682151136

THE VALIANT

ISBN: 9781939346605

VALIANT ZEROES AND ORIGINS

ISBN: 9781939346582

X-O MANOWAR

Volume 1: By the Sword
ISBN: 9780979640940

Volume 2: Enter Ninjak
ISBN: 9780979640995

Volume 3: Planet Death
ISBN: 9781939346087

Volume 4: Homecoming
ISBN: 9781939346179

Volume 5: At War With Unity
ISBN: 9781939346247

Volume 6: Prelude to Armor Hunters
ISBN: 9781939346407

Volume 7: Armor Hunters
ISBN: 9781939346476

Volume 8: Enter: Armorines
ISBN: 9781939346551

Volume 9: Dead Hand
ISBN: 9781939346650

Volume 10: Exodus
ISBN: 9781939346933

Volume 11: The Kill List
ISBN: 9781682151273

EXPLORE THE VALIANT UNIVERSE

VALIANT
HARBINGER
DELUXE EDITION 2

OMNIBUSES

Quantum and Woody: The Complete Classic Omnibus
ISBN: 9781939346360
Collecting QUANTUM AND WOODY (1997) #0, 1-21 and #32, THE GOAT: H.A.E.D.U.S. #1, and X-O MANOWAR (1996) #16

X-O Manowar Classic Omnibus Vol. 1
ISBN: 9781939346308
Collecting X-O MANOWAR (1992) #0-30, ARMORINES #0, X-O DATABASE #1, as well as material from SECRETS OF THE VALIANT UNIVERSE #1

DELUXE EDITIONS

Archer & Armstrong Deluxe Edition Book 1
ISBN: 9781939346223
Collecting ARCHER & ARMSTRONG #0-13

VALIANT
ARMOR HUNTERS
DELUXE EDITION

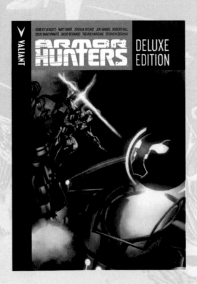

Armor Hunters Deluxe Edition
ISBN: 9781939346728
Collecting ARMOR HUNTERS #1-4, ARMOR HUNTERS: AFTERMATH #1, ARMOR HUNTERS: BLOODSHOT #1-3, ARMOR HUNTERS: HARBINGER #1-3, UNITY #8-11 and X-O MANOWAR #23-29

Bloodshot Deluxe Edition Book 1
ISBN: 9781939346216
Collecting BLOODSHOT #1-13

Harbinger Deluxe Edition Book 1
ISBN: 9781939346131
Collecting HARBINGER #0-14

Harbinger Deluxe Edition Book 2
ISBN: 9781939346773
Collecting HARBINGER #15-25, HARBINGER: OMEGAS #1-3, and HARBINGER: BLEEDING MONK #0

Harbinger Wars Deluxe Edition
ISBN: 9781939346322
Collecting HARBINGER WARS #1-4, HARBINGER #11-14, and BLOODSHOT #10-13

Quantum and Woody Deluxe Edition Book 1
ISBN: 9781939346681
Collecting QUANTUM AND WOODY #1-12 and QUANTUM AND WOODY: THE GOAT #0

Q2: The Return of Quantum and Woody Deluxe Edition
ISBN: 9781939346568
Collecting Q2: THE RETURN OF QUANTUM AND WOODY #1-5

VALIANT
JAMES ASMUS TOM FOWLER MING DOYLE
KANO JORDIE BELLAIRE DAVE LANPHEAR
QUANTUM AND WOODY!
DELUXE EDITION 1
MEH!

Shadowman Deluxe Edition Book 1
ISBN: 9781939346438
Collecting SHADOWMAN #0-10

X-O Manowar Deluxe Edition Book 1
ISBN: 9781939346100
Collecting X-O MANOWAR #1-14

X-O Manowar Deluxe Edition Book 2
ISBN: 9781939346520
Collecting X-O MANOWAR #15-22, and UNITY #1-4

VALIANT
JIM SHOOTER | DAVID LAPHAM
CHILDREN OF THE EIGHTH DAY
HARBINGER
VALIANT MASTERS

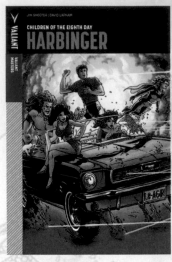

VALIANT MASTERS

Bloodshot Vol. 1 - Blood of the Machine
ISBN: 9780979640933

H.A.R.D. Corps Vol. 1 - Search and Destroy
ISBN: 9781939346285

Harbinger Vol. 1 - Children of the Eighth Day
ISBN: 9781939346483

Ninjak Vol. 1 - Black Water
ISBN: 9780979640971

Rai Vol. 1 - From Honor to Strength
ISBN: 9781939346070

Shadowman Vol. 1 - Spirits Within
ISBN: 9781939346018

VALIANT
KEVIN VANHOOK | DON PERLIN
BLOOD OF THE MACHINE
BLOODSHOT
VALIANT MASTERS

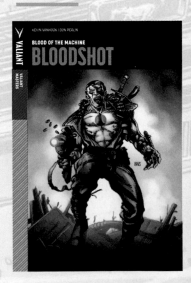

THE DEATH-DEFYING DOCTOR MIRAGE

READING ORDER

VALIANT
JEN VAN METER | ROBERTO DE LA TORRE | DAVID BARON
THE DEATH-DEFYING
DOCTOR MIRAGE
IGN
BEST OF
2015
BEST COMIC MINI-SERIES
WINNER

The Death-Defying Dr. Mirage

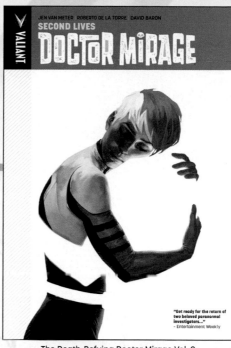

VALIANT
JEN VAN METER | ROBERTO DE LA TORRE | DAVID BARON
SECOND LIVES
DOCTOR MIRAGE
"Get ready for the return of two beloved paranormal investigators..."
- Entertainment Weekly

The Death-Defying Doctor Mirage Vol. 2
Second Lives

"★★★★...Equal parts clever and emotional as it sets up an impressive new hero..."
-Comic Book Resources

"Everything you could want in a paranormal story...with mystery and intrigue around every corner."
-Bloody Disgusting

READ DR. MIRAGE'S EARLIEST APPEARANCES

VALIANT
DARQUE RECKONING
SHADOWMAN

Shadowman Vol. 2:
Darque Reckoning
(OPTIONAL)

VALIANT
SHADOWMAN

Shadowman Vol. 3:
Deadside Blues
(OPTIONAL)

Go beyond and back with Valiant's spirited occult adventurer for a breathtaking, heartbreaking journey into realms of the unknown!

From Eisner Award-nominated writer
JEN VAN METER
(Hopeless Savages, Captain Marvel)

and

Visionary artist
ROBERTO DE LA TORRE
(Daredevil)

THE DEATH-DEFYING DOCTOR MIRAGE

VOLUME TWO: SECOND LIVES

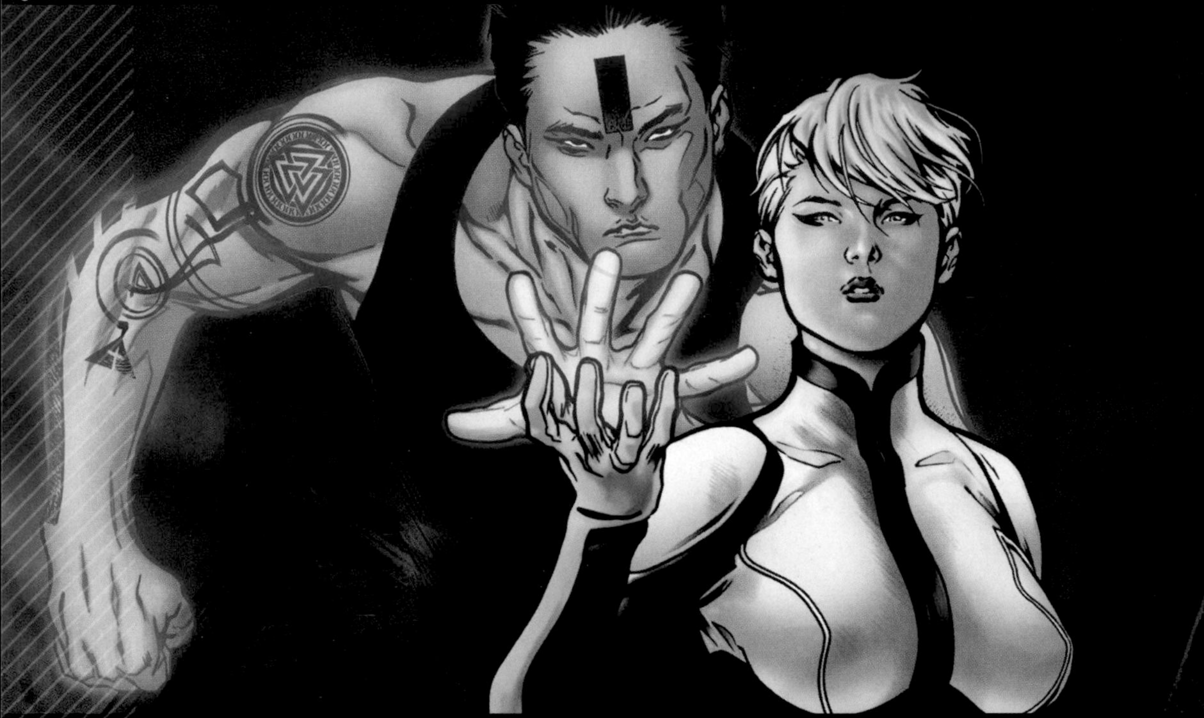

IN TIME, EVEN THE DEAD MAY DIE...

Occult investigators Shan and Hwen Mirage lived their lives in the thrall of an epic love that few will ever have...until Hwen died tragically before his time. Now, after a perilous trip through the underworld, Shan and Hwen are reunited... but Hwen is still an intangible spirit of the dead - incapable of opening a spellbook or even touching his wife.

Their options exhausted, the death-defying Doctors Mirage are about to enact a dangerous spell to restore Hwen's solid form...and grant his ghost a second life. But, in the wrong hands, their ancient rite will become a tool of terror - and unleash a force of pure, homicidal evil that lusts for the murder of the living and the dead alike... a torturous death that obliterates not just everything a person ever had in this world, but everything their ghost will be in the next!

After multiple 2015 Harvey Award nominations, the most sought-after couple in comics returns with an all-new adventure from Eisner Award-nominated writer Jen Van Meter (*Hopeless Savages*) and acclaimed artist Roberto de la Torre (*Daredevil*)!

Collecting THE DEATH-DEFYING DOCTOR MIRAGE: SECOND LIVES #1-4.

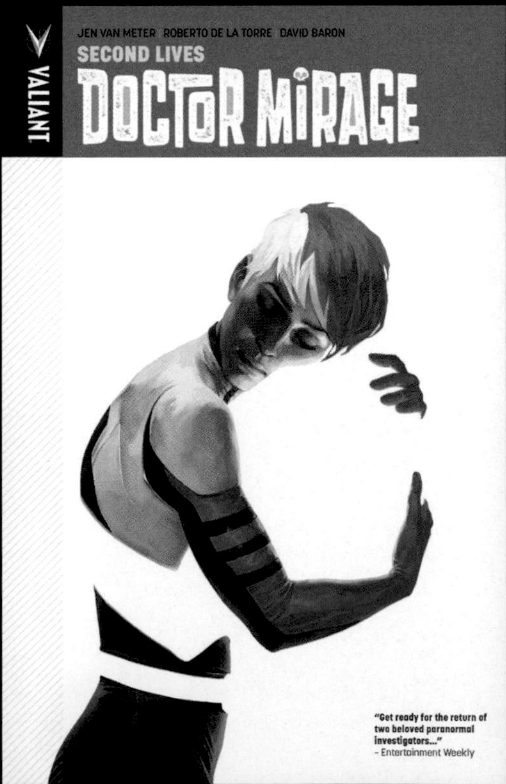
VALIANT
JEN VAN METER ROBERTO DE LA TORRE DAVID BARON
SECOND LIVES
DOCTOR MIRAGE
"Get ready for the return of two beloved paranormal investigators..."
- Entertainment Weekly

TRADE PAPERBACK
ISBN: 978-1-68215-129-7